A HISTORY OF
BRITAIN'S
FIGHT FOR A
REPUBLIC

ABOUT THE AUTHOR

Clive Bloom is Professor in Residence at the Larkin Centre for Poetry and Creative Writing at Hull University and also holds a Visiting Fellowship at the University of Western Timisoara, Romania.

He was the historical consultant to the BBC and a number of national and international newspapers on the G20 disturbances and the 2011 riots in Britain. He is an occasional feature writer for *The Financial Times*, *The Times*, *The Guardian*, *The Independent*, *The Irish Times* and the *London Evening Standard*, as well as being quoted in *The Washington Post*. He regularly appears on television and radio and he is quoted in *The Columbia Book of World Quotations*. He has also advised the British Cabinet Office on public disorder issues.

ALSO BY CLIVE BLOOM

Thatcher's Secret War: Subversion, Coercion, Secrecy and Government, 1974–90

A HISTORY OF BRITAIN'S FIGHT FOR A REPUBLIC

CLIVE BLOOM

For James,
who knows how the earth works,
and for Jonathan,
who knows how the world works.

Cover image by Ryan Miller on Unsplash

First published as *Terror Within* in 2007
First published as *Restless Revolutionaries* in 2010
This edition first published 2023

The History Press
97 St George's Place, Cheltenham,
Gloucestershire, GL50 3QB
www.thehistorypress.co.uk

British Library Cataloguing in Publication Data.
A catalogue record for this book is available from the British Library.

ISBN 978 1 80399 282 2

Typesetting and origination by The History Press
Printed and bound in Great Britain by TJ Books Limited, Padstow, Cornwall.

Trees for LYfe

Contents

Acknowledgements

Special thanks are due to: Rod Morley and John Culmer, Faversham Museum; Sandys Dawes, Mount Ephraim; Guy Gibb, Bossenden Farm; Kevin and Anita Kemp, Red Lion in Kent; Andrew Robertshaw, National Army Museum; Tish Collins, Marx Memorial Library; Wendy O'Cane, Derbyshire Records Office; Alison Kenny, Westminster Archives; Jill Barber, Hertfordshire Records Office; Vanessa Bourguignon, Cornish Studies Library; Alison Campbell, Cornwall Record Office; Wendy Thirkettle, The Manx National Heritage Library; Marian Martin and Barry Whelan, National 1798 Rebellion Centre; Samantha Chambers, London Metropolitan University; Geoffrey Bennett and Cornelius O'Boyle, University of Notre Dame; Graham Alexander, Malcolm Pratt, the Very Revd B. O'Farrall, Winchelsea Court Museum; Nigel Wilkins, English Heritage; Vernon A. Jones, National Library of Wales; Bruce Frost, the Littleport Society; John Edwards, Bath Postal Museum; Jane Halliwell, Dewsbury Library; Kim Streets and Clara Thomson, Sheffield Central Library; Judith Walker, Newcastle Local Studies Archive; Edward 'Bill' Moore, The Holberry Society; Nicola Mason, Huddersfield Library and Art Gallery; Roger Shelley, Derby Museum and Art Gallery; Fiona Hayes, the People's Palace and Winter Gardens, Glasgow; Professor John Simons,

University of Lincoln; Dr David Hume, the Grand Orange Lodge of Ireland; Howard Hyman, Howard Hyman Associates; Roger Appleby, the City of London Police; Charles Griffiths, Heddlu Dyfed-Powis Police; William Troughton, the National Library of Wales; the Guildhall Library; archivists at the National Archives of Scotland and Westminster Archives; the librarian, National Library of Scotland; the archivist, Celtic Football Club; National Archive of Ireland; National Library of Ireland; English Heritage; the librarians, the National Maritime Museum; the archivist, the London Metropolitan Police. Special thanks also to Alice Tyrell for helping me with books from the London Library, my agent, Malcolm Imrie, Christopher Feeney, for commissioning the book, James and Lesley Bloom, for their hard work and support, and Anna Saffer and Frances Kacher for helping with the footnotes. My thanks also to Paul Ford at Walsall Local History Centre, and Jennifer Thompson at Walsall Central Library and Museum; local historian Barrie N. Roberts; archivists at Greenwich Local History Museum; Nancy Langfeldt and the librarians at the Bishopsgate Institute; Jo Parker, Tim Foster and Gary Heals at the Vestry House Museum; Robert Thwaite and Renata Pillay, Bruce Castle Museum, Haringey Council; Nick Hamilton, Resonance FM; Malcolm Hopkins and William Hudson, Housmans Bookshop; David B. Lawrence, for his enlightening correspondence on revolutionary flags; and finally, Jo de Vries at The History Press, who put up with my nagging.

Thanks must go to the staff of the Bishopsgate Institute, Graham Smith of Republic.org, Paul Jump of *The Times Higher Education Supplement* and to my scrupulous editor for the revised edition, Chrissy McMorris of The History Press. Also thanks are due to Alice Tyrell, University of Notre Dame, Professor Michael Addo, University of Notre Dame, Paul Yowell, Benn Fellow & Tutor in Law, Oriel College, Associate Professor, Faculty of Law, University of Oxford and David Ibettson, Regius Professor of Civil Law, University of Cambridge.

My thanks go to *The Times Higher Education Supplement* for permission to reprint my article 'Imperial Lather' (28 April 2011).

Preface to the 2010 Edition

Restless Revolutionaries [now *A History of Britain's Fight for a Republic*] was first published in 2007 as *Terror Within*, a product of my own fascination with Britain's 'lost' republican history, a history that is violent, bloody and desperate. Ultimately, it is tragic too, not least because it has been a failure, but also because it is forgotten, ignored or even suppressed in official versions of British traditional narratives. The names in this book are only half remembered, the graves of their owners decaying and neglected, the scenes of their sometimes epic struggles overgrown and unrecorded.

Since this book was published at least two other books[1] have appeared purporting to tell the tale of British radicalism through the ages. Both, however, are general histories and neither detail the specific struggle of republicans, a struggle that ended in living memory when Ulstermen and Sinn Féiners came to their historic compromise in 1998 with the Good Friday Agreement and helped form a government in Northern Ireland; the guns and bombs have mostly fallen silent and the arms caches have been given up.[2]

In Scotland and Wales the struggle was abandoned in the last twenty years of the twentieth century and its renewal was avoided through devolution. In England, republicanism, which was spontaneously reignited with the death of Princess Diana and with the temporary distaste for monarchy, has faded into memory. The political struggles of the Cornish have long ceased, whilst the current counter-culture does not favour insurgency; the financial destabilisation, which began in 2009, has not encouraged revolution or created a revolutionary voice. Parliamentary reform is in the air and the monarchy seems more popular than ever in a destabilised age. The threat of Islamic terrorism driven by religious zeal seems, at least for the moment, a guarantee against secular revolution. The black flag and the red flag, the flags of republican Britain, are furled and put away.

It was only with the upheaval of the Civil War in the seventeenth century – which allowed ideas from the lower classes about freedom of conscience, religious toleration, removal of tithes, reform of the law, republicanism and the destruction of the 'class system' to finally surface – that the common people gained a political voice. The medieval period suffered its usual share of bread riots and work-related scuffles no doubt, but large scale political questions were beyond the common folk and generally passed them by. This changed during the Peasants' Revolt, but such an upheaval came at a peculiarly traumatic moment in the fourteenth century that was not to be repeated and that was, in any case, confined geographically. This was the last time for almost 300 years that the lower classes of society were able to make their economic grievances into a coherent political argument.

With the beheading of Charles I, previously seditious thoughts could be openly spoken. For a short time the grip of authority was loosened and rebellion might be contemplated by those lesser folk who had been taught for years to hold their tongues in front of their betters. New and dangerous ideas, circulated by the printing press and word of mouth, meant that the immediate worries about food, shelter and taxes could be put aside for long-term goals, which might be striven for by the lower orders, acting as a body and with only ideology or religion to guide them.

The Civil War threw up new men with values and ideas that separated them from their Tudor forebears: everything was to be questioned and everything debated. Thomas Venner was one such new man, born of the lower orders, bred in the fulcrum of the civil wars, reasonably educated, fiercely republican and deeply religious. Such men emerged from years of struggling with revolutionary ideas whilst in the army, which had itself become, for a brief moment, the revolutionary crucible. The turmoil of the seventeenth century is prologue to what followed in succeeding centuries.

Waiting impatiently for the Fifth Monarchy of the Apocalypse when Christ himself would reign, men like Venner gathered congregations and preached the coming end of the world. They were convinced by the signs of recent history and extrapolating from their own circumstances to the rest of the world that the End of Days was near. After the Civil War they had gained political strength and convinced many in the army, including Cromwell, of their position, but the various parliaments that followed failed to deliver the republic they demanded before Christ's coming. There was no wish from the country's leaders to get rid of taxes, lawyers and tithes or to hand over government to a self-appointed group of 'saints' who would convene a Sanhedrin to administer law, just as in ancient Israel. The 'saints' had a model of patriotism in which England was both the home of the twelve tribes but also the holy land itself. They were to be disappointed in everything: with Cromwell, with the peace with the Dutch, with parliament and its lawyers and with the betrayal of the army and final royal restoration. There would be nothing left to do but give in to fate and admit the time was not propitious for the Second Coming or rise and make history bend to their will.

Before and after the restoration of Charles II, Protestants feared that their position would always be precarious once a monarch with Catholic sympathies was back on the throne, and with that lingering doubt went the suspicion that fuelled rebellion or outright republicanism. Indeed, the belief in a Catholic plot that would effectively hand the crown over to French domination was not just a silly rumour but was backed up by proof of secret bilateral agreements with the French. Protestantism needed to arm itself in self defence.

One of the first attempts was the aborted rising at Farnley Wood near Leeds in October 1663. Its leader was one Thomas Oates of whom little is known except that he may have been a relative of Titus Oates, who emerges later in the Popish Plot. There were already rumblings in Scotland where the Covenanters feared destruction. They gathered, fought and died in the Pentland Rising of 1666, at Drumclog and Bothwell Green in 1679 and Ayrsmoss in 1680, setting up their fiery crosses against the hidden tides of Catholicism. Back in England, the 'saints' gathered to restore what had been 'promised' before the execution of Charles I.

Unlike the Levellers with whom they sometimes mixed, Fifth Monarchists were committed, not to an egalitarian tolerant republic under the army but to an intolerant religious republic ruled by a religious elite and with no army to interfere. The republican John Lilburne would be betrayed by Fifth Monarchy men, and Lilburne's supporters, the Levellers, had no reason to support that other alternative republicanism, whose aims were opposed to theirs. Indeed, they thought Ranters and such like merely religious fanatics and thus ridiculous.

For the most part, the Fifth Monarchists were gathered in London and had rebellious congregations at Blackfriars, Southwark, St Mary Overy's Dock and in a cellar near London Bridge. Venner preached in the Swan Alley meeting house, where having returned from New England he filled his listeners with ideas of rebellion. The congregations, which were packed

with both zealous men and women, were hotbeds of sedition
and closely watched. Their preachers were in and out of jail, but
it did not stop them, nor did it stop their printing presses.

Venner, like many of the Fifth Monarchists in London, was a
revolutionary at heart. At one time he planned to blow up the
Tower of London and chop off Cromwell's head. No opportunity arose for action until a Fifth Monarchist by the name of
John Pendarves was buried at Abingdon. The funeral turned into
a rally and Venner returned to London ready for war. By the
opening months of 1657 he had a secret organisation in London
– there was little interest elsewhere in the country – made up
of cells of enthusiasts. His plan was to attack some horse troops
and then parade through Epping Forest and eastwards gathering recruits. Eighty followers gathered at Mile End Green in
Shoreditch on the evening of 9 April but were interrupted by
soldiers, their arms taken and Venner whipped off under guard
to the Tower, where he cooled off for a time.

The affair warned the government but fired the 'saints'.
Female members of the group spread the word in secret, distributed pamphlets, and even wore armour and fought alongside
the men. These men and women believed themselves the chosen
people: they could not be thwarted. They planned assassinations
and risings anew. When Charles II was finally restored, it was
now or never for the Fifth Monarchists.

In May 1660, a preacher at Venner's meeting house was
openly preaching regicide, and on Sunday 6 January 1661,
Venner and fifty followers, all dressed in armour, marched
to St Paul's and waved their manifesto, which declared for
'King Jesus' alone. A fight with troops left them unexpectedly victorious, but with little idea what to do next they
retreated towards Highgate where they hid and trained, being
well armed and ready for more action. There may have been
up to 300 followers by this time but it appears only 50 were
ever seen together. These marched back to the City three days
later and fought a ferocious battle with soldiers where they lost

twenty-six men for twenty soldiers killed. At least one woman wore armour in the fight.

The end of the rebellion came when Venner, his fury expended, was arrested and put on trial alongside fifty others. Venner and twelve conspirators were hanged and their heads placed on spikes on London Bridge. The Fifth Monarchists were almost finished, but they fought on in minor skirmishes during 1661 and more plots were discovered in 1662.

Thomas Blood, the most famous and notorious renegade of the late seventeenth century was a confederate of the Fifth Monarchists, a believer in their doctrines and an active participant in their conspiracies and battles. He recorded the fact that he was wounded in the Pentland Rising in his diary and he was active in plots both in Dublin and London. At least one meeting in Petty France was the scene of assassination plans, which were thwarted by a spy, John Atkinson, whose attempts to seize the 'phanaticks' failed. This did not stop Blood plotting with a close friend called John Mason, who ran a tavern. Around 1670, Mason had thought up a scheme to attack Whitehall with fifty men, but nothing came of that particular dream. Instead, another scheme was about to come to fruition. This was the bizarre attempt to assassinate James Butler, 1st Duke of Ormonde, the most powerful man in England after James II, and a fierce royalist who had virtually ruled Ireland for years and come to terms with Irish Catholics.

The plan was to shoot him or haul him off to Tyburn to be hanged. He was hated by the Duke of Buckingham who may have paid Blood and Mason to do the deed in broad daylight. So this would be a political rather than a religious act in every sense.

On the evening of 6 December 1670, five armed men entered the Bull Head tavern in Charing Cross. The men drank heavily and waited for the Duke to arrive on his way from a banquet held to honour William, Prince of Orange, and Charles II's nephew, who was at the Guildhall that night. At around seven, the Duke's coach and entourage approached the pub on the way to his home in St James's. Blood and his accomplices bought three pipes, paid and left.

Moments later the highwaymen had stopped the coach and were struggling with Ormonde, who, although sixty years old, was tough enough to escape, avoiding two bullets as he did so. Blood, meanwhile, had gone to get a rope to hang his captor at Tyburn. By now the plot was in disarray, the Duke's household and footmen were now in the fray and success was impossible. The gang retreated to Fulham ferry which they took to the safety of Southwark and freedom. They were declared 'assassinates' and a reward of £1,000 was offered for their capture. A House of Lords committee identified the main culprits as a Dr Thomas Allen, Thomas Hunt and Richard Halliwell as 'desperate Fifth Monarchy men', Allen was one of a number of aliases used by Blood and 'Thomas Hunt' was none other than Blood's son Thomas. There were others also in on the plot: Samuel Holmes, John Hurst, a cook by the name of John Washwhite, a butcher called Thomas Dixey who came from Southwark and Fifth Monarchy radicals William More and William Smith. In the end there was not enough evidence to prosecute any of them. Blood was free and safe. He rewarded himself for the deed by a promotion from 'Major' to 'Colonel' Blood in accordance with his own growing notoriety. Finally, he retired from revolutionary activities and turned to spying for the king.

Anthony Ashley Cooper, Earl of Shaftesbury, was the last great republican conspirator of the seventeenth century and with his death in exile went a real possibility that a republican government would finally triumph. With the abortive rising of the Duke of Monmouth, it became clear that republicans were doomed to fail and that the fight of Levellers, Fifth Monarchy men and Diggers had all finally come to dust – fifty years of struggle wasted in the coming of the so called 'Glorious Revolution'.

Shaftesbury's plotting and his attempt to control parliament and the City of London aldermen ultimately failed and there was little to do except accept exile and defeat. Shaftesbury, nevertheless, with his taste for oligarchy, lack of mysticism and acute political sense, effectively forged the first political party and created the first mass political programme, which was republican at heart. 'The rights and liberties' of the people were to be tested against a free parliament which 'cannot enslave the people', for at bottom, 'Englishmen's minds are free and better taught in their liberties'.

No one in power listened and Shaftesbury was marginalised. He threw in his hand with the Duke of Monmouth, Charles's illegitimate son. Shaftesbury maintained his party through the close knit poorer communities of London and the press, the importance of this 'feminine part of revolt' having long been acknowledged. His followers printed and circulated pamphlets such as the one that reproduced the dying words of the Regicides. This was treasonable by the Licensing Act of 1662, which banned publications that attacked the Crown or Church. What emerged from government repression was the 'New Country Party' and it was a thoroughly revolutionary movement.

Shaftesbury made his headquarters at the King's Head at the edge of the City. Around him he gathered his 'Green Ribbon' men, demographically egalitarian and raffish in appearance, wearing their green cockades at a defiant angle called the 'Monmouth cock'. The Popish Plot, that nonsense dreamt up by religious fools and condoned by monarchy, began a situation that might favour the Country Party with the introduction of the Exclusion Bill into parliament. Charles II remained cynical about the affair, but his brother James thought it all a manoeuvre to get a 'republike'. The Scots covenanters were at war, and in London Justice Godfrey lay murdered, purportedly by a Jesuit plot. Now, to whip up the populace, Shaftesbury arranged a show of strength to frighten his enemies – a type of masque, the first real political rally, although it wore the clothes of religious bigotry. Through the City came a lone horse with the corpse of

Judge Godfrey upon it, the body stained with blood and held up by a 'Jesuit'. Behind this nightmarish vision came the real nightmare, a wagon bearing an effigy of everything Catholic and terrifying – the Pope as Antichrist.

There was, for a short moment, an apocalyptic air to London. It did not last long and the royalists regained their supremacy through three subsequent parliaments. Shaftesbury was finally arrested and put in the Tower. The Country Party held the City, but their grip was illusory and broken by the King's prerogative. There was nothing left but to declare a republic, rebel or shut up for good. The conspiracy started with a thought that found its voice in Londoners who felt a grave injustice. They demanded nothing less than the political programme of the original Levellers. To achieve it they would barricade the City and 'fight not to change persons only, but things' where a constitutional monarchy might reign if a republic could not. The rising was ambitious and unlikely, but if it had succeeded Shaftesbury would be 'prime minister' to the crowned Duke of Monmouth with James excluded and exiled. They argued and debated and they delayed until too late. The royalists had won and Shaftesbury was a marked man. He and his confederates left for Amsterdam and oblivion. Whilst in exile he died suddenly on 21 January 1683 and with him was snuffed out the last gasp of the Civil War's revolutionary ardour and the last best chance to gain a republic.

The dream was not dead and it was to reawaken in the likes of Tom Paine, Edward Despard, Arthur Thistlewood, Robert Wedderburn, Alice Wheeldon and Tom Wintringham, and in the apostles of Irish Independence, Physical Chartism and Social Democracy as well as in the national liberation struggles of the various nations of the United Kingdom. This is their story.

Clive Bloom,
2010

Why do esteem yourself above others? ... It is much safer to obey than to rule.

> (Thomas a Kempis, *The Imitation of Christ* (1441),
> tr. Leo Shirley-Price, 1952)

'The Queen is dead...'
'Does that mean I don't have to work tomorrow?'

> (Overheard by the author in a local takeaway on the
> day of Queen Elizabeth's death, 2022)

Introduction

Clap Hands, Here Comes Charlie!

I wrote this introduction between the Queen's Platinum Jubilee celebrations in June 2022 and her death on 8 September 2022, before the coronation of King Charles III. It was a period of mixed emotion. The jubilee, held in scorching summer weather, was taken as a moment for national and communal celebration after the Covid pandemic. *The Guardian* on 6 June 2022 rightly called the Sunday appearance of the queen on the balcony of Buckingham Palace the culmination of 'the people's day of jubilee', a 'tableau of the future of Britain's monarchy'. The queen said she was 'deeply touched' by the affection of the crowds; she had endeared herself by appearing in a video with Paddington Bear in which she revealed a marmalade sandwich in her handbag. It was brilliant publicity. Meanwhile, the prime minister, Boris Johnson, mired in corruption charges, would be forced to resign a month later.

Elizabeth's death at 96, after a reign of seventy years – meaning most people had known no other monarch, and whose image was known by everyone in the world – was a moment for serious contemplation. It was a moment of peculiar mixed emotions as Charles, Prince of Wales, ascended to become Charles III, the funeral arrangements of the deceased queen coinciding with the appearance of the new king. Thousands lined the various processional routes and millions watched the pageantry on television. There was a certain awe surrounding the proceedings and the crowds who gathered to witness events, for whatever reason, did so in a mood of sombreness, sobriety and silence. The period of official mourning was covered by every media platform, paying rapt attention to every detail. Epithets ran out as commentators, as well as ordinary people, described Elizabeth's reign as an exemplar of stability, stoicism, steadfastness and service. The term 'matriarch' of the nation was used by former prime minister Tony Blair (according to one source, her least favourite prime minister) and 'grandmother' to the nation was tweeted by Sir Mick Jagger. Ironically, her namesake Elizabeth I was called the mother of the nation for remaining a virgin.

She was both a symbol of idealised family life (with its ups and downs and pantomime heroes and villains) and of the national community. The appreciation of her service to her country became hagiographic; Queen Victoria might have recognised such sentiments. The rather old-fashioned term 'beloved', used in the new king's first speech to the nation, became a catch-all for every lost loved one and every much-loved companion.

Monarchy has to have 'mystery' and its ways have to be shrouded in certain arcana that offer it the gravitas that so impresses, but it also has to be seen – glimpsed at crowd handshakes, on balconies and occasionally in person at gala events. Just as in medieval days, the monarch had to make an occasional progress through the nation. A dead monarch was once surrounded only by courtiers, the king's effigy carried before their coffin to the grave as a sign of their undying sovereignty. Only burial was final. The modern monarch lies in state and their subjects file past in respect. So it was with Elizabeth, lying in state in Westminster Hall with her catafalque adorned with the Imperial State Crown and the orb and sceptre.

Queues to file past the coffin had waiting times of between five to twenty-four hours. The event (which I attended) gained its solemn dimension by the anticipation of the wait, the silence of the entry into Westminster Hall, the brightly lit tableau of soldiers, their heads bowed, and the reverence of the national community; some wept, many bowed or curtsied, others saluted, some crossed themselves. Those interviewed by the media talked of a 'surreal' experience. The monarch dead is a strange contradiction, as they are both present as a type of symbol and absent as a person. The glimpse of royalty here is that of a 'sacred' moment, a final glimpse of an inexplicable mysteriousness that might be related to divinity. It is, however, an illusion, of anticipation, of personal psychology, of place (Westminster Hall with all its associations), a brightly lit tableau, personal memories, royal regalia and religious symbolism. The illusion is created by the projection of psychological elements onto the catafalque, which itself is so arranged as to increase a mental picture formed by the mourners; it is not divine, but the illusion of divinity, hence it is, effectively, surreal.

For most people the monarchy represents tradition and stability, an unchanging rock throughout history (not just their own lifetime). Actually, the institution has constantly adapted to historical circumstances in order to survive. When it has failed, it has opened itself to attack and threats of abolition. The spectre of a republic has informed parliamentary protocols and statute laws. The Oath of Allegiance, which is a sacred oath, reinforces the relationship of religious duty and faithfulness to the monarch as an individual and the state as represented by the Crown and by Church precept. Its origins go back as far as the Anglo-Saxon king Edgar and it was certainly present at the time of Magna Carta. The oath binds the community to the monarch against the threat of papacy (during the reign of James I) or traitors (during the reign of George IV) and slightly changes as priorities evolve. The current oath (amended in 1978 following an Act of Parliament passed in 1888, which was itself a rewriting of an Act from 1886) has developed from oaths taken to past monarchs whose personal priorities were much more closely interwoven with the politics of state. It is supposed to be a binding oath spoken before God and therefore stressing a contract whose words cannot be gainsaid. By renouncing the Oath of Allegiance, republicans in the past, aware of grievances the monarch would not address, were themselves subject to the severest censure of Church and state. Whilst some sought forgiveness, others followed their own personal conscience, seeking to make an oath to higher principles than kingship.

This is a book about the republican movement in these islands and those republicans whose history we have mostly chosen to forget. They were radicals, and some downright revolutionaries, who wished to see a republican government in England and later the United Kingdom. Most were democrats, although the democracy they envisaged may not be exactly what we now desire. The republic they wanted was intended to be based on the rational principles of virtue. The people would be sovereign under the law. The radicals were not all internationalists or anticapitalist; many were aristocrats, but many were not. They all opposed tyranny, either through principles learned in the classics or through their deep reading of the Bible.

Republicans have argued about royal waste, entitlement and interference in parliamentary affairs. Some wished the monarch dead; others wished the monarch would abide by parliamentary will and the country's laws. All believed that a republic containing liberty of speech and freedom of conscience granted by a voted parliament convened by permission of the people was the only rational government. They fought their cause and were silenced, exiled or murdered. Many left to go to the newly founded republic of America, where they could speak freely and create a new world.

In 1993 Ipsos MORI polls suggested around 70 per cent of British people still favoured the monarchy, rising through the twenty-first century to a high of 77 per cent in 2012. Nevertheless, in May 2022 a poll conducted by SavantaComRes found only 57 per cent favoured monarchy against 29 per cent for a republic, but 14 per cent were undecided, making those favouring the status quo 28 per cent ahead in any contest. With the death of Elizabeth, a surge of support for monarchy kept numbers temporarily high in favour of royalty. Republicanism, however, has gained ground, and certain current members of the royal family have covered themselves with opprobrium, but the monarch has remained apart and untouched by controversy (unlike many senior politicians), denying republicanism an argument for abolition.

As mentioned, 2022 saw the death of Elizabeth II and the accession of Charles III. It was a period of mixed emotional responses. In Llechryd, Wales, they unfurled their 'God Save the King' banner, put carefully away since 1937; a chip fryer in Muir of Ord, Scotland, danced around with champagne, halloo-ing the death of 'Lizard Liz' and causing a near-riot before being escorted out of town by police; Symon Hill was arrested for protesting in Oxford during the local proclamation, only to be released without charge; football fans at Tallaght Stadium, in Dublin, burst into a spontaneous and derisory song when the news of her death spread in the crowd; another woman in Edinburgh was heard booing the funeral cortège whilst holding up a derogatory placard condemning the queen. On 9 November, a man threw three eggs at Charles and Camilla during their walk-about in York before the king unveiled a statue on York Minster to Queen Elizabeth. The eggs missed, the solitary protester was arrested, the king was insouciant and the crowd sang 'God Save the King' as the man was led away. The same happened some weeks later on a royal visit to Luton, and months later still whilst on a visit to Colchester, but, again, Charles was spared the embarrassment of a soiled coat.

Elsewhere, a number of radical commentators on social media took Queen Elizabeth personally to task regarding the legacy of slavery (although some seemed quite oblivious to the end of official imperial policy during her reign; the monarchy and its structure are far more ancient than Black slavery, although the accusation of invasion and genocide against the Anglo-Saxon ruling elite might hold water if discussing 1066). In Antigua and Barbuda, they quietly decided to hold a future referendum on the monarch's continuance as their head of state, whilst in Australia there were strident calls for the declaration of a republic. Yet, whatever one thought of the queen or the institution she led, such protests appeared merely crass, niggardly or simply ill-timed.

This book follows republican journeys mostly into unforgiving oblivion (with the exception of Ireland), but it starts where the original edition remained silent: what is a monarch and how has the role changed from the Anglo-Saxons until the House of Windsor? What changes have been made so that even now in the twenty-first century the voices of opposition are still little known and no statues to their memory exist in any public space? This is a book that records a struggle. It leaves the reader to make their own mind up regarding the value of heredity versus merit. Some political theorists (such as Rousseau) believed you could have a monarch in a 'republic' as long as the state was 'sovereign' and the law was supreme and universal. This has never really been an adequate solution to the question; in France the solution was the guillotine, while constitutional monarchy was the compromise in Britain. Both sides have their villains and heroes, but only one side might prevail, being diametrically opposed and with irreconcilable views. The question, simply put for past republicans, was this: should the monarchy end in blood or in reasoned argument, and here the home-grown republican movement reached an unexpected impasse.

Yet how did the peculiar institution of monarchy in these isles come about? What makes a monarch a sovereign? The quest for clarity takes us back to the Anglo-Saxon settlement of Britain. The original invaders were pagan and Germanic, and their leaders were the product of strength and alliance. From what we understand, leadership was patrilineal, but women in both Germanic and Celtic tribes sometimes held power. Lines of kings were not necessarily related by blood but had to make an argument that they were descendants of an ancient family and the more ancient god Woden. Most would have been chosen either by conquest or by a 'vote' in the Witenagamot, the council of wise earls who were the traditional advisors to the 'elected' ruler. The relationship with the Witan was, as always, a compromise of interests:

> The Witan consisted of those leading men and counsellors ... whom the King chose to summon; it advised him but only when he asked its advice. On the other hand a king was wise to ask and take advice; and a king who was on good terms with his Witan would find it easier to enforce his will.[1]

Such councils were not, as suggested by later writers, the upholders of English liberty, but they did have a power that was gradually eroded in the time of the barons. Five civil conflicts tried to resolve the issue and Magna Carta and the Provisions of Oxford resulted, as we shall see. Kings could rule only because of consent or conquest. They ruled by the values cherished by their ancestors. Rulers had to be warlike, protect their people, secure their borders and create contentment. Once tribal groupings were replaced by nations, kings became the embodiment of territorial right and a symbol of national identity. One might legitimately overthrow a king if these criteria were not observed. The new applicant for the throne would need to be acknowledged by the Witan and acclaimed by the people gathered as witnesses. The key word was 'election', one that subsumed the nature of consent, conquest and divine intervention.

Dying kings might designate those who would inherit their throne. This was often crucial to decision-making and, in England, might include non-Anglo-Saxons. Such contracts, often bound by sacred oaths, meant descent was no guarantee of overlordship. The most famous example is the election of Duke William by Edward the Confessor and the oath taken by Harold when he arrived at William's court. The Anglo-Saxon Godwinson family and the king's brother-in-law were side-lined in favour of a Norman count. Anglo-Saxon kingship was always a gamble with Scandinavian interlopers and conquerors, and the legality of the ruler just as often a matter of military tactics and placid acceptance in the face of overwhelming odds.

The difficulties arising from the idea of election are many, not least of which is the puzzle of its true meaning. 'Election' suggests choosing (Latin: *eligere*; Old English: *ceosan*) and it was probably a formal process already decided before by the present king and debate amongst his earls. Abbot Aelfric, living at the turn of the eleventh century, suggested:

> No man can make himself king, but the people has the choice to choose as king whom they please; but after he is consecrated as king, he then has dominion over the people, and they cannot shake his yolk from their necks.[2]

As historians point out, there was not a free choice by the people and tyrants might still be legitimately deposed.

Nevertheless, with the coming of Christianity to the islands, the nature of kingship changed. The election of the ruler was now by God's grace. The king had God's grace as an attribute. He was elected by the council, the people and God. Such a divine election elevated the monarch and made his rule sacred. His allegiance to God was, from now on, to be mediated not by a council, but by the Roman institution of the Catholic faith.

A coronation began with a formal demand for the people's acceptance, the Archbishop of Canterbury presenting the new monarch-in-waiting to the people, although this ceremony seems not to have existed at the time of Edgar at his coronation in 973. Nevertheless, this ceremony, known as the *collaudatio*, seems to have happened with the accession of William when he was presented by Archbishop Sigand, as the Bayeux Tapestry illustrates. This may have been a formal process only held before notables and churchmen who then swore fealty to the new ruler, as did the Anglo-Saxon earls at their meeting with William at Berkhamsted, although they had previously sworn fealty to Edgar the Aetheling – clearly a dangerous, but not disastrous, mistake.

Thus the secular side of rulership was established. The sacred part of the ceremony, which is the anointing at the coronation, then followed, as it still does. In 787 Ecgfrith, Offa's son, was 'consecrated' and anointed with chrism and holy oil just as Samuel had anointed David in the Old Testament when Saul had lost God's favour. Solomon, too, had been chosen or elected by God, even though he was no relation to the ruling family of Israel. Although holy oil administered by an anointed bishop was an essential component of election to the office of ruler, it also became the essential element within the faith. The crown, orb and sceptre were all borrowed from Roman imperial practice, but the anointing with chrism (oil and balsam) was a Christian adoption of earlier lost (and probably pagan) practices. The king was now shown to the people as God's anointed on earth.

As such, at the coronation of Edgar, two bishops led the king into the church whilst a choir sang or chanted an antiphon (short sentence). The king prostrated himself before the altar and the *Te Deum* was sung. Edgar then made his coronation oath:

> The church of God and all his Christian people shall keep true peace under our rule at all times; that I shall forbid thefts and every iniquity to every grade of man; that I shall ordain justice and mercy in all judgements, that the kindly and merciful God may grant to me and to you his mercy.[3]

After a further three prayers came a more solemn prayer calling on God to bless the reign and Edgar to act as his agent on earth, to keep the Church and to rule wisely. He was then anointed and the antiphon 'Zadok the priest and Nathan the prophet' were then sung. The ceremony continued with more prayer, the giving of a ring and a sword and the actual crowning, after which the sceptre and staff were given to him. Edgar then received the acclamation of his nobles, all would shout '*vivat rex, vivat rex in eternum*' and, before a further Mass, he had his now-sacred position explained by Dunstan, Archbishop of Canterbury:

> Stand and grasp your royal status which you have held till now at your father's designation, delegated to you by hereditary right on the authority of almighty God and by the present agency of ourselves, God's bishops and other servants ... so that the mediator of God and men may confirm you on the throne of this kingdom as mediator of clergy and people, and make you reign with him in the eternal kingdom – Jesus Christ ... Our Lord.[4]

Edgar's wife was then presented for her ceremony with further prayers and sacred vows.

Versions of this ceremony were repeated at various significant moments during the reign to remind the king of his role and reinforce his authority over his people. His duties may have stretched upward to heaven, but they were firmly fixed in duty to the community:

> The duty of a consecrated king is that he judge no man falsely, and that he defend and protect widows and orphans and strangers, and forbid thefts, and amend illicit intercourse, and annul and totally forbid incestuous relationships, and eliminate witches and enchanters, and expel from the land kin-slayers and perjurers, and feed the needy with alms, and have old, wise and sober men as his counsellors.[5]

It was on these occasions that a king might be reminded to be 'just, severe and merciful', as Edward the Confessor was reminded in a sermon preached in 1043.[6] Interestingly, Aethelstan was the first king to appear crowned on his coins, the king taking on the symbolic and visible role of guarantor of his currency.

In the early eighteenth century, a new element of the ceremony was introduced. The rise of British prosperity was put down to the special relationship of the 'British' and the 'Anglo-Saxons' in particular, who were now considered to be the representatives of the migration of the Jewish tribes to Britain at the Diaspora. England, particularly, was seen as God's chosen country and the English as God's chosen people. For George II's son, the Duke of Cumberland, after the victory over the Scots at Culloden, Handel (a German mythologising Englishness) created his *Judas Maccabeus*, and for the coronation of George II he wrote four anthems, one of which is 'Zadock the Priest' (a re-imagining of the earlier antiphon) played at every coronation between 1727 and 2023.[7]

The early Georgian monarchs, despite their German origins and lack of English language, saw themselves as God's chosen monarchs of God's chosen people, reinforced by text and imagery borrowed from the Old Testament and reinterpreted in Christian ceremonials. The only explanation for the rise of English dominance in the world had to be because they were actually the lost tribes of Israel, an ideology still peddled by fringe Christian groups today. In reality, Jews were not fully politically emancipated until 1860; they had waited almost thirty years since the idea was first mooted in parliament. In the years between 1833 and 1860, 'Jew' bills had consistently been rejected by the Lords and opposed by the majority of the Tory Party, including the Duke of Wellington, and, in the early days, by William IV.

Nowadays, the ceremony of accession (rather than coronation) is the descendant of those appearances of the new king to his magnates. King Charles III was officially acknowledged monarch on 10 September 2022 at a ceremony with the Privy Council, now bloated from Queen Elizabeth I's day to 700 members, of whom 200 balloted individuals attended. The

Accession Council, as it is called, is presided over by the Lord President of the Council, currently Penny Mordaunt. The ceremony had two parts, held at St James's Palace, and was carried out by chosen privy counsellors, but with the king absent. They proclaimed the new sovereign and were joined by all the great officers of state, including the Prince of Wales, Queen Consort, Archbishops of Canterbury and York, the Lord Mayor, high commissioners and some senior civil servants. The counsellors stood throughout both parts of the ceremony.

The meeting began with the Lord President announcing the death of the sovereign and calling upon the Clerk of the Council to read aloud the text of the Accession Proclamation (this includes Charles's chosen title as king). Then the 'platform party', consisting of Queen Consort Camilla, Prince William, the Archbishops of Canterbury and York, the Lord Chancellor, the Prime Minister, the Lord Privy Seal, the Lord Great Chamberlain, the Earl Marshal and the Lord President, signed the Proclamation. After which the Lord President called for silence and read the terms under which the proclamation was made and ordered where the dissemination of the Proclamation would occur, as well as giving various directions on the firing of guns at Hyde Park and the Tower of London.

The second part of the ceremony was Charles's first Privy Council meeting. Charles first made a personal declaration about the death of the queen and then took the oath to preserve the Church of Scotland (because in Scotland there is a division of power between Church and State). The Coldstream Guards, at attention in the yard of St James's Palace, then offered three cheers, the royal trumpeters played a salute and the chief herald read the proclamation to 'the people'. It was read again to the Mayor and Alderman of the City of London and later proclaimed throughout the realm. Unlike their medieval predecessors, modern constitutional monarchs are not rulers with 'just and severe' authority granted by God and the most powerful in the land, but 'servants' of the people, a reversal that takes away power to replace it with symbolic 'ceremony'.

Thus a king was (and still is) created through a ceremony. His *actual* role was another matter, and remains one of much debate. All medieval kings of England, including William the Conqueror, looked back to the righteous reign of Alfred the Great, to whom they frequently referred in legal wrangles and from whom they took as their ideal the concept of an ancient realm, peaceful, church-going, law-abiding, loyal and militarily prepared. Alfred's reign, and even his personality, quickly became distorted and mythologised as needs dictated.

Alfred was the idealised English king. Others fell below his standard. One who fell into disrespect was Henry III, ironically a cultured and peaceful ruler. Nevertheless, his insatiable need for money made him enemies. One was his brother-in-law, Simon de Montfort, who is credited with bringing some sort of 'democratic' and even 'republican' values to the politics of his time. He was, of course, neither a democrat nor a republican, but rather a fanatical crusader for holy causes (he wore a hairshirt during his latter years). Quick to take offence and quicker to see attempts at humiliation in every encounter, he was nevertheless accounted to be a brave and honourable warrior (notwithstanding his treatment of the Jews). Henry and de Montfort spent years wrangling over land, deference and money. Henry had none; de Montfort wanted more.

It was Henry's overseas ambition, especially regarding the Crown of Sicily that brought dangerous quarrels to a head. The king was becoming far too autocratic and ruling without due statesmanship or regard to his leading barons; law and order were collapsing, and de Montfort's crusading instinct grew, as did that of others. Except this crusade would be in England, not the Holy Land. Henry III and his son Edward were roundly defeated at Lewes (1264) and both captured. From now on, Henry would act as de Montfort's puppet, dragged around as a king without a crown. De Montfort was, for a short time, 'steward' of England, now able to impose his will – the new 'crusading' vision of the commonality of the realm – making decisions in concert to which a king would be bound.

Victory meant changes and new communally agreed 'laws' defended by barons and commoners alike: the Provisions of Oxford, which were the result of a 'parliament' held at Oxford on 11 June 1258, although De Montfort was not present. On 2 May, Henry had promised to try to impose the rule of law and legal justice, which had become corrupted by his nearest advisors who were seen as foreigners. The Provisions were as much about removing foreigners from English lands as about justice for the English. De Montfort had already shown contempt for the Gascons, the French and the Jews in his guise as a crusading knight. The hated foreigners this time were Henry's half-brothers, the Poitevins, who De Montfort wished to see banished, in the same way that the barons had demanded foreign mercenaries should be forced to leave as a condition of Magna Carta sealed during the reign of King John. This 'parliament' was the culmination of his crusading beliefs. Twelve councillors were chosen by the king and twelve by De Montfort's followers. From these, two were chosen from each side to then pick fifteen permanent council members.

The Provisions of Oxford, the rules for the very first attempt at governance by a 'parliament' of peers, freemen and burgesses, appear not to have been written down at the time. They are known from two corrupted texts published as late as 1684. The essence of the Provisions, agreed in 1258 (and confirmed a year later by the Provisions of Westminster), were the compromise that allowed Henry III to win support for his Sicilian ambitions. As stated above, they called for twenty-four 'signatories' to guarantee the contract between the monarch and his lords, half for the king and half for the barons. Each member had first to swear a sacred oath to uphold the Crown, but also 'the reformation and amendment of the estate of the realm'. The chancellor swore that he would uphold the law designated by the majority of the council and guaranteed by the magnates:

> This the chancellor of England shall swear.
>
> That he will seal no writ, excepting writs of course, without the commandment of the king and of his council who shall be present. Nor shall he seal a gift under the great seal, nor under the great [left blank], nor of escheats, without the assent of the great council or of the major part. And that he will seal nothing which maybe contrary to the ordance which is made and shall be made by the twenty-four or by the major part. And that he will take no fee otherwise than that which is given to the others. And he shall be given a companion in the form which the council shall provide.[8]

Moreover, 'that he seal nothing out of course by the sole [sic] will of the King. But he do it by the council which shall be around the King.'[9]

This was followed by a momentous comment that the king, robbed of authority, would be subject to the four barons who would choose the king's council subject to the agreement of the signatories to the Provisions. Three 'parliaments' were to be called each year, where the barons and 'commonality of the land' might meet to consider 'common need'. The king's judges were to sit for only one year, after which they were expected to answer for their actions. Another clause revised the relationship of the secular authority (of the new parliament) to the Church. All the clauses were to create a bond between magnates, the people and the king in order to safeguard 'the Charter of Liberty', a revised and more binding agreement than had been decided by Magna Carta, which had been continuously revisited and revised and had even begun to provide a legal framework for ordinary folk.

Yet, just as with Magna Carta, the curtailment of royal privilege rankled. Henry had declared himself satisfied with the Provisions, but his repudiation soon followed, backed by the weight of papal approval. Louis IX of France was asked to arbitrate and 'annulled' the agreement on 23 January 1264, but suggested that the laws of England before the Provisions should be adhered to – in other words, the laws as traditionally believed to have been handed down by Alfred the Great.

Henry III raised an army and war ensued. Simon de Montfort met a crusader's death at Evesham, where his body was ritually mutilated in an act of revenge. By the Dictum of Kenilworth at the siege of De Montfort's castle in 1266, the slate was cleaned for yet another monarch to reign as they saw fit. Things had changed, however, as rulers became more cognisant of priorities that they could not control by diktat and by laws and taxes that were not simply at their command to change or raise. A parliament was assembled at Kenilworth during the siege to make the new arrangements.

By the Dictum, and after continued sporadic warfare, Henry reconfirmed his allegiance to both Magna Carta and the Charter of the Forest (the main sources of royal restriction and general rights), and these were agreed in exchange for Henry to be able to have his personal prerogative in relationship to the appointment of his councillors. He, in turn, gave back confiscated lands taken from the rebels (but at agreed prices!). In November 1267, another parliament had been called, which confirmed the Statute of Marlborough, attesting to the reconciliation of rebels to the king and the restoration of lost royal prerogatives. It remained thereafter a central support for royal government.

Magna Carta, passed at Runnymede in 1215, continued to cast shadows over royal privilege. After King John's death, Prince Henry, his underage son, was left in the hands of a regency and the regency government decided to re-issue the agreement in 1216 that they had forced John to sign under duress, but this time stripped of its more radical clauses. When the First Barons' War erupted during John's reign, Magna Carta formed part of the peace treaty agreed at Lambeth in London. It was here that the contract was first named Magna Carta in order to distinguish it from the other 'contract' of rights, the Charter of the Forest. Henry III republished Magna Carta in the hope of gaining monies from new taxes. Edward I, Henry's belligerent son, nevertheless, issued Magna Carta again in 1297 and it was re-affirmed by each monarch thereafter, ironically losing its power as parliaments amended or changed laws regarding governance and prerogatives.

The system of feudal relationships that William I had had to set up to reward his followers was always fragile, with a tension between nobles who needed legitimisation from the monarch and a monarch who needed constant support from his nobles. The arrangements were complicated by land ownership, which could be withdrawn by the king at a moment's notice, and the practicality of being allowed to build a castle for which royal permission was required. Nobility itself was reinforced by the knightly class and other wealthy dependants, as well as by marriage ties. The inherent tensions of this pyramid of power, ratified and upheld by the Church, created divisions of loyalty that were not resolved until the mid-eighteenth century, when the Jacobites were defeated in Britain's last civil war. Ultimately, everything depended on the good will of the monarch and the acquiescence of the leading families, for without that there was no overriding authority (certainly not the law).

This, however, could have disastrous consequences. Although by the fifteenth century there was an established parliament, its function was to advise and ratify rather than create policy. It could not override the monarch's foreign ambitions, but it still could delay monies for foreign adventures. The conflict that broke out in the fifteenth century, known as the Wars of the Roses, was a direct consequence of the loss of England's French possessions and the machinations of a resurgent France, which allowed family rivalry to overspill into civil war and vendetta.

After his death, Richard of York's bid to overthrow Henry VI was followed by his son's bid to become king. Henry's two

mental breakdowns (he may have suffered from bipolar disorder) created a power vacuum into which nobles, now uncertain
of the stability of their position, fought for the Crown. Henry
ended in the Tower of London as the Yorkist faction took power
under Edward IV, only for them to fall at the hands of the Earl
of Warwick. Henry VI was taken from the Tower of London
and trotted round as the restored king in a 'Readeption' with
Warwick in charge, even though Henry was openly considered
'mad' by many of the common people; as early as 1442 a yeoman
from Kent had openly declared that 'the king was a natural fool'
and a Sussex man had suggested that Henry simply whiled away
his hours with a staff and bird 'as a fool'; 'another king must be
ordained to rule the land,' he argued.[10]

And so the power struggle began, even though Henry had
been ordained by the Church as God's regnal agent and therefore
could not be deposed, God had apparently removed His grace.
Edward had to eventually flee to Flanders, only to return to
seize the throne once again, making sure that this time Henry,
holed up in the Tower, would be silenced forever. He died in
mysterious circumstances. Each time one or other king returned
to the throne, he was acclaimed before parliament, which ratified his status.

The Civil War was extremely violent, with pitched battles
replacing sieges, and it lacked the codes of chivalry that determined the fate of the defeated during earlier centuries. To gloss
over the mayhem, chroniclers and courtiers renamed the era
after Arthur's Camelot. Nobles and gentlemen followers were
frequently beheaded, not as noble adversaries, but as traitors
to whichever king had won the battle. Edward IV finally triumphed with a mixture of love and 'dread', but the prolonged
wars had decimated the aristocracy and debilitated the country, which had suffered constant risings amongst the common
people. What was left of Edward's dream died with his brother
at Bosworth and the appearance of yet another contender for the
throne, Henry Tudor, now crowned Henry VII.

What was left of the highest magnates kept silent and waited on events they were no longer controlling. Much of the nobility of England was scattered abroad in Flanders, Brittany, Burgundy and Scotland. Those whom the new regime were to employ were those of the lesser 'county' gentry. These men were not nobles, but merchants and entrepreneurs from mercantile backgrounds who had risen to become town mayors, Members of Parliament, judges and landowners, but whose ambitions were European, based on trade and monetary adventures, and joined by new skeins of early European capitalism. These were, however, the type of men who still needed to align themselves with noble houses in order to gain prestige and royal patronage. As such, they too were unstable, but they had to be embraced by a febrile and nervous Tudor regime, constantly reminded that it was the instrument of French connivance and duplicity and prey to constant spying and threats of war from France and Scotland. Thus, it was these 'new' royal servants and money men who also chose to align themselves to Margaret of Burgundy and Charles VIII of France when it suited, in order to further their own precarious positions and place their puppet candidate in power, as was the case of the Perkin Warbeck conspiracy of 1499. Medieval politicians, with their ties of loyalty, land, revenge, chivalrous behaviour and justice, were being replaced by avaricious newcomers who needed royalty to justify their own importance, either as Englishmen or agents of France.

Henry VII's son, Henry VIII, however, seeing the difficulty of keeping noble alliances in place, also chose to counter them with chosen men, often from ordinary backgrounds whose only loyalty was to the throne. Thus, a new breed of obedient bureaucrats replaced the old families, whose jealousy could be appeased simply by dismissing the offender or, more likely, having them declared a traitor. Henry VIII was wise in one respect, for he left parliament alone if it didn't interfere with his personal business. He often took their decisions, although contrary to his expectations, with a knowing smile and a pinch of salt.[11] The only meaningful control any of the Lancastrian, Yorkist or Tudor monarchs could bring to bear was not a royal pardon, but the threat of immediate execution at the whim of the Crown.

By Queen Elizabeth I's reign, the arrangement of the country's governance had been stabilised. Almost gone were the days of the semi-autocratic rule of the Middle Ages, and so too were the worst excesses of her father's reign. Nevertheless, this did not mean that Elizabeth was not fully aware of her own significance, just that greater subtlety was needed, after her own life was considered to be a stake. Elizabeth worked through her advisors on the Privy Council, the epicentre of real power wielded on her behalf, and she listened and worked closely with them, cleverly avoiding the potential pitfalls of religious upheaval or foreign war or invasion. The council controlled the nobles in the Lords, introducing bills, reconciling differences and offering preferment, whatever got their way. The Commons supposedly remained the supreme house, but this was mostly a sham hiding disguised noble patronage.

Yet, it had the right to speak 'truth to power' and it could use 'free speech without danger', as Stephen Gardiner reminisced.[12] Even so, free speech was ill-defined. It meant one thing to some members of the Commons which it clearly did not mean to others. Was free speech – freedom to speak openly and even treasonously – freedom to speak from a position of loyalty or simply a form of bibulous madness? The debate was unresolved, with members of the Commons only too aware of their own prerogatives, which the nobility did not share. The Commons had a potent weapon in the right to withhold taxation requests, the one key area in which the monarch could not afford to offend the members of the lower house. Where Elizabeth's prerogatives were challenged, she would not sign an assent and sent the bill back for reconsideration, where it often just vanished from the agenda, but where her self-decided rights were not challenged, she left the Commons to its own devices. Yet, her particular tastes in rulership meant she had her way in some unnecessarily odd situations: 'Elizabeth's parsimonious preference for a lord keeper of the great seal instead of a lord chancellor necessitated an act of 1563 to confirm that the former had the authority as the latter.'[13]

Meanwhile, what did the Elizabethan parliament mean?

Parliament met to do certain things – to provide money, to pass bills, to discuss matters of concern. If it was to fulfil those purposes it needed organisation and guidance; to have failed to provide these would have been a plain dereliction of duty on the part of those who governed under the Queen and recognised the Parliament for what it was – a part of the Queen's administrative machine ... the Privy Council ... remained in control.[14]

The status quo was disturbed by the demands of a cash-strapped and God-obsessed Charles I, who felt his divine authority was more important than the system that Elizabeth had followed. Interference produced rebellion and its republican child. Monarchs who followed the debacle trod carefully, but built stronger lines of patronage and control, knowing what to leave be and where they could best retain old powers, create new sources of strength or gain powerful new adherents; they learned that one could control events through back-corridor confidences. *L'esprit d'escalier* served in England as it did in France.

The relationship between monarch and parliament was always likely to fracture if the balance of powers and prerogatives could not be maintained, either through a 'new' view of parliament's role or that of monarchy's *amour propre*. Such was the case in 1629 when Charles I dismissed parliament and ruled alone under the notion of the 'divine right of kings' for a further eleven years. He and his father James I were also convinced of their powers to heal the sick of scrofula and took their ceremonies of 'healing' very seriously. As might be expected, the king had to reconvene parliament in April 1640 in order to raise taxes to fight the Scots. Parliament sat for only three weeks but would not grant the subsidy, instead demanding that the house should be regularly called and it rights, and its voice, restored.

Two years later, on 1 June 1642, both houses passed the 'Nineteen Propositions', which demanded, amongst other things, that all royal counsellors, ministers, admirals and the Privy Council be approved by parliamentary debate; that the education and marriage of the king's children be subject to parliamentary approval, as well as all military appointments; and that, importantly, the Church should be reformed and the law upheld through parliament and not arbitrarily by the king. The Provisions were immediately dismissed by the king as an attempt to wrest power and leave him 'impotent'. He was outraged and refused to countenance such insubordination, despite the Provisions ending with the sweetener that parliament would grant the king money for his Scottish war.

Charles, in turn, decided to publish a 'Commission of Array' to raise soldiers (a direct act of war) and parliament retaliated by creating committees of public safety and passing legislation to raise its own armies. The king raised his standard on 22 August 1642 and the civil wars that encompassed the British Isles until 1651 began. These wars were about restoring parliamentary rule, the importance of traditional English legal and constitutional practice, the role of the monarch within parliament and the reform of the Anglican religion, and fear of Catholicism.

The war produced damage greater than anything seen before the First World War in proportion to the populations of England, then around 5 million, and Scotland, then 1 million. There were around 85,000 casualties, 100,000 dead from disease or wounds, 2 per cent of the population were made homeless and destitute and over 100,000 properties were destroyed. By 1649, the ideas that the Nineteen Provisions should stand had been forgotten and little had been resolved. Charles had been executed, leaving only unresolved and lasting resentments, and a desire for revenge by royalist outcasts, not the desired relationship of Crown and Parliament that had been sought. The anger and zeal of the victors found that there would be no compromise and turned the war into a fight for the idea of a republican commonwealth upholding the principles of parliamentary sovereignty and control by the peerage. This was as fragile as divine right had been. It would remain unresolved in the next reign after the interregnum of a republic that lasted from 1649 to 1660.

Charles II may have been portrayed in the popular mind as the 'merry monarch' following the supposed grimness of the last days of the Commonwealth, but his portraits show him as an ageing *roué* with a pencil moustache and a sneer, much more suggestive of the rather more paranoid and suspicious person he actually was. In one sense, of course, with the memory of his father's fate and with the gloomy thoughts regarding the security of the Stuart line once his brother James took over, he was justified in his suspicions. Yet the threat from extremist cults of apocalyptic Christians mixed in his mind (and that of his brother) with the potential damage to his authority inflicted by new philosophies of virtue, freedom and liberty coming from the pens of republicans, many of noble birth.

Despite his importance to republicanism, Algernon Sidney is now largely forgotten, and he is certainly less well known than his contemporary John Locke. He was born a Percy on his mother's side, a descendant of Harry Hotspur, whilst on his father's side his great uncle was Sir Philip Sidney. He spent his youth at Penshurst and soon developed a belief in merit as the key to rulership, perhaps because his brother, the future Earl of Leicester, was both dull and indolent. During the Civil War, Sidney joined the parliamentary forces and was severely wounded at Marston Moor. He was a commissioner for the trial of Charles I and, although concerned about the legality of the proceedings, still felt the execution was 'the justest and bravest action that was ever done in England'.[15] Cromwell appeared no better, however, and when he broke up the Rump of the Long Parliament in 1653, Sidney defied the soldiers. At the restoration of Charles II, Sidney was willing to bend the knee, but soon concluded that here was yet another 'tyrant':

> When I call to my remembrance all my actions relating to our civil distempers, I cannot find one that I can look upon as a breach of the rules of justice or honour; this is my strength, and, I thank God, by this I enjoy very serene thoughts. If I lose this by vile and unworthy submissions acknowledgment of errors, asking of pardon or the like, I shall from that moment by the miserablest [*sic*] man alive, and the scorn of all men.[16]

Pursued by the king's agents bent on his assassination, Sidney realised that his attitude was too deeply embedded to shake off and that his stubbornness might be his undoing:

> I know the titles that are given me of fierce, violent, seditious, mutinous, turbulent ... I know people will say, I strain at gnats, and swallow camels; that it is a strange conscience, that lets a man run violently on, till he is deep in civil blood, and then stays at a few words and compliments ... I cannot help if I judge amiss; I did not make myself, nor can I correct the defects of my own creation. I walk in the light that God hath given me; if it be dim or uncertain I must bear the penalty of my errors. I hope to do it with patience, and that no burden shall be very grievous to me, except sin and shame.[17]

Returning to England in 1677, once Charles thought him harmless, Sidney began his republic plotting as an almost sacred obligation. In 1679 he worked with William Penn to get parliamentary support for greater religious toleration, but he soon returned to the fight against tyranny, in fear that on the accession of James II parliament would be disbanded and Catholicism reinstated. In 1681 Charles dismissed parliament and decided to rule alone. The nightmare Sidney feared had come about. He turned to armed revolution, but the conspirators were arrested on 26 June 1683 and charged with high treason. Locke escaped at the last minute; Sidney was tried in front of Lord Chief Judge Jeffreys (the 'Hanging Judge') and after a farcical and illegal trial was sentenced to death. He was executed on 7 December 1683, but his real importance began with the loss of his head.

Sidney was a deep political thinker and, although his prose was of its time, his ideas were modern. Between 1681 and 1683 he composed a gigantic work of political theory in answer to another book supporting monarchy and divine right. *The Discourses Concerning Government* runs to over 500 pages, tightly packed with references to the classics and the Bible in order to refute tyrannical rule. His arguments differ from Locke and oppose Hobbs, the essence of the *Discourses* being the importance of virtue and honour in public life and the necessity of governance by true 'patriots', those freemen and gentlemen whose interests are best served by a free parliament, toleration in religion, free speech and universal law. Sidney believed humans to be able to run their lives and their country through reason. For Sidney, a freely elected popular assembly could not, by its existence, act unreasonably as long as it acknowledged the supremacy and universality of the law that restricted parliamentary excess and guaranteed individual liberty (political freedom).

His voice echoed years later in America where John Adams and Thomas Jefferson read the *Discourses* with attention in 1823. Adams wanted to publish Sidney in America, noting the slow evolutionary and painful progress of 'the advocates of liberty'. On a visit to the University of Utrecht, Sidney had written in the visitor's book, '*Manus haec inimica tyrannis. Ense petit placidam sub libertate quietem*' ('This Hand, enemy to tyrants, By the sword seeks calm peacefulness with liberty'). It is the official motto of the state of Massachusetts to this day.[18]

Thus, in this world of swirling resentment, frustration and conspiracy, one stepped with extreme caution. Republican enemies of monarchy, whose themes were parliamentary supremacy under the law (made by a free parliament) and rule by an oligarchy of 'patriots' (the name used to describe landed radical aristocrats), now saw themselves opposed to tyrannical government (i.e. that of the Stuart family). The consequences would be bloody indeed and rise to a crescendo with war between parliament's nobles and the Catholic James II. The final rapprochement was the Glorious Revolution, neither the bloodless revolution it was portrayed as nor glorious, which saw stability and peace restored in a compromise, the so-called new constitution, that would be continuously challenged by the exiled Stuarts from overseas up until 1746.

The accession of the Catholic James II created problems for the Church of England. On the one hand, they had been implacably opposed to the infiltration of popery, whilst on the other, they believed in the divine right of kings. For the most part, the Church urged simple acquiescence. The coming of William of Orange rendered their position bankrupt and destroyed their sense of purpose. Churchmen faced a serious quandary, for although the institution of the Church was guaranteed security, it was also threatened by the Toleration Act, the statutory establishment of Presbyterianism in Scotland and the Failure of the Comprehension Bill. Their willingness to back James II was a disastrous mistake of policy accounted for by blaming it on a diabolical plot to weaken the Church rather than realising that divine right was the stumbling block. In 1686, the diarist John Evelyn noted that the events surrounding the deposition of James II were the result of England falling 'from its antient zeal and Integretie'. On 19 April 1689, Evelyn wrote that the whole affair had been managed by 'some crafty, ill-principled men': 'The new Pr[ivy] Council having a Republican Spirit, and manifestly undermining all future Succession of the Crown, and Prosperity of the Church of England.'[20]

Nevertheless, by December 1689, Evelyn was in better spirits; his tone, however, had turned to one of resigned cynicism:

A Parliament (legally called) of brave and worthy patriots, not
influenced by faction, nor terrified by power, or corrupted by
self interest, would produce a kind of new creation amongst
us. But it will grow old, and dissolve to chaos again, unless
the same stupendous Provident which had put this opportunity into men's hands to make us happy, dispose them to
do just and righteous things, and to use their empire with
moderation, justice, piety, and for the public good ... These
[difficulties relative to preferment] and sundry other difficulties will render things both uneasy and uncertain. Only
I think Popery to be universally declining, and you know I
am one of those who despise not prophesying; nor whilst I
behold what is daily wrought in the world, believe miracles
to be ceased.[21]

As the 'high' Church crumbled under the strain of allegiances,
the 'lower' Church and dissenters gathered around the new
Newtonian sciences and attitudes they saw as ushering in a new
age; and with them and their secular supporters we see a turn
towards constitutional monarchy in its current sense.

Despite these new views, divine right or election by God's
grace was tempered, not abolished. Yet, as early as 1678, John
Bunyan mused upon the miracle of divine election where
'they said [Christ] had made many pilgrims princes though
by nature they were beggars born, and their original [*sic*] had
been the dunghill'. This resembled too closely the democratic
individualism in the last third of the seventeenth century and
such thoughts led straight to prison. Bunyan spent twelve
years in Bedford Jail. Here he wrote *The Pilgrim's Progress*,
published in London by Nathaniel Ponder six years after
his release and, for centuries, the most widely read book in
English after the Bible.

Bunyan's mission in *The Pilgrim's Progress* was to allegorise the
route to salvation and to deliver the self-directed pilgrim to the
'Gates of Heaven'. It may have been a 'dream', as he explains,

but this was a visionary dream, with a warning, or prophecy, of the future. Bunyan was an ordinary man, the son of a tinker (someone who mended household implements) and a 'private' in the Parliamentary Army with no pretensions to landed position, but had restated in muted language the revolutionary thoughts of radicals during the Commonwealth, but this time restated as allegory.

Despite restrictions on royal interference in national politics, it was still possible for T.H.B. Oldfield to complain in his 1816 six-volume study of representation that there was still 'the enormous and overwhelming influence of the crown'.[22] The Hanoverians, with their Germanic princely attitudes, could not see the need to avoid interfering in public life. George III's interference in colonial affairs is well known and his son was able to delay Catholic emancipation for years, whilst William IV simply dismissed ministers he did not like (in 1834, for instance), although he was the last monarch to dare do so.

On 26 August 1828, the Duke of Wellington wrote a despairing letter to Robert Peel: 'Between the King and his brothers the Government of this country is become a most heart-breaking concern. Nobody can ever know where he stands upon any subject.'[23]

Meanwhile governmental cynicism replaced remedial action. Lord John Campbell, on 26 April 1830, wrote to his brother:

The new reign will produce no change in the Government. The Duke of Clarence (I must say) magnanimously forgave the Duke of Wellington for turning him out of his office of Lord Admiral. The danger is that the Duke of Clarence will become deranged before he has been long on the throne. He was very nearly upset by his High Admiralship; and the excitement of a crown will be too much for him to bear. He will be difficult to manage for, though very good-natured, he is fond of meddling, and is very 'bizarre' in many of his notions. George IV is the model of a constitutional King of England! And when he is missed he may be mourned. He has stood by and let the country govern itself.[24]

On 14 July 1841, George Anson penned a rather sterner memorandum:

> The Monarchy of this Country has its sole foundation in the will of the people. Without that will it cannot stand and from that will it derives every prerogative and power. The Commonwealth has shown that the Country can exist and flourish without a monarchy and the Sovereign should be reminded forcibly by this fact, that the Sovereign of a free people cannot be the Sovereign of a party.[25]

By 1870 the monarchy was in trouble again: Victoria was 'invisible', according to William Gladstone, and her son was 'not respected'; the prime minister even had doubts as to the monarchy's ability to survive the year. Their 'credit [was] diminishing' fast, as he suggested in a private letter to Earl Granville on 3 December 1870. Little wonder that monarchy and the role of parliament became topics of serious debate during the nineteenth century. It was clear to all, both Whig and Tory, and later Liberal and Conservative, that the monarch appeared to be more and more a pointless appendage of the constitution, a remnant whose presence, ghost-like, disturbed the actual governors of Britain's parliament.

What was the role of the monarch and how did nineteenth-century monarchy see itself? Earl Grey set out the limits of parliamentary government in 1858:

> It is the distinguishing characteristic of Parliamentary Government, that it requires the powers belonging to the Crown to be exercised through Ministers, who are held responsible for the manner in which they are used, who are

expected to be members of the two Houses of Parliament, and more especially of the House of Commons.

By this arrangement the Executive power and the power of Legislation are virtually united in the same hands, but both are limited – the executive power by the law, and that of legislation by the necessity of obtaining the assent of Parliament to the measures brought forward.[26]

Nevertheless, Walter Bagehot argued that the monarch had a role in politics through three rights: 'the right to be consulted, the right to encourage, the right to warn' (three suggestions, now taken as statute law by some commentators). Yet, the monarch must also remain shrouded in mystery for 'we must not let in daylight upon magic'. Thereafter, the monarch was supposed to be a mix of Greek oracle and consulting detective. The young Prince of Wales, the future George V, was set the task of giving a precis of Bagehot's ideas in 1894 by his tutor, J.R. Tanner. It reads in part:

MONARCHY
1. The value of the Crown in its dignified capacity
    a. It makes Government intelligible to the masses.
    b. It makes Government interesting to the masses
    c. It strengthens Government with the religious tradition connected with the Crown …
    f. The existence of the Crown serves to disguise change & therefore to deprive it of the evil consequences of revolution, e.g. The Reform Bill of 1832.
2. The value of the Crown in its business capacity …
    b. During the continuance of Ministries. The Crown possesses first the right to be consulted, second the right to encourage & third the right to worn …
    c. He [*sic*] is the only statesman in the country whose political experience is continuance.[27]

A number of books quite rightly state that the monarch is there to be 'consulted', to 'encourage' and 'warn'. This, of course, is Walter Bagehot's definition, but Richard J. Aldrich states, in *Spying and the Crown* (2021), that monarchs enjoy the *'constitutional* [my emphasis] right to offer comments, encouragement and ... warning'.[28]

This is a fabrication. There is absolutely no constitutional precedent for such a statement. The statement of the monarch's 'rights' came full blown from Walter Bagehot in his book *The English Constitution*, which he published in 1867. Unbelievably, Bagehot, a journalist rather than politician, and a republican in sentiment as well, was hardly enamoured with the abilities of rulers. Nevertheless, his highly influential book helped define the role of monarchy as the highest appendage of 'crowned republic' (as H.G. Wells later put it in 1914) and gave the working class a sense of Victoria's purpose at a time when she had none. Such rights quickly extended to the vice regal representatives of the empire (and later Commonwealth) too.

These three dicta have no constitutional basis whatsoever, having never been debated or passed into law. They are a fabrication, which was made worse by the announcement by Queen Elizabeth II's private secretary, Sir William Heseltine, in *The Times* on 28 July 1986, that the queen enjoyed these 'rights' because they were a royal 'duty'. This was mere fluff, but it remained unchallenged. It was still taught as a school lesson to Prince William. The confusion over the issue is compounded by the problems surrounding penetrating royal privilege and prime ministerial meetings, as suggested by academics such as Anne Twomey of the University of Sydney. Twomey points out the ambiguity and ambivalence of the position:

> The secrecy surrounding royal intervention in the political process means that today, as for Bagehot 150 years ago, it is impossible to state with accuracy the true role of the sovereign in the political process. It is true, however, to say that

the sovereign's role is primarily one of influence, as suggested by Bagehot. The nature of that influence, at least in its formal description, has changed over time from limited rights to be consulted, to encourage and to warn, to more expansive rights and even duties to advise, advocate and urge changes in policy positions. Whether this change in description reflects a change in substance or is simply a more accurate reflection of what has always occurred behind palace doors will only be able to be determined once the documents concerning the reign of Queen Elizabeth II are eventually released.[29]

Yet it remains the case that there is no legal basis for the role except the willing acquiescence of those in power.

Victoria's reign was beset with national disturbances early on and every decision by the later Hanoverians was in part a decision taken through the lens of the French Revolution and the revolutionary tendencies at home. These did not subside until 1820 and were overtaken by the republican-tinged agricultural, industrial and political agitation, which continued beyond the Great Reform Act of 1832 until 1839, when militant Chartism collapsed.

All the threats to the regime in the first third of the nineteenth century were suppressed with draconian ferocity in an attempt to restore the status quo. Nevertheless, although violent anti-monarchical feeling had subsided with the working man's vote and unionisation, the queen's 'invisibility' and the ascension of radical politics during Gladstone's time in office brought republicanism dangerously to the fore both in the 1870s and 1880s. Victoria pleaded overwork for her silence, but the general public was not convinced. Monarchy resisted as the emblem of the 'social status quo', not least because of a rescue mission by Benjamin Disraeli.[30]

On 3 April 1872, Disraeli addressed a meeting in Manchester:

Gentlemen, since the settlement of that Constitution, now nearly two centuries ago, England has never experienced a revolution, though there is no country in which there has been so continuous and such considerable change. How is this? Because the wisdom of your forefathers placed the prize of supreme power without the sphere of human passions ... [the benefits of monarchy for the country follow] ... And you owe all these, gentlemen, to the Throne. There is another powerful and most beneficial influence which is also exercised by the Crown. Gentlemen, I am a party man. I believe that, without party, Parliamentary government is impossible ... I know it will be said, gentlemen, that, however beautiful in theory, the personal influence of the Sovereign is now absorbed in the responsibility of the minister. Gentlemen, I think you will find there is great fallacy in this view. The principles of the English Constitution do not contemplate the absence of personal influence on the part of the Sovereign ... The longer the reign, the influence of that Sovereign must proportionately increase ... who can suppose when such information and each suggestions are made by the most exalted person in the country that they can be without effect ...

Gentlemen, the influence of the Crown is not confined merely to political affairs. England is a domestic country. Here the home is revered and the hearth is sacred. The nation is represented by a family – the Royal Family; and if that family is educated with a sense of responsibility and a sentiment of public duty, it is difficult to exaggerate the salutary influence they may exercise over a nation It is not merely an influence upon manners; it is not merely that they are a model for refinement and for good taste – they affect the heart as well as the intelligence of the people; and in the hour of public adversity, or in the anxious conjuncture of public affairs, the nation rallies round the Family and the Throne, and its spirit is animated and sustained by the expression of public affection.[31]

This did not stop royal interventions. Victoria and Albert also couldn't resist forays into politics, the most famous example being the creation of the Great Exhibition, but also the none too clever negotiations between Victoria and the Irish unionists in 1886, which showed a clear monarchic preference in political life, unactable under the constitution. Victoria showed preferences, too, over the problem of Danish duchies in 1864 and the eastern question in 1880. As early as 1839, Victoria obstructed Peel when he tried to form a ministry. Although Victoria regarded herself as above politics, there was very little left for her to do except become the embodiment of empire, so interfere she did, as did Edward VII, and as has King Charles III with his famous indiscreet letter writing.

Victoria and Albert dreamed of a quite different world to the one they were forced to endure. Whilst Victoria called herself a 'liberal', she was utterly detached from Liberal values and a staunch opponent of democracy and radical change. The couple's imagination was fixed in past glories, such as their medieval Bal Masque held on 12 May 1842. According to Disraeli, the autocratic and Germanic Albert was the true monarch of Great Britain. He died unexpectedly on 14 December 1861:

> We have buried our sovereign. This German Prince has governed England for twenty-one years with a wisdom and energy such as none of our kings have ever shown ... If he had out-lived some of our old stagers, he would have given us the blessings of absolute government.[32]

As she aged, Victoria become an even greater opponent of democracy. A Whig at heart and reasonably 'liberal' in personal relationships with servants etc., Victoria could see no reason to tinker with the 'constitution' as it only encouraged radicals and fanatics such as socialists:

> These are trying moments and it seems to me a defect in our famed Constitution, to have to part with an admirable Government like Lord Salisbury's for no question of any

importance, or any particular reason, merely on account of the number of votes.[33]

On 11 September 1879, Victoria put her thoughts on her personal politics in correspondence with Lady Ely. This was Victoria's 'red line', beyond which she would not give a bill her consent:

> I wish the principal people of the Opposition should know there are certain things which I never can consent to 1. Any lowering of the position of this country by letting Russia have her way in the East, or by letting down our Empire in India and the Colonies ... 2. That I would never give way about the Scotch Church which is the real and true stronghold of Protestantism.[34]

Despite, or even because of, her hatred of radicalism, Victoria's motives also harboured a contradictory side regarding 'the Scotch Church'. This repeats an oddly republican affection for the 'Good Old Cause', reminiscent of Cromwell's description of his ideal solders in the New Model Army. That Victoria had 'republican' thoughts might have disturbed her; it may have amused her.

Victoria as the embodiment of empire was almost literally resurrected and animated by Disraeli, and crowds cheered themselves hoarse at her Golden Jubilee in 1887, where a camera caught her toothless, mask-like smile: the age of the media had begun, proof that she was simply an old lady after all. When she died, her funeral procession, complete with all the royalty of the world and the pomp of empire, was caught on newsreel, a last hoorah for imperial grandeur and an age gone by. Just as with the late Queen Elizabeth II, Victoria's reign had lasted people's whole lives: they knew no different, and the future instantly destabilised at her absence. A new and uncertain age seemed to begin. Modernity brought uncertainty and apocalyptic fears, in which a dynastic and hereditary monarch seemed even more invalid.

To lead the new century in, her son ascended the throne. Edward VII was old by the time he took over the reins of monarchy and he too had freely expressed his opinions when Prince of Wales. As king he belonged to that last great flush of European monarchy that still held sway over grand politics. Edward would write to relatives with cousinly affection, as if he still had a political role to play through family intimacy. He did not. He was abroad three months of the year for his 'health', enjoyed his royal status too much, made continual gaffes in important speeches and gossiped to the point where his government could not trust him with state secrets. He whined that the prime minister gave him no 'advice' (the very opposite of Bagehot's ideas) and he sat in political darkness without a helpful light to guide him. When he came to the throne, Henry James summed him up as 'fat vulgar Edward'.[35] His short reign was marked by political crises from the Cabinet crisis of 1903 to the constitutional crisis of 1909–10, the latter unresolved at his death, which was convenient as he believed that the Lords should solely be the possession of hereditary aristocrats.

Edward remained close to the right wing of the Liberal Party, was horrified by socialists and women's suffrage, but had the good grace to suggest 'taxing the rich' (just not him) and dropping taxation on food for the poor.[36] His personality was appreciated by ministers, but not his garrulousness. He grew more frustrated as his influence on domestic politics and foreign policy diminished in relationship to that of his mother or foreign monarchs. Where he could meddle, he did so, in both army and naval appointments. Indeed, it was in his reign that the legal status of the prime minister was finally defined, punished by being placed below the archbishops of Canterbury and York. In the end, he asked a simple question: what was his purpose?

George V was made of different stuff to Edward. He had learned the lessons of Bagehot and realised that if monarchy was to survive it had better keep quiet. George readily agreed to the 500 new peers for the Lords, who were required to be approved by royal prerogative to ensure the passing of the 'people's budget'. This resolved the constitutional crisis, though it was never acted upon. The new Labour government and its social-ist policies was accepted without a murmur; the Home Rule Bill was resolved after nearly fifty years of argument, although it effectively partitioned Ireland; and George accepted that the Lords would be recreated on a popular rather than hereditary basis. That the king wanted even 'peaceful picketing' made illegal did not alienate him from his Labour prime minister's loy-alty. All things considered, he was seen as, A.J.P. Taylor wrote, 'conscientious ... decent ... straight'.[37]

This was due to Asquith's government absolving him of all responsibility for 'the acts of the executive and the legislature', meaning that 'the King can do no wrong'. The idea effectively neutralised the monarch whilst at the same time allowing them any view they wished in private.

George V was the first truly constitutional monarch and his two sons quickly learned to be silent on issues that may have been previously seen as their prerogative. Thus, when Edward VIII abdicated, he did so quite constitutionally. His brother, unused to the idea of his being monarch, looked with some worry over his constitutional role, wanting to interfere in European poli-tics by suggesting he write a personal letter to Hitler, as if this were the time of Edward VII. He was blocked from such an ill-thought-out idea and interfered no more, but he was able to turn to America and President Roosevelt to cement the bond, which became the so-called 'Special Relationship'. Beyond reinforcing friendships, the monarchy had now finally lost its vital role in governing. Yet there was a parliamentary legacy of monarchy, which could stand in proxy for its innermost desires.

One area in which the relationship between politics and the monarch has actually grown in the twenty-first century is in the Crown's relationship to the state. This peculiar redefinition of the monarch's position was of little consequence until the last years of the nineteenth century, when a greater civil service grew up to administer imperial power and British order. Until the last years of Victoria's reign there were almost no real government departments but, as the century waned and the new century began, departments of 'state' grew to large proportions and their workings became more secretive. This new situation had been pre-empted by the creation of the 'Irish' Special Branch and its role in protecting Queen Victoria. By the First World War, there were the beginnings of 'state' departments, whose job was secrecy, disinformation and cryptanalysis, and so were born MI5 and MI6.

There had been no real state in medieval times and until the later nineteenth century such a creation (which was different from and had 'hidden' powers greater than that of the government) would have been unthinkable. The 'state' evolved to consist of family networks, with educational opportunities for those who went into the Church, military, secret service, diplomatic corps, finance and law, and at its head was the Crown. The intertwined strands were different from the government of the day, were powerful and, above all, were highly secretive. The monarch to whom the Oath of Allegiance was to be taken was only the living embodiment of a continuing tradition, so it might be said, of service, duty, honour and patriotism.

This was really only true in practical terms as these networks bound themselves more tightly together, those at the top being called, in the early twentieth century, 'society' and, later, the 'establishment'. This remains an ideological and totally undemocratic way of keeping power within small groups for whom the king (and 'country') represents the validation of their actions, however illegal, unconstitutional or immoral. To ensure those actions cannot be questioned, they are closely protected by the various security services.

Such secrecy at the heart of government only arose, in part, when Elizabeth I organised spy rings to protect herself and the realm from Catholicism. Although spying was normal in medieval days, this began a new era of surveillance. It did not last, as James I was indifferent (although paranoically obsessed with sorcery and witchcraft, later tiring of demonology once the damage was done) and later George III was uninterested in spy networks. Charles II used spies to assassinate or kidnap those who had condemned his father. For many years spying was seen as underhand and un-British, though a necessarily distasteful diplomatic weapon.

The First World War largely changed the climate. George V used spies and his extensive family ties within Europe to explore secretive activity to determine events and protect the British royal family from threats that might arise from 'aggressive' pacifists, republicans and Bolsheviks. His long-winded and unsuccessful machinations regarding the tsar left him scarred for life, and thereafter he wore a black armband to signify the loss of a close cousin rather than the millions of dead in France. His son's leanings towards frivolity, Nazism and divorced Americans led to surveillance on his activities. Hundreds of thousands of pounds were spent watching his actions, all the way through the Second World War, until his death. There was also a huge clean-up operation conducted by the royal family, personally and through relatives, to expunge any trace of embarrassing correspondence. They used agents such as Anthony Blunt, who was known to both George VI and Queen Elizabeth II as a Russian agent, but who was awarded a knighthood and allowed to live his days out in luxury.

George VI was kept up to date with all the secrets of the war, having become an enthusiastic enemy of Nazism, following a period of appeasement in which he tried to use diplomatic paths to write to Hitler as if he were a member of a European dynasty. Elizabeth II and Charles III were both instructed in the ways of espionage before becoming monarchs, as has Prince William. Elizabeth was aware of developments in nuclear war as well: the Crown as a symbol of state must be protected. Indeed, elaborate plans were formulated to rescue the royal family in the wake of a nuclear holocaust, including cutting down the avenue of trees in the Broad Walk in Kensington Gardens so that a small plane might land, while the rest of the population was to be abandoned to die of radiation poisoning. Elizabeth II was now centre of the stage of state, the mystic of monarchy preserved beyond life itself.[38]

These formal and informal networks have meant that the royal family has embraced secrecy in a way that would have astonished the Hanoverians. Scandals, such as those dealing with the Duke of Windsor, Sir Anthony Blunt, the death of Princess Diana and the behaviour of Prince Andrew have now to be closely monitored and controlled from within Windsor at the highest level. Such is the case with Harry and Meghan, whose withdrawal from public duties meant that they lost protection officers, Harry arguing, quite rightly, that he was born into royalty and did not choose the life. When Elizabeth the Queen Mother died, Princess Margaret simply put all her private notes and correspondence into black sacks and burned the lot. Secrecy at all levels of the firm is still paramount. Their safety, above all else, is vital too: the royal family, like the secret services, 'control and curate their own histories carefully'.[39] Yet, there is one more layer to royal authority and that is hereditary peerages.

William the Conqueror did not invent the system of hierarchy that dominated England before he arrived, but by installing his own Norman followers in place of the Anglo-Saxon nobility, he did make the system dependent on power and domination. This system, of course, produced the landowning aristocracy of the country (and of Britain), who dominated British politics for centuries in both the House of Lords and the Privy Council. Their squabbles have shaped our history.

From William's time onwards, the aristocracy of the country amassed for itself prestige and wealth (expressed in acquisitions, education, land ownership, great houses, art works, patronage, etc.) and has been closely aligned with monarchical affairs, by ironically and negatively trying to avoid royal interference in their own interests! Historically, aristocrats have been jealous of their privileges and entitlements, consumed with their 'rights' and wary of monarchical activity. They could not exist without the monarchy in the feudal and medieval periods as they took their rights directly from the king, who created certain nobles as 'tenants in chief' of the Crown and lesser nobility as tenants of greater nobles. This hierarchical pyramid required a monarch or who else had authority to decide precedent amongst equals and hand out land? When this system broke down civil war broke out as parliament, specifically the Commons, could not make such decisions without invoking its own version of sovereignty.

From the abolition of the Upper House after the Civil War until long after the restoration of its rights (including those of the Church leaders who also sat there), their lordships worried about their role in running the higher politics of the country. This meant creating revolutionary theories of oligarchic virtue all the way to the other end of the spectrum, with traditional downright stubbornness in the face of election reform, budgetary bills, women's enfranchisement, Ireland and minority political participation. As the Lords consisted of a relatively tight-knit group of men, ties of exclusivity born of blood ties, ancient and ancestral family connections, service to the state, the longevity of historical interventions at moments of crisis, education and securing their own future, the politics of the Lords was different from that of the Commons.

As recently as the 1990s, the hereditary lords faced one of their greatest challenges. Tony Blair, brought to power in 1997 by an electorate hungry for change and modernisation, brought in the House of Lords Act in 1999. It aimed to finally finish the 700-year-old automatic right of 750 peers to sit and vote on the red benches. The process seemed clear enough: finally get rid of an old and useless chamber. There would be no attempt at removing it altogether, as had happened during the Republic. Instead, the number of hereditary peers would be reduced to around fifteen.

There was no explanation why, but negotiations soon broke down as peers fought to keep their power – a right granted until their death. The compromise wrought from the government by

Robert Gascoyne-Cecil, 7th Marquess of Salisbury, descendant of one prime minister and Elizabeth I's first minster Robert Cecil, was that ninety-two hereditary peers would remain (all men, none from an ethnic background, half educated at Eton College) or all hell would break loose. Blair's government, like many left-wing governments and politicians in the twentieth century, were cowed by a Latinate education and blue blood. They agreed to a system where 200 aristocrats wait on a list until one sitting peer dies and they are eligible for a by-election to the vacant seat. These are coveted apparently. There were forty elections between 2002 and 2021. One elected peer is Viscount Stansgate, Stephen Benn, the son of Tony Benn, one of the great opponents of hereditary peerages and the automatic right to sit in the Lords.[40]

Blair had intended to pack the Lords with people with 'special abilities' instead of hereditary peers; these people would sit and aid, rather than hinder, government policy. However, the system was soon abused by bribery and corruption, nepotism and party considerations, resulting in almost 800 members, all of whom are entitled to large expenses. Titles, it seems, are the actual legacy that is left from medieval favouritism. Monarchy's legacy is as strong as ever, but hidden under a veneer of democratic choice.

Liz Truss arrived at Balmoral, the new leader of the Conservative Party and prime minister in waiting on 6 September 2022. She was, presumably, nervous. The queen still had the 'duty' of appointing 'her' prime minister and her new ministry, or rather the incoming prime minister still had the duty to be appointed. This took place at an audience in which the traditional acknowledgement of the new office holder was the 'kissing hands' ceremony, which has its roots perhaps in Anglo-Saxon monarchical practices and is now replaced by a formal handshake, followed by a quick chat between the monarch, the new prime minister and their spouse.

The government introduces its legislation at the opening of parliament at the Palace of Westminster and Acts of Parliament are presented in final form after the monarch's assent and in their name. It is the presiding ruler who has the right to prorogue parliament – a gamble Boris Johnson took on 28 August 2019, only to have the action deemed unlawful by the Supreme Court. All this is archaic and much of it historically redundant, but it still exists. Ordinary people are still not quite citizens nor fully beyond being subjects.

Elizabeth II had, unlike many of her ancestors, taken her coronation oath seriously. Others, perhaps more cynical, abided by it as it suited them. The queen took her role as defined by her coronation oath as literal, not as a symbolic gesture but as a moral imperative and guiding principle. Her attitude was nearer to that of Charles I or James II than it was to her father. In former times this might have led to trouble, but she wisely tempered her views by a form of reticence amounting to either repression or an inability to empathise, which manifested itself as something that she is always associated with: *duty* and *service* – two words whose meanings were filtered through her own Christian values (see, for instance, her early audiences with Billy Graham [1989], suggesting that she really believed it was her mission to rule, chosen by God as a family penance for the early death of her father).

This view she embraced ever more closely as she grew older, and it is a theme of much royal media management. The queen was carefully isolated in her moral duties by a long line of advisors and her own inclinations. No one expected either Philip or her children to follow her lead regarding what she saw as her duties and service. For the queen, her duty was first to God and her 'service' (never quite explained) was to 'her' people, always the subject of her royal gaze at walkabouts and Buckingham Palace balcony appearances.

The palace, as a media machine, made much of Elizabeth's service to the nation: her work during the war, her broadcast message after the death of George VI, her devotion to the Commonwealth, even her role as a grandmother. Much was made of her fortitude and spirit in the face of adversity, having been media-mixed from cold-hearted and cruel mother-in-law at the death of Princess Diana to frail, but hearty old lady, persevering despite the 'peccadillos' of her second son and the alleged toxicity between her grandchildren.

Just like Victoria with her family at her knees (as depicted by Franz Winterhalter), Elizabeth appeared to be an ordinary old lady, whose family caused trouble – the soap opera that the media created. She was fortunate in that her narrative was not created by history, but by the contemporary multiplicity of media platforms. She was both herself and a media character, as depicted in numerous films and plays, as well as the Netflix series *The Crown*. During the Platinum Jubilee, she travelled as a hologram in the Gold State Coach, just as she had done on the day of her coronation. Thus, she became a replica of herself again and again, fulfilling the projected role as assigned to her by others. On the other hand, we knew nothing really of the queen's actual thoughts, as she remained enigmatic and aloof.

She was a projection, but she also existed, her values cocooned in a world kept mysterious, for royalty have always understood that its most powerful tool is mystery, a theatrical property of religious ceremonies, now secularised. Prime ministers are overawed and presidents forget themselves and bow (as did Ronald Regan). Mystique is created by tradition, by deference and by the importance of surroundings and of place. It is a clear secularisation of religious ceremony and sacred totems. To be chosen by God to do this sacred work on earth requires the stalwart sacrifice that the queen adhered to as if she were in a religious order. She was unique: she was monarch and the social order follows, even if now it includes sport personalities whose recognition is granted by kneeling to be honoured with a sword tap on the shoulder as if they were knights of old. Deference creates gratitude.

The mystique of royalty is also that of power and entitlement, the fount of which is the monarchy as an institution (Diana, on the other hand, had 'glamour', the Hollywood ideal of visual enchantment). Despite the tawdry dents in the institution's current form, the mystique of the queen herself remained throughout her life, even to the point of seeing her advanced age as a value in itself: a symbol of an unchanging 'Britishness' adapted to and adopting new ways and peoples, stable and reliable in a changing world. We are reminded that the queen met fifteen prime ministers (including Winston Churchill and Liz Truss) and fourteen US presidents (including Kennedy), chatted with world leaders from Nelson Mandela to the Dalai Lama, and endured the Second World War and the Battle of Britain, the Falklands War and Iraq War. She gathered much kudos and respect from these meetings and this history, which is, after all, an accident of her position (yet no kudos has accrued for those who met the queen – it is a one-way arrangement). In death, Elizabeth now seems the embodiment of our post-war history – a repository of our past.

Every monarch reinvents the institution to accord with current times, or if they don't they are swept away, to be replaced by another contender. It is certain that the next coronation will be a less extravagant affair. The queen's wedding and coronation were filmed as none had been before, filmic and televisual affairs of extraordinary extravagance and lavishness that made former coronations look impoverished. They created the belief that all coronations were like this (Victoria's was a disaster, but mostly private. The crowd panicked outside William the Conqueror's closed affair in Westminster Abbey).

This royal family is, in terms of its personal land holdings, investments, art collections (that we, the people, own their art collections is risible), precious jewels, acquisitions, lifestyles, media presence, royal palaces and world reach, perhaps the most powerful monarchy we have ever had. It is wealthy beyond belief (far wealthier, in proportion, than monarchs of the Middle Ages and far more stable than monarchs of the seventeenth century). Surrounded by pomp and ceremony that is the theatricality of monarchy, the revelatory appearance of the monarch on the balcony of Buckingham Palace is anticipated by huge crowds of adoring 'subjects' gathered in the Mall, before the obligatory fly-past of the Red Arrows, resplendent in their red livery and spewing red, white and blue vapour. Even those in the heavens salute.

This is the apotheosis of what Charles I dreamed of when he commissioned the Banqueting Hall ceiling in Whitehall Palace or what James Thornhill envisaged in 1796 when he created his baroque extravaganza in the Painted Hall in Greenwich, for which effort of flattery he earned a knighthood. Ironically, it is the very wealth and power of the current institution, and its apparent uselessness, that secures its continuity. No one is threatened by monarchs any longer. Charles is the ruler of a new Britain: multicultural, religiously diverse, perhaps no longer attached to British 'core' values. He is the king of a country very different from the one his mother inherited, but he is king. How traditional will he wish to be?

With the death of Queen Elizabeth there have been changes. Not merely the reshuffle of royal titles and entitlements, but also of familial relationships fractured so severely by the apparent rift between Charles's sons, as well as Meghan's own resentments seemingly towards her obligations. In the end, Charles III, when he did address the nation, kept to the tradition of the Windsors and, despite referring affectionately to both brothers and Catherine and Meghan, did not suggest his reign would greatly alter the previous pattern. He referred to his religious role as nothing other than Christian (although his holistic and all-encompassing beliefs are far more in tune with current thinking) and he re-allocated titles in the usual way. His eldest son was named as the new Prince of Wales by the king's pronouncement alone, following precedent. Prince William may well have a full inauguration, as did his father, but this title of conquest seemed not to have been discussed with the Welsh Assembly, which may have had a view on a now contentious issue. On his visit to Wales, Charles was greeted by some republican protesters; the first minister of the Welsh Assembly, Mark Drakeford, is reportedly a republican too. Prince Edward became Duke of Edinburgh, again without discussion.

Prince William, in his turn, will probably become a modernised Scandinavian-style democratic 'ruler', slightly more glamorous than ordinary folk, perhaps more relatable to a younger generation and less attached to formality (see the hugs from the victorious women's football team when he presented the winner's medals at Wembley in 2022). But in the end, will his rather 'proper' wife, once turned queen, be overwhelmed by her middle-class feelings and demand a return to formal protocols? And what will be sacrificed in terms of wealth, possessions and prestige? There is still a lot of that around.

There are many royal personages that need attendance. The estimated cost of the monarchy alone is roughly £345 million and may be higher, according to Republic.org, and was certainly £87.5 million in 2021 – a rise of almost 20 per cent over the previous year. This, of course, might be the cost of a presidency, but a presidency would be accountable for the money, whereas the monarchy is not and there has to be no accommodation for the wider family. Until 2013, the monarch and other working royals were funded by a civil list payment and a number of grants to cover travel and property maintenance etc. These costs have since been rolled together into the payment of the Sovereign Grant. The grant does not cover day-to-day security nor regional visits, which are paid for by local councils. Amazingly, the income from the Duchy of Lancaster and the Duchy of Cornwall, despite being theoretically the nation's wealth, go directly to the monarch and Duke of Cornwall (now Prince William). During the last years of Elizabeth II's reign, the cost of the monarchy rose dramatically. The Sovereign Grant is determined by how much the Crown Estate real estate portfolio has brought in. It is paid for by taxation.

Property is still everything. The sitting monarch owns Buckingham Palace and Windsor Castle, which are effectively always family owned, and Balmoral and Sandringham personally. Hillsborough Castle in Northern Ireland and Holyrood in Scotland remain royal properties too. There are some strange and antiquated laws still extant regarding these buildings. The Palace of Westminster, although not a royal residence any more, has inherited the exemption from duty on alcohol drunk on the premises.

The list of royal family residences is extraordinary. Llwynywermod is the private Welsh residence of Charles III, who also personally owns a number of properties in Romania. Charles now also owns Craigowan Lodge and Birkhall in the Balmoral Estate, Clarence House in the Mall, Highgrove House in Gloucestershire, Tamarisk Hose on the Scilly Isles (where the inhabitants are his tenants), Kensington Palace (by right of monarchy), Amner House at Sandringham, Frogmore Cottage (a cottage in name only) and the Royal Lodge in Windsor and St James's Palace (as king), Gatcombe Park in Gloucestershire, Bagshot Park in Surrey, Ivy Cottage at Kensington Palace, Barnwell Manor in Northamptonshire, Wren House in Kensington Palace and Thatched House Lodge in Richmond.

The Guardian, on 7 May 2001, reported that Prince Michael of Kent had a grace-and-favour apartment in Kensington Palace for which he paid less than a council flat would cost. They performed no official duties. The 'flat' has nine reception rooms and seven bedrooms. The aged duke and duchess had lived rent free since 1979, until 1994 when the royal family had to pay for renovations out of its own kitty. Grace-and-favour residences are in the monarch or prime minister's hands and may be given out for services rendered or as recognition of a position. There are approximately seventeen grace-and-favour residences, including 10 Downing Street and 120 apartments where royal relatives and others often live rent free.

On his accession, King Charles gave up the title of Duke of Cornwall and gave the title, as a royal gift, to his eldest son.

William inherited a title to the vast estates and merchandise of the duchy. On 1 July 2022, the *Daily Mail* reported that the then Prince of Wales was getting a personal annual income from the duchy of £23 million, the enterprise itself being worth £1.2 billion and showing record profits during the pandemic of 2021–22. Charles only agreed to pay income tax in 1993. The enterprise itself pays no corporation tax and the estate has paid no inheritance tax, despite its changing hands through inheritance. Moreover, it is one of the very few areas that allows the duke to veto parliamentary will regarding any holdings within the estate, as the estate is considered 'private property'.

This, nevertheless, ignores the vast real estate holdings and tenancies administered on behalf of the royal family as a business enterprise. It was during the reign of Henry III that it was established that a monarch, to have full authority, had to be so wealthy from private income they had no need to go to a group of nobles or a 'parliament' of subjects to beg for monetary aid (often partially raised by loans from the Jewish community). This practice was important to English magnates and later parliaments as it curbed royal ambitions, especially throughout the Middle Ages. It was the overriding issue in the seventeenth and eighteenth centuries. The prince regent (the future George IV) was always petitioning parliament for monies to run his household and fund his personal foibles. By the compromises of the nineteenth century, the monarch was guaranteed fabulous wealth and privilege in order to silence such royal demands on parliament that might cause embarrassment.

Although it was during the reign of William III that royal revenue was bulked up by parliament and relief given for certain large royal expenditures (upkeep of the navy, for instance), it was George III who came to the conclusion that funding the royal estates, royal household, the government, civil service and even national debt was too expensive for him, and so in 1760 he surrendered control over his estate's revenue to the Treasury. In return he got a guarantee of funds through the Civil List. This was essentially a coup, and although his son always felt strapped for ready cash, it meant that royal decisions over money were no longer fraught with the fear of going back to parliament and being refused. The monarchy was now essentially protected from bankruptcy but also rewarded with unaccountable money guaranteed forever and always open to increases. It gave security, no risk and, as with almost every surrender of royal responsibilities, little in that respect has changed:

> Since 1 April 2012, under the terms of the Sovereign Grant Act 2011, the Civil List was abolished and the monarch has been provided with a stable source of revenue indexed to a percentage of the Crown Estate's annual net income (currently set at 25%). This was intended to provide a long-term solution and remove the politically sensitive issue of Parliament having to debate the Civil List allowance every ten years. Subsequently, the Sovereign Grant Act allows for all future monarchs to simply extend these provisions for their reigns by Order in Council.[41]

The vast holdings of the monarch are administered by the Crown Estate, in effect a corporation administered by the Crown Estate commissioners, who, in turn, administer the ownership of properties but are not the owners themselves. It is the major property business in the United Kingdom with a mixed portfolio, with its roots in feudal England. Nowadays, this is little different from any modern major corporation. Income from these hereditary properties is offered to the government against responsibility towards funding the government. The Crown Estate during Elizabeth's reign was worth £14.1 billion, of which £9.1 billion was invested in urban property. The estate administers 7,920sq. km of land, including mining operations, forests and farms, almost half the UK's foreshore, Ascot Racecourse and Windsor Great Park.

Therefore, despite recent reforms such as introducing the right for women to inherit the throne (legislation brought in as late as 28 October 2011 and requiring much amended past statutes going as far back as the seventeenth century), the institution is ancient and cannot be easily brought up to date regarding the distribution of its assets. Indeed, much of royal protocol remains hidden, obfuscated and downright occult. Why, for instance, are royal wills bound in secrecy and protected by privacy, as was Prince Philip's, whilst the rest of the population has to declare them publicly? The royal family remain above the law in more ways than one.

Queen Elizabeth's will, which is also a secret document (unlike regular wills), was the object of much speculation. *Fortune Magazine* estimated that she had bequeathed $500 million, but the final estimate may be nearer to £650 million. Her entire holdings went to Charles III to distribute as he saw fit. How this is divided between non-negotiables and amortised holdings, and how much is moveable finances, remains shrouded in mystery. The state gains no inheritance tax under an arrangement of 1993. Numerous requests to the deputy press officer to Charles III were left unanswered by time of publication. Indeed, the officials of Buckingham Palace seem prone to diffidence and obfuscation where any queries are involved. Such information requests are strictly forbidden to members of the public who are not journalists or 'writers'. It was reported that Prince Andrew wanted a share of the inheritance to bolster his shaky finances and to save him moving from his twenty-room home into Frogmore Cottage, vacated by the Duke and Duchess of Sussex.

How then does an opposition mobilise to remove the institution? High Treason is still statute law to protect the sovereign. It is defined by the following characteristics in England and Scotland (since 1708, effective from 1709), Wales and Northern Ireland, with a long history of amendment and subtle change:

> The Treason Felony Act 1848 (still in force today) created a new offence known as treason felony, with a maximum

sentence of life imprisonment instead of death (but today, due to the abolition of the death penalty, the maximum penalty both for high treason and treason felony is the same – life imprisonment). Under the traditional categorisation of offences into treason, felonies, and misdemeanours, treason felony was merely another form of felony. Several categories of treason which had been introduced by the Sedition Act 1661 were reduced to felonies. While the common law offences of misprision and compounding were abolished in respect of felonies (including treason felony) by the Criminal Law Act 1967, which abolished the distinction between misdemeanour and felony, misprision of treason and compounding treason are still offences under the common law.

It is treason felony to 'compass, imagine, invent, devise, or intend':

- to deprive the sovereign of the Crown,
- to levy war against the sovereign 'in order by force or constraint to compel her to change her measures or counsels, or in order to put any force or constraint upon or in order to intimidate or overawe both Houses or either House of Parliament', or
- to 'move or stir' any foreigner to invade the United Kingdom or any other country belonging to the sovereign.
- In addition to the crime of treason, the Treason Felony Act 1848 (still in force today) created a new offence known as treason felony, with a maximum sentence of life imprisonment instead of death (but today, due to the abolition of the death penalty, the maximum penalty both for high treason and treason felony is the same – life imprisonment). Under the traditional categorisation of offences into treason, felonies, and misdemeanours, treason felony was merely another form of felony. Several categories of treason which had been introduced by the Sedition Act 1661 were reduced to felonies. While the common law offences of misprision and compounding were abolished

in respect of felonies (including treason felony) by the Criminal Law Act 1967, which abolished the distinction between misdemeanour and felony, misprision of treason and compounding treason are still offences under the common law.

- It is treason felony to 'compass, imagine, invent, devise, or intend':
- to deprive the sovereign of the Crown,
- to levy war against the sovereign 'in order by force or constraint to compel her to change her measures or counsels, or in order to put any force or constraint upon or in order to intimidate or overawe both Houses or either House of Parliament', or
- to 'move or stir' any foreigner to invade the United Kingdom or any other country belonging to the sovereign.[42]

By these definitions, the monarch still cannot commit a treasonous act or a criminal action (as defined by the law), only be the victim of one (even Edward VIII could not be accused even though his loyalty was dubious). Interestingly, James Hewitt was pursued for High Treason for having an affair with Princess Diana between 1986 and 1991. As Diana was still married to Prince Charles, this seemed to fit the criteria and make a sensational, though unprovable, story, despite Diana admitting the relationship.

The death penalty for High Treason in the past was too terrible to contemplate. Catherine Murphy was sentenced to be burned alive for the offence of counterfeiting as late as 1786 (she was hanged and so not actually burned whilst alive) and the Cato Street Conspirators were hung, drawn and quartered as late as 1820. Of course, William Joyce was the last man hanged (on dubious grounds) for the offence in 1946. The sentence of death was removed from the statute books in 1998. It was theoretically possible to sentence someone for High Treason to be beheaded as later as 1973!

As a general rule, no British criminal court has jurisdiction over the sovereign, from whom they derive their authority. As Sir William Blackstone wrote in the eighteenth century, 'the law supposes an incapacity of doing wrong from the excellence and perfection ... of the King'.[43] Furthermore, to charge the sovereign with High Treason would be inconsistent, as it would constitute accusing him or her of disloyalty to themselves. The execution of Charles I was, by this definition, the result of an anomaly created by civil war rather than statute law. It was, by such a definition, illegal and unconstitutional, concepts his judges were painfully aware of at the time.

Those on the radical left have always opposed monarchy. Fewer have been openly republican once in parliament (with the exception of people such as Tony Benn and Jeremy Corbyn). This led to open opposition being expressed mainly by anarcho-comedians and satirists such as Russell Brand, whose book *Revolution* was a bestseller, but whose critique was confined to some rather childish, if amusing, abuse rather than the serious analysis the title suggested. Here are some of Brand's suggestions to the queen, reducing her to a type of middle-class foreign housewife with a big house and hiding a dirty secret:

> We should be calling her Mrs Windsor ... her actual name is Mrs Saxe-Coburg ... she might as well've been called 'Mrs Bratwurst-Kraut-Nan' ... Come on Frau Saxe-Coburg-Gotha, it's time for you to have breakfast with Herr Saxe-Coburg-Gotha. And you can make it yerselves. And by the way, we're nicking this f*cking great castle you've been dossing in and giving it to a hundred poor families. Actually you can if you want, they'll need a cleaner. You'll have to watch your lip, Herr Saxe-Coburg-Gotha, some of 'em ain't white.[44]

Marxists, on the other hand, have long called out the monarchy for what it is: the top of the capitalist system in Britain. They have long called for its abolition as the institution upon which British capitalism and imperialism pivots. This has been the case since Gerald Gould called for 'the coming revolution in Great Britain' in 1920, all the way to Tariq Ali's belief that the 'coming British revolution' was just around the corner in 1972.[45] Marxists see the practices of the monarchy not only as archaic, but as corrupt and corrupting of those below; they see it protect its own at the expense of others, who are treated as outsiders; they see it as the key to the establishment and the establishment as rotten to the core, hence:

> In summary, the kind of family Meghan and Harry have apparently fled is one where it is normal to display racism even towards one's own relatives; to willingly push a young woman to the brink of suicide; to punish a child for its parent's 'crimes'; to show cold-heartedness so extreme you'd cut your own child out of your life; to show a greater interest in the lives of horses than of human beings; and to willingly hinder a child sex abuse investigation.
>
> The concern of the royals for 'pure pedigree' has been exposed as racist white supremacy. Its 'cool detachment' is shown up as callous vengefulness …
>
> But this is not any old family. This family is a core institution of the British establishment. Its rottenness is the rottenness of the whole capitalist state. Its crisis is part of the crisis of the whole system, at the core of which it sits, putrefying. And its attitudes are the attitudes of a ruling class that has grown rich off of slavery, colonial plunder, and policies of racist division.
>
> The Monarchy is linked to the whole ruling class by a thousand threads – through a sordid network of public schools, wealthy institutions, banks, private clubs and family ties.[46]

Now, this all may have validity, but it sounds too angry, and therefore too extreme. It may be possible to align twentieth-century monarchs with capitalism and nineteenth-century ones with imperialism, but to simply pour all the accusations into a one-size-fits-all judgement will not really do. Monarchy as an institution (and that is the point) is centuries older than the calumnies it is collectively accused of perpetuating. It is the radical evolution of monarchical practice that defeats such analysis. It is the correspondence of establishment reorganisation and monarchical sleight of hand that suggest both tradition and continuity (represented by pageantry), as well as the ability to adapt to a multicultural and non-expansionist future. As much as the royal family deal with capitalism, they are capitalists, but as much as they deal with protocol, they are outside the grasp of anti-capitalist criticism. To attack the current royal family is merely to particularise a moment in royal history, which will soon change, blunting the attack and consigning it to history. A reformed monarchy might well address all the issues raised above, but still be the monarchy. What is needed is a critique of the institution as a historical, legal and religious entity.

Despite the rise of radical liberalism and socialist agitation in Britain during the nineteenth century, there were few popular disavowals of Queen Victoria or her reign. Much socialist and Marxist material from the period suggests her removal but none of the mainstream nineteenth-century communist groupings dealt directly with the problem of monarchy in a way that was freely indulged in by their confederates throughout revolutionary Europe. Neither Karl Marx nor William Morris tackled the subject directly and Morris, with his attachment to the medieval ideal especially, is artistically ambivalent. Morris avoided the subject, but this was a fault of Marx too, perhaps brought on by fear of deportation, unfamiliarity with British monarchy or of intellectual neglect (the monarchy as a side issue of capitalist practice); Morris's homegrown ambivalence was either an oversight (see the 'absence' of any debate in *News from Nowhere*) or dereliction of duty brought on by fear of accusations of sedition. Of course, one need not be a Marxist to be a republican, but one must be overtly anti-monarchical if one is a Marxist – clearly not the case for other radical movements.

On 24 October 2022 a 'Just Stop Oil' activist covered Charles's waxwork image in chocolate cake at Madame Tussauds (a play on 'let them eat cake' possibly), but this was wholly inappropriate given the king's stand on environmental issues and mental well-being when he was the Prince of Wales.[47]

One group that has attempted a more sophisticated approach, although with the same lack of success, is the long-running lobby organisation Republic.org, a small, mainly left of centre organisation dedicated to media advocacy for abolition. The group was founded in 1983 as Republic: People before Privilege, and had Albert E. Stanley as its first treasurer and secretary. Originally the group gathered disenchanted left thinkers disillusioned with aspects of life under Margaret Thatcher (whose own egalitarian, low Church views were certainly more 'republican' than those of legalistic, proto-Catholic Tony Blair), but it also gained intellectuals, celebrities, journalists and politicians (such as Claire Rayner, Peter Ustinov, Roy Greenslade, Jonathan Freedland and Tony Benn), who might speak at their various meetings.

The newsletter presented the organisation as dedicated to a 'peaceful, lawful, democratic Republicanism' and carried occasional jocular references to the French Revolution and the 440th anniversary of the English republic. It was a home-mimeographed affair produced on a shoestring, with a bookish sense of purpose. November 1989 was called 'Brumaire 440' (and required a footnote to explain to adherents who, perhaps, weren't really into the history of the movement). During the 1980s the organisation was often near to financial collapse, but it was buoyed by the satisfaction of seeing its hard work vindicated (even if it didn't produce results) and by its criticism of left politics.

Like all lobby groups, Republic has suffered its fair share of division and (if the restricted files held at London's Bishopsgate Institute are anything to go by) vituperation; nevertheless, the organisation has survived to a venerable old age and now apparently boasts 12,000 members and 100,000 Facebook followers. Its current CEO, Graham Smith, argues that, whilst it has not achieved its aims, it hasn't failed either. Interestingly, the first big spike in interest was William and Catherine's wedding in 2010, when they gained publicity for their 'Not the Royal Wedding Street Party'.

What the organisation envisages is a liberal and republican democratic state with a voted-in president, like in Ireland. The end of the monarchy would be decided by a referendum. There would also be a prime minister and the Lords would remain with a voted assembly of around 300 taken from all levels of the population. The current honours system and hereditary titles would be abolished to be replaced by a more democratic means of individual award; royal residences would become museums and their contents taken by the state. There would need to be a wholesale attack on abuse of power and position, greater accountability, transparency and a clear advocacy of the universal rule of law.

Nevertheless, there is, again, a definite refusal to look at the ideological relationship of monarchy to state organisations and the nature of a republican state after the end of monarchy. What would prevent it from acting as a sovereign power (not, as theorised by Rousseau, as the people united in a body)? As long ago as 1844, Max Stirner presented a prescient and damning answer to Rousseau regarding the benevolent 'sovereign' state in *The Ego and Its Own (Der Einzige und sein Eigentum)*, represented by Stirner as a corporate entity apart from the people and opposed to free will and individual effort. What would happen to aristocrats whose wealth had come from dubious means in the past and what about their stately homes? What would happen to the current royals who would still need housing and protection as they would still be celebrities, and what if they refused the offer of citizenship? What, indeed, about a potential royalist party willing to restore the monarch, by force if necessary? Would freedom of opinion backing such a view then be regarded as treachery to the state? There always has to be special legal precedents dreamt up to remove a monarch, as the English discovered in 1649, the French in 1793 and the Russians in 1917.

Prince Philip turned 90 on 9 June 2011 and, according to His Highness, bits were dropping off the old royal personage. In the same year, his ageing son, Charles, and daughter-in-law saw the shadow of the guillotine as angry students attacked their car in Regent's Street and posted the results on YouTube.[48]

On 16 April 2011, the Republican Socialist Convention, which had been set up by the Scottish Socialist Party in 2008 to bring together the disaffected multitudes of these isles, met at London South Bank University for their annual meeting: at first sight, the regular meeting of some defeated-looking blokes in woolly jackets who smelled of beer and cigarettes and a dog – or was it a room full of young, fired-up revolutionaries hot from Black bloc exploits?

I had been invited to talk about revolutionary flags, a topic so esoteric that it suggested I was an expert in some harmless but really nerdy hobby like milk-bottle collecting. Peter Tatchell, the campaigner on LGBT rights, was also a speaker and still the bad boy, letting forth on 'the case for republican secular democracy' whilst being filmed for Australian television. The event itself was organised by Steve Freeman, an economics lecturer at the University of the South Bank, who gave a subtle talk on English republican socialism. Revolutions are not what they used to be. Nowadays, they have fallen prey to sponsorship and this event had the backing of the Scottish Socialist Party (International Committee) and Bermondsey Republican Socialists, so that, should the revolution catch me unawares, I might be welcomed as a conquering hero along the length of Sauchiehall Street or behind the cheese stall in Borough Market.

As it happened, the convention worked out rather well. In the end there were around a dozen older men (no beer, no cigarettes, no dog, no Black bloc, one woman) who argued fiercely all afternoon about the differences between republicanism and absolute democracy. It was all rather jolly and interesting, actually, and the flag of the British Republic flew bravely above the proceedings. The republican movement has held on through thick and thin, a reminder of what Britain might have been and might be yet. The suffragettes even adopted the republican liberty caps and tri-colours of the movement (changing the colours from red, white and green to purple, white and green) and Oliver Cromwell is the hero of the lot, famous for chopping off a king's head, but even he succumbed to the seduction of absolute power.

We have happily put up with royal invaders, lunatics, serial philanders and Germans who spoke no English so long as we could have a monarch whilst everybody else quietly ditched theirs. This perverseness we call tradition – something we apparently do better than all the other countries of the world put together, if we believe the English Tourist Board, who insist that the royals are worth every penny to our economy. Even when they were associating with criminals, like Princess Margaret in the 1960s, when she mixed with John Bindon, or allegedly like Prince Andrew when he enjoyed dubious parties with oil-rich sheiks or wealthy American paedophiles such as Jeffrey Epstein.

UK Uncut and those who enjoyed the 'hospitality' of Fortnum & Mason during protests in 2011 were about to embark on a mass anti-monarchist rally somewhere in safe Tory-land, kettling the disability scooters of blue-rinse OAPs in the very heart of Waitrose country. Alternative plans involved nude flash mobs in front of the world's media, a mass 'zombie wedding' somewhere in central London and a republic street party in Red Lion Square. We lived in troubled times indeed. It was all up with the Windsors, but were we about to go revolutionary and fly the tricolour of the republic above Buckingham Palace? Not quite yet, perhaps. After all, we like to think of the United Kingdom as a reasonably peaceful place, traditional and loyal to its royal heritage. Revolution happens elsewhere. Yet something simmers below the surface.

In general, the discontents have not taken regular pot shots at the monarch for years. It was once an annual affair like the Henley regatta: somebody with a gun would stake out Buck House and have a pop. The latest is Jaswant Singh Chail, who was arrested in the grounds of Windsor Castle on 25 December 2021. On 2 August 2022 he was charged under section 2 of the Treason Act 1842 with 'discharging or aiming firearms, or throwing or using any offensive matter or weapon, with intent to injure or alarm her Majesty'. Such individuals are never the representatives of the coming revolution; in the past, many of them were deemed 'lunatics' and transported or sent to Broadmoor, for to shoot at the head of state was considered an act of sheer madness. There must have been a lot of 'lunatics', because people shot at George III and Edward VIII and poor old Queen Victoria must have become positively athletic dodging the numerous assassination attempts during her long reign, whilst even Princess Margaret narrowly escaped being kidnapped and shot as she travelled in her car from Buckingham Palace in 1974.

Even to advocate to abolition of the monarchy was a legal nightmare. In December 2013 *The Guardian* ran an article exposing the fact that, under Section 3 of the Treason Felony Act 1848, one may be charged with sedition and go to prison for life merely for suggesting in print that the monarchy should be abolished (it being deemed an 'act of war'). This, by the way, is not the case, as we will see. The law is now moribund, having fallen into silence since 1879 when it was last deployed (alongside laws banning 'incorrigible rogues' in the Vagrancy Act 1824), but it sat there in 2013, sleeping rather than dead, under the shadow of the Human Rights Act 1998, under which it has no legal footing.

There is no fourth plinth in Trafalgar Square sporting a revolutionary statue to rival all those equestrian monarchs cast in bronze and the only revolution anybody knows about is on stage at *Les Misérables*. The republican history of Britain isn't taught in schools. It isn't taught anywhere, but it existed, just as much as Good Queen Bess and the Merry Monarch: one a bald, old harridan who farted and the other a not very merry closet Catholic who nevertheless baited Catholics during the Popish Plot. In the last 200 years alone, many more people than might be expected have taken up arms and fought pitched battles in the streets of Welsh towns, the leafy lanes of southern England and the moors of Scotland before being overwhelmed by the forces of government and cast into the oblivion of official history.

Thomas Paine, perhaps our greatest republican and perhaps the first 'professional' revolutionary, made the republican case as long ago as 1776, in *Common Sense*, his awakening call to the colonies, when he pointed out that:

> The most plausible plea, which hath ever been offered in favour of hereditary succession, is, that it preserves a nation from civil wars; and were this true, it would be weighty; whereas it is the most barefaced falsity ever imposed upon mankind. The whole history of England disowns the fact. Thirty kings and two minors have reigned in that distracted kingdom since the conquest, in which time there have been (including the Revolution) no less than eight civil wars and nineteen rebellions.

And that was only up to the eighteenth century.

The ideals of Cromwell's republican commonwealth almost came true. The first twenty years of the nineteenth century, influenced as they were by the French Revolution and the dismal record of the Hanoverians, might have ended with a British 'Terror' and the heads of the royal family displayed on pikes, as Arthur Thistlewood and his Cato Street gang hoped when they plotted to kill the Cabinet in 1820 and declare London a Jacobin stronghold.

Victoria brought sobriety and respect to the royal family, but the death of Albert in 1861 and her retreat from public life for the next ten years as the 'Widow of Windsor' gave a huge boost to the republican movement during the early 1870s. The radical MP Sir Charles Dilke was cheered by a gathering of mainly working-class radicals and Liberal voters in Newcastle-upon-Tyne on 6 November 1871, when he attacked royal financial extravagance and called for the abolition of the monarchy altogether:

> I think that, speaking roughly, you may say that the positive and direct cost of the Royalty is about a million a year. In addition ... it is worth remembering that the Royal Family pay no taxes [an error on Dilke's part] ... In ... the Army, we have a Royal Duke, not necessarily the fittest man, at the head of it by right of birth, and the Prince of Wales, who would never be allowed a command in time of war, put to lead the Cavalry Divisions in the Autumn Manoeuvres, thus robbing working officers of the position and of the training they had a title to expect. Now, institutions are not good or bad in themselves, so much as good or bad by their working, and we are told that a limited Monarchy works well. I set aside, in this speech, the question of whether a Republic would work better; but I confess freely that I doubt whether ... the monarchy should not set its house in order. There is a widespread belief that a Republic here is only a matter of time. It is said that some day a Commonwealth will be our Government. Now, history and experience show that you cannot have a Republic without you possessing at the same time the Republican virtues. But you answer – Have we not the public spirit? Have we not the practice of self-government? Are we not gaining general education? Well, if you can show me a fair chance that a republic will be free from the general corruption which hangs about the Monarchy, I say, for my part – and I believe that the middle classes will say – let it come.[49]

Dilke had taken his cue for the speech from an anonymous pamphlet that had actually been written by another MP called George Otto Trevelyan entitled 'What Does She Do With

It?', a critique of Victoria's finances during the early 1870s. Trevelyan pointed out that Victoria appeared to be 'squirreling away £200,000' of her Civil List allowance without making any of the required appearances or undertaking any of the duties required. At the same time, her son, Prince Arthur, got £15,000 a year without anything to show and Princess Louise had been granted a wedding dowry of £30,000 (roughly £1.6 million in 2022). The point of Liberal republicanism was to erase poverty by saving on royal expenses and create a meritocratic society.[50]

The call for reform had begun in the early 1860s after the death of Prince Albert and had been regularly highlighted throughout 1862 in the radical press, especially *Reynold's Newspaper*. This was exacerbated by the fall of Napoleon III and the declaration of the French Republic, as well as by the non-appearance of Victoria at events such as the state opening of parliament. The Prince of Wales also faced disgrace in the divorce court, which even led Walter Bagehot to worry, at the end of 1870, that 'the Queen is invisible and the Prince of Wales is not respected'.[51] They were, in his words, merely 'a retired widow and an unemployed youth'.

Things went from bad to worse. Radical liberal opinion galvanised a working class that was hungry for change and a better life. This was not nascent communism, but rather the coming together of the radical wing of political Liberalism, which based its ideas on Tom Paine's writings, both *Common Sense* and *The Age of Reason*, a movement which had long since left behind the type of Whig politics that made Victoria comfortable. Alongside republicanism went the demand for a greater franchise, women's rights and, most controversial of all, atheism, as the Crown's profligacy was associated with the Church's indifference to monarchical abuse. There were soon seventy recorded republican associations across the country, including in London (part founded by the most advanced radical MP Charles Bradlaugh), Birmingham and especially the north-east, which always had a strong radical tradition. To avoid the pitfalls of treason or sedition, which had destroyed the radical associations of the 1790s, Bradlaugh urged followers to attack the principle of monarchy and avoid direct attacks on Victoria. As he pointed out, it was not unlawful to argue for the discontinuance of the Crown after Victoria died.

The press, for the main part, were hostile and 'Tory rioters' would attack republican meetings, although there were never any convictions for criminal damage or, in one case, manslaughter. Juries unanimously acquitted those accused. The difficulties that faced republicans were not helped by cancelled meetings or exaggerated numbers at protests. Where radicals counted 30,000 protesters, the police saw only 500 to 600 people. The movement finally fizzled out for several reasons: the Prince of Wales recovered from a serious bout of typhoid and so continuity was assured (and the general population seemed genuinely pleased at the recovery); the newspapers had garnered sympathy for a monarch suffering, they suggested, from chronic depression following her husband's death; Victoria appeared at a major thanksgiving service; the majority of the public remained unconvinced; Prime Minister Gladstone baulked at full radical reform; and Dilke's speeches in parliament on the issue were dull and confusing. Nevertheless, the movement stood for the best virtues of egalitarianism, individual merit, democratic participation and financial prudence, creating a platform for later agitation and actual reform.

In Britain, republicanism was reignited for a brief moment with the death of Princess Diana in a Parisian hospital following a car crash in an underpass on 31 August 1997, stirring the public's temporary (but latent) distaste for 'cold-blooded' (and a rumoured 'conspiratorial') monarchy, but it soon faded into memory. In Scotland and Wales, the struggle for a republic was abandoned in the last twenty years of the twentieth century and its renewal was avoided through devolution. Nevertheless, a version of republicanism as avowed by the Scottish National

Party may still get its way, freeing the saltire from the union, but ditching the monarchy might prove another matter. The political struggles of the Cornish have long ceased, although republicanism is sometimes revived amongst separatists. The current British version of the counterculture does not favour insurgency as a policy, whilst financial crashes and energy destabilisation, which began in 2008 and were revived by Covid in 2022, have not encouraged revolution or created a revolutionary voice. The monarchy seems more popular than ever in a destabilised age – a symbol of unflinching continuity and triumph in the face of adversity. The threat of Islamic terrorism driven by religious zeal seems, at least for the moment, a guarantee against secular revolution.

The old order slowly vanishes. Queen Elizabeth died on 8 September 2022, Prince Philip passed away on 9 April 2021 and their eldest is in his seventies. Charles III is William the Conqueror's descendant over about thirty-four generations, and the sixty-second monarch since the later Anglo-Saxon rulers. Yet, as the older generations of the royal family retain their grip on the monarchy's traditions, even as its role disappears, the very nature of the United Kingdom has started to fracture. Victoria was happy to call herself and her nation 'English' (not British), and Scots such as Sir Walter Scott were more than happy to be unembarrassed 'North Britons', revelling in a new-found Scottish identity based on tartan and bagpipes, but this will no longer suffice.

The challenge to English hegemony had come earlier with the French revolutionary message, which attracted intellectuals and workers to the Scottish Friends of the People, an illegal organisation set up to reconsider both the authority of the Georgians and the nature of their government. Here was a message that suggested a republican Scotland would have far more in common with a republican England, bonded by ideas of liberty – a franchise that empowered working men in voting for a free 'democratic' parliament, workers' rights and the redressing of poverty and hunger. Such was the hope, but the republican clubs were soon disbanded under duress and those that joined were hunted down and put on trial.

The rump of such sentiments lingered. For English radicals the dream was almost destroyed at Peterloo in Manchester in 1819, but for the Scots it continued another four years. In 1820, the remnants of those remaining from the days of the French Revolution decided enough was enough. This was a working labourers' revolt centred on the weavers of Lanarkshire, Renfrewshire, Dumbartonshire, Ayrshire and Stirlingshire, and centred on Glasgow. Pikes and other weapons were made and stored in secret; there would be a rising and a bringing to account. A date was set, but the enthusiasm for revolution evaporated at the sight of determined authority (and a constant, heavy downpour). Dispirited and with an 'army' of only fifteen, the uprising failed. James Wilson was named by the government spies as the leader of 'the provisional government' in Scotland; his house was the centre of plans and weaponry. He took his part as a Scottish 'working-class' patriot well. After a trial that found him guilty of treason in trying to compel the king 'to change his measures' (he was found not guilty of other treasonable offences), he was sentenced to be beheaded along with three others. Ninety-eight men were found guilty of treason and sent to the new penal colony at Sidney Cove, Australia. Twenty-four were hanged. When the headsman (who Wilson knew as an acquaintance) held up his head, the crowd booed and shouted 'murderer' before being dispersed. At his sentencing, Wilson stood up and defended his actions on the same moral grounds as had those who had gone before:

> My lords and gentlemen, I will not attempt the mockery of a defence. You are about to condemn me for attempting to overthrow the oppressors of my country. You do not know, neither can you appreciate my motives. I commit my sacred cause, which is that of freedom, to the vindication of posterity ... If I have appeared as a pioneer in the van of freedom's

battles – if I have attempted to free my country from political degradation – my conscience tells me I have only done my duty. Your brief authority will soon cease but the vindictive proceedings of this day shall be recorded in history … When my countrymen will have exalted their voices in bold proclamation of the rights and dignity of humanity, and enforced their claims by the extermination of their oppressors, ten, and not till the, will some future historian do my memory justice – then will my name and sufferings be recorded in the Scottish story – then will my motives be understood and appreciated; and with the confidence of an honest man, I appeal to posterity for that justice which has, in all ages and in all countries, been awarded to those who suffered martyrdom in the glorious cause of truth and liberty.[52]

Scottish republican sentiment has never been fully extinguished. Just before Elizabeth II's coronation, Scottish radicals complained that she was actually Elizabeth I of Scotland since the Virgin Queen had never ruled the northern kingdom. Such pettiness resulted in a bombing campaign against post boxes with EIIR cast on them, forcing the government to change the design to one with the Scottish coat of arms. MI5 blamed Scottish terrorists, the equivalent, as they saw it, of the IRA, and they blamed the extreme wing of the Scottish National Party.

The Victorian era saw labour quarrels as paramount, themselves coming to a head in the era of 'Red Clyde' after the First World War, but things again faded and 'culture' seemed to answer where politics had failed. Devolution changed national dynamics. The debacle of the 1979 Scottish referendum was annulled when the Scottish National Party took power in 2007, and Nicola Sturgeon renewed the push for full independence, even though she was again denied the opportunity by the Supreme Court in 2022.

Welsh nationalists during the French Revolution, too, have courted outright republicanism and Welsh intellectual thought

was both nationalist and European in outlook, Wales looking backwards to its old allegiances with France and modern
European regionalism. It saw itself in the nineteenth century as a
land of social democracy looking to Giuseppe Mazzini for inspi-
ration, but also took a darker turn when later thinkers turned
to Italian fascism as a way forward in their frustration at being
ignored by the Westminster government.

Nowadays Welsh politicians promote cultural difference and
'Celtic' particularism, whilst the SNP message is one of internationalism and economic autonomy from the rest of the United
Kingdom. Nevertheless, the SNP also include the retention of
the monarch in their programme, whose avowed 'Britishness' (or
Englishness) seems to contradict the party's desire for autonomy.
Nevertheless, who is the rightful monarch of Scotland? The end
of Stuart hopes on the field of Culloden still leaves intriguing
possibilities. The current Jacobite heir to the claims of the historical Stuart monarchs is Franz, Duke of Bavaria, of the House
of Wittelsbach. The senior living member of the royal Stuart
family, descended in a legitimate male line from Robert II of
Scotland, is Arthur Stuart, 8th Earl Castle Stewart. For now,
Charles and the House of Windsor will suffice. Perhaps it is judi-
cious, after all, to stick with who you know.

Ironically, when the Scottish parliament was abolished and
the two parliaments were amalgamated in 1707, the Scots became
'stateless', as they saw their country's identity obscured by the
shadow of creeping anglicisation ('England' was also formally
'abolished' in 1707 in favour of a new term: 'the Kingdom of
Great Britain', which replaced both sovereign states). However,
it also meant that the Scots were now politically independent
within a type of managed republicanism favouring aristocratic
landowners who styled themselves patriots and upholders of
liberty, and this long period of political independence free from
monarchical rule and interference from Westminster gave rise to
the Scottish Enlightenment.

It also allowed Scots a central role in British imperialism, Samuel Vetch reviving the term 'British Empire', which was first used by a Welshman. Charles II was crowned King of Scotland in 1651, but a monarch did not actually return to Scotland until 1822, when George IV was kitted out in full, and bogus, Highland regalia and the crowds cheered in rapture (possibly as many as one-third of all Scots attended the ceremonials). If Scotland does break with the English, Welsh and Northern Irish, it will cause a final blow to British identity as a unifying feature of these islands, but it will also create a crisis of identity in the nature of monarchy and the role the monarch has in the Commonwealth, as titular head of state in Australia, New Zealand, Canada and the Caribbean, where full independence is a topic high on commissioners' agendas.[53]

The flag of the British republic – red, white and green in horizontal bars – is last recorded flying amid bunting at the silver jubilee of George V in 1935, some bolshie householder no doubt spoiling things for the neighbours. The royal family seems to hold a mystique in times that need stability, but the ideas that informed the republican conspirators of the past and the desperadoes of the present are still alive; the struggle between revolutionaries and the 'secret state' over the last few hundred years is also the hidden history of British democracy. It is an honourable history, too, and should not be forgotten.

A comment is perhaps required regarding the documents that make up the paper trail of anti-monarchical sentiment. They form a selection of key moments in the history of democratic republicanism, from clauses in Magna Carta to the 'parliamentary' levying of the Provisions of Oxford, from the Nineteen Provisions and the Levellers' 'Agreement of the People' to Algernon Sidney's political musings, and from Thomas Paine's *Age of Reason* to Charles Dilke's attack on royal expenses. Together, they form a chain of commentary that, inevitably, leads across the Atlantic and into European radicalism.

Some of these may not have appeared to be radical at their reception or intended as 'republican' when conceived. Nevertheless, not only have these documents changed in relevance and meaning over time, but, crucially, they were all seen by their opponents as stages in a 'conspiracy' to undermine the established Church, the rule of law and, for our purposes, restrict or abolish the monarchy by either emasculating its prerogatives or abolishing its existence under cover of language apparently aimed at other targets. There is no suggestion that Magna Carta was a 'democratic republican' document, but King John clearly saw its hidden agenda and he used the pope and violence to get the document annulled as soon as possible. He saw it for what it was, just as the barons tried to disguise their oligarchic tendencies. This was a plain confrontation with the supremacy of God's anointed representative on earth. No wonder, then, that this stand-off in English history (seen as might versus rights), long remembered but marginal to British constitutional practice, has had such a central impact on politics in the United States. Simon de Montfort and his supporters took things a stage further, arguing that their obedience to Henry III and the stability of the monarchy was founded on a mutual relationship based on law, not right. Parliamentary, democratic and republican documents have evolved and supported each other retrospectively over many years, each building on and reinterpreting those that came before.

Together these documents form the legal and, later, statuary basis that argued for a reformed parliament; liberty of speech and belief; the universal rule of law regardless of social position; access to the law for all; accountability of representatives; universal equality with no divine election or right given to the monarch; and major restrictions placed on monarchy or the abolition altogether of the monarch and social hierarchy, including the end of a bicameral parliament that embodied the supremacy of the Church and the privilege and entitlement of aristocracy. No one document embodies all these principles; rather, taken together, they clearly demonstrate a disavowal of monarchical rule and political interference.

The documents, which are usually seen to mark the rise of parliamentary 'democracy', may also, quite legitimately, be seen to represent the 'republican' and egalitarian nature of mainstream political thought triumphing through historic evolution. The problem remains, however, that the documents show, for the most part, a move towards conciliation and rapprochement that obscures the thrust of some of the political thought that permeated Leveller thinking, green ribbon republicanism and even the nascent interests of the common people under Simon de Montfort's reforms. We still have a monarchy and it does well to remember that those who could not suppress republican ideals were often forced to emigrate to avoid being hunted down or murdered by royal agents.

The struggle for republicanism is therefore enacted in a Manichean universe: you chose which side is more evil and likely to do more harm. The monarchy will, no doubt, develop and change to meet the times ahead and there will be occasional decent monarchs, but the institution will always be dogged by a shadow that will not fade – that of a fully meritocratic republicanism and a fully egalitarian democracy.

The reader will become aware that when this book was first published I took the story of republican and revolutionary sentiment back to the seventeenth century with an emphasis on the last 200 years or so. There was also a greater interest in revolutionary 'terrorism' over other peaceful political solutions. I have decided not to change the emphasis of my original work, but instead, I hope this introduction has filled those gaps missing in the original. With this introduction I have taken the story back to the origins of monarchy on these shores and to the feudal and medieval origins of the republican struggle. It ends with the present king and the unwritten future.

Clive Bloom
2023

Chapter One

Children of the Revolution

It is Easter 1916. The city centre of Dublin has been reduced to ash by British artillery and Irish bullets. Pàdraig Pearse, soldier-poet and leader of the rising, and Michael Joseph O'Rahilly (known as The O'Rahilly),[1] reluctant last-minute volunteer, exchange a few words during a lull in the fighting. Pearse (later to be shot by firing squad) tells O'Rahilly, 'Well, when we're all wiped out, people will blame us for everything, I suppose.'[2]

This is how revolutions begin: with brave men who have 'stupid' dreams that apparently simply cannot succeed. Men who 'fight with a rope round [their] neck', as George Bernard Shaw put it, are outside our circumstances. Theirs is already a better world, somehow already achieved. They fight because others say that nothing has a hope of changing, and everything will remain as before. Yet to be a revolutionary you have to create a *moral* universe in which the future is different from the present, and better; a deed sufficient to win freedom or, if not, one in which 'our children will win ... by a better deed!' Such a moral dream is changed into political reality by history. In almost all the cases in this book, I must admit that I would have stood aside and let them get on with their better future (which so often led to exile, the gallows or the bullet). I might even have condemned them as fools, but fools in an honourable cause. Indeed, such 'foolishness' seems to arise more often than many from the left or right of the political spectrum have been willing to concede, a continuing thread in Britain's history. In the context of Britain and Ireland, heroism and foolishness are always very close.

This book presents for the first time the full story of republican 'terror' in the United Kingdom in the nineteenth and twentieth centuries, and the means and methods that have characterised the British revolutionary way, from assassination plots against the royal family, prime ministers and government to full-scale revolt and armed rebellion. It has long been a truism of political debate to talk of the 'presidential' style of our prime ministers. Such comments would be listened to with a sense of bitter irony by the men and women who feature within these pages. They would not see the people's utopian republic that they dreamed about through conspiracy, terrorism and war; instead they might remark that little had changed since the early republicans met in the heady days of the Corresponding Societies of the late eighteenth century. They might say things had got worse since England's first and only republic in the period known as the 'Interregnum'.

Since the 1790s, perhaps as many as 35,000 subjects born in the United Kingdom have fought and died both at home and in the Empire in the cause of the republic. Most were Irish, but many were Welsh, Scots or English, caught, as often as not, by government spies, police and informers before anything could happen, and brought ignominiously to trial and execution. There were also those, however, who had been exiled to Australia, Canada and the United States and who carried on the fight abroad. Nevertheless, more than might be expected took up arms and fought pitched battles in the streets of Welsh towns, the leafy lanes of southern England and the moors of Scotland before being overwhelmed by the forces of government and cast into the oblivion of official history. Their last glorious stand was (but where else?) in Dublin during Easter 1916; their reincarnation as a modern movement the consequence of that romantic debacle.

For over 200 years there has been a myth that British politics runs by the clock of steady compromise and consensus, that reforms are the result of rational debate, too slow no doubt for many, but nevertheless measured and correct. History consigns the agitators and violent incidents that led to change to a paragraph or two in official history, described in heroic or disdainful detail according to the historian's political credentials. While Peterloo, the Luddites, the Tolpuddle Martyrs and the Chartists remain in the collective memory as something vaguely attached to the Industrial Revolution, readers unacquainted with specialist histories are left utterly unaware of the long and violent struggles to make England, Scotland and Wales (not to mention Cornwall and the Isle of Man) revolutionary republican states, flying, not the Union flag, but the colours of the banner of the revolution: red, white and green. While every reader is aware of the struggle in Ireland, many will be surprised to see how central Irish revolutionary activities have been to the other nations in the British Isles, and how tragic have been the consequences.

Indeed, not counting the three extraordinarily bloody civil wars in Ireland, nor the bombing campaigns by the IRA in England up to the Second World War and from the 1970s to the 1990s, there have been two Welsh uprisings, one lowland Scottish civil war, one Highland 'rebellion', one uprising in Derbyshire and another in Kent, five attempts to assassinate the entire Cabinet and seize London, numerous attempts to assassinate the royal family and an almost continuous history of terrorism from the Fenians of the 1860s to the Tartan Army of the 1970s. Add to these events three French invasions (two of which landed), the attempt to seize Canada by an Irish army calling itself the IRA and the various revolts in Australia (a direct result of transportation), and the political history of the British Isles takes on a very different complexion. The story is truly international, played out at one time or another in the bars of New York, the jungles of Venezuela, the foothills of Afghanistan and the prison camps and gold mines of Australia.

Around a core of Irish nationalism and English republicanism there also remain the largely ignored or untold stories of Scottish and Welsh independence fighters and the violent revolutionary skirmishes and bombing campaigns that marked Anglo-Welsh and Anglo-Scottish relations from the 1790s to the 1970s. Equally ignored or sidelined have been the stories of men like Jeremiah Brandreth of Nottinghamshire and 'Sir' William Percy Honeywood Courtenay, who led the last purely English rebellion in Kent, which ended in the bloody battle of Bossenden Wood on 10 June 1838. Forgotten also by modern readers is the Suffragette conspiracy to assassinate Lloyd George and his Cabinet as they played golf on Walton Heath. The plot, possibly engineered by the secret service, included the use of poison darts and blowpipes from South America – the very stuff of a Sherlock Holmes mystery.

The first shot of revolution began with the birth of the United States. For Thomas Carlyle, working on his monumental study, *The French Revolution*, during 1837, the war in America was the key to all subsequent world revolution: 'the world is all so changed; so much that seemed vigorous has sunk decrepit, so much that was not is beginning to be! – Borne over the Atlantic ... what sounds are these; muffled-ominous new in our centuries? Boston Harbour is black with unexpected tea: behold a Pennsylvanian Congress gather; and ere long, on Bunker Hill, DEMOCRACY [*sic*] announcing, in rifle-volleys death-winged, under her Star Banner, to the tune of Yankee-doodle-doo, that she is born, and, whirlwind-like, will envelope the whole world!'

What began as a small-scale problem with honorary Englishmen soon kindled a desire for democratic republicanism that had its philosophical origins in the time of Oliver Cromwell's

Commonwealth; the French Revolution announced that the days of the old regime were finally numbered. Napoleon's threatened invasion gave hope to scores of British radicals who had formed secret cells ready to go into action to topple privilege, wealth, monarchy, aristocracy and Church and set up the Republics of England, Scotland, Wales and Ireland.

Trafalgar and Waterloo crushed these hopes and sent them underground; radicals divided into parliamentary reformers and republican terrorists. Many reformers and radicals were dedicated to the defeat of monarchic and aristocratic rule, the overthrow of authoritarian government and the realisation of national parliaments dedicated to liberty, equality and universal suffrage. In their way stood the full weight of royal tradition, the Church of England, successive governments, oppressive laws against combination and free speech, the army, the secret service and, from 1829, the new police.

We think we know our past, and the alternative version of British history at the core of republicanism seems a type of fiction. Nevertheless it is waiting in the wings to become the official version when the red, white and green flag of the republic replaces the royal standard and the Union flag. Extremism is usually considered not quite cricket and rather un-British; but our national character has a more sinister side, and if we remember only a convenient history that ignores this darker complexion, we also fail to see how the very system we live under has evolved and what titanic struggles mould it for good or evil. Despite a general belief in tradition and the feeling that our parliamentary system has somehow evolved, nothing is further from the truth. Indeed nothing would have changed at all without those who saw the need to challenge complacency and injustice in a Britain where the old ways seemed neither fair nor natural. Reform has too often been linked to violence and the media have long enjoyed 'hyping' the mild reformist into a 'loony lefty'. Yet agitators are dedicated to their causes, and where reform might fail, terrorism has sometimes triumphed.

Although often represented as martyrs to the cause of British democracy, the men and women of the extreme republican cause should not be lumped together with those working for reform. While the two groups are clearly connected and talk a similar language, their methods differ considerably, as do their attitudes to the cause. Republican extremists and those dedicated to various forms of national independence who advocate or actually resort to assassination and military uprising are not simply working for reform but are, in a fundamental way denying the very basis of it. Reform is *evolutionary* and *incremental*; revolution is a final, once-and-for-all settling of accounts to create a new world. Successive governments, panicked at such excess, have often treated reformers as revolutionaries, but the paths to republican democracy taken by reformers and revolutionaries remain distinctly different, even if policemen, judges and historians lump them together.

At this point it is worth differentiating radical reformers from the true revolutionaries themselves. On the whole, reformers wish to ameliorate current injustice by overhauling the system as it stands; revolutionaries wish to abolish the system altogether, and terrorists use armed force to do so. The authorities, meanwhile, often treat the two threats as similar in their use of repressive responses and, in so doing, turn the radical ideas of reformers into the revolutionary aims of terrorists. Revolutionary terrorism will therefore sometimes grow from the stopped-up channels of reform. Reformers rarely become revolutionaries in the strict sense of working in armed secrecy for the overthrow of a regime. Rather, the extreme revolutionary elements become attached to causes, using those causes as a rationale for their own wider aims. This is clear in both the extreme wing of the Chartists and the later anarchist outgrowth of the social democrat movement of the 1880s. In order to pursue their limited aims successfully, both the Liberal Party and, later, the Labour Party had to disassociate themselves from extremist agitation. Respectability was the key when representing the requirements of the working classes who voted first Liberal and then Labour. In this regard, reformers who aim at cooperating with the system in order to change it become the real traitors in the eyes of revolutionaries – collaborators who have sold out. Nowhere did this become more obvious than in the internecine warfare in the Labour Party and union movement that came to a head with the expulsion of Militant Tendency in the 1980s.[3]

There is a great and tragic irony in the early fight of revolutionaries against the state, for, as they fought it, it grew, the better to oppose them. Known as the 'Thing' to opponents in the eighteenth century, and the 'Machine' from the 1830s, the state was for over a hundred years little more than a chimera for revolutionary and nationalist proponents – a mystical stalking horse that hardly existed. Government there was, and power there was too, but it did not reside in bureaucratic layers of civil servants and red tape. When, in 1829, on the eve of the new Police Act, Carlyle attacked the rise of bureaucratic society, it was still a dream, and when Charles Dickens's characters in *David Copperfield* complained of being 'bound hand and foot with red tape', the government department was imagined run by only a father and son. In reality, the Home Office in 1811 had only the Home Secretary, his Permanent Under-secretary, two other under-secretaries, twelve clerks and a cleaner. Until the latter half of the twentieth century, government was feeble at best, incompetent and draconian at worst; in the eighteenth and nineteenth it was virtually unpaid and without a clear sense of purpose, other than to gather taxes for foreign wars and keep the monarch's peace. The inner government, the Privy Council, answered to the monarch, even if it did not always tell him what he wanted to hear; cabinets were clubs of similar-minded men from similar backgrounds. In the country a loosely knit world of magistrates and squires (usually the same thing) answered to a lord lieutenant of a county, and moral regulation was left to parish councils and the village squire's young brother, the local parson. Almost all government was in local hands, almost nothing in the hands of those at the top.

In an age that has seen totalitarianism we find it easy to equate the Regency and Victorian policed state with our own recent knowledge of history. The 'policed' state of the pre-railway age had no police force and relied on local militias, yeomanry[4] and other loyal forms of *amateur* enthusiast to maintain general law and order and political propriety. Dangers seemed to lurk round every corner of the kingdom, 'the Home Secretary smelled sedition and treason everywhere'. Revolution never came, only isolated revolutionaries. Yet here is one key to the growth of the British state. The state grew in direct proportion to the threat to social, political and economic order. Required to act as a mechanism to raise taxes, parliament also needed a structure to collect those taxes it levied and prevent the possibility of refusal. To do this, government needed the state. The people of the Regency period found the idea of the state so peculiar, they named it the 'Thing' in incomprehension. It included parliament, the army, magistrates and lord lieutenants, parish and vestry officials, workhouse beadles, prison commissioners and mad-house governors and, finally, the new Metropolitan Police: a hotchpotch of official and semi-official busybodies. At its head was the royal family, but they did not quite fit the new and gathering bureaucracy there to serve them.

The police were formed not to combat rising burglaries but to keep civil order. The creation of a political police, Special Branch, was directly linked to the fight against Irish republicans, and republicanism was a direct influence on the rise of the British state machine. Early terrorists fought a hazy and ill-defined enemy: the ruling elite. They fought the elite's monopoly of power and its control of the British way of life. This fight usually found identity in local machine-breaking or direct attacks on the person of the monarch or his representatives. Republicans were trying to break a spider's web of control. That very process forced those in authority to coalesce their positions and expand their remit in a purely defensive mode. Thus the modern state emerged, with its bureaucracy, police and secret service – professional, salaried and alert.

If the destructive element of British republicanism turned to the gun and bomb as a means to a final accounting with the rulers and their tyrannous system, it is not true to say that such action was the final resort of the frustrated and downtrodden. It is a truism that frustration breeds terrorism. This is not quite so. Terrorists see their actions as positive, clearly defined in aim and determined in purpose; terrorists are happy because they are certain of their cause, conscious of its outcome. Remarkable confirmation of this new-found psychological clarity of purpose experienced by armed terrorists comes from our own age in the testimonies of republican and loyalist volunteers during the troubles in Northern Ireland, men who felt elated and purposeful once armed. This is why they sometimes appear calm at their sentence or even exultant. They are not reformers who went to extremes. They belong to a different category and therefore may be viewed as a splinter of the various movements calling themselves nationalist or democratic in the British Isles. They act on behalf of the poor and disinherited but are usually not of them.

In the eighteenth and nineteenth centuries such revolutionaries (and their self-appointed enemies) were often men who considered themselves gentlemen and who had lost money and fallen into the void between the squirearchy and the respectable tradesmen class, failures in everything but their self-belief. James Tilly Matthews lost his tea business and his sanity working against the eighteenth-century version of the 'men in black'; John Bellingham, who killed Spencer Perceval, the prime minister, in 1811, insisted that his business had been ruined while on government business. For them, acts of entrepreneurial self-promotion were also deeds of altruism. Utopian ideals melded with self-image and produced a desire to find real self-respect by rising above the social respectability denied them in their business and social life. Failure in business is a curious thread that unites the extremists of our story, such failure becoming a positive foundation for a belief that the system itself is rotten and one's own failure is an exemplary instance of a common trend. Personal revenge is then sublimated into a general principle from which an ideology can be extracted with universal significance. The hopes of religious fundamentalists of an afterlife are here replaced for the secular republican fundamentalist (himself an authoritarian) by the concept of 'the future': 'The real goal is power over the past and, most of all, over the nature of the future. The past is disaster, unfair; but for all rebels the past should – must – end in future justice. The present is a constant humiliation; a similar future is intolerable.'[5] A revolutionary future forgives and justifies excess, just as the final showdown is needed to save the soul of the nation.

Terrorists act because they know that terror actually succeeds in getting results. The attempts at uprisings and killings described in this book are not therefore final acts of desperation but, once decided upon, are acts determined by belief in success and the will to carry out whatever is needed. Men turn to guns when they are certain and convinced of their cause and when they have found clarity of purpose. Such a mood represents a moment of no return, a self-made choice.

> Official denial that anything can be accomplished in politics by means of terrorism is, of course, inevitable: no government, whether it claims to rule by consent or imposes its rule by force, can afford to admit that its conduct of the nation's business is to be modified in any way by the use of force by any party of its opponents... . Such an admission would be a confession of failure to maintain law and order; and that its policies might have been mistaken.
>
> But the facts of history do not bear out this assertion of the uselessness of terrorism; quite the contrary, for at all epochs and in all parts of the world governments have, in fact,

repeatedly been forced by terrorists to change their policies,
and in some cases have been overthrown by terrorism.[6]

If terrorism is a ticket for success, that still leaves the question of
whose terrorism and for what purpose? After all, the terrorists
and revolutionaries described in this book either failed before
they began or were hunted down after their act. An explanation
can be found if we look at the difference between 'offensive'
and 'defensive' terrorism. Offensive terror, such as that used by
cadres and revolutionary organisations, is likely to fail, as they
lack the power of the state, its army, police, judiciary and economic base. Extraordinary outside pressure (such as Wolf Tone
hoped to get by a French invasion and the reformist Cobden
looked for in an economic 'accident') would be the only way to
overthrow a regime.

Defensive terror is that employed by the state itself. Here
we discover what every British revolutionary already knows,
that the state is deeply implicated in all revolutionary activity, not only watching it but fomenting it in order to increase
its own power further by mobilising its own structures and
the people it employs. This was clear to Scottish radicals in the
1790s sentenced to transportation because of the Government's
use of spies; it was clear to Joseph Priestley when 'Church and
King' mobs destroyed his laboratory; it was clear to those who
watched the formation of loyalist clubs and associations to fight
English democrats; it was clear to Edward Despard as he stood
on the gallows; it was clear to the Pentrich insurgents duped by a
Government stooge; it is clear to the Stevens Inquiry investigat-
ing state-sponsored assassination in Northern Ireland.

Indeed, the use of agents provocateurs, black propaganda,
scaremongering, spies and deliberate falsification of history is
almost the prerogative of the British state in its defensive posture. Amazingly, but not without reason, it might be concluded
that all revolutionary terrorism in the United Kingdom has had
state involvement since the Elizabethan age, either created in

the cause of entrapment (first of Catholics,[7] then of democrats, anarchists and communists, then again of Irish Catholic nationalists) or used to egg on a conspiracy of words to that of deeds. In Ireland, Scotland and Wales, national independence movements have long been infiltrated by intelligence organisations and quasi-official branches of the state.

Democratic freedom and state terror long differentiated by left-wing historians are too closely related, too intermingled, too interdependent to allow our story a simple ending. At its core is the complicity between the need of the British state to maintain order and the desire of republican cells to overthrow that order and build a new Jerusalem of equality and freedom. The use of terror is the virus of revolution and the toxin of republican sentiment, activity and assassination up to the present day. The ideas that informed the conspirators, the lives of the participants and the struggle between revolutionaries and the 'secret state' over the last 200 years also forms the hidden history of British democracy. Central to this hidden history is the interconnectedness between the French and the American revolutions and Scottish, Welsh and Irish nationalists and English terrorists, all of whom were prepared to use violent means to gain republican ends. Above all, the book tells a human, often tragic, tale of the thwarting of decent reformers by obstinate governments and the colossal self-deception of idealists mesmerised by utopian dreams which may, who knows, one day be realised.

The fashion among British communist or Marxist historians to see the revolutionary tendency as part of the rise of working-class socialism, in which such revolutionaries 'jumped the gun' in the historical process, is only part of the story and less fashionable as an argument after the collapse of the Soviet Union. After the fall of the Berlin Wall and the rise of international Islamic terrorism, the story seems a little more complex. The old story of republicanism, told as a tale of continuous struggle for freedom of expression and democratic voting rights undertaken on behalf of working people, has (at least in part) to be revised. New insights have offered themselves, first in terms of the nature of utopian ideological struggle and its impact on nationalism and republicanism, and secondly on the significance of the extremist groups themselves. With renewed interest in marginal groups now that the old left–right political divisions have broken down, we are starting to reconsider histories that were ignored in both the official and Marxist versions of the past because they did not quite fit.

In moving from the first and only English republic through the political debates over republicanism in the seventeenth and eighteenth centuries to the critical period of the American and French revolutions and thence to the assassination plots of Despard, the Cato Street gang or the risings at Pentrich or Newport, and onward to the machinations of the Irish Republican Army and Scottish National Liberation Army, this book weaves an uncomfortable, unstable, 'lumpy' history of the United Kingdom, in which neither the traditional nor the Marxist viewpoint quite works as a framework. To disrupt a seamless narrative of past events, in which cause and effect appear inexorably linked, is a worrying task because it leaves questions unanswered. 'Lumpy' histories are not easy to tell, because the heroes and villains are more difficult to discern and their viewpoints shift into contradictions without reconciliation.

Personality also recovers its place in human affairs, scanty records leaving us only tantalising glimpses of people who would willingly kill or be killed for a cause they had only read about in books or heard of as happening to a foreign people in a foreign land (including, most foreign of all, London itself). Moreover it is worth remembering that the men and women in these pages who dedicated themselves to revolutionary violence and political assassination were not wicked foreigners but English, Welsh, Irish and Scots who dedicated their lives to revolution, or who were converted to the cause by a combination of personal circumstances and sudden revelation. These are home-grown republican, fundamentalist and secular utopians who lived their lives in secret cells and republican cadres and who were engaged in the overthrow of government and monarchy by any means. They were inspired by hatred of the system and by social inequality and injustice. Almost all were class warriors dedicated to the overthrow of the economic system, but they represent a spectrum of those who upheld the old moral economy of fair market trading right up to those who were outright communists. In the eighteenth century the revolutionary potential of the newly proletarianised struck observers of the factory system early on. Observing a Yorkshire cotton mill, one aristocrat noted with alarm that, 'with the bell ringing, and the clamour of the mill, all the vale is disturb'd; treason and levelling systems are the discourse; and rebellion may be near at hand'.[8]

Yet it was also clear that, in the artisan clubs of London and Nottingham, Sheffield and Glasgow, Bristol and Leeds, rebellion was a more serious possibility. Edward Thompson in his ground-breaking book *The Making of the English Working Class*, which first appeared in 1963, was right to see these organisations as proving grounds for the new politics of social justice, but his view that here was an arena for a new working-class consciousness and solidarity and a new class culture has been a matter for debate ever since.[9] These self-employed men and their families did not simply vanish into a labour pool but often remained entrepreneurial small-time businessmen, sometimes precariously pitched above the abyss of the mass of labourers. It was from this group of small craftsmen, traders, shopkeepers, publicans and clerks that the lower middle classes arose. It was the neurosis of this class perched ideologically and socially, not to say economically, between the labouring majority and the squirearchy that proved the breeding ground for revolution as well as, rather ironically, the stoic virtues of Victorian sobriety.

It is, of course, difficult to discuss 'class' before class has made an appearance on the historical stage. 'Hierarchy' is a better word, perhaps. The lower middle classes had hardly a name to call themselves right up to the late nineteenth century.

Nevertheless, their outline can be discerned in new attitudes, social desires and cultural neuroses. Their numbers included those gentlemen who, though poor, did not *make* things and refused to labour for money, and those who did create with their hands and worked for wages. The author Walter Scott recalled, 'I was a gentleman, and so welcome anywhere,' but he was the son of a lowly lawyer, the descendant of cattle rustlers and a novelist to boot. He based his status on his father's ownership of a small plot of land. This emerging class might also include men such as William Lovett, the Chartist leader, whose mother was the daughter of a blacksmith and the wife of a sea captain. Lovett married a chambermaid and worked as a cabinet-maker. Such people had eyes that saw above as well as below in the social scheme of things. Families attempted to marry their betters even at this lowly level, and even if that only meant owning a small landholding, a shop or a horse. James Mill, defender of middle-class virtues, who blamed Peterloo on the lack of sober middle-class citizens in Manchester and who would never have tolerated such 'occasional turbulence', was himself the son of a poor Scottish shoemaker.

Middle-class virtue was, for Mill, the cure for all social ills. It was also the driving force behind social stability. And yet, the lower ranks of this new group were intrinsically unstable. If Britain was based on a cultural heritage of 'class, property and family', it was disturbed by 'the anarchical tendencies ... of virile individuality and informal government'. 'Enable me', prayed Patrick Fraser Tytler, the young Evangelical, in 1810, 'to discharge my duty amiably in that situation in life in which it has pleased God to place me.'[10] Robert Southey observed with satisfaction: 'I *am* in that state of life to which has pleased God to call me, *for* which I am formed, *in* which I am contented.'[11] The point was, however, that the lower middle classes, disturbed and disturbing, *never* knew their place.

The lower middle classes, not the mob or the aristocracy, were and remain the truly unstable modern class of British history, ignored by snobbish traditional historians and Communist Party annalists of the rise (and betrayal) of the British working class. Articulate, organised, money savvy, proponents of self-help and individual moral endeavour, a nation of shopkeepers is more likely to create a maverick than a nation of factory proles. The lower middle class that emerged from the artisan class chaffed at a political set-up inappropriate to their needs and they led the reform movement in alliance with disaffected aristocrats and gentlemen farmers.

Yet on their fringe were those whose chaffing and whose annoyance found no outlet in trade or reforming religion and who saw bitterly the uselessness of the mob and the disinterest of aristocracy. This subclass was itself divided. Thomas Paine, failed stay-maker and excise man, became a revolutionary but never a believer in terror. His books advocated neither regicide nor mob rule and he remained a supporter of justified republicanism and the rule of the property-owning respectable classes. The force of the American Revolution, on behalf of which he later became the voice, bumped him into a set of actions which in England he had not previously contemplated.

Men like Arthur Thistlewood, Despard and Honeywood were decidedly not working class in attitude or experience. Paine may have been an honorary citizen of Revolutionary France but he was marked for the guillotine because of his refusal to vote for Louis XVI's death; on the other hand, Thistlewood, a follower of Paine, planning to massacre the British government as it sat down to dinner, would have voted Paine's death with a clear conscience (in the name of the cause) and pulled the lever to release the blade. John Lilburne, the seventeenth-century soap-maker and brewer, Leveller leader and revolutionary ancestor of Paine and Thistlewood, who spent most of his life in jail, opposing Cavaliers and Roundheads with equal vigour, always insisted that his position stemmed from his rights as a gentleman. He opposed the execution of Charles I only on the practical ground that Cromwell would be seduced into taking the Crown. Even the seventeenth-century proto-communist Digger leader Gerrard Winstanley, forced to work as a labourer, prefaced his address to 'the City of London' with the autobiographical detail that he was an entrepreneur beaten by the 'cheating sons in the thieving art of buying and selling'. The class composition of Irish, Welsh and Scottish patriotic republicanism has similar divisions within the ranks of its lower-class leaders, who, despite playing the anti-capitalism card, often remain clearly on the fringes of their class, ideological warriors first and economic reformers second.

For whom was the revolution to be fought? On whose behalf were the revolutionary cadres to toil, fight and overcome? For whom might idealist martyrs be imprisoned or killed, knowing they died in a just cause? The answer was 'the people'. The people were not yet the working class and far less the proletariat. Indeed, the people were never quite to be exactly aligned with the toiling masses. Rather, the term came to represent those who worked with their hands or tilled the earth, artisans, factory workers, farm hands all grouped vaguely into a strange alliance against the 'general public', who were rapidly turning into the capitalists and the middle classes. Between the 1790s and the 1860s 'the people' were associated with all that was virtuous and wholesome about a nation. Rousseau had set the tone of all such thoughts with his belief that the people were the heart and soul of the nation and that 'they' spoke with one unalterable voice of liberty, equality and fraternity, unified by indivisible virtue. The ideal went to the heart of the French Revolution and, through it, helped shape the image of the working classes in Britain and the concept of a national identity in Ireland, Scotland and Wales.

The emergence of a 'Party of Virtue' in Revolutionary France created a new philosophy of social and political justice that, tied to the people, was nevertheless a philosophical concept to which an ideal (the people) was attached. In such a way, *ideology* emerged, half description, half idealisation, where the structure of a belief was attached to a vision of a society. The people (a singular entity) were not only the site of virtue but also indivisible. Those not of the people were seen as alien, foreign and a threat to its indivisible virtuousness. By such an argument all aristocrats, capitalists, priests and émigrés might be suspected of being of the Devil's party. Louis XVI went to the guillotine an 'enemy of the people', expelled from the body politic as an alien presence. The rebels in Ireland in 1798, in Scotland in 1820 and in Wales during the 1830s saw the British government in the same light. In later years, Irish, Scottish and Welsh nationalists came more and more to reconcile the people with their own version of the nation. In Wales this meant an emphasis on Welshness, especially the Welsh language, and in Scotland this meant a new sense of the oneness of Highlands and Lowlands. In Ireland, the people eventually came to comprise only Catholics; their oppressors were the Orange Order – Protestants backed by the British government.

Communism was the 'final' form of revolutionary ideology, in which social structure and political explanation were so entwined as to make a future wholly predictable. Thus the revolution took on its aspect of eternal struggle, never wholly completed nor truly begun, as Alexander Sullivan enthused to a secret meeting of the American-Irish Clan na Gael in Chicago during August 1881, where he stated that 'we mean war ... we mean that war to be unsparing and unceasing'. It was a sentiment with a heritage going back to the Jacobins, the society founded in 1789 to further the French Revolution and so called because it met in an old Dominican ('Jacobin') priory in Paris.[12] On 10 October 1793 Louis Antoine Saint-Just, the so called 'Angel of Death' of the French Revolution's Committee of Public Safety, had declared, 'the provisional government of France is revolutionary until the peace.' For the next two centuries, revolutionaries such as the Irish Republican Army plotted their plots, planted their bombs, hoarded their weapons, dreamed their dreams of power with the ghost of Saint-Just urging on the permanent revolutionary war.

The revolution was therefore to be enacted on behalf of the people if the people did not rise up spontaneously for themselves, finally enlightened about their oppression. To help them realise their destiny, revolutionaries took to journalism and pamphleteering before taking up the manufacture of pikes and bombs. Thus the people were to be taught that they alone were sovereign and all else that followed did so because of that one inalienable right, itself natural and in harmony with cosmic order. No king and no church could challenge such sovereign power. This new sovereignty bestowed upon the people the new rights and powers of citizens rather than subjects, and revolutionaries everywhere took up fraternal titles and signed themselves 'Citizen X' or 'Y', or 'a friend of the people'. Citizenship was international and joined the people of America, Ireland and France against the internal government of Britain, which was in cahoots with other despotic regimes across the world. Thus, patriotic revolutionaries might look to France or the United States to help in the 'liberation' of Ireland, Wales or Scotland, even when their own governments were at war with France or the United States. In this sense, patriotism was also a perverse form of treason.

As the nineteenth century progressed, 'the people' became more and more associated with the working class, poor artisans and factory workers and less with the labouring peasantry in the countryside. Part of the shift was the influence of the French Revolution, part the influence of the new socialists, who were based in the provincial cities and in London. From now on, much emphasis would be placed on what the factory hand could do. As early as the mid-1790s, radicals had agreed that the political struggle was attached to the fight against a 'capitalist' class – hoarders, exploiters and financiers whom they declared enemies of the people. By the late 1840s, this grouping was divided into a middle class and an entrepreneurial sector, to whom the emerging 'communist' parties gave the familiar revolutionary appellations of 'the bourgeoisie' and 'the capitalist class'. Now, however, the people were no longer in a hierarchic caste struggle with princes and popes but locked in a class struggle of 'two … hostile camps', as the *Communist Manifesto* put it, which was itself the expression of permanent revolutionary war.

The emergence of the citizen (first used in its modern sense by Louis-René la Charlotais in 1763) was also the emergence of world revolution. Thomas Paine called himself a citizen of the world and lived and plotted in England, America and France; Marx's war on the French and Prussian states was conducted from London's Soho. Paine aligned himself (as did Marx) with all those whom he believed to have had their political and human rights denied. Anacharsis Cloots, the Prussian émigré who sat alongside Paine in the national convention of revolutionary France, considered himself an elected representative of the 'human race' and demanded world revolution. The final years of the French Terror and the emergence of Napoleon tied the citizen firmly to the idea of national identity, but by the time of the Chartists, the term 'citizen', now old-fashioned, had metamorphosed into 'proletarian', a harder and less accommodating term, without the class-crossing application of the former word. With the emergence of a proto-proletariat, the struggle had found a new international perspective to take it forward.

To make the revolution a reality, most radicals sought two solutions. Either, the people, especially the 'workers', would spontaneously down tools, rise up and refuse to obey the bidding of tyranny, as the Chartist 'communist' George Harney believed, or a party of virtue would have to arise to force a revolution. Such a secret group would have to be highly organised and gather weapons ready for a coup. Such a coup might spontaneously alight the masses or the use of machine-breaking and strikes might make a coup easier, once the government of the day became rattled. Last, but not least, a foreign army (usually the French) might invade and bring liberty with it in its ranks, rallying the oppressed as it advanced on Dublin or London.

The combination of a belief in the power of the factory worker, the general strike, a revolutionary vanguard working in secret, international connections, spontaneity and a party of virtue coalesced in the ideas of the Communist League, a secret cadre of agitators who met to hold an international 'congress' in a public house in London on a drizzly day in November 1847. The fifty assorted delegates and foreign exiles included Karl Marx and Friedrich Engels, now working secretly to formulate their famous political manifesto. Like Robespierre and Saint-Just they preached revolution, but the revolution was no longer on behalf of republican democracy. Now that too had to be superseded in the vision of an international workers' state, where democracy no longer meant the parliamentary and representative order that previous revolutionaries had fought to create. 'In short, the Communists everywhere support every revolutionary movement, against the existing social and political order of things.... . Let the ruling classes tremble.... . The proletarians have nothing to lose but their chains. They have a world to win.'[13]

The Duke of Wellington had a nose for these dangerous upstarts; Napoleon was no gentleman and, on first meeting Horatio Nelson, Wellington dismissed him as a vulgar little man. Even Beethoven was, he believed, an overbearing newcomer, and the Duke remained a loyal, violin-playing fan of the more discreet Mozart (presumably ignoring the composer's actual vulgar personality). The Duke spent his civilian life reinforcing the windows and gates of his London home, Apsley House, ready for the day of revolution, and constantly called out the troops whenever radicals took to the streets and threatened civil war. By one of history's ironies, the disembodied Duke and his famous hook nose returned during the worst days of civil disorder in the late 1880s in the person and personality of Sherlock Holmes, the ultimate defender of wealth, property and sobriety against the new threat of foreign upstarts and entrepreneurial blackmailing murderers from the wrong side of the tracks. Sherlock Holmes made his literary debut in *Beeton's Christmas Annual* of 1887 in *A Study in Scarlet*. With his 'hook-like nose' and penchant for the violin, Holmes is the Iron Duke reincarnated in the age of the socialist menace. Not surprising that in the 'great cesspool' of London in this later age, the 'cold blooded' Mr Holmes should lament the fact that 'there are no crimes and no criminals' anymore, dull life for the fictional child of the hero of Waterloo.

Chapter Two

A Headless Corpse at Windsor

A casual visitor to Windsor Castle that April Fool's Day in 1813 might have been somewhat surprised to see a gaggle of gentlemen and workmen crouched inside an old burial vault in St George's Chapel. One, overindulged, overfed and over-coiffured, was the Prince Regent himself, affectionately known as 'Prinny' and later to be crowned as George IV. His well-dressed companion was the Prince's royal physician, Sir Henry Halford. To all intents and purposes, the two gave the appearance of hesitant but eager grave-robbers.

The occasion for this unusual outing had been the discovery (or more properly the rediscovery) of a vaulted royal burial chamber under the floor of St George's Chapel during the preparatory construction of a new vault. This had been ordered by George III and was intended to house the monarch and his descendants. In tandem with this work, another immediate interment was at hand. Prinny's mother-in-law and Princess Caroline's mother, the Duchess of Brunswick, had recently died and another vault was to be prepared. Work on both projects meant that the subterranean part of the

chapel was exposed and its dividing brickwork was acciden-
tally broken through when a passage was being constructed.

In the rediscovered and now newly disturbed crypt lay
what were assumed to be the coffins of Henry VIII and Jane
Seymour. A third coffin, still covered in black velvet, was
likely to be that of Charles I, but no one was sure. On top
of this was a smaller coffin, possibly holding the body of a
stillborn child of Queen Anne. Sir Henry was designated to
carry out the investigation, which he recorded in his memoirs
of 1831:

> On removing the pall, a plain leaden coffin, with no appear-
> ance of ever having been enclosed in wood, and bearing an
> inscription 'KING CHARLES, 1648', in large, legible characters,
> on a scroll of lead encircling it, immediately presented itself
> to the view. A square opening was then made in the upper
> part of the lid, of such dimensions as to admit a clear insight
> into its contents. These were, an internal wooden coffin,
> very much decayed, and the body carefully wrapped up in
> cere-cloth, into the folds of which a quantity of unctuous
> or greasy matter mixed with resin, as it seemed, had been
> melted, so as to exclude, as effectually as possible, the external
> air. The coffin was completely full; and from the tenacity of
> the cere-cloth, great difficulty was experienced in detaching
> it successfully from the parts which it enveloped.[1]

After some effort at removing the greasy cere-cloth, a face slowly
appeared, little decayed even after 164 years – the first time anybody had seen the face of Charles I since his decapitation.

> At length, the whole of the face was disengaged from its
> covering. The complexion of the skin of it was dark and dis-
> coloured. The forehead and temples had lost little or nothing
> of their muscular substance; the cartilage of the nose was
> gone; but the left eye, in the first moment of exposure, was

open and full, though it vanished almost immediately: and the pointed beard, so characteristic of the period of the reign of King Charles, was perfect. The shape of the face was a long oval; many of the teeth remained; and the left ear, in the consequence of the interposition of the unctuous matter between it and the cere-cloth, was found entire.[2]

The head, of course, was not attached to the body and was therefore taken out for forensic examination in a scene reminiscent of *Hamlet*, played as gothic horror for,

when the head had been entirely disengaged from the attachments which confined it, it was found to be loose, and, without difficulty, was taken up and held to view. It was quite wet, and gave a greenish red tinge to paper and linen which touched it... . It gave to writing paper, and to a white handkerchief, such a colour as blood which has been kept for a length of time generally leaves behind it. Nobody present had a doubt of its being blood.[3]

Halford duly sketched the coffins and did a portrait of the head. Its nose was missing. That would have been that, if this had not been the great age of the political cartoon. George Cruikshank could not resist and produced a tart little portrait of the Prince and Halford confronted by the disinterred bodies of both Henry VIII and Charles I, whose own skeletal body holds aloft the blood-dripping head. In the drawing, entitled 'Meditation amongst the Tombs', the Prince is shown addressing King Henry on how to get rid of an unwanted wife (in this case Princess Caroline), while Halford, holding aloft a burning torch (and goaded by a grinning devil) exclaims, 'How queer King Charley looks without his Head doesn't he?!!! Faith & Sure & I wonder how we should look without our Heads?!!!' The symmetry between the Stuarts and the Hanoverians was not easily ignored: one king beheaded by republican revolutionaries, another threatened by his own would-be regicides and a guillotine already red with a fellow monarch's blood.

What went through the Prince Regent's mind as he came face to face with that disembodied, noseless, red-haired cadaver in the vault of St George's burial chamber back on April Fool's Day 1813? Was there something darker lurking beneath the antiquarian desire to satisfy merely a doubtful point in history? Here, after all, was the face of another unhappy autocratic ruler, whose death on the block seemed only one step away from the guillotine that threw its long continental shadow across the present royal regime. Here, too, was the face of one of the family the Hanoverians had come to replace and whose presence had threatened to topple both the Prince's great-grandfather and grandfather. The House of Hanover had much to contemplate in the sorry fate of the House of Stuart. The lesson could hardly have been lost on the Prince. After all, the ageing lothario in the crypt had more reason than most to worry about revolutionaries, Jacobins and assassination plots. His father, the aged and occasionally insane George III, had succeeded almost single-handedly in being the most loved and hated monarch since Charles I.

The first and only republic of England began its life in 1649 with an Act of Parliament which passed through the single chamber of the Commons, the Lords and the monarchy having been abolished. On 19 May the House of Commons not only formally 'abolished the kingly office in England and Ireland' but also passed the following Act which made England a republic:

> It is declared and enacted by this present parliament, and by the authority of the same, that the people of England, and all of the dominions and territories thereunto belonging, are and shall be, and are hereby constituted, made, established, and confirmed, to be a Commonwealth and Free State, and shall from henceforth be governed as a Commonwealth and Free State by the supreme authority of this nation, the

representatives of the people in parliament ... and that without any King or House of Lords.

This new commonwealth was uncharted political territory and the script would have to be made up as it went along. Yet it had been over a decade in the making, had resulted from a protracted civil war and the far-from-inevitable beheading of a monarch, Charles I, 'King-Martyr'. There remained a legacy of confusion and exhaustion once it was all over. Worst of all, the new commonwealth brought with its vision of infinite possibility a darker and longer-lasting legacy of regicidal guilt and paranoia. From now on, blood-guilt and republicanism would always be associated.

On 20 January 1649, Charles I, appointed by divine right in his own mind and in the minds of most of his subjects, found himself at the bar in Westminster Hall, defending his life against a regime he had fought for seven years, against which he had no chance of acquittal and for whom he had nothing but contempt. He had been a prisoner for two and a half years already, now having travelled from the Isle of Wight via Southampton and Windsor to close arrest at Whitehall; he knew the scaffold was only days away.

The army was already firmly in control. It had marched on London and seized the capital on 6 August 1647, put down another royalist rebellion and, on 6 December 1648, sent Colonel Pride to 'purge' the Commons of all members unsympathetic to the army; and the army was determined that Charles would pay for his sins. An attempt to get Charles to agree to become a constitutional monarch had long since foundered when Pride's purge completed the army's coup d'état. This New Model Army was an ideological army and for some time had elected 'agitators', the equivalent of soviet commissars, to organise a political and growingly republican conscientiousness among the troops. When such debate became mutinous and threatened the social order felt necessary by the generals, Thomas Fairfax, Oliver

Cromwell and his son-in-law, Henry Ireton, had the mutineers rounded up and their leaders shot.

Charles was called by the army the 'Man of Blood' and the 'Grand Delinquent' and, as the war ground to its end and the peace had to be decided, the mood had become 'melancholy, spiteful and bewitched'. On 20 November 1648, the army demanded that the Commons (those that remained) bring Charles to trial. Charles was 'sensible into what hands [he had] fallen' and later prophesied, 'in my fall and ruin, you see your own'.

From the start there were difficulties. A trial of this nature was unprecedented and there were no rules as to how to proceed. A king, moreover, could not be tried by the Commons but only by the Lords, which had adjourned during the critical period and was then bypassed by the Commons, who assumed full responsibility. On 6 January 1649, the House of Commons issued its first Act, ignoring the Lords, to set up a High Court of Justice to try the King. Worse still, no one really cared to sit on the bench and pass judgement on their monarch, let alone do the unthinkable – sign his death warrant. A commission was called and after some debate agreed the following:

> Whereas it is notorious that Charles Stuart, the now King of England … hath had a wicked design totally to subvert the ancient and fundamental laws and liberties of this nation, and in their place to introduce an arbitrary and tyrannical government… .
>
> Whereas also the parliament, well hoping that the restraint and imprisonment of his person, after it had pleased God to deliver him into their hands, would have quieted the distempers of the kingdom, did forebear to proceed judicially against him; but found by sad experience, that such their remissness served only to encourage him and his [ac]complices in the continuance of their evil practices and in raising of new commotions, rebellions and invasions.

As an afterthought the commissioners (acting on behalf of the Commons) also accused Charles of making war against his subjects, in some ways a more serious and exact charge.

Throughout the trial, the commissioners (all but the republican diehards) had to be virtually dragooned into attending both the private deliberations and the public events. The Scots commissioners (Scotland had also been at war), urgently sent by the Scottish parliament to London, added their protest to the growing distaste for a regal trial. Meanwhile, on 4 January, the Commons made it clear that 'the people were the source of all just power ... and parliament represented the people'. This was something quite new and, to royalists and the constitutionally minded, somewhat disingenuous.

During the entire trial, Charles refused to recognise the authority of the bench, and his judges had to amend the accusations so that he would be tried 'in the name and on behalf of the people of England' rather than, traditionally, in the name of the sovereign. From now on, 'the people' were to be taken as the equivalent of the sovereign. As a final blow to the authority of the Commons, no one was willing to act as Lord President of the court. Eventually, John Bradshaw was chosen. He had been a rather minor official of the sheriff's court in London and chief justice for Chester. He took his time appearing before his fellow commissioners and then went out and bought an armour-plated hat, so fearful was he of assassination attempts. The commissioners ordered extra halberds from the Tower of London, and large numbers of troops under the command of Daniel Axtell patrolled Westminster Hall.

Bradshaw proved inept, when demanding of the King that he answer the charges that had been put by the chief prosecutor, John Cook, who had framed them for the commission. The Lord President demanded a reply, 'in the name of the people of England, of which you are *elected* king'. It was a disastrous mistake, which Charles seized upon: 'England was never an elective kingdom, but a hereditary kingdom for near these thousand years ... I do stand more for the liberty of my people, than any here that come to be my pretended judges.'

Charles was no fool when it came to law and, despite a stammer, was able, when allowed (which was not often) to hold his own. Indeed, the commissioners were always fearful that when Charles opened his mouth they would be made to look stupid. 'Remember', he reminded his accusers, 'I am your *lawful* king.' He was, of course, right and in arguing that in his person he guaranteed the ancient liberty of the people against usurpers, he was clearly a long way ahead on points. The court would have to make law as it went along. The King would not plead and so he was de facto guilty of treason, but real proof would need witnesses. These were never provided and were never needed and so the prosecution case simply collapsed into its own bluster. Charles might be guilty, but he could not be proved to be guilty.

Inside the hall, Lady Fairfax, wearing a mask but also the wife of the supreme commander of the army, barracked the proceedings. Axtell ordered her to be quiet or his men would shoot her; evidently he had not realised who the masked woman was. Elsewhere, people called 'God save the King', and the commissioners kept slinking off or excusing themselves from attendance. The trial had to be brought to a swift end before it became a farce. The King could not be seen to have even a modicum of right on his side. Cromwell had long before decided that 'we will cut off his head with the crown upon it' and Cook was determined that '[Charles] must die ... and monarchy must die with him'. Bradshaw summed up, the soldiers cried for 'justice', Charles was condemned because he was a 'tyrant, a traitor, a murderer'. He had also broken the social contract or 'covenant' between monarch and people, a new idea recently formed in his prosecutors' minds. Axtell signalled his men in the Hall and they shouted what they had rehearsed: 'Execution! Justice! Execution!' Charles was executed on 30 January 1649.

Was there at this moment of grim decision a suddenly clearing vision of a new dispensation, a new commonwealth and republic?

After it was over, there appeared the inevitable sense that the whole thing had been unavoidable, fated from the moment that the standards were raised and civil war followed civil war. It had all led, nevertheless, to the scaffold. With the fall of the headsman's axe, a new political consciousness was born. The nature of the political realm and the possibilities of a civil (and subsequent secular) governmental system had subordinate questions attached regarding liberty, property, self-determination and equality. The very nature of a commonwealth and of a republic could only be realised when, with the literal severing of the head of the head of state, a concept of future time, of a time different from the present, could come fully into focus. The emergence of this politics, conflict-based, future-looking and republican, would mark Westminster's deliberation for nearly 400 years.

The so-called Barebones Parliament was dismissed and Cromwell, backed by his generals, was dictator. The aristocracy were powerless and the Commons irresolute. Cromwell defended himself by arguing that his elevation was the work of God. The radicals were not impressed and began to plot. Cromwell's new status even succeeded in bringing the extreme republicans nearer to the exiled Charles II, with whom they thought they could cut a deal. It was an unlikely idea, but destined to cause trouble. By now, Cromwell had set his face against the extreme libertarians or 'commonwealth's men', whom he accused of wishing to 'level' everything to 'an equality'. Eventually, inevitably, Cromwell was offered the throne. 'The Humble Petition and Advice' was presented by Sir Christopher Packe, a prominent London merchant. The crown was refused, but a second chamber was restored and, if Cromwell had not died on 3 September 1658, the worst fears of the democrats might have come to fruition: a new, more powerful and more authoritarian 'monarchy' might have replaced the Stuarts for good.

The Republic of England was born in blood. Fairfax, not wishing to make war on the Scots, had resigned from the army, and Ireton had died worn out fighting in Ireland; only Cromwell had the will to continue to fight to secure the Commonwealth. He hacked his way through Scotland and Ireland until the republic was secure. This did not prevent plots from both royalists and millennial fundamentalists destabilising the situation. Things did not improve when Cromwell accepted the role of Lord Protector, interpreted by many as his wish to become the new monarch. Penruddock's rebellion occurred when 400 royalist sympathisers challenged this assumption. Needless to say, it was defeated, by a small troop of cavalry, even though 4,000 militia had been raised. More difficult to defeat were the nonconformists who expected the Commonwealth to herald the Second Coming and who saw their wishes undermined by Cromwell's action in becoming Lord Protector. During 1654 there were rumours that these Fifth Monarchists were going to rise in London in preparation for the coming of Christ (they were to hoist a banner of the Lion of Judah). The plan was foiled by Cromwell's secret service under John Thurloe,[4] and the religious group placed in detention.

Most dangerous of all were those men who could unite both sides of the spectrum of political opinion. One such was Edward Sexby, who enlisted in 1643 in Cromwell's regiment of horse. He had been born around 1616, probably in Suffolk, and soon became one of the leading agitators in the New Model Army. Agitators were the political representatives of the ordinary soldiers who, under the direction of the Levellers under Lilburne, debated with Cromwell and Ireton at Reading and at Putney. Sexby's main argument was that 'we have engaged in this kingdom and ventured our lives, and it was all for this: to recover our birthrights and privileges as Englishmen ... we have had little propriety in the kingdom as to our estates, yet we have had a birthright.... I am resolved to give my birthright to none.'[5]

At Putney, his sophisticated eloquence annoyed Cromwell. Sexby left the army late in 1647, but continued to be employed as a go-between for the Levellers and the troops. He rejoined the army in 1649 with the rank of captain and rose to become the governor of Portland. His regiment was at the siege of Tantallon Castle in February 1651, from which he emerged as a colonel. This was short-lived for he was court-martialled in June and left the army for the second time. His talents must have been such that he could not be easily missed and he was sent to France to aid the Huguenots and to oversee the translation of the 'Agreement of the People' (a key Leveller document) into French.

It appears he did not become a revolutionary until Cromwell had rejected an alliance with Spain (against France) during 1655, when he actually left for the continent pursued by Thurloe's agents. There he began his conspiracy against Cromwell, not only with the government of the Spanish Netherlands, but with Irish priests and Presbyterians and with Charles II (then in exile). Sexby's idea was to bring about a further revolution by assassinating Cromwell. By this means, the country would be returned to 'nature' and out of this primal chaos would emerge the true republic dreamed of before 1649. Sexby held to the view that one key catastrophic event would do the job of awakening the English.

In June 1656 Sexby came back to England to help establish an underground network of Levellers and others who would work in secret against Cromwell and the Protectorate. In the same year he formed a gang of assassins who hoped to kill Cromwell on 17 September as he rode to parliament. They rented a room in Westminster, but could not get at Cromwell because of the crowd around him. They continued to try but without success until January 1657, when they planted a bomb in Whitehall. This again was foiled. In the meantime a number of Sexby's associates were rounded up, including Miles Sindercombe, 'one of the Levelling party', who took poison while in prison in the Tower and died on 19 February.

Having made his escape, Sexby then took to pamphleteering. He produced the notorious political tract, *Killing No Murder*,[6] in which he attempted to justify the assassination of Cromwell, using biblical precedents. Cromwell's agents soon seized seventeen hundred copies and Thurloe called the pamphlet 'the most dangerous ... that ever has been printed in these times'. Despite the efforts of spies and government agents, the pamphlet was soon circulating among the disgruntled at inflated prices. The work itself was actually dedicated ironically to Cromwell from his 'slave and vassal'. Sexby also berated his fellow Englishmen for being 'servile' and not rising up and overthrowing the oppressor. Despite the popularity of the pamphlet, Sexby was picked up by Cromwell's agents on 24 July as he was attempting to escape to the Low Countries 'in a mean habit, disguised like a country man ... his visage altered by an overgrown beard'. He died (possibly by foul means) in the Tower.

This, however, was not the end of his incendiary pamphlet, which went on to inspire revolutions both in France and in Britain. There were new editions in 1659, 1689, 1708, 1715, 1734, 1743, 1745, 1753, 1808, 1810 and 1864. Two editions came out during the Jacobite risings and William Godwin and Percy Shelley read versions that were printed during 1792. The tract was translated into French and published in 1658, 1793 and 1800. An edition was actually addressed to Napoleon in 1804 and a version of a later translation found its way into the turbulent times of Napoleon III.

When Charles II returned to England in 1660 and was restored to the throne on his birthday, 29 May, there was general rejoicing. The regicides, however, were hardly in jubilant mood. Those who had died during the Commonwealth would be retrospectively punished, while those still living would be hunted down. There was no country where they might hide. Of the fifty-nine signatories to the death warrant, forty-one were still alive. Cromwell's body, which had been interred in Westminster Abbey on 10 November 1658, was dug up, dragged by sled to Tyburn, hanged and decapitated. The body was buried under the gallows and the head displayed on a spike outside Westminster Hall until it fell down in a storm many years later, only to be bought by an antique dealer and ending up in a Cambridge college. John Bradshaw, who had died in October 1659 and had also been interred in Westminster Abbey, was hung in chains at Tyburn.

Of the living, Sir Michael Livesey, who had fled to Holland, was hunted down by Charles's agents and assassinated. John Okey also fled to Holland but was extradited and, with Miles Cobet and John Barkstead, hanged, drawn and quartered in 1662. They had been preceded by the execution in October 1660 of ten regicides, of whom Thomas Harrison was the first (dying on the 13th) and Daniel Axtell the last, on 19 October. Samuel Pepys recorded in his diary for 20 October 1660, 'a bloody week this and the last have been; there being ten hanged, drawn and quartered'. Cavalier ballads gleefully celebrated the outcome of the 'horrid facts of treason' and sang verses, which elaborated each execution to the tune of the drinking song, 'Come let us drinke, the time invites'. Others were not as happy and many were concerned at the vindictiveness and savageness of the royal revenge.

Axtell had fought alongside Cromwell and Fairfax and had helped capture Granagh Castle in Ireland when Cromwell invaded in 1650. During the King's trial he had been the captain of the guard but had not signed the death warrant. A portrait shows him with shoulder-length bobbed hair and a pencil moustache. On 15 October 1660 he was on trial for his life. King's Counsel opened the proceedings with the charge 'that he did imagine and compass the death of the king'. He went on to mention Axtell's command of the soldiers and his ordering them to shoot at Lady Fairfax and cry out 'execution! execution!', asserting that 'if we prove any of these particulars to demonstrate unto you that he was guilty of compassing and imagining the king's death, it is equal as if we had proved he did actually cut off the king's head'.[7]

Axtell could hardly deny the role he played at the trial and, despite being 'ignorant of the law', he put up a reasonable defence. He was, after all, an officer carrying out the law of the land as set down by the House of Commons. The Commons, he argued, were the representatives of the people and he was therefore the instrument of a collective body, for 'if the House of Commons, who are the collective body and representation of the nation, all the people of England, who chose them, are guilty too; and then where will there be a jury to try this? ... if a House of Commons can be charged guilty of high treason as a community the distributive body must needs be guilty.'[8]

He had a point. Moreover, he was also acting as an officer of the army under orders. The court simply dismissed his pleas as irrelevant as he was considered to have acted in his own person. Things were oddly messy. Just as in the original trial of Charles I, logic quickly vanished, for it was obvious that the regicides were being collectively punished as private conspirators, not as the former law-makers of the kingdom. Axtell could hardly survive against the hyperbole of Sir Purbeck Temple, who reported that he heard of Axtell's soldiers 'spitting in the King's face'. Temple, speaking without irony, could 'think no bodies [*sic*] sufferings had been so like our saviour Christ Jesus'. Charles had by this time reached his apotheosis. The outcome was hardly in doubt and Axtell was hanged, drawn and quartered. His brother Thomas, meanwhile, was already living in Sudbury, Massachusetts, the founder of a wholly American family who remembered their dead English ancestor many years later as simply 'Uncle Dan'.

The execution of the King released dangerously subversive attitudes which previously had been unthinkable, left only to wild elements of society to whisper in tavern corners. These levelling tendencies found their most extreme form in people like Gerrard Winstanley, who had been born in Wigan in 1609, but had drifted to Walton-on-Thames and found work as a cow herder. Although a labourer, Winstanley was literate and articulate, producing pamphlets that argued for a redistribution of land among the poor because 'this creation made a common store house for all, [but] is bought and sold and kept in the hands of a few'.[9] The 'bondage of civil property' had to be broken if (in the biblical images he favoured) Jacob, or 'universal liberty', was to have justice against Esau, or ownership and property.

The English, to Winstanley, were like the enslaved Israelites. In his mind, the people of England were not just symbolic Israelites, but the actual inheritors of a long war with 'the Babylonian Yoke'. The whole thrust of history was this fight against enslavement, enacted in every age, 'and the last enslaving conquest which the enemy got over Israel was the Norman over England ... the Norman bastard William himself'. The curse of the Norman Conquest, which had extinguished or repressed old English rights, would be a refrain repeated for the next 150 years.

Winstanley, nevertheless, had a plan. With a group of supporters he decided to 'dig up [St] George's Hill [near Cobham, Surrey] and the waste ground thereabouts and to sow corn'. The waste ground was, in fact, common land, that is, land held in common by a number of taxpayers who rented the open space. It was not anyone's to use and after a year, from 1649 to 1650, this and similar projects by Winstanley's 'Diggers' were surprised by armed force. Winstanley's primitive communism, a forerunner of much recognisably left-wing modern thought about property and community, was extinguished and, after prosecution and a few more pamphlets, Winstanley simply vanishes from history.

The extremism represented by the St George's Hill experiment was not going to be tolerated by those who still saw hierarchy as the key to order, and order based on the recognisable distribution of property. Only by creating rules of cooperation (a commonwealth) would the return to primitivism (civil war) be avoided. Winstanley merely represented that anarchy and chaos that right-minded thinkers had had enough of in the years of civil war. Scholars spent the next fifty years trying to work out a political philosophy that satisfied the rights of parliament and the need for a concept of 'sovereignty' and that re-established a social order that everyone could accept. Civil war was to be avoided at all costs.

The writer who exemplifies these views is Thomas Hobbes, whose *Leviathan* (1651) completed and synthesised the political theories of his day. Hobbes had been born in the town of Malmesbury in 1588 and, after taking his degree at Oxford, had become tutor at Hardwick Hall to the man who one day would be the Earl of Devonshire. Hobbes was no Mr Chips and he travelled in Europe during 1629 to 1631 and again throughout 1634 to 1637. His political ideas, however, also meant that he would spend a necessary period in Paris from 1640 until the end of the Commonwealth. Even then the publication of *Leviathan* looked like getting Hobbes into hot water with parliament, a fate he narrowly escaped, being allowed to live to the ripe old age of 84 and dying as he began, at Hardwick, in 1679.

Leviathan is a long work. Its thesis is that a state of nature is a type of civil war. In order to avoid this situation, every person had to give up their total freedom for limited *guaranteed* freedom by joining with others in a commonwealth. Having contracted into a social order, everyone would be bound thereafter by their 'covenant'. Thus would be produced 'three kinds of commonwealth. For the representative must needs be one man or more: and if more, then it is the assembly of all, or but of a part. When the representative is one man, then is the commonwealth a monarchy: when an assembly of all that will come together, then it is a democracy, or popular commonwealth: when an assembly of a part only, then it is called an aristocracy. Other kind of commonwealth there can be none.' Such covenanted forms of society avoided the 'horrible calamities, that accompany a civil war'.

Thus, in the unstable mid-years of the seventeenth century, Hobbes outlined the options for a government. Yet what did one do with the monarchy that was about to be destroyed; how would order be maintained? Hobbes answered this problem with the idea of 'sovereignty'. A sovereign in this formulation was not a monarch but the symbolic name given to the body to whom everyone in the community had covenanted their liberty. Thus, parliament could be a sovereign power whose laws guaranteed the liberty of those it represented. In order to keep 'peace and concord', everyone had to agree to abide by the sovereign power's rules. Hobbes then argues the logic of this position that whether the sovereign is 'a man, or assembly', its power cannot be challenged, for to do so would be to destroy the covenant of the commonwealth and return to civil war. Indeed, 'no man that hath sovereign power can be justly put to death'. In an age when choosing sides might mean ruin or fortune, and when people with political ideas like Hobbes's might spend years in exile, this was a brilliantly sophisticated way to justify the actions of either side and thus square the circle of revolutionary doubt.

The nature of sovereignty haunted the seventeenth century and the image of the martyred king was never far from the eyes of the power brokers and their advisers. It was a vision that shimmered before the eyes of conspirators and revolutionaries too – a promise and a warning. One such potential conspirator was John Locke, the greatest of all seventeenth-century political theorists. Locke's family came from Somerset, where his father had been a captain in the Parliamentary army during the 1640s. Locke went to Westminster School and then on to Oxford, where he taught until he was 34. When he left Oxford, however, he fell in with the powerful, conspiratorial and dangerous Anthony Cooper, Earl of Shaftesbury, who was then plotting to maintain the throne for Protestantism against the hereditary desires of James II, who was a Catholic. Locke's involvement with this dangerous aristocrat left him vulnerable to arrest and, perhaps, to an indictment for treason, so in 1683 he took the better part of valour and left for Holland. It was only with the successful supplanting of the Stuarts by William III that he returned in February 1689, living a quieter life until his own death in 1704.

Locke's ideas were encapsulated in the *Second Treatise of Government* (1690). In it, he attacked absolute monarchy as 'inconsistent with civil society', but if he was unwilling to go back to the time of Charles I, he was not willing to return to the 'state of nature' and anarchy. In the compromise he sought between the tyranny of an individual and the tyranny of absolute freedom, he too looked to the nature of a commonwealth. The choices for society lay between democracy, oligarchy and monarchy and Locke was clear that '[he] must be understood to mean, not a democracy'. Whatever the shape of the commonwealth, and Locke favoured oligarchy, it must be 'made by the consent of the people' and especially by the 'consent of the majority'. Locke does not spell out what this means, but essentially it is the entrusting of government to those with a stake in the country. In those days this meant the landed and mercantile interests and particularly those aristocrats gathered around his mentor, Shaftesbury. The chief end of a commonwealth, Locke tells us, is 'the preservation ... of property'. That itself is the end of government responsibility. Moreover the agreement of the majority itself consists of an act of 'incorporation', a mercantile term used since the Tudors. The threat to property is a direct route to the anarchy that Locke feared and that in itself would be the end of order.

With a glance at recent Stuart history, Locke argued that when the ruler attempts to 'destroy the property of the people', he was, in fact, declaring civil war and it therefore 'devolve[s] to the people ... to resume their original liberty'. Nevertheless, the appropriate legislative protection of property rights (and therefore social hierarchy) was also the 'best fence against rebellion'. By playing the middle against both ends, Locke had, by a clever sleight of hand, defended a new compromise dreamed up by Shaftesbury and his conspirators when they had met many years before at the King's Head Tavern in London's Chancery Lane in the 1670s.

Locke's arguments went further than he or his allies intended. In effect, the logic of government by the people, majority rule, protection of property and separation of powers provided a ready-made political language for Samuel Adams and others when, in the 1770s, they began debating the first phase of the American War of Independence in Boston. London was not far behind, as the issues driving the colonies were live issues for merchants and politicians in the imperial capital. Questions regarding taxation, freedom of speech, alienation from central government, the prerogatives of unpopular ministers and the overbearing presence of the King suggested a congruence of interests that did not go unnoticed and that came to a head with the publication of the Stamp Act, a tax not agreed to by the colonists, which had to be scrapped only two years after it was passed in 1767. Things did not improve with the Townshend Act, which imposed duties on things such as tea, made legal judgments dependent on a judge rather than a jury and forced billeting of troops on private Americans, who rightly feared the sort of foul play found at home regarding the standing army.

By the late 1760s there were those who declared themselves friends to America and who gathered to counter the feeling of those in Britain who, as Benjamin Franklin pointed out, 'Seem to consider [themselves] as ... sovereign over America; seem to jostle ... into the throne with the king, and talk of our subjects in the colonies'.[10] These 'Patriots' designated themselves the 'Real' (or 'Honest') Whigs or 'Commonwealthmen' and worked to protect American liberties at home. In this they were also upholding the constitutional settlement of 1688, the limited power of the King and a detestation of the corruption of parliament, while defending the traditional liberties of the English (Lord Bute, the prime minister, was a Scot). Such groups contained colonials such as Joseph Quincy and Franklin, but also included radicals such as Richard Price and Joseph Priestley. They all supported the Bostonites after the 'Boston Massacre' (a riot that ended in five dead) and declared that the Bostonites were an 'outraged, free ... people'. Their hero was the English popular politician John Wilkes, who had succeeded in annoying the Government with a libellous article, had found himself

exiled and in prison and had been the subject of a riot in his support. He was also an alderman of the City of London, finally
elected lord mayor, and a contestant for the most radical seat
in England, that of Middlesex, which he won. It was around
Wilkes that the Real Whigs gathered and placed their hopes of
liberty at home and liberty in America. Thus they were travelling further away from the Government position and more
and more believing in the tyranny of the executive. Whiggism
became the norm for protest in the capital, with the City alderman as much against the Government as the small tradesman.
By the 1770s their anger was directed at a peculiar mix of Jews,
Catholics (Jacobites), placemen and jobbers, and against a system
they saw as more and more oppressive. In this atmosphere they
also began agitating for parliamentary reform.

London was at the centre of the agitation, with a large, literate and politically educated population. A pamphlet of the time
suggested that 'every man, woman, and child, is by instinct, birth,
and inheritance, a politician'. London declared itself for Wilkes
and America. The Robin Hood Club of tradesmen declared their
'love [for] the Americans because they love liberty'. The Club of
Honest Whigs included men who agitated for continental rights.
It also included Price, whose pamphlet, 'Observations on the
Nature of Civil Liberty', was said to have sold 60,000 copies when
published in February 1776. Congress took the extraordinary step
of offering him citizenship of the United States on 6 October
1778, in order to 'receive his assistance in regulating their finances'.
It was Franklin who was to go and ask. Meanwhile, Wilkes and
others were in continuous touch with America. Indeed, it was
felt that sympathy for America was a touchstone of what it meant
to be 'a patriot' at home and an address was sent to the King on
24 May, complaining about the 'evil councillors' who were inappropriately advising George on his American policy.

The Boston Massacre occurred on the same day as parliament finally decided to repeal the Townshend duties (5 March
1770), with the exception of the duty on tea. At the same time

a new society was created: the Society of the Supporters of the Bill of Rights, whose plank was that rights won at home would be rights won in America. Having entered into a correspondence with a similar society in Charleston, Carolina, the British Society penned the following letter in February 1770: 'We shall ever consider the rights of all our fellow subjects throughout the British Empire in England, Scotland, Ireland, and America, as stones of one arch, on which the happiness and security of the whole are founded.' The letter went on to enumerate the problems of English history, including the moment that Saxon liberty was lost, comments that would be often repeated by radicals and specifically included in Paine's *Common Sense*: 'the Norman troops of the first William kept the English in subjection'. The Boston Committee of Correspondence, under Sam Adams, was therefore directly influenced by the English Bill of Rights Society, whose sense of grievance they embraced and whose form of agitation they espoused.

The Boston Tea Party saw the imposition of martial law and the hardening of attitudes on both sides. Things did not improve when the Government proposed the Quebec Bill to clarify that province's borders, sort out relations with the Indians (as Native Canadians were then generally known) and confirm the Catholic religion and the Church's retention of its privileges. This seemed to acknowledge the belief in a Government conspiracy to arm the Canadian French Catholics against the Americans. The bill became law, however, on 22 June 1774. Nevertheless, Londoners felt a sense of betrayal, a sense which included a strong element of the anti-Catholic feeling which would spill over into the Gordon Riots of 1780. On his way to parliament to give his assent to the bill, King George was assaulted by a mob, who were 'very abusive, and some persons, dressed at least like gentlemen, held out their fists at the king, and cried out "Remember Charles I! Remember James II!"'[11]

Feelings were hardening on both sides; it was felt by many Englishmen that the Americans had gone too far and Franklin was dismissed from his job as postmaster general for America, while other Americans abroad lay low. Londoners had their say during October, when Wilkes was elected MP for Middlesex, partly, it was said, for his championing the American cause. Ironic, then, that Wilkes blew hot and cold on America and called it a 'howling wilderness'. Meanwhile, Edmund Burke, in belligerent mood, declared on the hustings of Bristol, 'I have ever held, and ever shall maintain, to the best of my power, unimpaired and undiminished, the just, wise, and necessary constitutional superiority of Great Britain. This is necessary for America, as well as for us.'[12]

In this he was supported by the West Indian lobby, the non-conformists (whom Priestley tried to excite) and the merchants who had turned their back on the City where Wilkes had his power base. Things looked ugly and the old Real Whigs became more agitated. In January 1776, a fanatically pro-America periodical appeared called *The Crisis*. Its printer, Samuel Axtell (perhaps a distant relative of the regicide), called on troops to mutiny and not to 'butcher their relations, friends and fellow-subjects in America'. Astonishingly he was not prosecuted. Yet by far the most influential writer on constitutional matters was the Irishman Edmund Burke.

Burke had been born to a middle-class family in Dublin in 1729. His father was a bad-tempered Protestant, his mother a long-suffering Catholic. Burke was brought up a Protestant, but nevertheless married a Catholic, Jane Nugent. He was accused of being a closet Catholic (a 'Blade in a Jesuit rug') for the rest of his life. A brilliant legal mind, Burke soon aligned himself with the radical Whigs around the Marquis of Rockingham. The 'Rockingham Whigs' saw themselves as the inheritors of the compromise that had been 'the Glorious Revolution of 1688'.[13] Rockingham became prime minister and found Burke a 'rotten' or pocket borough (Wandover), from which he progressed to represent Bristol and then back to a pocket borough (Malton). Although a fierce advocate of freedom and a fearless ally of the American colonists, he was unwilling to embrace the revolutionary potential of colonial events and arguments, preferring to believe that the American fight was one for usurped, ancient liberties that they wished to regain. By the time of the French Revolution, he had settled on a partial return to Rockingham principles.

Burke, upholder of the rights of Americans, withdrew any support when it came to the needs of Britain. With the 'dislike [he felt] to revolutions', he penned *Reflections on the Revolution in France* in 1790. Written as a reply to the radical sermon given by Richard Price to the Revolutionary Society, it foresaw the danger of the French experiment once the king had been arrested. Burke's book was a robust defence of the British way of politics. The British would not follow the 'newest Paris fashion'. Indeed,

> the people of England will not ape the fashions they have never tried, nor go back to those which they have found mischievous on the trial. They look upon the legal hereditary succession of their crown as among their rights, not as among their wrongs, as a benefit, not as a grievance; as a security for their liberty, not as a badge of servitude. They look on the frame of their commonwealth, *such as it stands*, to be of inestimable value, and they conceive the undisturbed succession of the crown to be a pledge of the stability and perpetuity of all the other members of our constitution.[14]

For Burke, 'revolution will be the very last resource of the thinking and the good'; moreover, 'the very idea of the fabrication of a new [revolutionary] government [was] enough to fill [him] with disgust and horror'.

Burke was clear that the settlement of 1688 was permanent and reasonable, as it upheld the 'ancient' rights of the nation. Indeed, 'the Revolution was made to preserve our *ancient*, indisputable laws and liberties and that *ancient* constitution of government which is our only security for law and liberty.' The events of 1688 had secured the liberties already claimed by parliament as the 'Petition of Right' during the reign of Charles I and enshrined in the 'Declaration of Right' during the time of William and Mary. Liberty was an 'entailed inheritance ... specially belonging to the people' and it was the product of a policy which was the 'happy effect of following nature'. All that was now needed was conservation (and tradition) and adjustment (and, of course, the established Church).

The English, Burke thought, should refuse all continental talk of liberty or citizenship. On Jacobins, Burke wrote to William Smith on 29 January 1795 that

> my whole politics, at present, centre in one point, and to this merit or demerit of every measure (with me) is referable – that is, what will promote or depress the cause of Jacobinism. What is Jacobinism? It is an attempt ... to eradicate prejudice out of the minds of men for the purpose of putting all power and authority into the hands of persons capable of occasionally enlightening the minds of the people. For this purpose the Jacobins have resolved to destroy the whole frame and fabric of the old societies of the world, and ... to obtain an army for this purpose, that everywhere engage the poor by holding out to them as a bribe the spoils of the rich. This I take to be a fair description of the principles and leading maxims of the enlightened of our day who are commonly called Jacobins.[15]

Radicals were merely 'little, shrivelled, meagre, hopping ... troublesome, insects'. The British were 'not the converts of Rousseau ... not the disciples of Voltaire'. France was too close geographically and intellectually for comfort, but her ideas were now 'polluted'. France 'has always more or less influenced manners in England; and when your fountain is choked up and polluted, the stream will not run long, or not run clear, with us or perhaps with any nation'. What had died with the arrest of Louis XVI was plain respect and a common decency that was inherent and natural. 'As things now stand, with everything respectable destroyed without us, and an attempt to destroy within us every principle of respect, one is almost forced to apologize for harbouring the common feelings of men.' What had happened to the 'spirit of a gentleman and the spirit of religion'? They had been 'cast into the mire and trodden down under the hoofs of a swinish multitude'. And with that one phrase, Burke revealed all. He never lived it down. In inventing political conservatism he also went a long way in defining class war.

Chapter Three

Pig's Meat

In Massachusetts, things were going from bad to worse, martial law had been imposed and General Thomas Gage had been appointed captain-general and governor with 2,000 troops to occupy the city of Boston. On 19 April 1775, he sent out a substantial force to seize arms and ammunition in Concord. They made their way via the little town of Lexington. Meanwhile, riders on the night of 18/19 April had warned the local militia and a small contingent under Captain John Parker stood waiting for the redcoats on Lexington Green. The accidental shooting that started between the Government troops under Major John Pitcairn and the minutemen soon escalated into a full-scale battle along the road to Concord and back. Five thousand armed civilians fought a running battle which lasted all day and left 19 British officers and 254 men as casualties, and 49 colonists killed and 41 wounded.

The events of the day had no precedent and left both sides bewildered but decided. The printer Isaiah Thomas, working for the Provincial Congress, published an account and took a series of depositions from the witnesses. The conclusion was clear. For the 'provincials' it was the final straw, 'when the troops of Britain, unprovoked, shed the blood of sundry of the loyal American subjects of the British King in the field of Lexington'. What was left when the British seemed to 'thirst for blood, but to stand up and fight'. The first account of the 'massacre' was printed soon after by an American: 'Then the provincials (roused with zeal for the liberties of their country, finding life and everything dear and valuable at stake) assumed their native valour and returned fire .... And all this because these colonies will not submit to the ... yoke of arbitrary power.'[1]

For those traditionalists for whom democracy was anathema, no more decisive proof was to be found of its corrosive effects than on the battlefields of the American Revolution. The militiamen and minutemen sneaked around on the battlefields, were overly fond of ambushes and, most vulgar of all, shot at officers as their usual form of target practice. This latter tactic was distinctly un-European and was considered particularly unfair given that, without direction regarding attack, retreat and parley, an army became a rabble. The democratic weapon of choice in America was not the unwieldy and obsolete pike of the sans-culottes and Irish republicans, but the more deadly rifled musket seeking its gold-braided redcoat: 'An altogether higher rate of kills was achieved by riflemen who were shooting at carefully selected targets. The thump and whistle of a musket shot was much less feared by troops standing in line than the crack and buzz that told you that jaegers or American backwoodsmen were at work. In America, unlike ... Europe, the life of an individual was sought "with as much avidity as the obtaining of a victory over an army of thousands".'[2]

American troops fighting under the new conditions of guerrilla warfare simply reverted to their lesser state as tradesmen and farmers when having to face British bayonets in open battle. One English officer called Nicholas Cresswell reported regarding the Americans after a skirmish on Staten Island on 22 June 1777, 'our people then rushed upon them with their bayonets and the others [the Americans] took to their heels; I heard one of them call out *murder*!'[3] It was not sporting.

Thomas Paine, looking for an excuse for a revolution, argued that 'Europe, and not England, [was] the parent country of America', but on this particular day, the argument would have appeared mere sophistry. Of the militia and 'minit' men who fought that day, and who had come from the villages named after those in Essex, Norfolk, Lincolnshire and Cambridgeshire in the old country, that is Stow, Billerica (after Billericay in Essex), Chelmsford, Dedham, Lynn, Lincoln and Cambridge, nearly all had family names linking them to England.

News of the incident reached the Isle of Wight on 27 May and was widely reported in London two days later. The official version got to London on 10 June, but it was all enough to convince William Lee, an American, that another 'civil war' had begun, a refrain taken up by other radicals and patriots in London that a 'civil war [has] commenced in America'. Its cause was no less than the intransigence of George III himself. At the Middlesex annual elector's feast held on 27 July 1775, the toast was, 'General Putnam, and all those American heroes, who like men nobly preferred death to slavery and chains'. John Horne Tooke, acting on behalf of the Constitutional Society, even took out an advert in a number of newspapers which stated that it was for 'the relief of the widows, orphans, and aged parents of our beloved American fellow subjects, who, faithful to the character of Englishmen ... were ... inhumanly murdered by the king's troops at or near Lexington and Concord'.[4] The King was generally hissed when going abroad, an occurrence that shook him and which he could not understand.

On 12 June 1776 the Virginia Convention met to ratify a draft Declaration of Rights prepared by George Mason. It unanimously approved sixteen propositions that would have been quite recognisable to Lilburne and Cromwell and would have seemed reasonable to Hobbes and Locke. The proposals contained the statement that 'all men are by nature equally free' and have certain inherent rights, including the possession of property, and the objective in life to pursue 'happiness and safety'. In the opinion of the Virginians, this was the purpose of 'a state of society'. To secure this, it had to be accepted that 'government is ... instituted for the common benefit' and that 'all power is vested in ... the people', magistrates being only 'trustees and servants' of that original power which lay in the sovereignty of the people. Equally, no man was 'entitled to exclusive ... emoluments or privileges' and no official was 'descendible' or hereditary. Following Locke's novel formulation, it was also accepted that 'legislative and executive power of the state should be separate'. Only by consent of the people should laws be suspended or changed and no 'unusual or cruel punishment' allowed. Moreover, general warrants, used freely to search premises in England (and used most notoriously against Wilkes), were declared illegal and their target, the freedom of the press, recognised as 'one of the greatest bulwarks of liberty'. Finally, under 'love and charity towards each other', religious belief was to be affirmed as a private matter untouchable by the law. In one thing alone the convention faltered and this was in the matter of elections. Like their British counterparts, they wanted proof that voters had a 'permanent common interest' (that is, they had property) in the community. It was vague enough to mean anything the Virginians wanted it to, but it was also a great leap forward from anything that Westminster might recognise. Such a Declaration of Rights was in clear lineal descent from Magna Carta and, as such, belonged to a still discernible British tradition of radical protest and correction. The next step belonged to the new and untried path demanded by Paine – full independence. The decision would be made by Congress meeting in Philadelphia.

The second Continental Congress, meeting in June 1776, appointed a small group, including John Adams, Thomas Jefferson, Roger Sherman, Robert Livingston and the lapsed Anglophile Franklin, to take the final step of separation from

Britain. These men would draft a Declaration of Independence separating, once and for all, the former English colonists from the empire and creating a new nation. Fifty-six members of Congress (three less than the signatories of the death warrant that created England's only republic) signed the Declaration, duly prepared on parchment on 2 August. It had already been adopted on 4 July of the same year.

George III was declared by Congress to be 'a tyrant ... unfit to be the ruler of a free people', who, by 'declaring [the American colonists] out of his protection', had waged war against them. He had trampled on the rights of the people, refused laws and made 'judges dependent on his will alone', so that laws for the public good had been blocked. Moreover, George had destroyed the very foundations of a commonwealth, the uniting of natural and social reason: the 'certain unalienable rights ... of life, Liberty and the pursuit of Happiness'. To the Americans, looking back to Locke and Hobbes, and looking also to the republican ideals of ancient Rome as well as the contemporary common sense of Paine, all this was transparently clear, self-supporting, consciously moral and reasonable; in a word, it was just.

An American in England was no longer merely a displaced Englishman. Indeed, Americans had long called themselves by the name to distinguish themselves from Englishmen. Of course this did not prevent them from rising in prominence in the City as merchants or even in higher circles, as did Benjamin West, who was the favourite Court painter and who became second President of the Royal Academy despite being without any formal education. It was, however, time for displaced Americans to be counted.

With feelings running high and with constitutional means towards a solution unlikely, Americans (who were still technically 'British' and therefore capable of committing treason) turned to sabotage in order to foment revolution at home: 'The people at home will rise, and their heads [those of the Government] will be on Temple Bar before Xmas.' The estimation was wildly optimistic and little help came from the people who had been so supportive before 1775. There would be unlikely support from a one-man bomb factory called John Aitken. Here was one person dedicated to the American cause and deeply embroiled in the American spy network that stretched from Paris to Downing Street. Aitken went under a number of pseudonyms during his life, from James Hill to James Hind and James Boswell, but he was best known as John the Painter. Aitken was born the twelfth son of respectable Edinburgh crafts people in 1752. Given a good education, which marked him out for better things, he was nevertheless assigned by his guardians to the humble role of a house painter. There was little work and he turned to crime. He was a highwayman, a thief, a deserter and (by his own admission) a rapist. After an abortive attempt at emigration to America as an indentured servant, he became a fervent revolutionary in the American cause with plans to destroy England's dockyards and burn down Bristol and Portsmouth in 1776 and 1777. Possibly the more successful because of the cunning bred by working on his own and not trusting anyone else, he came near to spreading panic in England. He was caught and hanged after becoming the most notorious criminal revolutionary in Britain. Aitken was never a republican, despite working for the American cause. What he wanted was the preferment denied him after his education finished and he was set adrift. When caught, he blamed American spies sent from Paris for his entrapment.

The most serious potential incident was the attempt to subvert the soldiers in the Tower, kidnap the King on his way to parliament and hold him hostage. This hare-brained affair was thought up by Stephen Sayre, a long-standing supporter of independence, who contacted Francis Richardson, an adjutant in the Guards stationed in the Tower. Richardson was an American, but he was also a loyalist and blew the plot. Sayre was arrested on 23 October 1775. On the day of his arrest, thousands of leaflets were distributed in London urging the population to rise. Sayre was obviously not alone, but no one else was arrested. Owing to judicial incompetence Sayre was acquitted and actually allowed to sue for compensation, a case he won, although he never received the money.

Wilkes and his brother-in-law George Hayley were also up to no good, evidently in discussions with the French and possibly smuggling money to the rebels. An approach, however, to supply military information was declined. Another incident was reported in Woolwich, where moves were afoot to smuggle deserters to America, but the plans were discovered. By now, the leading Americans still in London, the brothers William and Arthur Lee (both from a wealthy Virginia family and both educated at Eton), were suspected of being behind most of the plots and were watched closely by Government agents.

While some plotted clandestinely, others were more open. The London Association was formed in the summer of 1775 and began circulating information that accused George of breaking the spirit of 1688 and of destroying 'liberty'. The club was formed by tradesmen such as Thomas Joel, a teacher and journalist, Henry Maskell, 'a dirty little apothecary', Robert Turner, a draper, and Benjamin Crompton, a wallpaper manufacturer, men with only an altruistic attitude to the colonies, but men, nevertheless, who had knocked around in radical circles for a decade. The mayor of Worcester, on hearing of their letters to the newspapers, thought that they 'intended to recommend and abet in this country the rebellion which now exists in America'. This was treason, but the association fizzled out within two years, before any prosecutions.

Through the meanderings of time, the republican hopes of the English regicides had evolved into this new world. The impact on English, Scottish, Irish and Welsh republicanism would be immense, not merely because the United States would be a haven for those pursued by the forces of British justice, but also because, for the next 200 years, it would be the breeding house and treasury for the long struggle for Irish independence.

America was now the practical consequence of revolution. It was seen as a special case and formed no particular precedent. This would be supplied by France. It would be in France that the great leap forward would create a new and more dangerous form of British republicanism. The revolution's starting point would, ironically, be the idea of English liberty.

The death of Charles I was surrounded by an almost religious awe that had resonance a century and half later, when the French revolutionaries cast about for a precedent for their own regicidal intentions. On 13 November 1792, Louis Antoine Léon Saint-Just, just 25, a fervent Jacobin, stood before the Legislative Assembly to demand the death of Louis XVI because he was an 'enemy of the people'. Saint-Just spoke in the most fervid, yet fearsome, tones of those who failed to protect the people's government: 'Today, respectfully, we conduct a trial for a man who was the assassin of a people, taken *in flagrante*, his hand soaked with blood, his hand plunged in crime. These same men who are to judge Louis are charged with founding the Republic. Those who attach any importance to the just punishment of a king will never found a republic.'[5]

Saint-Just's conclusion: 'this man must reign or die'. Indeed, continued Saint-Just as he warmed to the subject, 'monarchy is an outrage' and 'every king ... a rebel and a usurper', no better than others who seize the throne. 'Do kings themselves treat otherwise those who seek to usurp their authority?' he asked, and, 'Was not Cromwell's memory brought to trial? And certainly Cromwell was no more usurper than Charles I, for when a people are so weak as to yield to the tyrant's yoke, domination is the right of the first comer, and is no more sacred or legitimate for one than for any other. Those are the considerations which are great and a republican people ought not to forget when judging a king.'

More perversely and more pointedly, if this was a trial by a 'council' representing the people themselves, who were now citizens, then 'Louis [must be] an alien' as 'he was not a citizen before his crime'. That there was no French precedent for either his crime or his trial was not to put off those tasked with judgement, for there was 'nothing in the laws of England by which to judge Charles I'. Yet like Charles, Louis had made war on his people and broken his sacred contract. Saint-Just continued with his tirade: 'Louis waged war against the people: he was conquered. He is a barbarian, an alien, a prisoner of war; you have seen his perfidious schemes; you have seen his army; the traitor was not a king of the French, he was a king of a band of conspirators. He raised secret troops, he had private magistrates, he regarded the citizens as his slaves.'

Saint-Just had been preceded by others with a taste for English history. Jean-Baptiste Maihle, a lawyer and rapporteur for the Committee of Public Safety, looked to clarify the matter of the new French constitution, article 3 of which had declared the 'person of the king inviolable and sacred' (exactly the same was said of King Charles's person), but since Louis's attempted escape on 20 June 1791, the constitution needed amending. The prerequisite for such amending was a long historical memory that included the drama in Whitehall. Indeed, virtually without case law to go on, the French were quickly thrown back on English history to find a suitable example. In this respect the ghost of Charles haunted the whole proceedings, with the various speakers trawling English regicidal 'law' to make their points in the debate. Maihle used the example of Charles when he rose to speak on 7 November 1792, pointing out that in the seventeenth century, 'there were no written laws to declare the punishment of a king'. There was scarcely more now, and a history of Charles's execution circulated in Paris during 1792 to remind Parisians of their duty. Charles's memory was again disturbed on 13 November when Charles François Gabriel Morrison rose to speak, but when Robespierre spoke on 3 December, he sternly warned the Convention that they must not 'be led into error' by examples from 'foreign lands'. It was a timely and sensible intervention and forced those present to think about a coherent argument, rather than one based on historical precedent. In that, he also broke with the past.

Paine sat in the Convention as the Deputy for Pas-de-Calais. He too wished to speak on this momentous occasion as the greatest of all English revolutionary voices and as a hero of the American republic. Since he could not speak French, his speech was delivered by his friend Maihle and concerned itself with an attack on international monarchy. His vision (which did not include the death of Louis) was determined by what he saw as a British conspiracy centred on a petty German princeling (that is, George III): 'We have already penetrated into some part of the conduct of Mr Guelph [George III's surname], elector of Hanover, and strong presumptions involve the same man, his court and ministers, in quality of King of England.'[6]

Having reminded the revolutionaries of their alliance with the Congress of the United States during the American War, Paine suggested that Louis might settle down on a farm in America and earn an honest living as 'Mr Louis Capet'. Allowed to 'practice the duties of domestic life', the ex-king should 'let ... those United States be [his] safe guard and asylum', where 'fair, equal and honourable representation' would mend his 'crimes' and 'treason'. Paine submitted his proposal as a 'citizen of the world' and as a 'citizen of America', but he failed to understand the austere Robespierre, the tyrannicidal Saint-Just and psychopathic Collot d'Herbois, whose revolution was not to be finally modelled on American experience and whose exterminating extremism frightened and threatened this English-American Francophile. Paine miscalculated his more determined associates, failing to realise that he was no longer persuading Jefferson or Franklin.

In language identical to that used over a century later by Leon Trotsky, Paine called for endless revolutionary war, with Britain as the first target: 'France is now a republic; she has completed her revolution; but she cannot earn all its advantages so long as she is surrounded with despotic governments [that is, Austria,

Prussia and Britain]. Their armies and their marine oblige her also to keep troops and ships in readiness. It is therefore her immediate interest that all nations shall be as free as herself; that revolutions shall be universal.'

Robespierre, joining the debate late, spoke in words that made him the direct heir of the English prosecuting lawyer John Cook:

> Louis was king, and the republic is founded. The great question with which you are occupied is settled by this argument: Louis has been deposed by his crimes. Louis denounced the French people as rebels; to punish them he called upon the arms of his fellow tyrants. Victory and the people have decided that he alone was a rebel. Therefore, Louis cannot be judged; he has already been condemned, else the republic is not cleared of guilt. To propose a trial for Louis XVI of any sort whatever is to step backward toward royal and constitutional despotism. Such a proposal is counter-revolutionary since it would bring the revolution itself before the court.[7]

For Robespierre, as for Cook, such monarchs were 'enemies of the people', their death, as Cromwell is rumoured to have muttered standing next to Charles's coffin, one of 'cruel necessity'.

Cromwellian thoughts came easily to mind when the debaters looked to the consequences of Charles's beheading. The delegates were well aware of the problem of dictatorship (Marat was already contemplating a limited version to safeguard the Revolution) and few wished to replace a dead king with a live Robespierre. Maihle had already pointed out that Cromwell desired to be king and that, but for the genius of the National Convention, any man might set himself above the nation. The 'nation' was supreme and must rule supreme, for anything other would be a tyranny. Saint-Just, rising to speak on 13 November, reminded delegates that the nation had to protect its liberties and no longer show nostalgia for its 'chains', as in the days of Cromwell, whose own death saw kings 'reborn'.

Never should France yield to the dictates of an individual such as Cromwell whose whole demeanour was an attempt to undermine parliament, as Pierre Victurnien Vergniaud pointed out on 31 December at the end of an exhausting debate. In the end seven votes separated the parties regarding proceeding with the sentence immediately, but it was enough for Louis to die.

The ghosts of Charles and Cromwell continued to return to haunt debates over reform for thirty years after the French Revolution and, according to one's tastes (royalist or republican), mould one's rhetoric. A comic broadsheet offered the following entertainment during the 1790s:

> A new and entertaining farce, called
> LA GUILLOTINE [*sic*]
> Or
> GEORGE'S HEAD IN THE BASKET!
> Dramatis Personae
> Numpy the third …
> (Being the last time of his appearing in that character)

By the passing of the Reform Bill on 4 June 1832, the joke was in earnest. The Tory journal *John Bull* pronounced in apocalyptic mood that 'on the banks of the Tyne, in Birmingham, in Dudley, in Bradford, the mob is omnipotent … . We want another year of Whig misrule … to reduce the standard of national feeling to the level of the Marseillois [*sic*] of 1793 … . A little longer period of ministerial tuition will teach us the ready use of the lamp-post and the guillotine.' Cromwell also came to mind when the radical Samuel Bamford visited a session of the House of Commons in 1819:

> I looked on a dimly lighted place below. At the head of the room, or rather den … sat a person in a full loose robe of … scarlet and white. Above his head were the royal arms, richly gilded; at his feet several men in robes and wigs were writing

at a large table, on which lamps were burning, which cast a softened light on a rich ornament like a ponderous sceptre of silver and gold ... those persons I knew must be the speaker and the clerks of the house; and that rich ornament could be nothing else than the 'mace' – the same thing ... to which Cromwell pointed and said, 'Take away that bauble; for shame – give way to honester men.'[8]

Charles's shade returned from its French leave during the Reform Bill debates of 1831 and 1832. Both sides, with historical precedent in mind, sided either with Cromwell or Charles. For the more ultra (or simply more cautious) Tories, concessions to the 'people' were dangerous and would lead to the ruin that befell the Stuarts. Against their arguments, men like Thomas Babbington, Lord Macaulay claimed that Whiggism would prevent any such disaster from occurring. The Whigs were 'composed of the vast and intelligent body of the middle classes. That party, with the flower of the aristocracy at its head and the flower of the working classes bringing up its rear, takes up its impregnable position between the main body of the aristocracy and the mob. It will have reform; it will not have revolution.'[9]

For the Duke of Buckingham, however, any concessions would bring down monarchy and, having brought into his speech the memory of a 'patriot king' (Charles I), he continued, 'so will it be now if we break with the king ... [government] will be in the hands of sullen radicals, of domestic tyrants of canting Puritans or of some ascetic statesman who retires now because his plots are not ripe and spins his web until the country is fixed in his toils, that the destinies of England will be placed'.[10] All that would remain would be 'republicanism' where 'all the beggars of London could vote'. For men like Buckingham and Wellington it looked as if the bad old days of the British Jacobin clubs might start again. Without concession and common sense, however, things might indeed have returned to those insurrectionary days. A cavalry trooper recalled, 'It was rumoured that the Birmingham Political Union was to march for London that night... . We had been daily and nightly booted and saddled with ball cartridge in each man's possession ... ready to mount and turn out at a moment's notice. But until this day we had rough-sharpened no swords... . Not since Waterloo had the swords of the greys undergone the same process.'[11]

Some, like John Singleton Copley, Baron Lyndhurst, named after the great American loyalist painter, had less historical acumen than Macaulay and more sense of pantomime. Much could be made by mixing up old historical enemies and religious intolerance. Thus it was 'unnecessary to add that the conduct of those whom the Roman Catholics of Ireland had hitherto sent into parliament sufficiently shows that those members will also be in the scale of extreme democracy ... they might disband the army, expel non-compliant members in the fashion of Cromwell'.[12]

The heady atmosphere of the French Revolution, reported in newspapers and broadsheets, commented upon in pamphlets and hotly debated in tavern and workshop, rekindled the revolutionary spirit of its British enthusiasts. For them, British history offered plenty of examples of republicanism and fraternalism that they could emulate. The ideas of men such as Winstanley, half-forgotten in detail but only dormant in spirit, returned in the millennial egalitarian hopes of men such as Thomas Spence, whose primitive communism would mingle with Paine's common sense to provide an incendiary mixture for more adventurous republicans.

Spence was a small man, only 5ft tall, but he had big ideas, which included the creation of the Republic of England, for which he published a constitution in 1803 based on the desire that if 'the people wished to have the government in their own hands, they must begin by taking the land into their own hands'. It was a doctrine from which Spence never deviated, inherited from Winstanley's ideas about common ownership and Locke's ideas about nature and just as with Winstanley, Spence would get no nearer to his utopian dream of 'a new

Jerusalem or future golden age'. Nevertheless Spence would be the first Englishman to create a practical model for the ardent republican who was looking for a 'Rights of Man ... that goes further than Paine's'. In the climate of the 1790s such a man might be considered mad, but his pamphlets aimed at 'the plebeian race of mankind' living in 'poor wrangling Britannia', his distaste for colonialism in America (called in his pamphlets 'Fridinea') and his call for combination represented a potentially dangerous challenge to authority.

Spence was born on 21 June 1755 in a house on the quay at Newcastle upon Tyne. Both his parents had arrived in Newcastle from Scotland; his father was a net-maker from Aberdeen who had made his home in the city in 1739, while his mother came from the Orkneys. Although they were both poor, they were rich in children, producing eighteen brothers and sisters for Thomas. The family were brought up to read and write by a father whose views were coloured by the extreme religious group to which belonged. The Glassites believed in the coming of the millennium and in the communal ownership of goods. Their views were simple, separatist and apocalyptic – a community of true believers adrift in a sea of faithlessness – and their ideas went deep into Spence's later secular hopes for his republic and for the half-humorous system he laid down in his guidelines for the utopia of 'Spensonia'. Alongside his Bible, Spence also kept James Harrington's *The Commonwealth of Oceana* and Thomas More's *Utopia*, the first steps in a self-taught political education.

The possibilities opened up by this reading were reinforced by Spence's acquaintance with a sectarian preacher from Edinburgh called James Murray. Murray had come to Newcastle in 1765 having lost a position in Alnwick in 1761, presumably for his outspoken ideas about civil rights, and built himself a meeting house in High Bridge Street. From here he preached the Gospels, interpreting them in the political language of the time, arguing that they encapsulated everything from the widening of

religious freedom, to the condemnation of taxes, the illegality of
enclosures and refusal to pay church tithes. He also condemned
the rich and supported the food rioters of the 1770s, later, pre-
dictably, supporting the American colonists in their struggle.
Preachers like Murray and poor tradesmen like Spence senior
kept a radical tradition alive that went back to the revolutionary rhetoric of the Commonwealth, mixing religious zeal with
a hard-nosed sense of contemporary politics. It would be this
mixture that would flow in the very life blood of the new working-class movements – the northern and Welsh self-help utopian
groups that would create the cooperative movement, the Labour
Party and the Salvation Army.

Spence grew up in a harsh environment of grinding poverty
but he was also educated and entrepreneurial. He was literate
enough to become a private tutor and then a schoolmaster, travelling around the north until returning to Newcastle to set up a
school on the quay. His eye for business also saw him opening a
toy shop and running an employment agency for maidservants.
By this time he was married to a Miss Elliott, whom he had met
as a teacher in Hexham, and they had a son (who later helped
in his father's radical activities). Spence was already fulfilling the
criteria for a radical: born in poverty, educated and business-
minded but not very successful, unsettled in work and marriage
(his was not a happy partnership), resentful of the injustice
he saw around him but incapable of intervening; a man of no
class, no place and no future but fired with an intense vision of
how things might be if only he were listened to and his ideas
implemented. Such a situation led to anger and frustration, and
eventually to the notice of authority.

Radicalism in Newcastle had grown in the ten years between
1765 and 1775, and societies with names such as the Recorder's
Club, the Cappadocian Club and the Robin Hood Club debated
the political problems of the day. These clubs supported Wilkes
and sent donations and signed petitions when he was imprisoned
for his attack on the Government. On his release they paid for

wassails and fireworks to celebrate. In 1774 Newcastle Town Corporation was stopped by them from carrying out enclosures which would have destroyed the traditional rights of commoners. The fight, which ended in the Newcastle Town Moor Act, was supported by the radical clubs, preached by Murray and propagandised by Spence. When, in 1775, a philosophical society was started, Spence paid his membership fee and prepared for his first lecture.

On 8 November 1775 Spence tried out his ideas for the first time in a public forum. 'The Real Rights of Man' argued for the communal ownership of the land and its produce through the creation of local parish councils whose responsibility was to lease out plots for farming and use the revenues for welfare provision and security. The gathered audience must have been outraged, for Spence was asked to retract his demands and, after persisting with them in public, he was finally expelled. At the same time, he was putting his new ideas to another debating society, which held its meetings in his school. Here, too, he met incredulity and one member, the future engraver Thomas Berwick, challenged him to a fight with quarterstaffs *à la* Robin Hood and Little John. Needless to say, Spence was beaten up.

A new start was called for when, in 1792, Spence left Newcastle to live in London. His wife had died the same year and Murray, his greatest supporter, had already been dead for a decade. Once in London, Spence decided to begin again as a publisher and bookseller, selling his own compositions, as well as the work of Paine, from a stall in Chancery Lane, where he supplemented a slow day's trading by selling a hot milk drink called 'saloop'. Later he moved indoors and sold books from shops in Holborn and Oxford Street. Happiness seemed just around the corner. He married, this time to a servant girl, but she deserted him and so he was left with his son to carry on the good work that he had started in his lecture on land reform all those years before, in Newcastle. Frustrated, he would even go out sometimes at night and chalk slogans on walls and pavements. In answer to Burke's

attack on the 'swinish multitude', Spence brought out a periodical called *Pig's Meat*, in which were published excerpts from
radicals of the past. In addition to Paine's work, Spence sold his
own pamphlets, poetry and political spoofs, which continued to
argue for his own brand of land reform.

His idea was simple. All land would be taken back from the
'present idle classes' and monopolisers and returned to the 'citizens'. These citizens would form themselves into parishes to lease
out the confiscated land to individuals willing to pay a rent. Each
parish would act as a cooperative link with all the other parishes
and each would limit the power of central government, much
as the various states did in America. At the heart of government
would be 'the people', whose local autonomy, wealth and hatred
of aristocratic privilege would ensure perpetual internal peace.
The basis of this harmony would be a type of primitive agrarian communalism only superficially communist, for at its heart
would be equality of opportunity and a morally guided individualism, rather than soviet-style collectivism. With land reform
providing the basis for local autonomy and the end of poverty,
and the surplus allowing for the redistribution of resources, it
would be possible, so Spence argued, to create a social welfare
system. Spence's 'welfare state' was taken from Paine's ideas as
outlined in his *Rights of Man*.

Republican democracy would surely follow, with a citizen
militia to prevent the return of aristocratic predation. There
would be universal suffrage, secret ballots, annual elections,
abolition of property entitlements, equal constituencies and
payment for members of parliament. In this, he anticipated the
Chartists by many years. It was true that he ignored the rise of
the factory system, but his was an artisan's vision of a plebeian,
parochial world based on agriculture. His extreme ideas soon got
him noticed by friends of whom he might have had had cause to
be wary, and enemies he had cause to fear.

Spence's activities as a bookseller got him attention from
those he least trusted. During the morning of Thursday

6 December 1792, Spence was working on his stall in Chancery Lane, selling books and distributing hot cups of saloop, when two Bow Street Runners, dressed incognito, bought the *Rights of Man*. The act of selling the book made him liable for prosecution for distributing seditious material. After he had been hauled off to the Hatton Garden police office magistrate, it turned out that the detectives had actually purchased Spence's *Rights* and not Paine's, and the case was thrown out. The purchasers were left grumbling that they had not been compensated for their mispurchase by their superior, John Reeves, a man hated by all radicals and castigated by Spence as 'the chief political inquisitor of England'.

Next day, the detectives were back to buy the correct book, which Spence sold them! Again he was hauled off, this time to Bow Street and thence to wait around in a pub, where he was searched and then (according to his account) assaulted. 'What country am I in?' asks Spence in his later pamphlet outlining the details of his temporary incarceration. Surely this was the 'age of bloody Queen Mary', surely it was better actually to unmask British tyranny and open 'bastilles' than violate British laws in the name of a fake liberty and loyalty. The following Thursday (13 December), Spence was again at his stall when, he tells us,

> a gentlemen ... seeing a young man with the first part of Paine's *Rights of Man* in his hand ... seized the book and ... abused Mr Spence, hustled him about, tore his shirt and dragged him to an adjoining shop where, joined by more of his brutal fraternity, he robbed the poor man of two other books. One of the villains hastened to the police office to fetch some runners, while the others guided the persecuted man, uttering violent threats.... Perhaps these were some of the immaculate members of a certain inquisitorial society; at least they must be sanctioned by a dark and mysterious group not less diabolical than themselves.[13]

All this was the start of a long and painful acquaintance with Reeves, Bow Street Runners and the joys of English law. His arrests on 6 and 10 December 1792 were subsequently followed by further arrests and trials in January 1793, December 1793, May 1794 and in 1798. The last two were more serious, being related to alleged treasonable practices, for which seven months were spent in jail without Spence ever being convicted. In April 1801 Spence faced the law again, accused of undermining private property and spreading seditious discontent by the publication of *The Restorer of Society to its Natural State*. For this supposed infringement of the rights of Englishmen, the state finally got its conviction and Spence spent a year in Shrewsbury jail. He was still fighting his cause on his release in 1803, defending his 'dangerously incendiary common-sense' in a 'foolish trial' against the 'property-owning classes', those Burke had designated alone to be the 'general public'. Against the propertied middle and upper class, Spence spoke as a 'labourer' putting forward a viewpoint little more seditious than a parliamentary bill.

No doubt worn out with fighting his cause and languishing in damp prisons, Spence finally died of an intestinal disorder on 8 September 1814. Although he never joined any of the branches of the London Corresponding Society (LCS) or the Constitutional Clubs, partly because he was independent and bloody-minded, partly because he remembered his troubles in Newcastle, his name was associated with 'Jacobins' such as Thomas Hardy and Thomas Evans of the LCS, who advocated republican forms of government. He was also bracketed with French Jacobins such as Jean-Paul Marat, who was in Newcastle at the same time as Spence.

Spence's difficulties arose partly from his association with men like Evans, whom the authorities considered dangerous. By 1807, however, Spence had a small group of followers of his own, who formed the 'Free and Easy Club' and met in the Fleece Tavern in Windmill Street in London's Soho. Among the members were Evans, Dr Thomas Watson and his son, Francis Place,

Allen Davenport and Arthur Thistlewood. After Spence's death, the group was reconstituted around the land reform proposals as the Society of Spencean Philanthropists, with a membership of 150. From its central cadre came proposals to remove the aristocracy and implement the Spencean constitution by force. By a quirk of fate, the revolutionary who stood 'unconnected with any party' was now the martyred leader of a cell of hard-line revolutionary terrorists who would attempt two armed coups (one at Spa Fields on 2 December 1817 and the other at Cato Street on 23 February 1820) and who would be relentlessly targeted by 'government spies, executions and transportations' until they had been annihilated. Spence's ghost was not so easy to exorcise and his ideas continued to influence the National Union of the Working Classes and the East London Democratic Association, the demands of Chartists and the insurrections of 1842 which so impressed Engels and Marx.

Chapter Four

Suspended on a Volcano

Revolutions are not one-sided affairs; there are those who make them and those against whom revolutions are made. Between the hot passion of Lexington Green and the cold calculation of Louis XVI's beheading, new creatures had emerged from the political chrysalis of radicalism. These were nothing less than fully formed revolutionists, speaking a new language dedicated to 'the people', replete with a vocabulary of strange and dangerous words and phrases: 'democracy', 'equality', 'fraternity' and 'inalienable rights'. They demanded constitutions and republics and threatened open warfare with pikes and firebombs if they did not get them. Radicals could try their persuasion to cajole or bully or plead for some place at the table of state; republicanism required sterner stuff – a dedication to a life of ceaseless motion, in which their new world seemed ever closer, ever further away.

The enemy wore faces then, too early yet for the gathering of the proletarian masses against the capitalist plutocrats. That would come, but later. The early revolutionaries knew their enemies face by face and one by one. There was the king himself, his family and royal hangers-on; nobles, aristocrats, county squires and magistrates; bishops, vicars and tithe collectors. These were the enemy alongside the 400,000 or so readers of Burke, who, being the top layer of society, were then accepted as the 'general public', separated from the rest of mankind by their money, connections and education. Come the day and the whole lot would be on the rotting wagon to the gallows, guillotine and city lamppost for a little bit of last-minute political education.

Know your enemy. The state always wished it did. The new revolutionaries – Jacobin, social democrat, anarchist and communist – were each in turn seen as exotic, alien and other, unknowable cancerous growths to be cut out of the body politic by hangman's noose, imprisonment, transportation and exile. To catch revolutionaries it was necessary to fit a face to an action, but how much simpler to foment revolution with the use of spies and agents provocateurs and wait for the faces to offer themselves up as volunteers for the cause – bagged in one go and with far less effort. Since Queen Elizabeth's secret war with her Catholic subjects, the rule had remained simple: embroil your enemy in the conspiracy of your choosing, watch them stew, arrest them and, if needs must, destroy them.

The new revolutionaries, however, came from all walks of life, from humble cobbler to radical aristocrat. Jacobinism was everywhere, as Jacobitism had once been. To catch those men who called themselves patriots but spoke the language of England's enemies – the Americans, the Irish, the French – it would be necessary to create a machine (finally a bureaucracy) working for the state, but somehow 'outside' of the state, using the already well-worn tactics of eighteenth-century thief-taking, but now enhanced with surveillance, black propaganda, misinformation, letter-opening, code-deciphering and outright spying using semi-professional informers. Yet before all this, another monarch had to die.

At 11.47 a.m. on 5 September 1793 an ominous darkness fell over the politicians and peoples of London and Paris. In the strange blue of an eclipse, the French Revolution[1] was about to enter its most dramatic and deadly phase and the English language was about to gain a new and fearsome term for political extremism, for it was on this day that the Commune of Paris initiated the Reign of Terror. The Terror was intended to curb the disintegrating situation surrounding the nascent republic. It would, its authors hoped, restore a national sense of purpose, revive the political will of the 'people', curb division and civil unrest, defeat anarchy, remove the possibility of the restoration of a monarch and allow France to come victorious through her international wars. Terror was the instrument of governmental policy to defeat the chaos of political disorder. First and foremost, it was seen as the only means whereby the republic might finally enjoy the stability of a nation-state, one moreover driven by a new ideology of an equal, free and fraternal citizenry in which all traces of the old ways – the old regime – had been cleared away. Terrorism, the name given to the policy of the Terror, was intended finally to bring the light of reason to men's minds and actions.

As the sun again appeared over the French capital, a large group of Jacobins and common folk, led by the mayor, wound their way to the Tuileries, where Robespierre and the Committee of Public Safety sat in almost permanent conclave. Robespierre and the Committee listened in silence as the visitors demanded that the government act to protect 'the people' from the ravages of war, hunger and the depredations of the rich. With the 'electric commotion of patriotism', one speaker noted that once the people were aroused they would 'exterminate [their] enemies', while to the cheers of '*Vive la République!*' the hero of the sans-culottes, Danton, demanded more money for arms and ammunition in defence of 'the sublime people'. Yet it was the arrival of the delegation of the more extreme Jacobin Club that sealed the discussion. Their view was clear, the enemy was not only external but the Frenchmen dedicated in secret, or in open rebellion, to the overthrow of the republic; their demand, to 'make terror the order of the day!' Thus would the people be vindicated with an extermination leading all the way to the royal family, giving a final purpose and goal to the hundreds of executions already carried out by revolutionary courts.

Louis XVI had already been guillotined in the place de la Révolution (now place de la Concorde) on 21 January 1793. With as much dignity as he could muster, Louis had shrugged off the attempts by the guards to prepare him and began to make a speech when the drums were ordered to beat to drown out his words. These seemed to put courage back into the crowd, which had fallen silent, and amid jeers and hoots, Louis was forced into the jaws of the guillotine and executed. His confessor reported that 'the youngest of the guards, who seemed about eighteen, immediately seized the head, and showed it to the people as he walked round the scaffold; he accompanied this monstrous ceremony with the most atrocious and indecent gestures'. The body, meanwhile, was taken off to the cemetery at the Church of the Madeleine, thrown into a pit and smothered in quicklime.

On his way to the scaffold, Louis was accompanied by his confessor, the Anglo-Irish priest Henry Essex Edgeworth, the vicar general of the diocese of Paris, a man also known as l'Abbé Edgeworth de Firmont. Edgeworth, son of a Protestant convert, was one of the many thousands of expatriate Irish, but he would become the symbol of the tragedy of the Terror, fêted by émigrés and governments alike, for whom such a witness was proof enough of republican motives 'in this land of horrors', as Edgeworth described France. Just like Louis, his 'wretched master', Edgeworth found that 'Almighty God [had] baffled [his] measures' and tied him to the apocalyptic landscape of revolutionary revenge. He had no choice but to prepare for his own martyrdom.

The expected bloody end did not, however, occur and, having uttered the line 'son of St Louis, ascend to heaven', for which he would become famous and yet could not actually remember saying, Edgeworth found he was able to make his way through the crowd around the guillotine and escape, only to find, some days later, his expected martyrdom creeping ever nearer when the Jacobin Club demanded his head. Finally, dressed as a civilian and travelling under the name of Henry Essex, he escaped to London on 17 August 1796, where he became the embodiment of the émigré cause, being offered a state pension by Pitt and an invitation from his brother, Ussher Edgeworth, to return to Ireland in triumph. All this came to nothing, however, when Louis XVIII, then living in exile at Blankenburg, asked him to act as his chaplain, an offer which took him, alongside the French royal family, to Mitau (now Jelgava) in Russian Latvia. By a quirk of fate, perhaps not lost on the priest, he caught jail fever after administering to French prisoners of war and died on 22 May 1807. Louis XVIII provided the words for Edgeworth's monument, the testament to Louis's impotent rage against his own father's 'impious and rebellious subjects' now memorialised on the stone of a priest's grave.

The Terror was a direct response to internal instability and external war, but it was also an expression of political vision: democratic republicanism. To defend democracy, however, the people had to suspend toleration and, as a people's army (created by the *levée en masse* of 23 August 1793), defend itself against the professional armies of every other European aristocratic power. Terrorism was thus a political and judicial response to the appearance of total war, of which mass conscription of individuals fighting as a people's army was the military expression. Thus surrounded by foes, France kept faith with the only other two republics then in existence, the United States and Switzerland, and offered, for a time, a safe haven to that most famous of all English insurrectionists, Thomas Paine, whose polemical writings had helped turn the American war into a revolutionary struggle.

Of all radical thinkers of the period from the 1770s to the 1820s, none was so hated or so revered as Paine, his works becoming the bibles of revolutions everywhere, dangerous to read and even more dangerous to practise. Possession could result in imprisonment and ostracism, knowledge in damnation. By the beginning of the nineteenth century, he was the most feared man in Britain, not for what he did but for what he wrote. He systematically set about destroying the belief system and outworn traditionalism of the past in a language at once elegant and clear: 'my motive and object ... have been to rescue man from tyranny and false systems and false principles of government, and enable him to be free.' This led him to one conclusion and that the most radical of all: 'I believe in the equality of man.' It also led him to reject the Bible (but not God) as so much cruel tosh, 'a history of wickedness, that has served to corrupt and brutalize mankind'. Indeed every fellow citizen was entitled to his own opinion. To his enemies this merely confirmed him as a blasphemer. The past, with its pretensions of kings, church and property, suddenly seemed the merest chimera, a shadow; Paine abolished the past and replaced it with a world of reason and common sense in a language that was both accessible and direct.

Paine had been born in Thetford, Norfolk on 29 January 1737, to a family of Quakers called Pain (the extra 'e' added after his stay in America). For the first half of his life he drifted, first as a stay-maker and then as an exciseman, a duty for which he was ill suited and for which he was sacked for misconduct. It was polemical journalism that was his forte, something he drifted into when acting on behalf of his fellow excisemen. Even then, it took copious supplies of brandy or rum and water to get him into the mood and one is left with the impression that, despite his seemingly adventurous life, Paine was essentially a man who was relatively lazy and only drifted into rebellion, a vocation that he soon realised was his real calling. He was the first professional revolutionary, working at it and learning its rules on the way. Having moved to America in October 1774, looking for work as a school teacher, he soon sniffed the wind of change. It was clear that Americans must 'declare themselves independent'. *Common Sense* immediately stuck a chord and became the bestseller of the eighteenth century on its publication in January 1776. It not only made the war in America one for independence, but it gave a revolutionary and republican rationale to the proceedings.

Paine returned to Britain and was tolerated so long as he was tactful, but the French Revolution changed that and he travelled to France to take his place at the Convention on 13 September 1792, alongside John Frost, a radical lawyer, and the Frenchman Achille Audibert, an official from Calais, for which district Paine was to sit as representative. Although possessing no French, Paine was the famous revolutionary leader and a great catch, if a difficult one to predict. So troublesome did he become that he was imprisoned in the Luxembourg Palace on 28 December 1793, and was only released on the word of James Monroe, then ambassador to France and successor to Gouveneur Morris, who had acquired an antipathy for Paine which had nearly ended with his death in prison. As it was, he left the Luxembourg more dead than alive and had to be brought back to health by the Monroes. By this time, Paine had developed a marked distaste for the abandonment of the principles of the revolution: 'The just and humane principles of the revolution, which philosophy had first diffused, had been departed from... . The intolerant spirit of church persecutions had transferred itself into politics; the tribunal styled revolutionary, supplied the place of an inquisition; and the guillotine and the stake outdid the fire and fagot of the church.'[2]

Ironically, it was no longer safe for revolutionaries to be in France. Tightening their grasp on the powerful committees they controlled, Robespierre and his colleagues on the Committee of Public Safety began their struggle with the counter-revolutionaries. The Law of Suspects was passed on 17 September. It identified those who were to be arrested as those who 'by their conduct, relations or language spoken or written, have shown themselves partisans of tyranny or federalism and enemies of liberty'. Anybody suspected of neglecting their civic obligations to the republic or discharged from office, all aristocrats not fully committed to revolution, as well as émigrés who had returned to France, were liable to arrest and imprisonment in one of the holding centres or 'national buildings'. Republican extremists demanded that the prisons (now holding over 100,000 enemies of the state) should simply be mined and blown up. Even when such calls were silenced, there was still the business of execution. Considering the very large population in France in 1793 and the exterminating zeal of the ideologues, relatively few met their deaths actually on the guillotine – perhaps no more than 16,594 men and women, of whom 878 were aristocrats. The death of the King and Queen merely signified the most important of those executed.

As Saint-Just put it during the Convention meeting of 10 October, 'the provisional government of France is revolutionary until the peace'. The resolution was formally accepted by the Convention, and terror and revolution, as well as the terror of permanent revolution, entered the mentality of all the revolutionaries and revolutions that marked the history of republics, whether nationalist, democratic or socialist, throughout the nineteenth and twentieth centuries.

In its original form, terrorism was the defence of democracy by a government on behalf of the people, by those entrusted by the people, the agency of the political will of democratic republican statehood. Precisely because of this, it was the opposite of anarchy, inequality and exploitation by tyrannical monarchs and their governments. Carried along by the mystique of the people, the body and soul of the collective nation, terrorism was essentially secular by nature, replacing religious belief with a political vision of a civil way of life determined by a social contract born not from tradition and conquest, but from free relations between equal citizens, protected neither by monarchs nor nobility, but by law and free markets.

Such a vision affected those across the Channel in different ways, creating not only a new vocabulary but one that would itself be forever a site of conflict, the language itself identifying the angels from the damned. To be a Jacobin, democratic or republican during the early nineteenth century was enough to make you an enemy of the state in Britain; to be an anarchist, socialist or communist would be damnation enough for a further hundred years. Surrounding such words, the concept of terrorism and the image of the terrorist bomber were never far away, evoking thoughts of conspiracy, images of civil disorder, assassination and the crime of treason. Yet such enemies of the British state and of the traditional values of the British way of life were also the heroes and heroines of national struggles in Ireland, Scotland and Wales, and of a strain of republican socialism that tempered parliamentary excess and social inequality even as it struggled to overcome both.

The terms of political debate are as fluid as the situations from which they arise and the term 'terrorism' has long been disassociated from the actions of the state. Indeed the term 'state-sponsored terrorism' is used nowadays to differentiate the actions of individuals or revolutionary groups from those of nations whose actions do not meet with international approval. Nationalist republicanism contains within it a dualism between non-aggressive parliamentary legalism and armed struggle, the two sometimes, but not always, linked, while democratic socialism contains many varieties of Marxism-Leninism, each group struggling to keep the flame of pure belief ablaze, branding others as revisionists, defeatists and collaborators. At the close of the eighteenth century the very mention of the words 'Jacobin' and 'democrat' had the same dangerous connotations as 'Bolshevik' and 'communist' to the twentieth. Ironically, all the subsequent parties of the 'left' originated in the simple seating arrangements of the French Convention. Revolution would be associated more and more with the activities of the extreme left, while the right came to stand for reaction, counter-revolution and, finally, fascism.

In such an atmosphere, the word 'anarchy' came more and more to stand for the demon of chaos. Whether the state was ruled by a monarch or by the people, anarchy stood for the collapse into nature, where all common feeling and civic duty broke down. It was caused, all agreed, by the loss of reason and direction when the body politic literally lost its head. The restoration of that stability provided by an actual head of state (monarch or dictator) as well as the principle of headship (the people and the commonwealth) was the sole duty and responsibility of government. Charles I's great crime was to instigate 'civil war' from above, thereby returning his realm to a state of nature. It was this connection with chaos that attached itself to the nineteenth-century proponents of anarchism and their advocacy of a new social order, regulated by absolute liberty of conscientious, cooperative government and the absence of central authority. The ancient term was, therefore, never quite replaced by the strictly political usage of 'scientific' anarchism. In effect, therefore, as the apparatus of government (the bureaucracy that acted in proxy for the people) came to replace personal loyalty to a monarch, any political action that threatened the principle of headship (the state) would from now on be labelled anarchism, terrorism and subversion.

Nothing would so disturb the state in the early years of the nineteenth century as the term 'democrat'. Its subversive and deadly threat (so deadly that Queen Victoria was its implacable foe until her death) was early summed up by the Corresponding Societies that grew up in England to demand political reform and that were based partly on support for American independence and partly on the French Jacobin Club. Even the term 'republican', quite early accepted as respectable in regard to the United States, was less anathema than the term 'democrat', suggesting as it did the overthrow of political order, the end of Christianity, the pursuit of scientific materialism and the annihilation of monarchy – anarchism indeed. Democrats and 'infidels' with their views on free love and free markets were to be shunned and feared. From the moment of solar eclipse in 1793, all the actions of the French government would be labelled terrorism. The early meaning of terrorism, nevertheless, was clearly related to the required allegiance of subjects to a nation-state whose institutions acted on behalf of a sovereign people. Such allegiance has always been subject to the vagaries of interpretation in Britain, the relationship of state to monarch nowhere as clearly defined as might be imagined.

From now on, treasonable action had to be interpreted as transferred from making war on the person of the monarch (whose actual and spiritual body represented the nation: '*L'état c'est moi*,' as Louis XIV indecorously put it) to that action that threatened a government. This was stated early on by the English republican government of 1649:

> If any person shall maliciously or advisedly publish, by writing, printing, or openly declaring, that the said government is tyrannical, usurped, or unlawful; or that the Commons in parliament assembled are not the supreme authority of this nation; or shall plot, contrive, or endeavour to stir up, or rise force against the present government, or for the subversion or alteration of the same, and shall declare the same by any open deed, that then every such offence shall be taken, deemed, and adjudged by the authority of this parliament to be high treason.[3]

Ideas of democratic government so threatened the political order of the eighteenth century that a defence of the old order had to be mounted. Such a defence was based on traditionalism, precedent and caution and presupposed a final settlement following the Glorious Revolution of 1688. Anything other than this seemed to suggest revolution itself. Burke's own sense of government, for instance, was based upon a limited number of statutes. The first of these was the Declaration of Breda, signed on 4 April 1660, restoring Charles II, in which the monarch reasserted the 'just, ancient and fundamental rights' of the people, agreed to a 'free parliament' and forgave past 'notes of discord', as well as upholding 'liberty in matters of religion'. The Bill of

Rights, passed in 1689, confirmed William and Mary of Orange as King and Queen of England and also confirmed 'freedom of election [to] parliament', the supremacy of the Protestant religion, and the 'ancient rights and liberties' of the English, as well as the 'freedom of speech and debate' in parliament. It affirmed the 'ancient and indubitable rights and liberties of the people'. The Toleration Act followed in 1689, allowing some leeway to forms of dissent, as long as tithes were paid and dissenters were Protestant. Finally, the Act of Settlement of 1701 provided for a Hanoverian succession and again restated the rights of the English. These Acts, with the common law and tradition, were Burke's final settlement of the constitutional question as far as it applied to the aspirations of the French republicans looking for a workable English model. It was their breaking with that model that so upset Burke, who believed strongly in 'reformation' not 'innovation'.

At the heart of Burke's views was an appeal to patriotism best exemplified by Franklin when he was entertained at Versailles by Louis and Marie Antoinette in quieter times: 'I would have you think me so much pleased with this king and queen as to have a whit less regard than I used to have for ours ... no Frenchmen should go beyond me in thinking my own king and queen the very best in the world, and the most amiable.' Yet it was this same attitude that in the end led Franklin towards rebellion: 'Here ... were all the ingredients of the Patriot political philosophy: a determination to rise above particular interests and seek the common good, an intense loyalty to the patriot king and his patriot minister, and, above all, a healthy distrust of the French.'[4]

Both Franklin and Burke believed in balance above all things, but this led Burke to a conclusion that he nevertheless feared, that is, that if all else failed, then nothing stood between chaos and order except the 'interposition of the body of the people', the very situation that created the only English republic in the first place, and exactly what Burke was trying to avoid. This was a revolutionary move and Burke knew it and rejected it. It was the move that Franklin, however, embraced. How else was arbitrary power to be avoided? It was also the logical conclusion to the Glorious Revolution of 1688 and Burke's own (unacknowledged) constitutional position. This had once been Frankin's view, too, when he was one of those patriots who gathered at St Paul's Coffee House. Ultimately, Franklin was simply taking Burke's ideas to their logical conclusion, ideas that Burke himself could not acknowledge. It was while Franklin was in England that the French began debating their own revolution.

It was Burke's constitutional model that appealed to one of the founders of the French revolutionary movement, Jacques Pierre Brissot. The English way held considerable appeal to those, like Brissot, who wanted a limited settlement with their king. Born in January 1754, the son of an innkeeper, Brissot studied law and followed the teachings of Voltaire and Rousseau. Travelling to London, he hoped to learn about the constitutional settlement so lauded by Burke. He started a paper, *Journal du Lycée de Londres*, which was intended to express the views of the Enlightenment and its adherents, but, having returned to Paris, Brissot soon found himself in trouble with the Government for his advanced views. The King threw him into the Bastille. Released, he again travelled back to London, where he entered the lists on behalf of the slave abolitionists, founding the Société des Amis des Noirs, of which he became president in 1790 and 1791. He also visited America, whence he returned to the Revolution, then just in its early stages, and it was Brissot to whom the keys were given when the Bastille fell – a fitting and ironic conclusion to his self-imposed exile in London, where he learned the rudiments of his revolutionary ideas. Brissot was a moderate all his life, favouring Burke's constitutional system, and yet he declared war on both the Austrian Emperor (20 April 1792) and Britain (1 July 1793) and made those declarations revolutionary in nature. Indeed, it was Brissot who popularised the wearing of the red 'Phrygian' cap of the working man and it was he who popularised the terms 'sans-culottes' and 'citizen'. The leader of the moderate Girondists, Brissot was outmanoeuvred by more extreme elements and he, along with his fellow 'right wingers', was arrested on 2 June 1793, going to his execution on 31 October 1793.

Whatever the belief in British constitutionalism in France, much was made of the possibility of a truly democratic French parliament and associations were formed in Britain to correspond with the French and thus kick the British into completing their own revolution. Nevertheless, when Burke published his *Reflections on the Revolution in France* in November 1790, it was already too late: both sides had become entrenched and the British had begun to produce abusive lampoons which showed the French in cahoots with everyone from the Devil to the Jews. The French also reacted against the British who originally supported them, rejecting those who wished for international cooperation and branding them as apologists for a system the French had already gone beyond. The result was a war lasting the best part of twenty-five years.

Brissot and Burke shared a friend from South America who also believed in the British constitutional model and whose adventures and eventual betrayal would be the first great epic of that continent's liberation. His name was Francisco de Miranda and he was born on 28 March 1750 in what is now Venezuela. It was a perfect childhood, with Miranda destined to be a scholar or a soldier. The Venezuelan aristocracy despised his Spanish blood, which smelled of the corruption and arbitrary violence that permeated Spanish rule in South America. In January 1771, he travelled to Spain and arrived in Cádiz, whence he made his way to Madrid and into the ranks of the Spanish army as a captain. In 1775 he was sent to Morocco, where the Moroccans were fighting the Spanish, but he was rude and surly and got himself confined during the siege of Gibraltar.

It was from Gibraltar that in 1779 he was despatched to North America to fight the British, where he distinguished himself. Meanwhile, friends in Venezuela sent letters telling him of the dreadful state of things under the new captain-general, Bernardo Galvez, 'a new Nero'. Miranda decided to return to try and remedy the situation by overthrowing Galvez and liberating Venezuela, but on his arrival he was arrested on trumped-up charges of smuggling and sentenced to ten years, which luckily his friends were able to overturn. Effectively under constant surveillance as a subversive, Miranda next planned to return to Spain to plead his cause with the King, travelling via the United States. When he left, in June 1783, it was considered tantamount to desertion from the Spanish army and therefore marked the beginning of Spain's determination to bring Miranda to justice. In effect, Miranda was Spain's number-one potential terrorist, apparently plotting to bring down the Spanish empire in South America from bases in the United States and Britain.

In America, Miranda met Washington, Hamilton and Paine and saw the sights, but was not impressed with Congress, which he thought lacked virtue. Eventually he arrived in England, long seen as a haven for the disaffected and at that time covetously looking to the closed markets of South America for trade. A continuous, unspoken trade war had gone on for years and Miranda, in England to plead his case (via letters) to the King of Spain, knew that he might find allies in his cause. Ensconced in a hotel, this charming and educated man was soon mixing with the Government, advocating a vigorous policy of action not only to liberate Venezuela but actually to liberate the whole of South America. The *Political Herald and Review* noted that 'this gentleman, having visited every province in North America, came to England, which he regards as the mother country of liberty, and school for political knowledge'.

Miranda was now a celebrity, a friend of liberty and an educated and highly civilised companion. Britain recognised his cause but shunned military action to achieve it. So Miranda went on a grand tour, where he met Frederick the Great and possibly became the lover of Catherine the Great, trailing his book collection and his lovers behind him, with Spanish spies always on his coat-tails. He was back in London in 1789 and found lodgings in Jermyn Street. More importantly, he was invited for an interview with the British prime minister, William Pitt, for whom he drew up elaborate plans (including a prototype Panama Canal) ready for the day Britain would equip a fleet. In his political views, Miranda advocated a mixture of monarchical and republican models, similar to British constitutionalism, and he constantly played on Britain's sense of fair play and self-interest. When it was necessary, he flattered: 'we must expect soon to see a respectable and illustrious nation [that is, South America] emerging worthy of being the ally of the wisest and most famed power on earth.'[5] The idea was very attractive, as the Spanish monopoly on trade would be finished and the whole continent opened to British goods. The question was whether Britain cared for a showdown with Spain. The answer, not surprisingly, was no, and Miranda remained in England until 1792, living in Soho.

At the same time, Brissot was also in London and recognised that the French Revolution could be spread to South America. At his invitation, Miranda travelled to Paris and found himself almost by accident the head of one of the revolutionary armies. With the rise of the Jacobins, Miranda was, however, dismayed with the extremism of the French and wrote to Alexander Hamilton in the United States that 'the introduction of extremist principles ... would poison freedom in its cradle and destroy it'. Miranda foresaw the dangers of the Jacobins, and his identification with Brissot and the Girondins got him arrested on 19 April 1793 for not being revolutionary enough. Marat's *L'Ami du Peuple* had accused Miranda of looting but he was defended at his trial as 'an irreproachable republican'. Even Paine travelled to Paris in order to defend him, 'because the cause of the French revolution is intimately tied to the favourite cause of his heart, the independence of South America'.

The advocacy worked, as did Miranda's own eloquence, and the guillotine was cheated. Again brought to trial on 13 July, this

time for apparently plotting with royalists, Miranda nevertheless cheated the executioner for the second time. The French
Revolution had gone too far, but Miranda had met and admired
Napoleon and wished to emulate him. Napoleon for his part distrusted Miranda as an adventurer and a spy. Arrested yet again in
April 1801, Miranda finally took the hint that he was not wanted
in France and returned to Britain, Pitt and promises. His view of
Britain always continued to be complimentary and the liberal-
ity with which ideas were discussed in Britain seemed to him to
be revelatory: 'When you leave England do not for a moment
forget that outside this country there is in all the world only one
other nation where you can breath a word of politics ... and that
country is the United States.'[6]

During the Napoleonic Wars, two British expeditions
were sent to South America, but both were aborted and neither was for the liberation of Venezuela. When the Peninsular
War began, Arthur Wellesley (later the Duke of Wellington),
who had agreed to lead an expedition, found himself an ally
of the Spanish and the plan was dropped. Miranda believed
that Wellington would be beaten in Spain but it was not to
be, and the South American liberator was again left in limbo.
Miranda's own attempt at a revolution came in 1806 when he
and a small flotilla of American and British ships set out for an
invasion. Inevitably this little force was defeated and many of
his men were captured and tortured by the Spanish. Miranda
was back at the beginning, and back in London in 1808, but
this time he had recruited Burke to pamphleteer on behalf of
South American independence.

Hailed by now as the 'Washington of the Latin American
Continent', Miranda awaited the imminent overthrow of
Spanish tyranny. In Caracas, the capital of Venezuela, a provincial government had been set up after the French overthrow of
the Spanish government. At Martin's Hotel, Miranda, the old
revolutionary, met a group of Venezuelans looking for allies.
These included an admirer, Simon Bolivar. Miranda was no

doubt flattered by the younger man's attentions, but Bolivar was hysterical, histrionic and unstable.

In 1808, France overthrew the Spanish monarchy; the revolution in Venezuela was in full swing and Bolivar and Miranda had to get back there. Two years went by. They still hoped for British help and met Marquis Wellesley (the Duke of Wellington's brother), who was Foreign Secretary, on 17 July 1810. Bolivar was titled the 'Spanish American Representative' for the visit. The meeting was purely diplomatic on the British side and again the group went away empty-handed. Indeed, the British refused to recognise Venezuela as an independent republic because it might encourage others on the South American continent to revolt. Bolivar and Miranda returned to Venezuela as heroes and in February 1811 Miranda was appointed lieutenant-general by the new government in Caracas. Nevertheless, a royalist counter-revolution had broken out and Miranda and Bolivar took to the field with their revolutionary armies. They were defeated.

In the meantime, a constitution was passed which enshrined liberty and equality, freedom of the press and equality between races. It was a giant leap beyond British constitutionalism. At 62, Miranda was again called upon to lead an army finally to defeat the royalists. His luck ran out: the British were now suspicious of his revolutionary ideas (they sounded too much like the Jacobinism that the young Miranda had himself despised) and, worse still, he had to agree to an armistice. Once Miranda had come to an agreement with the royalists, Bolivar became his implacable enemy. Miranda, in a dangerous position, thought it best to escape aboard the British frigate *Sapphire*, but was arrested by Bolivar's men the day before embarkation. Bolivar handed Miranda over to the Spanish; they finally had him and he was duly transferred to Cadiz. The Peninsular War was over and Ferdinand VII was on the throne, the worst of all revengeful despots. Miranda was not to escape, despite his pleas to all his old friends and to the British whom he loved. Lord Castlereagh wrote to Henry Wellesley (ambassador to Madrid), a self-serving and subservient letter in which he looked to diplomatic means to bring Spain to her senses regarding South America and insisted that nothing was to be done that would upset the alliance with Spain. In all this, Miranda was simply a diplomatic memory. Abandoned and suffering from typhus, Miranda died on 14 July 1816 after four years in jail, his body being burnt to avoid spreading the disease. Today there is an empty tomb in Caracas as a reminder of his courage, and of Britain's willingness to encourage revolution but do nothing about it and finally to deny all knowledge of it.

Meanwhile, there was another Frenchman in England. Among the most famous of all French revolutionaries to be influenced by British radical circles was Jean-Paul Marat, who came to live in England during 1765. Born on 24 May 1743 in Neuchâtel, Marat was Swiss by birth, but changed his surname from Mara to sound more French. While in Britain, he mixed with the likes of Angelica Kauffmann, the famous artist, and with aristocrats such as Lord Littleton. Two physician friends helped him obtain a doctorate from St Andrews University, then notorious for selling awards to the highest bidder.

Marat was a true son of the Enlightenment, interested in such diverse issues as the passage of Venus, the rights of slaves[7] and the political philosophy of dualism. He was also widely travelled and had probably visited The Hague, Edinburgh, Utrecht, Amsterdam and Dublin before he finally settled in Soho and began a career as an author. He also travelled to Newcastle, where he received the citizenship of the town for helping in an epidemic and where he would be influenced by the primitive communism of Spence, whose circle of followers met to discuss the political questions of the day. Marat, already a frequenter of various clubs and debating societies, could not have missed the speeches (or their reports) that emanated from Spence and his friends. Indeed, he would have been only too aware of the scandal surrounding Spence's expulsion from the Newcastle Philosophical Society on his publishing the lecture 'Property in

Land, Everyone's Right', which the *Newcastle Chronicle* reported on 25 November 1775, although by this time Marat was living in London.

Between 1770 and 1773, Marat practised medicine and took part in the reform (and scientific discussions) that marked Newcastle's intellectual life. First among these was electoral reform, then beginning its long history of struggle. Among its demands were three-yearly parliaments, equal representation, disqualification of 'placemen' and the release from prison of the reform hero Wilkes to take up his parliamentary seat of Middlesex. Marat, by now a thorough Anglophile, joined in the debate and published *The Chains of Slavery*, which he advertised in the *Public Advertiser* on 3 May 1774 as an 'address to the electors of Great Britain'. It was published under the name of a fictitious English writer called 'Doctor Mariot', and illustrated by the great engraver Bewick. Bewick himself remained a radical and, although he never met Marat, it seems he took his ideas to heart. Marat for his part absorbed the philosophy of constitutional monarchy, which he greatly admired, and the belief in personal liberty that was the watchword of that second civil war, the American Revolution.

At some point, probably 1777, Marat travelled to France and became doctor to the Count d'Artois. He continued to publish and followed the scientific fashion of the day by experimenting with electricity, one demonstration of which was attended by Franklin. Thus far, 'Marat was a complacent, conservative spirit, endowed with a goodly share of middle class virtues.'[8] For Marat, nevertheless, the stirrings of revolution would prick his own philosophical ideas. He was a rationalist who saw the monarch as a figurehead and as a chief magistrate accountable to the people, who were *sovereign*. The monarch acted on behalf of the people only. Although no communist, Marat also mobilised Spence's arguments in terms of a 'moral economy' of just division: 'The right to possess is derived from that to live. Therefore everything that is indispensable for our existence is ours, and nothing superfluous can belong to us legitimately as long as others lack necessities. This is the legitimate foundation of all property, both in the state of society and in the state of nature.'[9]

None of these views was particularly new or novel, but Marat pursued them with vigour and with an intensity born of a suspicious nature and a personality that was marked with the righteousness of his already developing martyr complex. By degrees, Marat ceased to be a spokesman for constitutional monarchy and the compromise solutions of the middle classes from whom he had sprung, and became instead the voice of the urban poor and the sans-culottes. However, Marat was not yet quite a revolutionary. 'If the constitution leaves to the king any share in the legislative power, it ought to be only in the right to approve or to reject the laws which are passed, as is the practice today among the English,' he concluded.

The fall of the Bastille on 14 July 1789 began to change Marat's mind. Perhaps the King's veto was not such a good idea; perhaps a constitution other than 'English' was needed. By August 1789, Marat was advocating the sovereignty of the people and that idea became more insistent as he worked as editor on his journal *L'Ami du peuple*, but he was also suspicious of France's old ministers and the possibility of a republic built around their power. Marat remained torn between the accusation that he was not sufficiently republican and the equal accusation that he was too much a Spencean primitive communist. If he addressed himself to 'simple labourers' because they alone had 'courage and feeling', he certainly did not advocate that they should rule, for 'agrarian law' was 'destructive of all civil society', a point he made in his *Profession of Faith* on 30 March 1793.

Yet Marat had begun an unstoppable process that had its origins in Newcastle and would return to Britain, clothed in the language of French Jacobinism: that urban artisans were no longer a criminal or a mere indiscriminate mob, but a force and a power, coming slowly to that class-consciousness that would create a new and dangerous collective mentality and collective ideology. Marat was this group's advocate and hero, even president of the Club des Jacobins during a short period in April 1793. Power came from the people and from now on power had to come from *below*:

> Expect nothing from rich and opulent men, from men brought up in luxury and pleasures, from greedy men who love only gold. It is not of old slaves that free citizens are made. There remains only the farmers, small merchants, artisans, and workers, labourers and proletariat, as the insolent rich call them, to form a free people, impatient of the yoke of oppression and always ready to break it. But these people are not educated; and nothing is so difficult as to educate them. It is even an impossible task today when a thousand venal pens are working only to mislead them in order to put them again in chains.[10]

Marat's new federal republicanism could be nothing if it did not defend itself and did not choose a leader. By 1790, Marat's paranoia saw traitors everywhere. Everyone not on Marat's side had to be purged. In March 1793 Marat's vision of a people's court was finally established with the setting-up of the Revolutionary Tribunal. Marat's rhetoric of murder became almost heroic. On 27 May 1791 he declared, 'Eleven months ago five thousand heads would have sufficed; today fifty thousand would be necessary; perhaps five hundred thousand will fall before the end of the year. France will have been flooded with blood, but it will not be more free because of it.'[11]

This was the language of modern revolution and modern dictatorship. The people must choose a dictator to lead them towards the apotheosis of the republic. Once his work was done, like Washington, the dictator was to resign and retire. Curiously, when elected to the National Convention, Marat was not a fully committed republican, even when the Convention declared France a republic on 22 September

1792. A republican by slow degrees, Marat finally threw in his lot with Robespierre and Saint-Just once Louis was dead. Indeed, he had voted for the execution and with it was finally convinced of the reality and ideology of the republic. He 'believe[d] in the Republic at last!'[12]

Having cast in his lot with the Republic, having called for a Committee of Public Safety and a Revolutionary Tribunal, he too would be hunted by the police in that hothouse atmosphere and brought to trial as a traitor. With real and imagined enemies on all sides, having successfully purged the 'right wing' of the revolution under Brissot, and having survived (for the moment) the attention of judicial committees, Marat watched the tempest of revolution as it swirled around him while he dictated his ideas or met his guests in the luxury of his famous bathtub, which he used to ease an acute skin complaint.

Civil war raged in the Vendée; the Revolution was still in great peril. Marie-Anne Charlotte de Corday d'Armont was from Normandy, a conservative, Bible-reading and martyr-dom-seeking assassin who felt the revolution had gone too far. Her plan was simple: to come to Paris and kill as many of the Jacobin leadership as possible. She found Marat in his bath on 13 July 1793, and got his attention with a report from Caen. While he was reading the report, she pulled out a knife and thrust it into his lungs. Revolutionaries do not live long; Saint-Just was dead at 28, Marat had just turned 50. Corday was 25. She died on 17 July, her Bible at home allegedly open at the story of Judith the decapitator.

Looking back at the events of those years, Bewick, Marat's one-time illustrator and Spence's eccentric friend, could still conjure up the depths of emotion and commitment that fired the friends of liberty who watched the events in France with the eagerness of men looking to their own immediate libera-tion: 'The government of this free country and free people ... had readily found pretexts for entering into a war in support of despotism; and war was begun, in the year 1793, against the

republican government of France.... In this state of things, with
Mr Pitt at their head, and the resources of the British Isles in
their hands, it was calculated as a certainty [that it] would soon
put a stop to the march of intellect, and ... extinguish the rights
of men.'[13]

The war in America was a shock, but it was a shock only after
it became a fight for full independence. British radicals, including
those such as Wilkes who later retreated from their radicalism, supported their American compatriots, aware that ancient
English rights had been breached. The war was one of redress,
and its consequences the result of obstinacy and distance. The
young United States proved an irritation but hardly a threat, its
resources unable to challenge British power for over 100 years.
The Americans had stood up for good ancient English principles
and if the pernicious creed of democracy had been imported, it
had, after all, been Englishmen who had first preached it. The
French Revolution was different. If the American disaster had
created a smouldering fuse, the French Revolution provided the
gunpowder. The seizure of the French King directly challenged
traditional British constitutionalism, and delighted the English,
Scottish and Irish extreme republicans longing for a showdown
with the old European order. A rapidly developing situation put
monarchy and privilege on alert and threatened 'world' convul-
sion and the coming of a new order. The beheading of Louis and,
later, his queen was clear proof not only of France's grand civil
designs but also of her intention of taking revolution abroad.
While the British looked on with curiosity, sometimes enthusiasm and sometimes horror, they might well have reflected that
it was they and not the French whose ideology had first sparked
the revolutionary turmoil.

The French had little to learn from the lessons of 1688, and
what they did learn proved the undoing of many of their leading revolutionary leaders. Instead, constitutionalism seemed to
provide the first magic words in an incantation that would utterly
sweep away the old compromise that had served Britain and, in so

doing, it served also to reveal that compromise was a mere sham, a piece of illusory theatre to trick the nations of England, Scotland, Ireland and Wales into a slave-like subservience to the demon of 'tyranny'. The Corresponding Societies watched with anticipation the manoeuvres, both political and military, of their fraternal French cousins, increasingly drawn to the drama of revolution.

To create a British revolution, there had to be four ingredients. British revolutionaries were needed in France to pass on the message and to participate fully in the necessary correspondence that would keep the radical societies up to date as to the swings of revolutionary thinking in Paris. There should be continuous participation of those British radicals abroad at the centre of events in Paris with the aim, ultimately, of persuading the members of the Convention (later National Assembly) and Committee of Public Safety to commit troops to an invasion of Ireland or England in order to liberate the people from the tyranny of Dublin and London. An information network was required that would help revolutionaries at home arm and drill an army of volunteers for a war of liberation to be fought by the now enlightened 'people' against the King, his ministers and cronies. Finally, there had to be a blueprint for national assemblies for England, Ireland and Scotland, so that the ideological warriors in Paris might return to their capitals ready to declare the everlasting republican union of France with the newly proclaimed republican nations of England, Ireland, Scotland and (as an afterthought) Wales.

All this was to be accomplished in a few feverish months between the death of Louis XVI and the final beheading of Robespierre, amid the din of Austrian invasion and civil war, the purging of political opponents and the massacre of royalist towns and cities. Trying hard to stay at the heart of events was a group of around fifty British émigré revolutionaries centred on their club at White's Hotel (also called the Philadelphia Hotel) at 7 passage des Petits Pères in Paris. At their centre was a committed revolutionary called John Oswald.

Oswald was one of many Britons who sympathised with the Revolution, seeing it as a new dawn. Most travelled to and fro across the Channel as events unfolded, making sure that sympathisers in England, Scotland and Wales got the latest from Paris almost as it happened. Most, but not all, of the British 'fellow travellers' were constitutionalists whom the French suspected and who abandoned the Revolution when the Terror began. Almost all followed the latest intellectual fads from mesmerism to druidism, and from free love to masonism. Oswald was both a vegetarian and a possible Buddhist and he was certainly a bigamist. He was also an early advocate of the Terror. Indeed he half-jokingly advocated it to Paine, who suggested that lack of meat in Oswald's diet had turned his head. Born the son of an Edinburgh coffee shop owner, where there was opportunity for political debate, he graduated to the army, where he saw service in India and discovered that he had no proper religious beliefs. Having fought a duel with another officer, Oswald returned to England and thence Scotland to settle down as a poet.

It was in England that he first met Brissot, then trawling the masonic lodges for converts to his Lycée. He also met Miranda. When the Revolution finally broke out, Oswald, by now a democrat, was one of the first to travel to France to witness events, and it was here that he met Paine and Danton and became a central figure in the early Convention. He was still a constitutionalist and looked forward to the day that there would be a 'federal Britain' allied with France and the United States, then still the model for revolutions. Oswald believed Britain to be 'suspended on a volcano', ripe for revolution either by internal insurrection or by invasion or, better, a combination of the two. By now he was frequently travelling the Channel and working as a newspaper correspondent as well as producing his own pamphlets, including a draft constitution for France. Nevertheless, the Revolution was in danger and Oswald, by now an advocate of ideologically strong measures ('philosophic war') to defeat the 'Counter Terror', volunteered to lead a regiment against the royalists in the Vendée (a war that was to last until 1804). On 14 September 1793, Oswald was killed leading a charge. When he died, his fame was such that his friends actually thought that he was Napoleon.

By late 1793 France had run out of friends. Paranoia had descended and Englishmen and women were rounded up, imprisoned and sometimes executed. The French had some reason to fear. The English and Scots headed for safety in the rue Helvétius near the Bibliothèque Nationale, and it was from there that women like Arabella Williams secretly worked with her lover the Baron de Batz to undermine the revolution on behalf of Pitt. In England, meanwhile, Robespierre, denounced as a dictator, was imitated at one masked ball being pursued by a 'Charlotte Corday' brandishing a knife.

Chapter Five

Theatre of Catastrophes

The consequence of the Terror in France was a considerable increase in trials for treason in Britain, an attempt by successive administrations from the mid-1790s to the brink of the First Reform Act of 1832 to suppress dissent. On the whole, such repression was successful in scaring dissidents into silence, although evidence was often obtained by dubious means and convictions, except in blatant cases of violence, were rare. A charge of treason was often replaced by the vaguer charge of conspiracy, itself regularly rejected by juries suspicious of the connivance of magistrates and spies, and fearful of the brutality of the judiciary. Nevertheless, if the charge of treason was a blunt instrument in the hands of governments, it was also one whose consequences for the accused were dire. The ritual of hanging, drawing and quartering, traditional punishment for traitors, was replaced in the late eighteenth century by mere hanging and beheading, even that violent age no longer able to witness the horror of the full ritual. Such public displays of state revenge did not cease, in fact, until 1820. The lesser charge of sedition was often substituted as a means to secure conviction when treason seemed too extreme, and for this there was always transportation. There was a belief that if you were in the dock, you must be guilty, judges frequently directing juries to reach a guilty verdict, while juries were sometimes placemen who knew their civic duty in advance. More to the point, the accused was allowed no defence or preparatory help other than in cases of treason.[1]

The situation was somewhat different for those accused in a treason trial. This was for three reasons. The first and most important was that judges acted on behalf of the Crown as appointees and so were biased already towards a guilty verdict; the second was that most treason trials (at least before the eighteenth century) were against aristocrats, people of substance and standing; the third was the miscarriages of justice that occurred during the Popish Plot of 1678, when a number of innocent people went to their deaths because of trumped-up charges. To remove such apparent corruption, the Government passed the Treason Act in 1696, whose main amendment to the law was to give the defendant the help of defence counsel. As the penalty for treason was a particularly unpleasant death, and as the accused were men of status (and therefore a wrong verdict would destabilise the country), special care had to be taken. Steps had to be taken to put a barrier between the defendant and the bench. Another was that the prosecution already employed lawyers to work for it, so the safety of a verdict was dependent on money and bias not the facts. One jurist commented that '[a] s many council as can be hired are allowed against [the accused], ... [it] is a wonder how any persons escaped; it is downright tying a man's hands behind his back and baiting him to death'.[2] Allowing the defendant lawyers evened up the odds against him and allowed him to fight back just as he was prosecuted – with lawyers. Last but not least, treason required two witnesses to the 'act'. But what was an act of treason? Opinions differed and this required lawyers to avoid 'constructive treason' charges – that is, charges imputed by reason of motive or action. In effect, the treason trial was the origin of all modern criminal trials.

The effect of the Treason Act between 1793 and 1820 was that when treason was invoked it became usual to grant the accused proper legal representation, at least in points of law. The judges remained as biased as ever, always intent on getting a conviction – a conviction that was, nevertheless, often warranted by the facts as presented to them. On the other hand, jurors were wary of 'noose-happy' judges and often acquitted the defendant altogether, unless a lesser charge could be substituted. Judges also had the right to commute a sentence of death to one of transportation, and very often did.

An offender, once apprehended, was brought before a magistrate to be charged. A grand jury was called and a decision was made as to whether the accused had a case to answer. Before or during this process, the accused might also be taken to London to answer to the Privy Council. If such a case was made, the defendant was placed in jail until the assizes, sometimes a wait of six months in which jail fever might finish what the law had started. Although crude, brutal and blunt, the law was effective. However, used as a blunt instrument during the period, it lost much of its effectiveness, being brought into disrepute not by its procedure but by the barbaric nature of its effects: hanging and beheading.

An example of the difficulty of getting a fair trial (there was no recourse to appeal) is illustrated by that of William Orr, arrested on 15 September 1797 for administering the oath of the United Irishmen to Hugh Wheatly and John Lindsay. This was to be a show trial, orchestrated by Lord Castlereagh, Viceroy of Ireland, to scare those dissenting groups. The trial judge was Baron Avonmore (Barry Yelverton), who had been a Volunteer and Patriot. Orr's solicitor, James McGuckin, was a Catholic solicitor who himself would become an informer. He, in turn, instructed the barristers, John Curran and Arthur Wolfe (who would die on the pikes of Robert Emmet's rebellion).

The jury were undecided whether Orr was guilty or not and the foreman, Archibald Thompson, simply 'left the prisoner to his lordship's mercy', which, being unacceptable to the judge, left only one verdict: guilty. Meanwhile, Curran raised legal objections to the verdict, namely that the Insurrection Act, under which Orr had been charged, had expired and that Orr could not be tried in law under a statute that no longer existed. Yelverton rejected this, as he did also the affidavit, which said that Thompson had been threatened and two bottles of whiskey had circulated in the jury room. Indeed, Thompson was 'quite distracted' about the verdict. These mitigating circumstances, apparently overwhelming, were not admitted, yet when Yelverton passed sentence he was said to have cried, an emotional outpouring considered mere crocodile tears by his opponents. Yelverton felt that he was trapped by the letter of the law. Despite every attempt to save him, Orr was executed at 2.45 p.m. on 14 October 1797 on an ancient three-pillared cross on Gallows Green, near Carrickfergus.

If the law was rough and ready in England, it was non-existent in Yelverton's Ireland, where contempt stood in for justice. Here, the rules of civilised behaviour were utterly absent and a type of savagery that would not have been tolerated in England was the rule. The army in Ireland was shambolic, ill-disciplined and volatile, and quickly being divided on sectarian lines. General Sir Ralph Abercrombie, commander-in-chief, had described the forces under him in a secret memo as 'formidable to everyone but the enemy'. During the Irish War of Independence, the situation degenerated still further. Ulster had the misfortune of having General Gerald Lake in charge of operations. A veteran of numerous conflicts, Lake had learned that the direct approach got quick results and it did not matter how those results were obtained. He was, without doubt, a brutal martinet who would follow orders to an almost psychopathic degree and who could induce others under him of a like-minded persuasion to carry out what would now be considered war crimes. It was Lake's plan 'to excite terror' in the civilian population. In this he succeeded. Thus he went about the burning of towns and villages and the public killing and torture of suspected rebels, or indeed anyone looking suspicious. His methods were novel: a travelling garrotte on which the victim was hoisted by a rope around his neck; the pitch cap, a mixture of tar and gunpowder applied to the hair and then set alight; the triangle, a type of crucifixion where the victim was whipped, usually until he died. These methods he applied 'systematically', a policy so successful in its awfulness that resistance in Ulster collapsed. Lake focused brutality as latent as it was unexpected. It shocked some, but reassured others and Lake was soon the supreme commander in Ireland.

What had brought Ireland to this catastrophic situation? There had been a movement for reform in the late 1780s and early 1790s, brought on by the war in America and the Revolution in France. It had flourished in Belfast, celebrated Paine's *Rights of Man*, and united Catholics and Presbyterians despite the sectarian violence in Ulster. It had finally faded and the 'volunteers' had had to put away their blue revolutionary uniforms and braid.

The fabric of Ulster was meanwhile slowly unravelling as Catholics and Protestants faced up to each other. Protestant gangs such as the Oakboys, Steelboys and Peep o' Day Boys raided and killed Catholics on the excuse of looking for hidden arms. The Catholics, for their part, formed the Defenders, who took the fight to the Protestants. It was soon rumoured that an organisation called the United Irishmen was being formed across Ireland, and Protestants grew queasy, fearing an attempt to dislodge them. In 1795 there was an extended brawl between Peep o' Day Boys and Defenders outside an inn in the little village of the Diamond. The Protestants won but, fearing the power of the Defenders, formed the Orange Boys, which by degrees became the Orange Order. This was a semi-secret and Masonic-like organisation defending the interests of the Protestants in the north, who had long retreated from their fraternal attitude to Catholics, who feared the United Irishmen still operating in Belfast, who had had enough of revolutionary ardour and who looked to confirm their loyalty in the historical atmosphere of William of Orange's Protestant victory over James II at the Boyne.

In 1798 it was Dublin, rather than Belfast, that was the centre of operations for the United Irishmen (both Catholic and Protestant), who numbered, it was said, 200,000 men, armed with pikes secretly made by the village smithies, and inspired by the vision of a Gaelic republic. Their motives were mixed: a hatred of landlords and landlordism, of the English, of the tithes to the Church of Ireland, a fear of magistrates and cruel laws, contempt shown by hatred of those who ruled, and simple poverty. These at least were the motives of Catholics; among Protestants, many of whom were wealthy and some of whom were of the ruling elite, there was the idea of a free and inde-pendent Ireland which would be rich, confident and republican, joined to its French counterpart by example and to England by family ties and tradition. The old Anglican families were not about to give over their privileges and control to Presbyterians, just as the English were not prepared to relinquish their hold on the colony, to give the slightest concession on the way it was ruled or allow Catholics to dictate terms to Protestants. The country had its own parliament, but was ruled by a viceroy who carried the veto of Westminster and the king. He could not rule without the consent of the loyalist gentry and they could not rule without the power of England behind them. It was a deli-cate balance of power.

The danger to this balance lay not in the ranks of the disaf-fected peasantry, but right at the heart of the establishment, at the centre of the Protestant ascendancy itself. Lord Edward Fitzgerald was the twelfth child of the Duke and Duchess of Leinster, the premier family of Ireland, intimately related to almost all the major political and social figures in England, and great-grandson of Charles II. The Duchess, enamoured of the liberal ideas of Rousseau and the new-fangled idea of a loving family, as well the idea of the noble savage, brought up her chil-dren to be happy, free and self-confident, and to believe in the nobility of human beings. 'Natural reason' and the free expression of emotion were part of the cult. Her romantic vision of human nature rubbed off on her favourite child, who took his mother's views to the American war, where he was wounded at the Battle of Eutaw Creek on 8 September 1781. Here, he was found by a black slave named 'Tony Small', who nursed him back to life and whom Fitzgerald rewarded by making him his personal servant and confidant when he returned to Ireland. For Fitzgerald, Tony was the epitome of Rousseau's natural man. In contrast, Fitzgerald was already a cosmopolitan figure, relatively wealthy, well connected, extremely personable, dangerously fluent in French and from a family whose attitudes were liberal and on the whole unpatriotic. Fitzgerald always regretted fighting in America 'against the cause of liberty'.

His interests in reform began with his acquaintance with his cousin Charles Fox, and he was soon unsuccessfully pressing for reform in the Irish parliament. He got the idea of independence through reading Paine's *Common Sense*. In 1788 he was in Nova Scotia with the army and was struck by the lack of social hierarchy. He wrote home that 'the equality of everybody and of their manner I like very much'. What intrigued him was the fact that 'there are no gentlemen' and that 'every man is exactly what he can make himself … by industry'. From there he travelled to Detroit to meet Joseph Brand, the Indian who had helped the British and who combined the life of a country squire with that of a full-blown Iroquois chief. On his return, Fitzgerald felt alienated and isolated, clinging now to the familiar features of Tony, whose 'black face is the only thing that I yet feel attached to'. By degrees, a creeping sense of injustice was overtaking his thoughts. 'I ought to have been a savage', he wrote, 'and if it [wasn't] that the people I love … are civilised … I really would join the savages [and] be what nature intended.'[3]

With the coming of the French Revolution, Fitzgerald found his cause. 'He is mad about French affairs,' his family complained. He was now insisting that the mob be referred to as 'the people'.

Paine's *Rights of Man* convinced him of the need to restore man's natural rights and renovate the 'natural order' of the world. Paine became Fitzgerald's idol and Fitzgerald soon sought out and befriended him, by now adopting the plain civilian clothes and tied-back hair favoured by the revolutionaries. By September 1792, Fitzgerald was in Paris, applauding the new Republic and making a beeline for Paine's lodgings at White's Hotel. Fitzgerald's brother Robert, as natural a Tory as Edward was a republican, and assistant ambassador to France, lamented that the world was divided between 'men and Frenchmen'. Edward chose to become a Frenchman in spirit, giving up his title and becoming plain 'citizen' after a drinking session at Whites on 18 November. It was a decision he never regretted, as he did not regret marrying a relatively poor but convinced French republican, Pamela de Genlis, alleged bastard daughter of the Duke of Orleans (who had reincarnated himself as Philippe Egalité), and considered 'his dangerous little wife' by those who knew them.

It was in Paris that Fitzgerald met the Sheares brothers and other leaders of the United Irishmen, the organisation formed by Theobald Wolfe Tone, and it was here that he decided to fight for an Irish republic. He did not become a United Irishman until the autumn of that year. Here he also met the American Eleazer Oswald, who proposed raising an army to defeat England. The proposal came to nothing but the idea would stick. With the suppression of the 'open' United Irishmen, the society went underground and by 1795 they were a force to be reckoned with, uniting as they did Protestants with Catholics and merchants with the peasantry. They were also cultivating Fitzgerald, who became by degrees their commander in Ireland when others fled to France. The old Defenders were also joining the ranks and a reform movement lurched into revolutionary mode, with pikes (deadly in an ambush or street fighting) being manufactured, the old blue uniforms being dusted off and the hidden brass cannon of the old volunteers being retrieved from long neglect in barns and outhouses.

Two parties now spoke for Ireland at the council tables in France. On the one hand there was Fitzgerald, and on the other, quite unaware of the first's deliberations, was the party led by Tone, already long in exile. Born in 1763, Tone was raised as a Protestant and educated at Trinity College to be a lawyer, but the revolutions in America and France persuaded him of the need for Irish independence and Catholic emancipation, ideas he pursued when he formed the United Irishmen in Belfast in 1791, an act for which he was eventually banished first to the United States and then to France. Here he consolidated his ideas for a war against the English oppressors and pressed the French to mount an invasion.

The second suppression of the 'secret' United Irishmen meant that the rebel leaders were arrested or scattered. Lake's strategy of torturing his way to peace was succeeding and the well-made pikes of local blacksmiths were rapidly rusting in heaps as the population crumbled. Those suspected of being ringleaders went into hiding and Fitzgerald took on numerous disguises as he travelled around Dublin from safe house to safe house. What was to be done, when there was no effective leadership and Fitzgerald was the most wanted man in Ireland? Spies were around every corner and the Government soon found its grass in the shape of Francis Magan, a Catholic barrister, whose identity long remained a secret. Fitzgerald was hunted down for the reward and trapped by Major Swan on information from Magan. Seizing the dagger he kept by his bed, Fitzgerald slashed at Swan, who shouted for help from a Captain Ryan. Ryan clasped Fitzgerald round the waist only to be hacked to pieces by Fitzgerald, seemingly unable to let go. Swan pulled out his pistols and shot Fitzgerald twice in the shoulder, after which the dagger was dropped and the most wanted man in Ireland was taken prisoner. Fitzgerald languished in solitary confinement, his bullet wounds untreated and the Government quite undecided as to what to do with a celebrity at once so famous, so popular and still looked upon with such favour by his influential friends, who quickly rallied round. It was to no avail, for, with the bullets still unremoved, Fitzgerald developed septicaemia and died as the rebellion raged all around him, on 4 June 1798.

Everything seemed lost with the United Irishmen but, as Fitzgerald lay dying, the revolution spontaneously began, in many places taking the Government by surprise with its ferocity. The Government fought back with annihilatory determination, quelling most of Ireland and reducing the countryside to mere pockets of resistance. Nevertheless, in ambush the Irish were deadly, giving no quarter to the hated (usually Protestant) yeomanry; none was expected on either side. Everywhere the fighting was piecemeal, sporadic, violent and unexpected, flaring and then dying away, a trail of smouldering buildings and desolation in its wake. In the south, loyal Protestants were the target of Catholic vengeance and local sectarian feuds were settled by a burning or by a murder. The county squirearchy banded together as best they could for defence, but they were often the victims of attacks long dreamed of by their tenants and now undertaken with immunity. Such new-found liberties made the Catholics wild and ferocious opponents, their ranks often charging up to the cannon's barrel before being blown into oblivion, around their necks leather pouches enclosing good-luck prayers. Local priests were often in the front rank, although the Catholic Church remained on the side of the English and threatened their flocks with excommunication.

As the fighting died away in British triumphs, County Wexford in the south-east of the country finally and unexpectedly rose. Led by a reluctant middle-aged priest, Father John Murphy of Boolavogue, the locals had ambushed and scattered a troop of yeomanry and by degrees had organised themselves sufficiently to have captured the ancient town of Enniscorthy and massacred its garrison, setting up a great camp on Vinegar Hill, which overlooked the town. From there, Wexford also fell and, with it, its strategic harbour. The south-east was now in rebel hands. In the town, the magistrate, Bagenal Harvey,

himself a Protestant landlord, but now in jail and suspected of
being a United Irishman, found himself dragged from his cell
by the rebels, only to be proclaimed president of the Republic
of Wexford and the head of the Committee of Public Safety.
Meanwhile, over 400 Protestant prisoners were rounded up,
all of them considered Orangemen. A catechism separated the
republicans from loyalists:

> Question: 'What have you got in your hand?'
> Answer: 'A green bough.'
> Question: 'Where did it first grow?'
> Answer: 'In America.'
> Question: 'Where did it bud?'
> Answer: 'In France.'
> Question: 'Where are you going to plant it?'
> Answer: 'In the crown of Great Britain.'

The town was full of rebels; some 15,000 were in the streets,
dressed in green and sporting hats and flags with '*Erin go Bragh*'
(Ireland For Ever), while on Vinegar Hill there was a Liberty
tree and the singing of the 'Marseillaise' and the 'Carmagnole',
song of the sans-culottes. They may also have sung a new song
called 'The Swineish [*sic*] Multitude'. Yet they were isolated, the
rebel armies in the north suffering defeats and no overall strategy to take things forward. At the Battle of Ballynahinch, the
Republic of Ulster had been extinguished. On the battlefield
were found the bodies of two prostitutes dressed as the Goddess
of Reason and the Goddess of Liberty. Only Wexford was left
and the atmosphere there was getting poisonous as the tales of
Protestant atrocities filtered into town. Were the Orangemen
plotting to massacre all Catholics? Whether true or not, it was
sufficient reason to drag most of the Protestant prisoners onto
Wexford Bridge and pike them to death as traitors to the new
republic. The Republic lasted barely two months. General Lake
was on the move and soon had sufficient troops to rout the camp

at Vinegar Hill on 21 June and retake Wexford. All the rebel leaders that were captured were summarily executed. Harvey was hanged from Wexford Bridge on 28 June.

Tone remained helpless in Paris. He had been sent to France as a friend of the new Republic and as a good revolutionary. Two years had gone by since he had first convinced the French to invade. He had gone expecting immediate help, but had been left kicking his heels as the Revolutionary government shilly-shallied over aid and as their civil war in the Vendée increased in intensity. Eventually, however, Lazare Hoche, a young revolutionary who hated Britain, offered to lead an invasion of Ireland. Tone joyfully accepted and an expedition was got together with 1,500 soldiers and a substantial navy. It left Brest (in the centre of the civil war) on 16 December 1796. The noise of distant cannon-fire could be heard as they sailed. Unfortunately for Tone there was no gusto for the invasion on the part of the French admiral, Justin Morand de Galles, so that despite avoiding the Royal Navy, as soon as a gale blew up the expedition turned round and went home, reaching Brest during January 1797. Tone was furious.

Other plans were cooking, such as an invasion of Cornwall or a raid on Newcastle. These, too, were dropped until a scheme was hatched to invade Wales, where there was meant to be a body of revolutionaries. William Tate, a 70-year-old adventurer from Carolina, was chosen to lead the expedition, which this time consisted of an army mostly recruited from the prisons. Tone could hardly believe the stupidity of it.

Two of France's most modern frigates would lead the expedition, followed by corvettes and armed luggers, and would attempt to attack Bristol before going up the coast of England and dropping off soldiers to invade Chester and Liverpool. The invaders left Brest again on 18 February 1797 and were in the Bristol Channel by the next day. Misfortune forced them to avoid Bristol but raids were made on Ilfracombe. It was decided that they would continue to make their way up the coast and attempt a landing in Wales. The expedition arrived at Fishguard in Pembrokeshire on Wednesday 22 February. The local fort fired a warning and the people of the town prepared, but they were hardly in a position to resist, as the little fort had only three rounds of ammunition for each gun. At 5 o'clock in the evening the invasion force began to disembark and, by 2 o'clock on the morning of Thursday 23 February, everybody had landed and the last invasion of Britain had begun. It did not take long before the troops started looting and drinking. On the British side, the locals started mustering, especially the Pembroke Fencibles, a volunteer infantry regiment. Yet there were only 250–300 soldiers to meet an invasion force of approximately 900 men and, what was worse, their commander, Thomas Knox, had never been in any situation more difficult than an argument over a broken fence. He led his men back to the fort and waited.

Meanwhile, preparations were being made in Haverfordwest, the mayor having set up an internal command in a local inn. The navy, too, was organising and harassing the French luggers and word was got to Knox to hold the enemy and await reinforcements under Lord Cawdor, who commanded the Castlemartin Yeomanry, more amateur soldiers. In the meantime, the French got more drunk and more disorganised. Seemingly paralysed, Tate did not move position and a group of locals tried their own sneak attack, but to little effect. Things were now out of Tate's control as skirmishes broke out and drunken Frenchmen fired at the local clock, mistaking it for the enemy! Local women now joined in. Jemima Fawr (Jemima the Great), a middle-aged cobbler with pitchfork in hand, rounded up twelve Frenchmen. The British had organised little in the way of resistance, but Tate was under the impression that his force was surrounded and sent his second in command to negotiate a surrender. Cawdor, realising his luck, talked his tiny force up. In actuality, Tate not only outnumbered the British two to one, but after his surrender went on to pretend that the British force consisted of 7,000 well-trained regular troops. It was a victory for the yeomanry, who were awarded the battle honour in 1853, and for Welsh women, several of whom had helped in the humiliation of the French. Prisoners were exchanged over the next two years. Tate returned to America, but vanished into history, perhaps dying on the trip back.

Thereafter it would be harder to convince anyone in the French Directory of the point of an invasion. The Irish émigrés persisted, nevertheless, and with the war in Ireland raging and a republic already declared in Wexford, they felt that they had cause for optimism. They did not know that the fighting was dying down and that the Wexford experiment was already history. Still the French prevaricated. The moment might be lost in delay. Then a miracle happened and the fleet was gathered. On 6 August General Joseph Humbert and 1,000 men sailed for the west coast. They arrived on the 23rd and declared for a third time a republic on Irish shores. This time it was the Republic of Connaught. Again the rebels took heart, especially when the French routed a force of British at the 'Races of Castlebar'. On 17 September, Tone and a further force left Brest. Meanwhile, the clouds of disaster again descended. Humbert was defeated at the Battle of Ballinamuck and surrendered. The French were treated honourably as prisoners of war and fêted in Dublin; their Irish allies were merely butchered. Tone was captured on 12 October when his ship, lurking off the north-west coast was taken by the British. He was rushed to Dublin, but was able to cut his throat in jail, dying in agony on the 19th. The rebellion was at an end as, one by one, the rebel leaders were hunted down and executed.

Ireland was left a ruin: over 30,000 had died; villages and towns had been burnt to the ground; families were wrecked; thousands were homeless, without food or shelter; the country had been turned into an armed camp, with Protestants and Catholics at each other's throats; torture and murder were commonplace and hardly to be commented upon; death touched everything. There was to be no more nonsense about Irish wishes either. Indeed, the Irish parliament was disbanded and control handed over to London, its main buildings turned over to other uses. Without sufficient numbers at Westminster, the Irish vote dwindled and was silent for almost 100 years. Tony Small, Fitzgerald's loyal friend, was free to roam the world after his master's death, but he was also rootless and homeless. He and his family went to London, where his wife, at least, made a living as a seamstress. Small died some time later of an illness, unknown and unremarked.[4]

Chapter Six

The Woman Clothed with the Sun

The end of the 1798 insurrection was a problem for the Government, who now had many thousands of prisoners too dangerous to leave in Ireland. They opted for transporting them to Australia, now the main penal colony since the loss of America in 1786.[1] Defenders and United Irishmen soon began arriving – no ordinary prisoners, but articulate, often enfranchised men who could read, write and plot. Moreover, the Irish rebels numbered among them many priests, who were also educated and influential. The fear that the British had effectively exported revolution was never far away and the idea of a convict republic continued to be a worry for almost sixty years. To make matters worse, there were very few women and even fewer people who had emigrated of their own free will. Australia was therefore a gigantic social experiment where attitudes had to be relaxed. As so many of the prisoners were Catholic, they were allowed to hear open mass. Many were granted parcels of land to work. Nevertheless, where sedition was suspected, the authorities were harsh. In 1806, for instance, one Joseph Smallsalts received 100 lashes for merely saying that he agreed with Thomas Paine.

Irishmen resumed the war against the English in Australia and began to plot for a convict rebellion. Samuel Marsden, the 'flogging parson', caught wind of this plot and decided to flog his way to the evidence. Indeed, he thought of all the Irish as merely an 'ignorant and savage race'. Maurice Fitzgerald, a middle-aged Cork man, was flogged until the 'flesh and skin' blew into onlookers' faces. Paddy Calvin (or Colvin), another victim, got 300 lashes, until his 'haunches were … jelly'.

Marsden, although cheated of his pike-heads, was correct that the Irish were plotting. On 4 March 1804 the Irish rose, led by Philip Cunningham, a storeman. They took Castle Hill, a little settlement, with the intention of moving on to Parramatta, a convict colony, and marching on Sydney. A password was sorted out, 'St Peter', and, on receiving this, those inside Parramatta were to rise too. Yet again, however, the United Irishmen were infiltrated by a spy, a thatcher called Keogh, and he alerted the garrison. Encouraged by Cunningham's 'Now my boys, Liberty or Death!', the rebels, between 250 and 400 strong, marched on Parramatta, gleaning weaponry from homesteads and farms on the way and even attacking a notorious 'flogger' and beating him up. The very reverend and very worried Marsden thought prudence best and took a boat downriver to Sydney. News had preceded him, however, and Governor King ordered a detachment of fifty-two soldiers of the New South Wales Corps to march to Parramatta, where they arrived at dawn on 5 March, led by a Major Johnston.

Meanwhile, the rebels had gathered on a mound which they called Vinegar Hill, after the battle back in Ireland. The major and a Catholic priest now went to negotiate. The two sides were wary of each other but Cunningham and Johnston went to parley nevertheless. The major and his adjutant were both on horseback and, instead of negotiating, promptly beat the rebel leader with the butts of their pistols and dragged him into the ranks of soldiers, who then opened fire. The subsequent 'battle', for mêlée it more properly was, saw fifteen rebels dead and

Cunningham badly wounded. The rebels broke and ran; the soldiers hunted them down. Cunningham was immediately seized and strung up from the door-frame outside the local government office in Parramatta, while the rest were rounded up and tried on 8 March. Eight others were finally condemned and hanged too. The hangings were distributed around the colony to show 'what the declared slogan of Death of Liberty really meant'. The bodies were, moreover, hung in chains like common thieves. Others were flogged or forced to work the coal seams as virtual slaves on Coal River (later Newcastle). Interestingly, four Protestants and two Englishmen were among the hanged, the whole series of events being as much an English as an Irish affair. Needless to say, no pike-heads were ever found.

Troubles in Ireland, artisan discontent and even the threat of French invasion, however serious, were merely sideshows to Britain's main defence policy during the Revolutionary wars. What would be the effect if the Royal Navy went on strike, rendering Britain defenceless? This, however, was precisely what occurred.

Naval life was harsh, dirty and violent but it was also comradely and communal, where any action by an officer considered too tyrannical might spark an on-board revolution. In April 1796 the men of the *Shannon* complained in a letter about their captain's over-authoritarian manner. The letter stated that the sailors were all 'true Englishmen ... born free but now "slaves"'. The sailors evidently knew their *Rights of Man*, by hearsay if nothing else, and were certainly willing to make it clear that their duties were undertaken by mutual trust, not by mere demand. With French Republican armies triumphant in Europe and a French fleet capable of reaching Ireland, the Lords of the Admiralty were quite aware of their responsibility for the security of the realm. So also were the sailors, men very often dragged into the service. Of 120,000 personnel (sailors, marines and officers), only one-fifth were volunteers. The scarcity of men willing to serve had forced the Admiralty to bring in a quota system which began to impress better-educated men, men who could write and who could articulate their grievances. Tyrant officers, poor food and pay arrears sparked the first disturbances at Spithead, off Portsmouth.

The sailors began forming discussion groups and then protest groups on the anchored warships, and boats rowed between with news of debates aboard each vessel. A petition was then sent to the Lords of the Admiralty asking for redress of a variety of grievances, a central feature of which was low pay. The petition, anonymous except for the names of the ships, was sent via Lord Howe, but the 'sailors' friend' ignored the request, in possible anticipation of his replacement by Lord Bridport. Bridport in turn reported the appearance of 'disagreeable combinations' (that is, unions) on board the ships of the fleet, and Earl Spencer, First Lord of the Admiralty, warned him to look out for troublemakers.

Spencer decided to send the fleet to sea to keep the sailors busy. Bridport feared a mutiny and that the sailors would refuse to sail. Spencer insisted and sent orders to arrest mutineers. The sailors meanwhile made it clear that they would sail only on redress of their demands. They insisted they were loyal but also that they were getting impatient with their lordships: 'we flatter ourselves with hopes that we shall obtain our wishes for they had better go to war with the whole globe than with their own subjects'[2] was the message sent from the sailors' committee of the *Royal Sovereign* to the *Defence* during April. Their lordships became increasingly concerned that full rebellion was only moments away. They were correct.

During the next few days, a full mutiny in a number of vessels was beginning to paralyse the Channel Fleet. Delegates from the crews toured each ship and every sailor signed up to their demands; rules were devised and officers unwilling to abide by the sailors' wishes or who had made themselves disagreeable were sent ashore. Meanwhile, ships' discipline was to be maintained by the crews themselves and officers were to be treated with respect.

Leader of the delegates was Valentine Joyce, a 26-year-old quartermaster's mate from the *Royal George*, and it was with him that
Lords Bridport and Spencer would have to negotiate. By now,
the red flag flew on the mainmast of every ship.

Joyce and his delegates met Spencer at the Fountain Inn in
Portsmouth and, after some discussion, got concessions on pay
but not conditions. They also, however, demanded a full royal
pardon (in order to escape punishment), for which Spencer
would have to return to London. Finally the pardon was
obtained and read aboard each ship, allowing Bridport again to
gather a fleet to sail against the French. On 24 April a part of the
Channel Fleet finally got under way, those ships still paralysed
by disputes with officers left at anchor until a resolution could
be found.

Things were not quite as they seemed: other squadrons
of the fleet began to mutiny until, having had enough, the
Admiralty ordered captains to prepare their marines (on-board
soldiers acting as police) for action. It was a provocative stance
and the consequences were dire. Instead of taking their lead
from Bridport's move into the Channel, the ships still anchored
refused to sail, their crews running up the red flag and jeering at
their officers. Spencer wrote despairingly to Pitt, 'total destruction is near'. Bridport collapsed under the strain: 'I cannot
command a fleet as all authority is taken from me.... My mind is
too deeply wounded.... I am so unwell that I can scarcely hold
my pen to write these sentiments of distress.'[3]

Two French fleets, one at Brest, the other at the Texel in
Holland (then the Republic of Batavia), were reported as preparing for the invasion of Ireland. Pitt needed to act fast, and he
did, getting an Act of Parliament improving pay and conditions
passed through all its stages by 10 May, when it received royal
assent. Lord Howe and his wife toured the disaffected ships, and
tempers were cooled when Howe agreed to dismiss the long list
of blacklisted officers. The red flag was run down and eight more
fighting ships joined the line. On 14 May the Spithead Mutiny

ended in the great cabin of the *Royal William*, where toasts were drunk and a ceremonial dinner arranged for the following day.

From a sailor's perspective, the mutiny had been a success and recriminations non-existent; from a Government perspective, the entire affair must have left a bitter taste. Indeed, the Government had been convinced from the start that the trouble was all the fault of a revolutionary minority. To this end they had commissioned a London magistrate, Aaron Graham, to leave his work in Hatton Garden and go as a spy to Portsmouth to discover the ringleaders. Graham was to search out Jacobins and United Irishmen. Thomas Grenville, brother of the Foreign Secretary, was convinced of such a conspiracy, writing during May that 'I cannot help fearing evil is ... deeply rooted in the influence of Jacobin emissaries and the Corresponding Society. I am more and more convinced that Jacobin management and influence is at the bottom of this evil.' Burke jumped to the conclusion that Valentine Joyce was a 'Belfast clubest [*sic*]', one of the 16,515 known Irishmen in the naval service, of whom Burke assumed the majority were troublemakers. He was wrong on both counts: Joyce was a Jerseyman and no United Irish propaganda ever surfaced.

Meanwhile, Graham arrived in Portsmouth on 11 May, settled into an inn and immediately began reporting to his boss, John King, Under-secretary of State to the Home Department, who then passed on what had been discovered to the Home Secretary, Lord Portland. Having 'hastily devoured a mutton chop', Graham was on the case, an early version of Sherlock Holmes. His first act was to try to speak to Joyce, but the plan was too crude, so he struck up a friendship with Joyce's mother, hoping thereby to trick Joyce into a compromising admission. This too failed, so he tried bribing the delegate-leader of the *Pompee*, Quartermaster Melvin. Again failure, as Melvin knew of no prior conspiracy by United Irishmen or Jacobins. From now on, Graham took to disguise, travelled the taverns and hospitals, chatted up sailors and their girls and was ever busy – all to no avail. Exhausted, Graham finally concluded that so great is the abominable itch (among all descriptions of persons) for inventing something new, and so common is the practice of circulating as a matter of fact what is considered only as a story of the day, that treason itself might easily be planned, executed, and publicly talked of long before it would be seriously noticed by the magistrates... . I am persuaded from the conversation I have had with so many of the sailors that if any man on earth had dared openly to avow his intention of using them as instruments to distress the country his life would have paid forfeit. Nothing like want of loyalty to the king or attachment to the government can be traced in the business.[4]

Burke and Grenville might have been miffed by the news, but Lord Portland and Pitt could relax, and Graham could return to more leisurely meals at the Hatton Garden magistrates' office.

The navy's troubles had certainly not gone away. Almost immediately following the conclusion of business at Portsmouth, other mutinies began to break out. On the whole, these were contained, all except those of the Nore squadron anchored off the Thames. Here, the demands made at Portsmouth took on a political tone much more threatening to the defence of Britain and much more worrisome for the Government. Here again, the red flag fluttered at each main mast, committees of delegates formed, ships were seized and officers ejected. Worse still, at the height of the disturbances it appeared that some ships might even sail to France and join the enemy, while an actual gun-fight did indeed break out between the squadron's own ships. The fact that these mutineers also protested their complete loyalty and played loyal music on the King's birthday would avail them nothing.

As at Portsmouth, each sailor signed an oath of loyalty to the cause, itself punishable by death or transportation and clearly interpretable as conspiratorial. Having bound their fate to that of the cause, the sailors looked to their delegate-leaders to write

to the Admiralty setting out their demands. This they did in a
'manifesto' delivered on 6 June to Lord Northesk. It stated in
uncompromising language the new doctrine of 'human rights'
learned from the American and French experience and so distasteful to the Government: 'His Majesty's Ministers too well
know our intentions, which are founded on the laws of humanity, honour and national safety – long since trampled under foot
by those who ought to have been friends to us – the sole protectors of your laws and property.'[5]

The manifesto, nevertheless, repeated the loyalty of the
crews, who 'do not wish to adopt the plan of a neighbouring
nation [i.e. France]', despite the spreading rumour that that was
exactly what they wanted to do. With things left unresolved by
7 June, revolutionary fervour had begun to affect the delegates,
the committee leaders resolving:

> shall we who have endured the toils of a tedious, disgrace-
> ful war, be the victims of tyranny and oppression which vile,
> gilded, pampered knaves, wallowing in the lap of luxury,
> choose to load us with? Shall we who amid the rage of the
> tempest and war of jarring elements, undaunted climb the
> unsteady cordage and totter on the topmast's dreadful height,
> suffer ourselves to be treated worse than the dogs of London
> Streets? ... No, The Age of Reason has at length revolved.
> Long have we been endeavouring to find ourselves men. Now
> we find ourselves so. We will be treated as such.[6]

Sailors may have wanted redress of grievances and may have
become militant; they did not become revolutionaries and the
central committee's order to blockade London, sail to Holland
or join the revolutionary apostles of the 'rights of man' fell on
deaf ears. Nevertheless, the fleet did not sail as ordered on 9 June,
but by 16 June the last ship had thrown away its red flag and surrendered. This time, the Government would make examples of
the mutineers.

First on the list was the leader of the central committee, Richard Parker, the son of a respectable Exeter baker and corn factor. Parker had enjoyed a 'liberal education' but had defied his parents and gone to sea. While on service, it was said he had argued with his captain, 'gone over to France and was a spectator, if not an active agent, in what passed there in the time of Robespierre',[7] or so his accusers said. More significantly, it was also said he wanted to be the 'Naval Oliver Cromwell', finding his opportunity on being elected 'President of the Committee of Delegates' at the Nore. Despite being a 'worthy good man', something not disputed at his trial, Parker clearly allowed himself to be deluded into taking on the mantle of a revolutionary hero. His wife actually suggested to magistrates that he was 'deranged' (perhaps a play for leniency), but his belief that he could lead the fleet as a prize for the enemy or blockade the capital suggests someone whose own destiny was coming unhinged from the more mundane demands of colleagues.

Parker himself was unable to answer for his growing extreme conduct, except to excuse it as a moment of madness. In a letter bearing his own signature, he insisted that all the sailors were loyal and 'an oath has been taken by the delegates ... that they never had any communication with Jacobins or traitors'.[8] Yet here, too, was a certain irony, for Parker must have known that his actions would be such that they would be precisely those that would get him accused of being a Jacobin. Parker, after all, was a well-educated if capricious man, who had been a naval volunteer and then, after failure as a teacher in Scotland and landing in debtors' prison, had bought himself out of debt by joining the navy under the quota system. Thus Parker fitted the revolutionary profile almost perfectly: well-educated, impoverished, intelligent and rootless. Inherently a Jacobin by lifestyle and choice, if not also by acquaintance with the radical literature of his time, Parker was a revolutionary despite his own conscious desires, the nature of revolt in his blood, first and last leader of the so-called Floating Republic. Unlike Joyce, Parker was tried and hanged, his body suspended from the yardarm of a warship on 30 June 1797. Of his colleagues, sixty others were flogged, imprisoned or transported and fourteen hanged. In all, 400 courts martial were conducted at the Nore.

One mystery remains at the very heart of both the Spithead and Nore mutinies. What was the significance of the hoisting of red flags on the mainmasts of all the ships in revolt? Although it was often used as a sign of no quarter (black flags were more often used), the adoption of the flag as a symbol was sufficiently strange to require explanation at Parker's trial. All agreed that the use of a red flag was one of 'defiance' and 'mutiny'. One officer quizzed by his lordships was asked, 'Have you ever understood what the red flag meant?' His reply was itself a matter of personal confusion, for he had been told that the sailors 'wished to establish it and fight under it, for the Dutch had stolen it from the English and they [the sailors] wished to restore it'.[9] A dumbfounded silence must have followed in the court as the officer concluded, 'That was the reply made to me.' One of the first appearances of the red flag of the people was as odd and mysterious as its explanation.

Massacres in Ireland might be expected, but rebellion in the navy and during a war was unthinkable. The times were out of joint and there were many who interpreted the events of the past few years as heralding the Apocalypse and the Second Coming. There were now political citizens, but there were also a growing number of citizens of the soul. The visionary hopes which germinated before the Civil War left a legacy of seventeenth-century religiosity that greatly appealed to the sectarian and nonconformist nature of republicanism, especially to those whose actions were prompted by personal morality alone and a feeling of self-selecting grace. The new revolutionary elect created their own historical myths and acted to make them reality; contemporary events became elevated to steps in a predestined plan and signs and wonders could be found everywhere. It is in this light that William Blake's 'Jerusalem' from 1804 may be read

– a strange apocalyptic call to the last judgement couched in the language of St John, Elijah and the Industrial Revolution. The poem balances desire for a future Jerusalem with the restoration of the 'lamb of God' to 'England's green and pleasant land'. This revolutionary conservatism looked to ancient times in order to oppose Toryism and capitalism or Georgian exploitation and corruption. Blake's mysticism, secular and yet spiritual, combined elements of Emanuel Swedenborg's teaching and Joanna Southcott's weirdness. The combination, mixing slowly with the more radical elements of Methodism formed one pillar of the growing labour movement that finally found its political voice in the Labour Party. Such visionary delights and their self-affirming sense of rightness gave working-class radicals a sense of communal solidarity as the religion of Dissenting chapels became the ideology of proletarian struggle. The proletariat became the embodiment of authenticity when all other classes proved false, corrupt and illusory.

The last years of the eighteenth century seemed out of joint to more than just people of quality. Just as in 1649, there was a visionary air about the time. Meetings of the London Corresponding Society might well include Swedenborgians or followers of the prophetess Southcott. Nonconformism attracted the free-thinking, the fundamentalist and the eccentric. Borne up by revolutionary ideals were those who saw the millennial in the mesmeric wands of Franz Mesmer or in the Celtic mists of Ossian and druidism. Occultism became central to many secret societies and the machinations of the continental Illuminés gave the revolution hermetic and occult thought that was drawn in part from the Welsh deism of David Williams. Some dreamed of the conversion of the Jews on the last days. This was one of the dreams of Priestley, whose ideas crossed the Atlantic and re-emerged in the spiritual revival of the 1840s.

Many of these strange, evanescent, but powerful ideas fed the iconic tale of the period, Mary Shelley's *Frankenstein* (1818). Its first edition (not yet revised and Christianised) betrayed its political intent to contemporary readers: the people, to Burke, were 'a species of political monster'. Victor Frankenstein himself was the product of the Bavarian university of Ingolstadt, itself the home of the Illuminati, blamed by many as the fount of the Revolution. Shelley's creature may have been a fictional and symbolic monster but it, too, was based on the strange revolutionary sciences of mesmeric fluids, ether and electricity. One influence on Shelley's fable was Andrew Crosse, who spent his time at his home in Somerset experimenting with the invisible fluidity of electricity. Both Franklin and Priestley had done the same, Priestley producing *The History of Electricity* in 1767. In 1807 Crosse began a series of experiments in electro-crystallisation, leading, apparently, to an attempt to produce electrically induced life. He succeeded to his own satisfaction in 1853, when working on crystals of silica.

The Terror of the French Revolution was unprecedented and, to many, inexplicable. Its nature gave vent to every sort of conspiracy theory. Abbé de Barruel wrote one of the first conspiracy theories with his *Memoirs of a Jacobin* (1800). He believed the Revolution was a conspiracy by Templars, Bavarian Illuminati and heretics to destroy religion. The puppet-masters had Robespierre and other leaders under their control and sacrificed them when they could no longer be controlled. A strange Scotsman called John Robison followed with *Proofs of a Conspiracy* in 1801, in which he blamed the Illuminati for the Jacobin Club and the French Revolution as well as the creation of the mysterious 'aetheric fluid' used to undermine the British constitution.

The result of these theories was a political and cultural paranoia. Paranoid fantasies parasitically attached themselves to the new scientific materialism and, in a psychologically potent reversal of the facts, turned materialism itself into an occult and mystical ethereal 'machine' for the control of history. The secret cabal of puppet-masters was hiding in the sewers, in gothic laboratories or even in the room next door. Such was the fantasy of James Tilly Matthews, who in the 1790s took a fancy to the idea that the Jacobins had installed a machine below parliament and were hypnotising its leading politicians. Thomas Erskine, 'outrageously French' in his sympathies, had risen to criticise the Government only to sit down in mid-sentence, and Pitt appeared to be sleepwalking. Could this be the Jacobins' secret weapon, a brass cylinder giving off an invisible gas which united all things and could be harnessed to cause 'fluid locking'. Such delusion got Matthews locked away, but other ideas just as strange were released by revolutionary hysteria.

Crosse's insectoid creatures dancing in front of a microscope were strange indeed, but not so amazing now that there existed a revolutionary gaze capable of seeing the invisible unity of things. The French Cult of the Supreme Being was a manifestation of an obsession with nature. For William Wordsworth, newly arrived in Britain and escaping from a pregnant French girlfriend, nature was all-in-all, its essence pantheistic, expressed in the ordinary and ignored aspects of rural life. Wordsworth's romanticism was an expression of the obsession with imagination and its ability not only to create from nothing, but also to penetrate to the heart of the invisible, connective threads of cosmic reality.

Such invisible threads were central to the discoveries and practices of Mesmer. Mesmerism was the bridge between the occult and scientific, the spiritual and material realms that French and British revolutionists sought as the philosopher's stone of a new consciousness. The cult of mesmerism was directly related to the cult of the imagination and the intriguing possibilities of imaginative susceptibility. What could be influenced could be mesmerised and what could be mesmerised could be controlled. Was it beyond the realms of possibility that invisible influence could be use in place of pikes and pistols to destroy a dynasty or kill a cabinet? The age of paranoia had begun – a never-ending conspiracy of the mind against itself.

Alongside madness and mesmerism there was religious mania too. The 'prophet' Richard Brothers was born in Newfoundland in 1757 and educated at Woolwich before becoming a naval lieutenant in 1783. Discharged on half-pay (the usual course of events when naval officers were not wanted), he refused to take the money if it required his swearing an oath to the Crown. Penniless, he was therefore sent to the workhouse, where he declared himself the 'Napoleon of the Almighty' and began to prophesy. Brothers became so troublesome that he was actually indicted for treason, but was found to be so entirely mad (perhaps he was schizophrenic) that he was confined as a criminal lunatic. Yet, even in this state, he gained a number of followers, including John Finlayson, with whom he finally came to live and in whose house in Marylebone he died in 1824.

He was not the only one to see the light of revelation. Of all those who believed that the millennium was coming, the most significant was Joanna Southcott. She was born the fourth child of William and Hannah Southcott of Ottery St Mary, Devon, in 1750. She grew up to become a proud, hard-working girl who had a gift for prophecy that brought her to the attention of a wider public and inevitably led to accusations of lunacy and fraud. Joanna had begun prophesying in 1792. There can be no coincidence with the date. Priestley, for instance, published the sermon, 'The Present State of Europe Compared with the Ancient Prophecies' in 1794. In that, he had seen the French Revolution as the fulfilment of the apocalyptic message of Revelations. Southcott had already identified Napoleon as the anti-Christ and had distributed papers on which she had written 'seals' to protect the wearer. On 22 October 1803 the *Leeds Mercury* noted that 'The object of her visit is to distribute Celestial Seals to the faithful: and as these seals ... will protect the possessor from all danger even at the cannon's mouth, we recommend the Volunteers to lay in a stock preparatory to the arrival of Bonaparte and his sharp-shooters'. In a credulous and worried age, with rapid change and constant war, Southcott appealed to all levels of the population. Indeed, most interestingly, her appeal seems to have been to the more educated middle class, who found solace in her teachings. Many of her dreams, for instance, related ordinary domestic activities (the squabble of a cat and dog) to the wider picture of the war with France.

Finally unable to persuade the Church that her revelations were real, she 'became' pregnant at the age of 65, declaring the baby the 'Prince of Peace' and calling him Shiloh. Despite her age, many believed her to be pregnant and her followers laid aside numerous gifts for the baby. So famous was she at this point that there was even a cartoon by Thomas Rowlandson (8 September 1814) and she was soon the talk of medical society, who were unsure if it actually was a pregnancy or a cancerous tumour. Inevitably she died on 27 December 1814, with no sign of Shiloh. The 'woman clothed with the sun', as Southcott called herself, died with devoted followers who still eagerly awaited the birth of the Saviour.

One of these followers was her faithful companion Jane Townley, the daughter of the High Sheriff of Lancashire, who became Southcott's supporter and eventually believed that Shiloh was the Prince Regent himself. There was also the Revd Thomas Foley, an Anglican churchman and guardian of Southcott's mysterious closed box, which was to be opened when twenty-four bishops were willing to sit in judgment at a time of great crisis. Foley remained faithful to the end and even today the box is advertised in newspapers awaiting its opening.

William Sharp, an engraver and friend of Paine, and John Horne Tooke, a member of the Society for Constitutional Information, also believed in Richard Brothers. There was also George Turner, who was so sufficiently problematic to be committed to a Quaker asylum. After his release, he too predicted the coming of Shiloh but died in 1821 still awaiting his appearance. It was an age of superstitious belief and credulousness. A Leeds woman by the name of Mary Bateman, a disciple of Brothers, even claimed that her hen was laying eggs with the message 'Christ is Coming'. Such beliefs were taken seriously by many.

More importantly, it was from this milieu that many of the revolutionary voices came. Thus around Oldham at the time there were a number of free-thinking religious groups who had little affiliation with more mainstream religion but who believed in the Second Coming, and who rejected original sin and even the afterlife. John Wesley, preaching Methodism, came across these groups in the 1750s and noted a 'whole clan of infidel peasants'. Such chapels were often attacked by loyalists, as was the one in Dobb Lane, Manchester, the mob apparently crying out to the radicals that 'you are Jacobins, Painites and Presbyterians, you are enemies of your King and Country and deserve to be killed'.[10]

Chapter Seven

Drinking Blood with Monsieur Robespierre

The British reform movement of the 1790s centred on two quite different societies led by two very different men. One was the Society for Constitutional Information (SCI), a gentlemen's organisation chaired by John Cartwright, a Lincolnshire country squire. The other was the London Corresponding Society (LCS) founded by a poor shoemaker called Thomas Hardy.[1] The SCI was known as the Hampden Club, after the great seventeenth-century parliamentarian. Soon Hampden Clubs were springing up all over the country.

Despite his radical credentials, Cartwright belonged to polite society. He had a family with a Tudor pedigree, received an education at minor, but respectable schools and was commissioned as a midshipman. His younger brother Edmund went to Oxford and invented the first steam-powered loom, thus completing in the two brothers both the cause and the cure of the economic and political discontent of the early Industrial Revolution. By 1762 Cartwright was a lieutenant on HMS *Guernsey*, stationed off Newfoundland, where he noted the fact that land speculators exploited both the Irish who had emigrated and the local fishermen, until they turned 'the wantonness of their cruelties' on the 'Red Indians'. When he returned from Canada, Cartwright was a changed man. He had become a reformer. In 1774 he wrote his first political pamphlet on American independence, in which he declared, '1688 ... gave Englishmen their liberty', which itself was 'inherent and inalienable'. Cartwright knew he was on dangerous ground and so he published anonymously. He would not remain in the shadows for long, for he now had a purpose – reform: 'Mine was a Tory family I am told, and Popery was once its religion; but as for myself, I shall be neither Papist nor Tory, until I can believe in the infallibility of popes and kings.'[2]

By 1776 Cartwright was a major in the Nottinghamshire militia, upholding the Establishment, and, at the same time, a radical producing *Take Your Choice!*, a book dedicated to parliamentary reform. The book argued for an electoral roll to include men over 18 (although not women), equal constituencies and yearly elections. The corrupt nature of government was, the book argued, almost wholly the fault of its history, which dated back to the supposed usurpation of English rights by Norman invaders. The Norman yoke had to be destroyed if reform was to be possible. This recovery of imagined lost freedoms had one inherent logical consequence of great significance, for it clearly suggested 'a momentous transition: from the recovery of rights which used to exist to the pursuit of rights because they ought to exist: from historical mythology to political philosophy'.[3]

Cartwright needed an organisation to put his message across. He already participated in the debating societies that discussed such things as colonial rights and electoral reform, but these issues were not central to the political agenda until Charles Fox, the leader of the opposition Whigs, decided to create a reform group, the Westminster Committee, to focus discontent against the current government. Cartwright joined what was for Fox a partially cynical exercise, but which took off in earnest, adopting Cartwright's own reform ideas. Cartwright himself then formed a group to publish the pamphlets and books that would propagandise on behalf of the cause and it was this group that became known as the SCI. The reformers included three dukes, three earls and three lords. There were no working men, but working men soon took note. The SCI had its first meetings during 1780, with the Gordon Riots still fresh in the minds of its members.

Thomas Hardy made his living at a workshop in Piccadilly and it was here that he first heard about reform in the chit-chat of his wealthy clients. Hardy was the son of a sailor who had drowned in 1760. Thomas had learned to read and write but had had to become an apprentice to a shoemaker, and finally left to work his trade in Glasgow. In 1774 he gave up life in Scotland (having also learned bricklaying as a sideline) to travel by fishing boat to London. He was a tough 6-footer eager for work, and slowly but surely he built up a business. It was never very successful but it kept Hardy and his new wife, Lydia, from the poverty which hovered just beyond his door and which would later threaten to destroy him. Religious by nature and nonconformist by persuasion, Hardy and his wife attended chapel meetings in Covent Garden and Hoxton, but by slow degrees Hardy was becoming a political animal; the French Revolution would see to that.

Some of the impetus came from the rhetoric of Unitarian preacher Richard Price, son of Welshman Rhys Prys, himself a founding figure in the revival of Welsh culture. Price had addressed the London Revolutionary Society at the London Tavern with a sermon on liberty. Although the revolution celebrated in its name was the Glorious Revolution of 1688, by 1790 the society was a debating group for various radical dissenters. Price had congratulated the French National Assembly, who had asserted the 'inalienable rights of mankind'. He must have been only too aware that such comments were likely to encourage Tory reaction. It soon came. First, a bill to repeal the Test and Corporation Acts (excluding non-communicants of the Church of England from holding local office) was defeated, as was a bill to widen the franchise slightly. Looking to answer the near sedition of Price's sermon, Burke penned his classic defence of conservatism. He, in turn, prompted Paine's reply, *Rights of Man*. The stage was set for conflict between reformers and traditionalists, between defence of the old ways and a chance of the new.

Meanwhile, Price's book supporting the Americans, *Observations on the Nature of Civil Liberty* (1776), had greatly influenced Hardy, as had Price's call for a network of corresponding reform societies, which had first appeared in *Discourse on the Love of our Country*. The demands of the Corresponding Societies were not merely political. Already, Hardy was pondering the link between political reform and economic betterment. As Hardy considered what to do, he may have discussed his plans for a new society with a lodger, Olaudah Equiano, a former slave and now one of the up-and-coming black middle class living in London in the eighteenth century.

Hardy founded the London Corresponding Society of the Unrepresented Part of the People of Great Britain (later known as the LCS) in January 1792. Hardy, his wife and a few friends and relations met at the Bell in Exeter Street, near the Strand. One of those present, William Gow, a watchmaker, asked Hardy, 'Is it a revolution you're thinking of like the Frenchies?' Hardy had replied in the affirmative but as yet without the intention of having the King's head in a basket. The society's second meeting saw nine working men eating bread and cheese, drinking ale and discussing how to alleviate their poverty by reforming politics. Subs were collected: 8*d* (perhaps one man was too poor to pay). Hardy was elated and told Lydia that night, 'There! With those eight pennies we are going to reform the House of Commons!' Unlike the SCI, the LCS was a working man's organisation. It soon had sixty members divided into six neighbourhood 'divisions'. New LCS divisions kept opening and soon there was a British network, with societies such as those in Sheffield, which had been founded earlier in 1791, enjoying a membership of

2,000. Membership was restricted to the sober and the God-fearing, smoking being strictly forbidden at meetings, as was alcohol later. Hero of the LCS was Paine.

Cartwright of the SCI thought Paine a mere hooligan and had already made plans in 1792 to join with local landowners in Lincolnshire to put down a labour dispute on his farmland. He was for reform, not revolution, and on 11 April he formed a middle-way reform group called the Friends of the People to ward off the dangerous revolutionary tendencies of the LCS, even though Hardy himself was nothing other than a constitutional reformist. Things were coming apart and old political allegiances becoming unclear. Panic was to set in when, on 14 May 1792, after publication of Paine's second part of *Rights of Man*, his printer, J.S. Jordan, was summoned for sedition. On 21 May, a proclamation was issued by the Government against the publication of 'seditious writing' and its use by those corresponding with 'sundry persons in foreign parts'. Despite Cartwright's attitude, the SCI printed 1,200 copies of Paine's own self-defence of the book, as well as 6,000 copies of its own attack on the King's proclamation. In August, Paine was made a French citizen and invited to represent a French constituency (Pas-de-Calais). The Government issued an arrest warrant but missed him by twenty minutes as he left Dover.

At the same time, the LCS had grown sufficiently to suggest a threat to the Government. They were hounded by magistrates and refused the licence of public rooms. They were also honeycombed with spy networks. One spy, called 'Mercator' (possibly George Lynam), reported that the LCS debated Paine's ideas and talked 'rebellion'. Another, George Munro, thought the membership 'the very lowest tradesmen', who seemed to be almost entirely made up of 'Scotch shoemakers'. By the winter of 1790 the LCS had grown to over 600 members who were dedicated to reform, many recruited as a result of the crass propaganda put out against the society by the Government. On 1 November 1792 a delegation of the LCS met the French ambassador; on

21 January 1793 Louis XVI was guillotined; on 1 February France was at war with Britain. Membership of the SCI or LCS now looked little less than treason.

The revolution in France cast shadow or sunshine according to one's political disposition and economic or social standing. The activities of the French National Assembly were watched carefully by all sides in Britain and Ireland. Every change in what was a fluid situation was debated with urgency, not only by the ruling elite, but by ordinary shopkeepers and artisans, who had gained the name 'sans-culottes' across the Channel because they wore the unfashionable trousers disliked by gentlemen.

A British reformer of the period from 1789 to 1791 could look to France to see an example of a working constitutional monarchy, a fully elected assembly, almost universal democratic voting rights, a church stripped of its state power, a proper legal system and reform of local government. Yet there were more ominous warnings that threatened to undermine the Declaration of the Rights of Man which had been passed by the French in August 1789. Things were to change dramatically from 1792 until 1800.

During 1792, Louis XVI began to plot to regain his former power. France was embroiled in a foreign war which would last until Napoleon's downfall at Waterloo in 1815. Parts of France were already suffering a civil war and a major rebellion, aided by the invasion of Austrian and Prussian troops and supported by a landing at Toulon by the British. France's defence of the principles of the Revolution, however, included the storming of the Tuileries by the Paris Commune and the massacre of prisoners when the jails were overrun. The factions in the National Assembly were also at each other's throats and after the *coup d'état* carried out by the Paris Commune, the Committee of Public Safety and its local surveillance committees began an internal cleansing of political opponents. The new France was destined for 'the creation of a new race' and 'the republican state was ... the vehicle for the moral regeneration of the citizens who composed it'.[4] The virtuous minority who ran the Commune and the Committee of Public Safety saw themselves as the guardians of the Revolution and they knew instinctively the needs of the people, even if the people did not. Such ideological certainty (itself a new phenomenon because it was secular, all religion being abolished) treated all enemies as 'aristocrats'. During 1793 to 1794, 2,000–3,000 people were executed in Paris alone and 14,498 in the Paris area, south-east and west in total;[5] what was done was done *'dans le sens de la révolution'*. By 1799 the Terror had exhausted itself and Napoleon was dictator of France.

Before 1793, British reformers looked to France, if at all (they had the example of America), for a compassionate solution to political inequality. Britain had traditions of radicalism that France did not. If the politicisation of British and Irish individuals happened in the 1790s, then the legacy was at least as old as the seventeenth century, and that legacy itself was under severe pressure by the time of the war in America. French sansculottism was not quite the same as British Jacobinism, despite the use of a French *nom de guerre*.

Cartwright and the SCI argued not for a new set of rights and liberties but for a restitution of those that they believed had been usurped by William the Conqueror. Hardy of the LCS did the same; both men realised that the situation in France did not exactly match that of Britain, despite the fact that in November 1792 it was said that 5,000 'republicans and levellers' took to the streets to celebrate the victory of France's army of sansculottes against the might of *ancien régime* Prussia and Austria. The reformist tradition in Britain did not look forward as it did in France to a utopia based on moral regeneration, but to a recovery of a lost utopia. The SCI used a language perfectly understandable to the Diggers of the seventeenth century and their leader, Winstanley. This argument lost none of its mythic and symbolic force in the pamphlets of the SCI and LCS:

> This identified an original and highly democratic constitution shaped by the originally pure English spirit in the days

of the Saxons with their direct democracy of the Witan, their people's militia of the fyrd, their people's king chosen for ability and their scorn for aristocracy except a non-hereditary aristocracy of service. Corruption set in with William the Bastard and his Norman bandits ... the free Saxon spirit ... had finally been perverted at 1688 by coup d'etat of landowning malefactors.[6]

Winstanley would also have recognised the language of nonconformist Bible readers in the 1790s, steeped as they were in the prophetic language of the Old Testament. Winstanley's call to free Israel (the English) would be repeated by Hardy's call to arms, 'to your tents, O Israel'. It was a far cry from the French abolition of Catholicism and their creation of the Cult of the Supreme Being. British radicalism was also moribund once the American issue was settled. The French Revolution revived rather the older British reform movement, now tinged with a new visionary revolutionism few mainstream reformers cared about: 'What was needed now was an educational campaign to create "uniformity of sentiments" in favour of universal suffrage and annual parliaments, which would finish off Old Corruption. The French had begun with nothing but Catholic tyranny. Revolution was a necessity and the terror, therefore, comprehensible.'[7]

While the French were 'slaves' ... we [the English] were men'. Unlike the French, the English believed themselves 'drenched in the rhetoric of liberty, constitutionalism and the freeborn Englishman'. Indeed the term 'Frenchified' became fashionable during the period for everything un-English, foppish and intellectual, as William Godwin pointed out in his radical novel, *Caleb Williams*: 'They told me what a fine thing it was to be an Englishman, and about liberty and property ... and I find it is all a flam. Lord, what fools we be! Things are done under our very noses, and we know nothing of the matter; and a parcel of fellows with grave faces swear to us that such things never happen but in France.'[8]

As we have seen, when Thomas Carlyle came to write his history of the French Revolution, it was the revolution in America that he actually saw as decisive and which indeed was decisive for a British understanding of French events. Yet the American Founding Fathers had no desire to overthrow the 'natural' order of things. Indeed, Paine upheld property rights, but his writings unleashed another more radical set of sentiments which saw that property went hand in hand with political oppression, and both had to be tackled to produce social justice. The French Revolution clarified matters and turned debate into a European war. The Republican Convention of France was not a reform of government but its overthrow, precisely the annihilation of the old order and the destruction of its social hierarchy. Natural order based on property rights had been destroyed. What might follow? Wealthy British reformers looked to restore ancient rights seemingly usurped by the monarchy; the artisan class and then the poor looked for something quite different.

It was the British constitution that was central to radical British minds and for many its reform certainly came before its overthrow. Republicans were always marginal to the desire for reform and they drifted away from the American example that so suited the British debating and agitation societies, into the arms of French extremism and revolutionary sans-culottism. Here was meat for desperate men, men who thought the world stood on the brink of a new secular revelation. For men such as Godwin, father to Mary Shelley, father-in-law to Shelley and former Calvinist preacher, 'everything rung and was connected to the Revolution in France ... everything was soaked in this one event.' It was from this cataclysmic 'event' in history that Godwin developed his own brand of republicanism, without property or government and, perhaps, without God. 'There will be no war, no crimes, no administration of justice ... and no government,' Godwin declared in his *Enquiry Concerning Political Justice* of 1793. These were thoughts Godwin had developed since 1793 with radicals such as Horne Tooke and Thomas

Holcroft, who had been arraigned for treason in 1794. In such thoughts was an attempt to replace the arbitrary power of des-potism with reason and 'political justice'. It was a blasphemous and dangerous mixture of individualism and natural rights. It was also the origin of the later anarchist movement. The term 'citizen' now became a fashionable and subversive term for those with more than reform in mind.

Despite its aggressive stance between 1794 and 1820, the Government had few weapons with which to fight radicalism. The Cabinet was a tiny affair, a small gentlemen's club, which ran an even tinier civil service and which occasionally turned to a House of Commons where everybody knew or was related to everyone else, and the House of Lords, which effectively con-trolled the Commons and was itself home to the ruling class of Britain (and later Ireland). This was an effective machine for defending the status quo, making occasional tweaks to keep things running smoothly and more likely to approve private bills for canal building or enclosure rather than any major amend-ments to what had been laid down in 1688.

Without a police force, the Home Office ran a loose, ama-teur spy network, as did local magistrates, who reported to the various lord lieutenants of the counties and the Home Secretary. With the opening of hostilities with France, most town and country areas raised companies of yeomanry made up of gen-tlemen, farmers and retainers, or companies of militia, foot soldiers, consisting of artisans and workmen. It was vigilantism. Vigilantism was often all that stood between the aristocracy and their destruction. Wellington advised the Hampshire mag-istrates, for instance, 'to put themselves on horse back, each at the head of his own servants and retainers, grooms, huntsmen, game-keepers, armed with horsewhips, pistols, fowling pieces or what they could get, and to attack ... these mobs ... destroy them, and take and put in confinement those who could not escape.... It is astonishing how soon the country [will be] tran-quillised ... by the activity and spirit of the gentlemen.'[9]

More significantly, the local populations, especially in rural or county town locations (rather than Sheffield, Birmingham, Manchester or Bristol) were tightly knit, hierarchic communities where almost feudal bonds might still hold. Such bonds implied social obligations within a paternal system of rewards and responsibilities and within a system where many more householders held some sort of civic responsibilities (there was no real local bureaucratic structure) and therefore had a stake in the peace and prosperity of an area where their family might have been settled for centuries. In a world where everyone knew their place and the local squirearchy and established church were related by family ties and political affiliation, anyone threatening to 'turn the world upside down' would soon become a dangerous pariah. The best defence against such people was to hound them from the district, and magistrates and local squires would help the matter along by raising 'Church and King' clubs and then, with the promises of drink or pay, turned the groups loose in a semi-official riot.

British reformers of the 1790s divided into the wealthy, whose sense of justice was irked by political anomaly, and the middling and artisan groups for whom political reform would provide a platform for economic redress. Wealthy reformers, less tied to the economic worries of war and trade depression and who could weather poor harvests, could debate principles that had hard practical consequences for shoemakers, tailors, coal heavers or warehousemen. To the ruling county elite, both their gentlemanly opponents and the almost unmentionable 'working mechanics' were determined to smash up an old, trusted and natural order which had had its guarantee in the settlement brought about by William III. Lord North, speaking in the Lords during the debate on reform on 18 April 1785, defended the preponderance of 'country gentlemen' in parliament. They already represented the people both of the county and in the 'large boroughs'. According to North, 'the bulk and weight of the [Commons] ought always to be in the hands of the country gentlemen, who were ... the best and most respectable objects of the confidence of the people... . They were fitted by their education and their situation in life more peculiarly for members of parliament than almost any other description of men in the kingdom; besides, they had the greatest stake in the country.'[10]

By the 1790s, however, an almost religiously adhered-to consensus had been broken by the actions of the Americans and the French and the reading matter that had been pouring into Britain from abroad. No wonder that anyone opposed to the order of society was tarred as an atheist and blasphemer. It would not be the radicals, gentlemen or artisans who would make the situation revolutionary but the Government itself, which, perhaps quite rightly, saw its position, which it genuinely believed to be benevolent and right, under a sustained attack by the forces of secularism and democratic anarchy.

No better example of the reaction against radicalism can be found than in the government-inspired 'Church and King' clubs that arose when war broke out with France. The first of these, the Association for Preserving Liberty and Property against Republicans and Levellers, was founded by John Reeves, a barrister associated with the Government (and who was despised by radicals such as Thomas Spence). The first meeting, packed with Tory MPs, aristocrats and barristers, which met at the Crown and Anchor tavern in London on 20 November 1792, passed the following resolution: 'to support the laws, to suppress seditious publications and to defend our persons and property against the innovations and depredations that seemed to be threatened by those who maintain mischievous opinions founded upon plausible but false reasoning.'[11]

Reeves had been around government circles since July 1785, when he had drafted a bill 'for the better prevention of crimes, and the punishment of them', effectively a bill for a new police force and a stronger executive. Reeves was now chairman of the leading loyalist association. He was a product of Eton and Oxford, had been a commissioner of bankruptcy, counsel to the

Mint, law clerk to the Committee of Trade and was presently Receiver of the Public Offices. Reeves was a good organiser, but an unbending Tory of the old school. His association was clearly a front for Government propaganda, even if Reeves never admitted Government help: 'none of the king's ministers knew or heard of this association, till they saw the first advertisement in the public prints. It was planned without their knowledge, and has been conducted ... without their aid.'[12] Approval of the association and its activities came immediately. It was, of course, disingenuous of Reeves to talk as if the loyalists acted independently, for they were controlled (at the very top) by the people who had most to lose and had both family and social connections with those in political power.

Such unofficial Government spokesmen could be relied on to raise and help pay for militia, join the mounted yeomanry for use against insurrectionary meetings, cancel room bookings intended for reformist groups through their connections to local magistrates, and destroy printing presses or even reformers' houses by whipping up a Tory mob. Mobs like these regularly burnt effigies of their main hate-figure, Thomas Paine, but they would also turn their attention to likenesses of Priestley or the Pope if the mood took them. They might even be persuaded to demolish property and threaten life if required, the mob not merely being made up of ruffians and the dregs of society, but also including large numbers of journeymen, crafts people and apprentices who might see their way of life threatened by free thinkers and dissenters.

The danger from such groups was not to be discounted. It showed its force on 14 July 1791, in Birmingham. The cause had been a celebratory dinner honouring the fall of the Bastille (14 July 1789). It proved sufficient provocation (with some other grievances) to get the 'booby-faced Birmingham mob'[13] baying for the blood of Catholics ('No Popery'), and dissenters such as Priestley, the Unitarian preacher, scientist and radical, who lived nearby. Rioting lasted beyond 18 July, when the 18th Dragoons finally arrived and Priestley's house and chapel were already gutted. The Revd William Jesse wrote a report of the events for the Earl of Dartmouth during July 1791. The report leaves a strong sense of Jesse's outrage and obsequious disbelief that such things were possible in England:

> All Birmingham is in an uproar. The meeting of the Revolutionists to celebrate the infamous revolution in France has given occasion to the most dreadful riotous proceedings. Previous to the meeting, the republican Dissenters circulated a paper ... . This paper gave great offence, as did the toasts at the meeting, which were immediately known all over the town. Someone had written in large characters on the church, 'to be let' or 'this barn to be let, or pulled down'... . So great was the offence taken at this writing ... that the mob assembled and destroyed all the windows of the hotel where the Revolutionists met... . Many I was told had suffered. The military are sent for. There is a report, which I do not credit, that the Republican party have pulled down a church at Coventry. Though I smiled and was very much pleased to read the old toast 'Church and King' on every house ... I cannot help feeling sad apprehensions in view of the spirit which is prevailing through Europe.[14]

The result of the riots was £100,000 worth of damage (millions of pounds in its modern equivalent) and two hangings. The Anglican backlash against dissenters with money resulted in magistrates either doing little to quell the disturbance or, worse, egging it on. Conservative and traditional, local justices may well have seen this as the just deserts of nonconformist free thinking, the riots silencing dangerous voices of dissent and scientific atheism promulgated by the intellectualism of Priestley and his fellows. Priestley, a long-standing supporter of American independence and French republicanism, was finally confirmed as a 'traitor' when he became a member of the French

National Assembly, after taking citizenship in 1792. In 1794 he left Europe and settled in Pennsylvania, where he died in 1804.

When the Royal Navy under Admiral Howe defeated the French fleet on the 'Glorious First of June' 1794, crowds in London attacked the homes of radicals who refused to celebrate by the statutory lighting of candles in the windows. Hardy's house and workshop were attacked and his pregnant Lydia had to be dragged through a backyard window to escape. Some years later, on 16 October 1797, mobs again returned to destroy Hardy's house, but the LCS organised a stouter defence. It consisted of 100 sympathetic members of the society, among whom were a large number of Irish armed with shillelaghs. Fighting went on all night.

Loyalist mobs, whipped up by people like Reeves or vindictive magistrates, made genuine loyalism seem ugly. Yet almost all Britons were loyal and 'Church and King' supporters. The painter Tom Haydon's bookselling father 'believed England to be the only great country in the world and swore Napoleon won all his battles by bribery'.[15] Wellington and Blücher finally crushed Napoleon at Waterloo on 18 June 1815, which left Haydon to reminisce that 'boys were born, nursed and grew up hating the name of Frenchmen... . We had thought of France from youth as forbidden ground, as the abode of the enemies of our country.'[16] Loyalism was not merely a cynical ploy in the struggle for power but overwhelmingly a genuine and deeply felt sentiment of the British (and even sometimes the Irish) people. It was the assured counterweight to revolution.

Republicanism was a type of virus the Government struggled hard to contain. It was already in England and soon spread to Scotland, where the Society of the Friends of the People wished to set up an independent parliament and break away from England.[17] No longer were the Scots inspired by Jacobitism. Now they had been bitten with Jacobinism.

Robert Burns was an early adherent and joined the local yeomanry supposedly to spread the revolutionary creed. Many

Scots had taken part in the American War of Independence and returned to do the same for Scotland. Indeed, Robert Watson formed the first Scottish Corresponding Society, wishing not merely for reform at Westminster but a clean break from it altogether. Scots figured abroad too. John Paul Jones of the American navy came from Kirkcudbright and many Scottish Catholics served in the French army, using Gaelic for orders. Dr William Maxwell accompanied Louis when he was on the gallows, after the monarch's death sending back to Kirkconnel a blood-soaked handkerchief as a souvenir. The Earl of Lauderdale and the Earl of Buchan also went to Paris and met French leaders. Both returned and began setting up revolutionary clubs, Lauderdale later being named as one of the Provisional Government of Scotland. Paine's writings were translated into Gaelic and immediately banned.

The United Irishmen inspired the United Scotsmen, who called themselves the Friends of the People and openly advocated the repeal of the union. It was a dangerous move, as Lord Daer pointed out to Charles Grey: 'the Friends of Liberty in Scotland have almost universally been enemies to the Union with England.' The first society meeting was on 26 July 1792 and its membership steadily grew until it was broken up. Its leading figure was Thomas Muir, who had been a friend of Lafayette and who had opened communication with France. In October, the French sent a secret agent to report on the likelihood of an uprising. His report was reproduced in the *Moniteur* on 3 January. It would be hard for the Westminster government to ignore such provocation for long. In December the first general convention was held in Edinburgh, with 140 delegates. The United Irishmen sent a delegation. At the meeting, William Skirving was elected as secretary.

Swearing 'to live free or die' might be all very well, but the situation in France was deteriorating and the Revolution was in danger. Muir therefore decided to go to France to investigate. The declaration of the Republic on 20 September had brought a declaration of war from Austria, in which Britain soon joined, goaded by the French foreign minister, Brissot. The Government issued an arrest warrant for Muir and began arresting others for forming clubs that promoted 'equality and freedom'. Muir was tough and decided to return to Britain to fight his case. He returned on an American ship and was tried for sedition on 30 August 1793. Tried by a partisan jury, he was sentenced to fourteen years' transportation. He was removed to London to avoid the possibility of rescue. His speech from the dock was long required reading for American children. Another member of the Friends was Thomas Palmer, who also was tried for sedition and sentenced to transportation. The Convention continued to meet, was raided and thereafter met in secret, as more and more members were arrested. Among them was Maurice Margarot, who had been living in France and had been an early member of the LCS. The London delegates had elected him to travel to Edinburgh as their representative after a meeting at Chalk Farm on 24 October. His companion was Joseph Gerrald, the son of a planter from St Kitts, who had lived in America and befriended Paine. He had returned to London when Margarot was found guilty and, despite poor health, refused to run to avoid his own trial. He appeared at the proceedings with his hair unpowdered and loose in the French Revolutionary mode and caused a sensation. It was a powerful statement, but he too was found guilty. With so many of the Convention in jail or in hiding, there seemed nothing now to wait for and, with the example of the Irish, the Scots prepared to rise. Pikes were collected and plans made but the rising in Paisley failed and its leaders were tried, and executed or transported. With the arrest and conviction of George Mealmaker, a radical weaver from Dundee, in January 1798, 'the deep and secret conspiracy' of the United Scotsmen came to an end.

Muir, Skirving and Palmer were joined by Margarot in the old, abandoned eighteenth-century navy anchored in the Thames. These ships were known as 'hulks' and they represented the first stage before transfer to a naval ship out to Australia. From this floating city, the Scots prisoners were transferred to boats like the *Surprize*, moored out at Spithead, near Portsmouth, on their way to Botany Bay. Margarot hoped to take his wife along and, to this effect, he wrote a rather insolent letter to the Minister for the Home Department, in which, after asking that she be treated with 'the utmost delicacy, attention and respect', he concluded: 'However you think proper to punish my body, my mind preserves its independence and remains ... attached to the cause of the People, and to a thorough parliamentary reform, which you but accelerate by such repeated severities.'[18] There was no reply.

On board the *Surprize*, the prisoners were visited by Hardy. They were cheerful, except Muir, who was 'dull and pensive'. The ship sailed for Botany Bay in February 1794. Out at sea, Margarot had a nervous breakdown and turned informant against his fellows. His accusation of a plot to cause a mutiny got the others short rations and incarceration in the ship's 'cage'. In Australia, convicts were often granted plots of land to work and the governor offered the prisoners a number of acres to farm and the use of any earnings to invest. Once in Australia, Margarot started a campaign against the authorities, whom he considered corrupt, but by 1809 he had saved enough from his smallholding to return to Britain in 1810 (arriving in 1811), where he gave evidence to the government commission into transportation and, it was said, secretly plotted to contact Napoleon finally to set up the Republic of Scotland. In 1816, he died in poverty, disturbed, disappointed and defeated.

Muir had friends in high places and, when news reached Scottish Americans of his transportation, they contacted the President, George Washington. Washington ordered USS *Otter* out of New York on a mission halfway around the world. The idea was to rescue Muir and invite him to practise law in America. The *Otter* arrived in New South Wales on 5 February 1795, Muir was located and the escape made a reality when he swam out to the ship. On the homeward journey, the ship foundered near Panama. Muir and two others survived, only to be taken prisoner by Indians. Muir again escaped and made his way to Havana, where he was assisted by the governor to board the frigate *Nymph*. Out at sea, the *Nymph* was attacked by British warships and boarded. Muir was badly wounded and lost an eye, but the surgeon that boarded the ship turned out to be an old friend and hid his identity to avoid his recapture. He was repatriated as a Spaniard at Cadiz. Remarkably, Muir recovered from his wounds and was soon writing to the French government to assure them of his continuing freedom. He made his way to Paris, where he joined the community of British and Irish émigrés at White's Hotel. After all his adventures, he nevertheless quarrelled with his colleagues, especially Wolfe Tone and Napper Tandy, over who should speak on behalf of the United Irishmen (despite his being Scots). In the heady atmosphere of the times, he fell from favour and finally died penniless in 1799.

Palmer was joined in Australia by his wife and by a loyal friend, John Boston, and together they tried their hand at boat-building and soap manufacture. After refitting an old Spanish ship, Palmer found a crew and set sail for home, only to find his hopes dashed when the ship was impounded in Guam by an unfriendly Spanish governor, and its crew held as prisoners of war. Thrown into jail, he died of cholera (or possibly dysentery) in June 1802. Gerrald, transported in 1795, was so ill that he was simply abandoned to his own devices on arrival and, although given a harbour cottage out of benevolence, he died in 1796. Skirving died three days later.

Loyalist reaction to the cause espoused by the Scots and English radicals was predictable and violent and was often enough to scare off middle-class, respectable reformists such as the Pattison family of Witham in Essex, who, hearing of the news of the sentences imposed on the 'Scottish Martyrs', concluded that 'things are now arrived to such a crisis that there are difficulties on either hand, opposition conducted by moderation seems useless, or worse than useless, it appears as if it encouraged our governors to be more oppressive, on the presumption that good-men will suffer much rather than hazard such dreadful scenes as have been exhibited in France'.[19]

The alternative for radicals and reformers seemed plain: dissenters and radicals (often one and the same) should quit Britain and, like the Pilgrim Fathers before them, travel to the United States. After a friend had visited Palmer in the prison hulks, she reported what she had seen to Elizabeth Pattison, who wrote back to her that

> a few days before, Mr R— had dined on board the hulk with Mr Palmer, he says he found him in good spirits though strongly impressed with the probability of his departure to Botany Bay… . If the Governor of Botany Bay is an intelligent, liberal minded man he will rejoice to receive such a set of convicts and think the people of England are mad or they would not part with them. While some are forced from England, others are voluntary quitting it to seek in America, that security and peace, there is so little probability of enjoying in Europe.[20]

Christian forbearance, Elizabeth concluded, would get the reformers through and, like Christ's disciples, enable them to take their reforming zeal and their revolutionary evangelism elsewhere. Yet the revolutionaries would need more than just forbearance.

Most Britons remained convinced that the practicalities of life were best served by a tried and tested traditionalism. Even William Cobbett, who had been imprisoned as a radical and who had fled to America, deeply distrusted the theoretical nature of a future reformism led by airy-fairy 'feelosofers', as he called them. The curious emotional attachments of loyalty were beyond rational explanation, a matter of the heart and of a certain gut feeling. The mystique at the centre of English traditionalism even nowadays has a strong appeal, represented as it is in symbol, ritual and landscape, eulogised today by conservative apologists such as Roger Scruton:

> The English aristocrat was not a courtier, kowtowing to his sovereign in the city, but the heart and soul of the landscape ... bearing a title that ennobled the country as much as it ennobled himself.
>
> Monarchy was ... not a form of political power, but a work of the imagination, an attempt to represent in the here and now all those mysterious ideas of authority and historical right without which no place on earth could be settled as a home.[21]

To radicals all this would have been so much bunk; to republicans it would appear as a moist-eyed fantasy.

Chapter Eight

The Black Lamp

Radicals smelled corruption and disdain in high places and they were right. The Hanoverians were a family that never took to democracy. George I refused to learn the language of his adopted country, while George II would kick his hat or even his ministers when frustrated. George III also felt the acute pangs of frustration that only a monarch can feel in an age where the cry is constantly 'liberty and democracy'. When offended by petitioners early in his reign, he would turn and present his backside, a practice known as 'rumping', an early form of mooning. He had come to the throne at the age of 22, determined to rule 'adored by a happy, free and generous people', as long as he and he alone, through hand-picked aristocratic ministers, ruled the country. He did not enjoy criticism but found he had little else, assailed by the carping of a vociferous Whig opposition and a London mob that took to the streets at every opportunity.

There was Wilkes, the cross-eyed member of the Hellfire Club, whose best friend was Francis Dashwood, the Chancellor of the Exchequer, of whom it was said (by enemies and friend alike) that he could not even add up his tavern bill. There was also Fox, swarthy and overweight, and not only a dedicated king-baiter (he called George 'Satan'; others called the king 'Farmer George'), but also the heir apparent's best friend and a constant visitor to Carlton House. Fox was the son of Henry Fox, Lord Holland, the Paymaster General during the Seven Years War. Notorious for his profiteering even in an age of profiteers, the elder Fox was utterly ruthless as a politician and totally indulgent as a father. Fox the younger was coddled to the point where he nearly lost the family fortune gambling. A thorn to George III, Fox held major office only once, during the so-called Ministry of All the Talents (1806–7), in which he was secretary to the Foreign Office in the negotiations to bring the war with France to an end. Fox was dead, however, before a conclusion could be reached. Meanwhile, while he remained in opposition, he was the noisiest and most caustic opponent of the Court party, an attitude he maintained when holed up in Brooks's, his club.

Prince George had long kept a separate court down the road from his father, and here he plotted the undoing of every Tory ministry with Fox and the Whigs. In the spring of 1784 the King watched as Pitt went to the country over the issue of who should run the East India Company. Fox, leader of the opposition, essentially wanted to bring it into public ownership. The King was livid at being 'dictated to by Mr Fox' and did all he could to threaten, cajole and bribe MPs not to support the Whigs. He found his Tory in William Pitt junior, the son of the Earl of Chatham, also a William. Pitt the Younger was only 24 and known as the 'immaculate boy'. George III was quite capable of using any and every means to bring down political opposition. He had a secret fund of £1,000 a month put aside from the Privy Purse to purchase seats, and paid at least £30,000 to agents (including one payment of £14,000) in sealed boxes sent from Windsor Castle. He candidly told one agent that he 'thought this the most secret way of doing it'. The election of 1784 was contested using £9,000 of royal money to buy votes.

Bribes, trumped-up charges of corruption (although Fox was hardly whiter than white) and the threat of withdrawal of royal patronage finally got the King the ministry he wanted, but Fox retained his seat and had a triumphal parade. Fox, once a Tory, now a democrat (of sorts), was accompanied by a brass band, flags and a bodyguard of twenty-four butchers. There was free beer in the West End and blue flags, ribbons and cockades everywhere – the sign of everything the King hated. To make matters worse, the very next day, Prince George held a huge fête in his gardens at Carlton House, a sight which was designed to affront his father, who was then making his way to open the new parliament.

To add to the bickering, backbiting and jockeying at court and the jibes of his son and his son's radical friends, there was the populace, which had shown itself less than generous in its appreciation of George's benign rule. Observers noted that the English had been exercising their independent political opinions for years. During 1726, a Swiss traveller, César de Saussure, had noted that 'all Englishmen are great newsmongers. Workmen habitually begin the day by going to coffee-rooms to read the latest news. I have often seen shoeblacks and other persons of that class club together to buy a paper. Nothing is more entertaining than hearing men of this class discussing politics and news about royalty.'[1] The German traveller Johann von Archenholtz, travelling in England during the 1770s, was 'sometimes dumbfounded to hear people of the meanest sort very seriously discussing laws, property rights, privileges, etc.... . Often nothing is more difficult than to make an Englishman converse; he replies to everything with Yes or No; but if one has the address to start him off on politics, suddenly his face is alive, he opens his mouth, he becomes eloquent.'[2]

The Hanoverian family inheritance was a deeply politicised, cantankerous and easily inflamed populace, who knew and demanded their rights on pain of a broken window or a broken head. What differentiated them from their ancestors was the growing sense of politics as a secular activity determined by questions of property, equality and liberty under law. Political choices were no longer a matter of religious conscience. A secular politics had slowly developed and then broken away from the old theological model. The new politics brought with it the question of social need and this in turn was associated with the idea of democratic government.

The war in America became the very model for the reforms needed in the British Isles. The King could only see yet another group of ingrates unable to appreciate his dedication to his people. In later life he brooded over his failure to reconcile the colonies to his way of thinking. Of himself and the aged and blind Lord North (who had been prime minister during the war), he lamented that 'he, poor fellow, has lost his sight, and I my mind. Yet we meant well to the Americans; just to punish them with a few bloody noses, and then make bows for the mutual happiness of the two countries.' What was so irksome, he believed, was 'want of unanimity at home' but he failed to understand that the lack of political will was caused by real and similar demands at home, which he naively thought could be quelled by a 'few bloody noses'. Thus was George reduced to the language of a prize fighter.

The American democratic disease had long been dormant in Britain and now united the English with the Irish, Welsh and Scots in ways unthinkable only half a century earlier, when Jacobite armies had threatened the Hanoverian throne. Indeed the English and Scots had long hated each other. When James VI of Scotland had become James I of England, he had asked parliament to endorse a new term for the united country of England, Scotland and Wales: 'Great Britain'. Its inhabitants would be known as the British. Parliament had unanimously voted to remain English. The 'Scotch' were disliked and distrusted almost as much as the Welsh, and tales were circulated about their cannibalistic manners, a myth long preserved in the story of Sawney Beane and his troglodytic family of flesh-eaters. The 'plundered and oppressed' Irish, as the writer 'Junius' called them,[3] were despised as bog-trotting Catholics, a threat to English weavers, who regularly rioted to keep Irish workers out of their industry.

Despite this prejudice against anyone not English, the national interests of England, Ireland, Scotland and Wales had slowly been coalescing over the eighteenth century, so much so that by the late 1780s these countries were emerging as a new, single entity. With the voluntary liquidation of Ireland's parliament during 1801, and the Act of Union passed on 2 July of that year, the four countries formed a new nation:

> Article First, That it be the first Article of the Union of the Kingdoms of Great Britain and Ireland, that the said Kingdoms of Great Britain and Ireland shall ... for ever after, be united into one Kingdom, by the name of the *United Kingdom of Great Britain and Ireland*.[4]

Yet George was unwilling to push any imperial pretensions:

> His ... Majesty, George III, was advised, at the time of the Union with Ireland, in compensation for H.M.'s abandonment, then voluntarily made, of the title of King of France, which had been so long annexed to the Crown of England, to assume the title of Emperor of the British and Hanoverian Dominions; but his ... Majesty felt that his true dignity consisted in his being known to Europe and the world by the appropriate and undisputed style belonging to the British Crown.[5]

Principles of liberty, representation and independence infused every political debate around the new principles of democracy. A national political arena united the various radical groups, who now spoke with one voice; United Irishmen spoke the same political language and supported their brethren, United Englishmen. The respect was reciprocated. Thus, the closer the

United Kingdom grew politically, the more radicals spoke the language of separatism, but a separatism based on a vaguely federalist, republican and American model to which radicals looked to measure their own needs and in which the monarchy and its aristocratic and theological base would play no part.

Much of the blame for the House of Hanover's unpopularity fell on the head of the Prince of Wales, who seemed to his enemies merely a slowly fattening, lecherous libertine. A supporter of the Whigs as long as they backed his spending sprees (why not? – they were always included), the Prince had little to do and a kingdom in which to do it. His mistresses were liberally handed over to friends, such as Fox. From only one could he not be parted. The Prince of Wales secretly married the wealthy Catholic widow Maria Fitzherbert on 15 December 1785 at her home in Park Street, Mayfair, the Revd Robert Burt 'presiding', having been freed from the Fleet prison (in which he was lodging for debts) and given a £500 bribe for services and silence. Mrs Fitzherbert and her new husband remained happy, despite the rumours that circulated about the illegality of the proceedings and the possible birth of an heir (whisked off to serve as an officer in India). Having married a Catholic wife, against the wishes of his father and the prohibition of the Royal Marriages Act of 1772, the Prince continued as before.

With his pleasures unabated, the Prince constantly petitioned parliament to clear his debts, which at one time amounted to £600,000. Secret marriages and the Royal Pavilion at Brighton apart, the Prince also contemplated suicide. In January 1796, the 'Prince of Whales' (so fat had he grown) wrote out his will. In it, and despite his new love, Lady Jersey, he left all he owned to Mrs Fitzherbert, 'my wife, the wife of my heart and soul ... my true and real wife ... dearer to me, even millions of times dearer to me, than ... life'.[6] By that time the marriage had already been secretly annulled. It might have cost Prinny the throne and destroyed the Hanoverians once and for all. In the Act, which made him Prince Regent, was the ominous clause, 'that if ...

[he] at any time marry a Papist … all the powers and authorities vested in [him] shall cease'.

The Prince's will had been completed only three days after his official wife, Princess Caroline, had given birth to a baby girl, Princess Charlotte, herself tragically destined to die in childbirth in 1817. When Charlotte's parents met for the first time, George was so horrified that he went white: 'I am not well,' he whispered. 'Please get me a glass of brandy.' The royal couple were married on 8 April 1795 at St James's Palace in London. Princess Caroline was dark, podgy and big-bosomed, wore the diaphanous clothing of the time in a manner neither fashionable nor flattering, was an embarrassment to the Prince from the start and ended in virtual exile alongside her hirsute lover, Bartolomeo Bergami, who, at 6ft tall, towered above his roly-poly royal girlfriend. Nevertheless, Caroline was universally liked by the populace, who considered that the Prince had treated her with undeserved contempt. When she died, the crowds did not throw flowers (as for Princess Diana), but rioted instead to show their hatred for the royal family.

George III had his first taste of lunacy in the late spring of 1788 and, progressively but intermittently, continued to suffer until his death. After years of this rollercoaster, Prinny was formally declared Prince Regent by Act of Parliament on 5 February 1811. His father was in the third period of delirium and enough was enough; the King was almost blind and, at 72, a model for King Lear himself. The Whigs, miscalculating, waited to form a government. They had a nasty shock: the Prince of Wales had turned Tory. The House of Hanover wobbled on its foundations as opposition that had remained dormant, at least in England, began to surface again. The Prince was quite sure that only the most draconian laws might restore his kingdom to sense. His ministers agreed and went to the task.

Things were rapidly getting out of hand and a 'Committee of Secrecy', based at the Home Office and packed with Pitt's allies, was organised by the Commons to consider what to do. The committee first met on 16 May and in its possession were the books and proceedings of the 'two societies, calling themselves the Society for Constitutional Information, and the London Corresponding Society'. Both were 'closely connected with other societies in many parts of Great Britain and in Ireland'. The threat 'to the internal peace and security' of both Britain and Ireland was immediately noted by the committee. It was clear to them, using information gained from spies, that the societies were attempting 'systematically' to work towards 'the subversion of the established constitution'. The evidence included the information that 'the [SCI] applaud the intention of publishing a cheap edition of the first and second parts of the *Rights of Man*'; and resolve, 'that a copy of Mr. Paine's letter [informing them of this intention] together with these resolutions, be transmitted to all the associated societies in town and country'.[7]

The SCI had also been corresponding with the Society of Jacobins in Paris and had sent their Parisian counterparts a letter of congratulation on the Revolution, which had been followed (on the brink of France's declaring war on Britain) by the setting-up of a 'Foreign Correspondence' committee. English and Irish revolutionaries were also noted by agents at the harbours as taking boats to France. One was an Irishman, Father James O'Coigley, picked up in the Government's sweep of United Irishmen as he escaped across the shingle of Whitstable in Kent. Another, apprehended in 1793, was the John Frost (not to be confused with the Chartist of the same name) who had accompanied Paine on the cross-Channel packet. He was a radical lawyer and had already twice addressed the French Convention. Some French revolutionaries were also accorded honorary membership of the English Corresponding Society. The meaning of all this seemed clear enough; it was not merely unfortunate, it was inflammatory:

> From a review of these transactions [the] Committee feel
> it impossible not to conclude that the measures which have
> been stated are directed to the object of assembling a meeting

which, under the name of a general Convention, may take upon itself the character of a general representative of the people. However at different periods the term of parliamentary reform may have been employed, it is obvious that the present view of these societies is not intended to be prosecuted by any application to parliament, but, on the contrary, by an open attempt to supersede the House of Commons in its representative capacity, and to assume to itself all the functions and powers of a national Legislature… .

When, in addition to these considerations, the Committee reflect on the leading circumstances which they have already stated, of the declared approbation, at an early period, of the doctrine of the Rights of Man, as stated in Paine's publications; of the connection and intercourse with French Societies and with the National Convention: and of the subsequent approbation of the French system; and consider that these are the principles which the promoters of a Convention evidently make the foundation of all their proceedings; they are satisfied that the design now openly professed and acted upon … must be considered as a traitorous conspiracy for the subversion of the established laws and Constitution, and the introduction of that system of anarchy and confusion which has fatally prevailed in France.[8]

The die was cast. Government had little choice, or so it felt, to act decisively. It was Pitt's government that began the process of rolling back the nascent British revolution. He had a war to win and a way of life to preserve and he was in no mood for complacency or compromise. Radicalism would be stamped out.

The Committee of Secrecy had acted after the wholesale arrest and trial of as many members of the English and Scots radical societies as the Government could catch. The sentences passed against the Scots radicals failed against their English colleagues, but the Government, an alliance of 'right-wing' Whigs and Pittites, were not going to lose this fight. The arrest of nearly

200 people for seditious libel or treasonable activity during the mid- to late 1790s constituted a violent politicisation of the legal process. The state trials achieved the effect of bringing in state-sponsored terror – 'Pitt's Terror', as the radicals called it.

Pitt was determined to hear no more of democrats, conventions and petitions for electoral reform. Habeas corpus was suspended. It had been brought in by a confused vote in 1679, but been seen thereafter as a bulwark of ancient rights. Habeas corpus guaranteed that anybody arrested had to be brought before a court of law to establish a charge. It was a cornerstone of Burke's perfect constitution. Without it, the Government could arrest and detain anyone indefinitely. This is what they now did. Suspension of habeas corpus nevertheless took sixteen divisions of the House and a third reading. It passed the Commons on 18 May 1794 by 146 to 38, and passed through the Lords four days later, becoming law on 25 May. It was regularly suspended thereafter, from May 1794 to July 1795, April 1798 to March 1801, and again in 1817.

Pitt found his excuse to clamp down on 29 October 1795, two years into the war with Revolutionary France. George had been riding in his closed state coach to open parliament. On both his outward journey and return, a crowd of a few hundred of 'the lowest and worst sort' had chased the King's carriage. Tempers had run high and there had been some hissing. There had also been shouts of 'No War! Down with George' and 'No War! No George!', as well as continuous stone-throwing. A central witness in the later hearing had been Christopher Kennedy, a Bow Street constable and, since 1792, a spy in the LCS. Kennedy was a carpenter by trade and needed the Government's money.

It was during the procession to parliament that a small missile, travelling too fast for a stone, was said to have hit the coach's window. This became known as the 'popgun plot'. Two special constables, John Walford, a haberdasher of Pall Mall, and John Stockdale, a bookseller in Piccadilly, both agreed that a bullet had been fired at the coach from an open window in the

Ordnance Office, making a hole in the glass the size of a marble or bullet, and itself coinciding with a stone that also broke the glass at the same time. They concluded that the bullet had come from a pistol or rifle. James Parker, a footman stationed on the outside of the coach, believed the weapon was 'a wind gun [air rifle], for [he] heard no report'. If this was not worrying enough, the mob appeared to some of the witnesses to be an organised gang with subversive intentions. After arresting one 'young man in a grey coat and a black collar' who seemed too familiar with the strangers around him, Stockdale suggested the sinister possibility that 'several of them seemed to know each other as if they belonged to the same gang, if I may be allowed such an expression. My reason for it is that there were several standing together. The young man taken up was resting his shoulder on one of his companions in a friendly manner. I asked him at St James's, "if he knew the person whose shoulder he was resting on?" And he denied having any knowledge of the persons he was standing with.'[9] This was suspicion enough.

Another possibility also raised its head. The chairman of the committee, Lord Grenville, needed to check: 'Did you conceive any of them spoke with a French accent, so as that you might think they were Frenchmen?' The reply was clear: 'No, I did not.' In the end, the affair was never brought to a satisfactory conclusion and no culprit was ever found. Moreover, the five people arrested for rioting that day were all released without charge.[10] To the radicals, this seemed just another royal charade, created in order to bring in even tougher laws.

Almost immediately (in November 1795) two laws were brought in to stop all protest of any sort completely, including even a mild remonstrance. The first was the Act for the Safety and Preservation of His Majesty's Person against Treasonable and Seditious Practices and Attempts (Treasonable Practices Act), which more closely defined the meaning of treason, and the second, the Seditious Meetings Act. These followed the 'assassination' attempt and were the direct consequence (a little too convenient perhaps) of 'the daring outrages offered to [his] Majesty's most sacred person'. The two laws were enacted to stop (or 'gag') 'the continued attempts of wicked and evil disposed persons to disturb the tranquillity of this your Majesty's kingdom, particularly by the multitude of seditious pamphlets and speeches daily printed, published, and dispersed ... tending to the overthrow of the laws, government, and happy constitution of these realms'.[11] The Act declared any such person to be a 'traitor' and liable to death or transportation.

It only took two witnesses for a convenient conviction. The Seditious Meetings Act 1795 had been brought in because 'assemblies of diverse persons, collected for the purpose of or under the pretext of deliberating on public grievances, and of agreeing on petitions, complaints, remonstrances, declarations, or other addresses, to the king, or to both Houses, or either House of Parliament, have of late been made use of to serve the ends of factious and seditious persons, to the great danger of the public peace, and may become the means of producing confusion and calamities'.[12] A magistrate could, without a specific reason (on a 'general warrant'), demand to search premises where such meetings might be held and could, anyway, withhold a licence for such meetings in advance when a public lecture hall, theatre or upstairs public-house room was to be booked. Any talk of public grievance was effectively silenced. The law did little to stop continuing carping and greatly increased the number of hardliners, while silencing only the faint-hearted. The challenge would come at the turn of the century.

As things turned out, it was an old friend of the nation's war hero, Horatio Nelson, who posed the greatest threat. Edward Marcus Despard was a younger son of a wealthy Irish Protestant landowner. Bought a commission in the army, as was the practice for younger siblings, Despard found himself shipped out to Jamaica, where his constitution seemed to thrive in the hostile environment. Indeed, he was soon noticed by the governor and rose in the ranks until he commanded a small engineering company and later found himself a full colonel in the British army. Intermittent war with Spain and the fluid nature of Caribbean politics meant that an opportunity arose to attack the Spanish in Central America, ostensibly to protect the British settlers working the mahogany trade, but also to disrupt the Spanish hold on South America. Nelson was in the fleet as part of the expedition and accompanied Despard inland (sharing his plans and his tent), as the little British force captured Spanish forts. The result was that Despard, having organised the local natives into an effective fighting force, secured Honduras (Belize) for the British Empire, and he was soon installed as its 'Superintendent'.

Unfortunately, things did not run smoothly and disputes began to arise between the loggers and the various groups of slaves and Indians. The Superintendent acted so fairly with regard to justice, rather than colour prejudice, that he enraged the landowners and was toppled in an election after bringing in a constitution that they disliked. He then stood again, as a magistrate rather than superintendent, and won, but it was a victory for principle only and he left for England hoping to clear his name and recover the vast fortune he had had to pay from his own pocket to keep the colony going. Here, at some point unknown, he married a black woman called Catherine, who would prove a tireless advocate of her difficult husband's later needs. They had one son, called James.

Despard's arrival in London was hardly triumphant. He spent his time shuffling between government offices with promises of a hearing, but little else. He prepared a dossier but it was two years before anybody read it. When his case was eventually heard, it was agreed that Despard was innocent of the 'tyranny' of which he stood accused but, equally, pressure from the loggers meant that he would not be reinstated. A half-pay colonel, washed up in London, Despard was now bankrupt, and bankruptcy meant jail. In 1792, he found himself lodged in the King's Bench Debtors' Prison at Southwark. Here, the life was not too bad; the prison had wine cellars and even a post office. Its free and easy atmosphere meant that reading matter was not censored, and Despard wiled away his time reading Paine's *Rights of Man*, dangerous stuff for a man incarcerated for an injustice and with time on his hands to brood. The book turned a loyal servant of King George into a radical who recognised in the principles by which he had governed Honduras the applicability of Paine's doctrine to a wider world. Despard emerged from prison no longer the coiffured, bewigged gentleman of polite society, but instead wore his hair in the new natural style of the 'democrat'. What Catherine said is not recorded, but it seems a different man had come out of jail.

This 'new' man found and joined the LCS at the age of 43 and soon became a member of the inner circle, a gentleman among the workers who made up the membership. During the summer of 1797, reports started to come in about the possibility of an armed rebellion in Ireland. At the same time, the United Irishmen had been joined by a shadowy group which intended to revolt in London and whose leader was, according to infiltrators, called Despard. His organisation was called the United Britons or, alternatively, the United Englishmen. Despard, it was said, recruited disaffected soldiers in pubs and it was in the George at Clerkenwell on 18 April that arrests began for the big purge to wipe out the LCS. The treason trials were a political and propaganda disaster for the Government. They would not let it happen again. Despard was again picked up and thrown into Coldbath Prison in Clerkenwell. This time, prison was no picnic and the redoubtable Catherine recruited Sir Francis Burdett, the leading radical advocate and a great admirer of Fox, to get her husband justice. Even the loyalist John Reeves was recruited to the cause and Despard was finally released. He had been arrested when habeas corpus had been suspended; the Government next passed the Habeas Corpus Suspension Indemnity Act to protect themselves from acting unlawfully.

In February 1802 Despard's family was living in Lambeth and, if spies are to be believed, he was plotting again, his organisation, the United Britons, recruiting soldiers in pubs. One informant was introduced to Despard as 'the Colonel that was confined so long in the Bastille [Coldbath Fields]'. They were plotting, so it was said, to assassinate the King on his way to parliament and capture the Tower. The group were required to take certain secret oaths to protect the 'constitution: the independence of Great Britain and Ireland; an equalisation of civil, political and religious rights [and] an ample provision for the heroes who shall fall in the contest'.[13]

In the background an even more sinister organisation was gathering in the north. It was called the Black Lamp and it was waiting for the signal from London that the King was dead. This shadowy organisation was based in Yorkshire, where drilling was taking place and pikes were being manufactured. Years later, Government agents met men in the north who claimed to know of the Despard plan and were merely waiting for the nod. The authorities, not knowing what was truth or fiction, decided to act and, on 16 November 1802, arrested thirty men at a meeting at a pub in Clerkenwell. Among them was Despard, dressed like a gentleman and holding his characteristic (and then fashionable) green umbrella. He was charged with high treason and taken to Whitehall to be interrogated, and thence to Newgate. It was alleged that the King was to be assassinated, and the London garrison would then rise and take control of the Houses of Parliament, the Tower of London and the post office. Communications out of London would be blocked, which would be the signal for revolutionary cells in the rest of the country to rise.

The charges were grave but implausible, more pub talk than reality, and Catherine again went to work to organise a defence committee. Burdett was early on board and even Nelson appeared as a character witness for the defence. Spencer Perceval, the attorney general and later the only prime minister to be assassinated, prosecuted. Despite flimsy evidence, Despard and his companions were convicted and sentenced to be hanged, drawn and quartered, a sentence commuted to hanging and beheading. After he was dead and laid in his coffin, Marie Tussaud took his death mask for exhibition in her 'Chamber of Horrors'. Of Catherine and James, nothing else is recorded, except the glimpse of a 'flashy creole' getting into a carriage.[14]

The law did nothing to silence Ireland either. Stronger measures would again be needed for Britain's 'traitorous' subjects. Robert Emmet was born a wealthy Protestant in 1778 and became by degrees a United Irishman. He had been exiled in France since the 1798 rebellion and, like Tone, had argued for an invasion, but to no avail. His opportunity came when European war was renewed in 1803 and he returned to Ireland to lead a rebellion, which was organised for August but was already riddled with spies.

Misinformation and mismanagement saw the rising begin on 23 July and almost immediately be put down. The rebels' only 'success' was the piking to death of Lord Kilwarden and his nephew (mistaken for the Lord Chief Justice), who had been pulled from their coach. Emmet was caught during August, and tried and executed on 19 September. Fifteen men were hanged with him, men with humble trades (seven carpenters, two tailors, a farm labourer and a factory worker, a baker and shoemaker, a roofer and a coal facer). These were the sort of men the Seditious Practices Act sought to silence in England. They could be silenced nowhere. Emmet is remembered less for his deeds than for his heroic speech from the dock of the court, but the rising was considered by many to be an act of the utmost folly. Henry Grattan called it an act of 'stupidity and barbarity' and O'Connell told his wife that Emmet had caused so many useless 'murders' that he had ceased to be an 'object of compassion'. Cobbett, too, was disgusted. The famous and patriotic version of Emmet's speech from the dock did not appear until September in *Walker's Hibernian Magazine*. Ireland had again taken England by a surprise that it was to repeat throughout the nineteenth century. No gagging laws and no amount of force would suppress her.

The Seditious Meetings Act was renewed in 1817, in order to silence the Spencean revolutionaries:

> As unlawful combinations and confederacies, highly danger-ous to the peace and tranquillity of this kingdom, and to the constitution of the government [have taken place] ... be it enacted, that from and after the passing of this Act, all societies or clubs calling themselves *Spenceans* or *Spencean Philanthropists*, and all other societies or clubs, by whatever name ... the same are called or known, who hold and profess ... the same objects and doctrines, shall be ... utterly suppressed and prohibited, as being unlawful combinations and confederacies against the government of our sovereign Lord the King, and against the peace and security of H.M.'s liege subjects.

Between 14 and 17 June 1817, Lord Fitzwilliam, then Lord Lieutenant of Yorkshire, was regularly reporting to Lord Sidmouth,[15] the Home Secretary. Fitzwilliam reported not only on 'the war of No Property against Property' but also on the dangerous use of Government spies and agents. The mass of the people, the Lord Lieutenant concluded, were 'sound' and a simple expedient might save the situation from degenerating into chaos: 'I may presume to offer an opinion of my own with respect of measures fit for the purpose, none can be resorted to that will prove so expeditious and permanently efficacious for putting an end to all seditious planning, and revolutionary machinations in the country, as to make it known, to have it loudly promulgated, that there is not in existence a revolution-ary committee in London.'[16]

By 1816 the word radical had become a noun (it had been an adjective since 1769), and radicalism had become a very dirty word in royal circles. Thus, Lord Holland's secretary, writing of the Prince's former association with the Whigs, could state that '[the Prince of Wales had] no communication with the radicals'. Who were the radicals but those who put forward 'those damnable doctrines of the hell-begotten Jacobines [*sic*]', as the Prince put it in September 1792 after reading a lampoon called 'The Jockey Club'? He might indeed fear 'these times of democratic frenzy'; after all, his father had been shot at. The Prince Regent would also be the target for an alleged assassin's bullet in 1817, when he travelled in his coach to open parliament. The Prince was no longer a harbourer of radicals. He was now a Tory, heart and soul.

Exasperated by the events in Manchester on 16 September 1819 that became known as 'the Peterloo Massacre', Lord Liverpool, prime minister since the death of Spencer Perceval, and a traditionalist and authoritarian, had expressed to George Canning on 23 September the urgent need to increase the absolute control of the Government over meetings and over propaganda: 'When parliament does meet, it will be indispensably necessary to consider what measures can be adopted for averting those evils with which the country is so seriously threatened by the frequency of these seditious meetings, and still more perhaps by the outrageous licentiousness of the press.'[17]

On 14 November 1819 Liverpool wrote a letter to Lord William Grenville, in which he explicitly made the connection between the new industrial 'refinements in machinery', the topsy turvy labour market and the French Revolution, which had turned 'the attention of the lower orders ... to political considerations' and had destroyed 'all respect for established authority and ancient institutions'. Burke's class war was no longer a distant nightmare but a daily political reality. To combat the continuing and growing unrest that threatened the Hanoverians with a bloodbath, civil war and a republican democracy, the Government passed the 'Six Acts' in 1819. The first and most important of the six was 'to prevent the training of persons in the use of arms', because 'in some parts of the United Kingdom, men clandestinely and unlawfully assembled have practised military training and exercise'.

Between Pitt's first ministry and Lord Liverpool's last, Britain had become a 'policed' state, at least to its critics. As George III lay dying on 29 January 1820, he had no reason to believe that his son might see out his reign with his head on his shoulders. Years later, now George IV (and a laudanum addict – in 1826 he was taking 200 drops a day), the Prince would reminisce with the arch-Tory, the Duke of Wellington, about his imagined participation at the Battle of Waterloo. He believed he had led a cavalry charge and saved old Europe. Wellington is said to have drily replied, 'I have heard you, sir, say so before: but I did not witness this marvellous charge.'

It must have been irksome to the gallant royal hero of Waterloo that even as his dream cavalry were charging the French, there were many well-placed, middle-class or even aristocratic Britons who applauded Napoleon and were miserable at his defeats. William Hazlitt remained an admirer even after the crowning of Napoleon as Emperor, so did Byron. After Waterloo, Hazlitt wore a black crêpe armband, refused to wash and drank in excess for weeks. Mrs Elizabeth Inchbald, Britain's most famous popular novelist, a Catholic and a radical supporter of the French Revolution's principles, watched dismayed as the King of Prussia and Tsar of Russia paraded with George III in Hyde Park after Napoleon was banished to Elba in 1814. She was delighted when Napoleon returned in March 1815 to France, prior to Waterloo. A portrait of Napoleon by David and Lefebvre was exhibited in Leicester Square in October 1814. It sold out tickets for six months at a shilling per person.

Godwin in his primer *A History of England*, written in 1807, included the following passage: 'The French Revolution produced one very extraordinary man, Napoleon Bonaparte, as the English civil war against Charles I produced Oliver Cromwell.' Such remarks could not be made openly and Godwin worked under the name 'Baldwin' to avoid discovery and imprisonment. He remarked that 'I believed it necessary to substitute a feigned name ... on account of the clerical and anti-jacobinical prejudices which are afloat against me'. In spite of this precaution, in 1813 he was charged with teaching pernicious ideas to the young. It is ironic that two of Napoleon's supporters, Fox and Byron, both had mothers related to Charles I.

George IV died on Saturday 26 June 1830, concerned, it seems, for the good taste of his surroundings. He is said to have exhaled 'surely this is death' before breathing his last and, presumably, before his final mistress, Lady Elizabeth Conyngham, tried to wrest the key from the chain around his neck in order to rifle the jewellery box to which she supposed it belonged. The country was close to revolution, or at least the radicals and their foes believed it so. George's brother, now William IV, hardly helped. At his coronation feast he offered a strange and perhaps drunken toast:

> *Les yeux qui tuent,*
> *Les fesses qui remuent*
> *Et le cul qui danse –*
> *Honi soit qui mal y pense.*

The House of Hanover seemed about to come crashing down. The Iron Duke, hysterical about reform (but later a reluctant reformer himself), thought the 'revolution [had] begun' and, having covered the windows of Apsley House with bulletproof shutters, sat back with the thought that 'if we are in luck we may have a civil war'. John Wilson Croker, an early Tory spin doctor, wrote to Lord Yarmouth that 'there can be no longer any doubt that the Reform Bill [of 1832] is ... a *stepping-stone* in England to a republic, and in Ireland to separation'.[18]

Victoria came to the throne in 1837 unencumbered with a scandalous past. She was fresh, correct in manners (she was unlikely to 'rump' her ministers) and observant of social propriety, yet she had reigned only two years before warfare broke out in Wales. In 1840, she herself became a target for republican ire.

The Queen was out in Hyde Park, enjoying the sunshine with her new husband, Prince Albert, and being driven in an open carriage, when a 19-year-old republican idealist named Edward Oxford aimed and fired a pistol at the royal couple. The Queen and Albert were, presumably, less than amused and Oxford was soon in custody. In his pocket was a proclamation for an armed rising on behalf of 'Young England' (not to be confused with the ultra-Tory group of the same name), with instructions on finding weapons and using disguises. It was a last distant echo of the United Britons.

Oxford was merely the first of a series of men who plotted to kill Victoria, most of whom were Irish and Fenians. All were classified as 'madmen' by the authorities. Oxford was proclaimed insane on the grounds that only lunatics fired at monarchs and thus he was disarmed of any political intent he may have felt. The tactic had already been used in deciding the fate of George III's assailants. Those who opposed the established order were de facto deranged. Sometimes they actually were.

The Georges had a knack of attracting deranged assassins. Margaret 'Peg' Nicholson presented a petition to George III in 1786 and then attempted to stab him with a blunt knife. She claimed the throne for herself and told her captors that England would be drowned in blood if she failed. She failed, and spent her years quietly in the Bethlem Hospital (Bedlam) where she died quite contented at 94. James Hadfield, massively brain-damaged after the Battle of Vincennes of 1793, attempted to shoot the King on 15 May 1800 as his majesty entered Drury Lane theatre. Blowing a kiss from the balcony, George nearly had his head blown off as the bullet embedded itself in the royal box.

Hadfield's brain injury had been exacerbated by a Pentacostal preacher's hell-fire sermons and he had been urged on by Messianic visions. Hadfield had first attempted to kill his son before turning on the King to herald the Second Coming; he was charged with high treason. Hadfield's mental state was plain and, as no law covered the case, he was set free on grounds of insanity. A new law was soon passed to cover such eventualities, the Act for Custody of Insane Persons Charged with Offences, and so the criminal lunatic was legally born. Hadfield went to Bedlam, escaped in 1802 and got to Dover, where he was recaptured and put in Newgate. After fourteen years, he was transferred to Bedlam's new criminal-lunatic wing. There, the governors bought him a wig to cover his head-wound; he kept pets, argued with fellow inmates and finally died in 1841. Oxford spent the next twenty-seven years in Broadmoor, being discharged on 27 October 1867, when he was presented with a one-way ticket to Australia, exile and silence.

Chapter Nine

To Go a-Revolutioning

Tales of riots and disturbances spread quickly in pre-railway England. Despite isolated villages, muddy roads and poor literacy, news travelled fast and rumour travelled faster. The first turnpike was the Bath Trust of 1707, and this was followed by the Bristol Trust in 1727 and the Bridgewater in 1730. By this means, roads were maintained and improved for the new mail routes between London, Bath, Bristol and Exeter. In 1729 the London to Bath route took two and a half days, but a half-day was shaved off that by 1739. Coach services were expensive but regular until the 1760s, when 'flying coaches' carrying passengers and luggage created a regular service leaving three times a week. Post-chaises would then meet the coaches and take passengers on to their destinations.

The change of pace really came in 1784, when Samuel Palmer introduced Royal Mail coaches taking passengers, luggage and the post (including all secret service letters) to destinations along reasonable roads, having the right of way, paying no tolls and benefiting from the accuracy of being documented at every stage of the journey. Travelling at 7 miles per hour and with a repeated change of horses, a journey from London to Bristol could be expected to take sixteen hours. Palmer was appointed Controller General of the Post Office in 1786. The speed of the mail coaches created competition and other coach firms were determined to beat the time set. Most coaches carried, alongside the passengers, newspapers and gossip and, by 1811, 200 vehicles regularly plied the mail coach routes, keeping carefully to time and guarded by ex-soldiers riding 'shotgun' to protect the money box. These guards were provided with a chronometer so that strict time could be kept, and spot checks were frequent. Thus the stoppage or lateness of a coach would presage trouble and was often used as a signal for rebellion. More to the point, many radicals, from Jacobins to Chartists, travelled 'up top' on the coaches, moving around England to address secret covens of conspirators or huge open meetings. Roads also improved, with the methods of John McAdam saving passengers from the discomforts of mud, dirt and potholes. By the early nineteenth century, all the major cities of Britain were joined by a network of fast, efficient and regular mail services. Indeed, news was not universal but the new coach trade made it flow with ever-increasing rapidity.

Information, transmitted by a network of freelance spies, also travelled from town to town on these coaches, as they looked out for troublemakers and provided tales for the credulous. News from strangers was almost oracular in those days and far less likely to be met with suspicion than might be imagined. It is a feature of this era that spies were at the centre of almost all the conspiracies and plots. The credulity of the local population was always a help to them. In their rumour-mongering, they were helped by the efficiency of the mail service and the eagerness of their listeners for news of the outside world. By the 1830s, speed was at a premium and the 122 miles from London to Bristol could be covered in thirteen hours. Things were not to change until the coming of the railway.

If one had no horse and could not afford the fare on the coach, then there was always Shanks's pony. Skilled men, such as stone-masons, hatters, cabinet-makers, printers and a host of other workers would 'go on the tramp' from town to town and village to village, looking for work. As they travelled the country in search of 'work, hospitality and help', with a 'chit' to prove their professional affiliation, they could expect a welcome at a designated inn, a tankard of ale, some cash and a job. These skilled men were mobile and influential and in some areas dominated the vote.

At the same time, such 'free' labour was both democratic and traditionally jealous of its rights. Above all, the watchword was liberty of movement and of trade. The disturbances following the French Revolution brought conflictual thoughts into such traditionalism and made for danger in the future: 'The democratic aspect of craft tradition gained radical impulse from economic discontent. Its new organisational form growing in an age of international upheaval, was a force to be feared by government and, in the era of the Napoleonic Wars, to be repressed... . Those who did look to the future in a visionary way looked with a view tinged by ideals of fellowship and a way of life being relentlessly undermined.'[1]

Such trades were always tight-knit and jealous of their privileges and disliked 'illegal' cheap labour. In 1792 the word 'scab' was invented to describe someone who was 'to his trade what a traitor is to his country ... he is an enemy to himself [and] to the present age'.[2] Such was the type of mobile organisation that could prepare rapidly but whose structure relied on peripatetic strangers. In such an atmosphere, rumour could become fact, what one village was thinking becoming a matter of action in the next as the traveller brought rumours across fields and along hedgerows. Dreaded 'combinations' spread, the origin of trade unionism and the bane of government, with their secret signs and initiation ceremonies, held beyond the gaze of magistrates or ministers in back bar-rooms or on moors, which put fear into those who governed. Secrecy was the key to such combinations and secrecy attracted all sorts of potential conspirators and revolutionists; ideas were ultimately spread not only by the mail coach but by the tramping system.

Men would gather at pubs on a set day of the week, to discuss and smoke. Such rooms as they hired were called 'clubhouses', where the national papers were available to read and where the news of the country could be garnered. All correspondence made its way to the clubhouse and all such correspondence was deemed subversive by the spies and magistrates who watched over these activities: 'During the period of the Combination Acts government agents opened the letters and copied, resealed and sent them on. The employers were not as discreet as the government, and in 1817 London master hatters met the postman outside the clubhouse, paid him off and rushed the letters to the magistrates ... when the magistrates refused to open the letters, the masters did so.'[3]

Such fears were not altogether fanciful. During the high point of Chartism, police and spies infiltrated all such secret organisations, one policeman reporting of a meeting of local masons that it '[had] nothing of the republican in it'. Indeed, it is recorded that the trades that tramped were acutely aware of the state of England and of its political needs. They, of all people, travelled and observed and were often advanced in their views, advocating forms of primitive socialism, rarely drinking and frequently appearing to those who spied upon them to be atheistic. As Government agents watched them, they noted the number of 'seditious ceremonies' and itinerant participants and became more concerned at the secrecy that attended such meetings of working men.

It is easy to imagine the Industrial Revolution as either the satanic landscape of William Blake or the Mancunian hell of Friedrich Engels. This would be misleading. Oldham, for instance, situated near the Pennines and with abundant water and coal, developed its cotton industry around a group of merchants and factory owners whose families went back into the seventeenth century and who had subsequently been tied by intermarriage. Of forty-two cotton mills built in the years between 1776 and 1811, all but two were owned by 'yeomen' families which already had capital to spend. Such interrelationships created clans before they created classes and were much more traditionally based than might be expected from the description left us by Dickens in *Hard Times* (1848) of hard-faced, self-made scoundrels. Old families dominated production and trade *as* families; loyalty was personal and particular. From the manufacturing families in Oldham also came the infrastructure of power, including the Church, the law and military, with the Oldham Volunteers led by twenty-one grandees of the leading local families.

Such families rode out as best they could the highs and lows of investment which dogged the years 1785, 1788, 1793, 1797 and 1800, while their workers struggled with a depression that went on intermittently from the 1790s to the 1820s and that saw their purchasing power halve. Mere grumbling led to machine-breaking and rioting and increasingly focused on wage demands which went hand-in-glove with the more traditional demonstrations over food supplies (bread riots). Nevertheless, on the whole, working relationships were localised and familiar and, at the beginning at least, dependent on mutual tolerance.

Within this system of mutual tolerance, which contained both benevolence and loyalty as well as meanness and discontent, leading families kept order as best they could. However, the parish church and Sunday school observance did little to rein in those who refused to attend, or those who dutifully attended but then went to meetings of Hampden Clubs or combinations at the ale houses, whose owners happily took the chance (when the magistrate was not looking) to take money from both sides. On alternate days and without a blink, landlords might rent out rooms to a Loyalist Association, the Freemasons or a trade dinner (all attended by the same families), and to a meeting of a Hampden Club, illegal union or radical dinner to toast Henry Hunt or William Cobbett.

Both sides (that is those on the side of Government and those against it) recognised the advantages of self-support, but only one side found all of its self-support mechanisms to be considered illegal. From the 1790s onwards, both sides appreciated the need for secrecy, a secrecy that lasted long into the century but which was especially acute up until the 1820s and then again in the

1830s. Working men clubbed together (in secret) to fight wage restrictions or the introduction of machinery, to discuss political reform and to organise resistance to what was perceived as growing coercion and displacement. Local solutions seemed doomed to failure. A Bury businessman, Thomas Ainsworth, wrote in 'low spirits' to Sir Robert Peel on 12 March 1801 that 'every link that bound subject to government seems broken – no confidence – no interest felt in the welfare of the country – feeling pinching hunger – seeing rising markets and no prospects – but the hand of oppression ... continually upon them – any kind of change they say must be for the better'.[4] On 14 March 1801 his colleague, a local magistrate (whose illegible signature proclaims his haste), again wrote to Sir Robert regarding the rioting taking place outside Bury garrison: 'I am sorry to say that what I have seen and heard today, convinces me that the country is ripe for rebellion ... and I firmly believe if provisions continue at the present high price a revolution will be the consequence.'[5]

If economic hardship were not sufficient cause for revolutionary action, then hunger could at least be harnessed to that revolutionary cause. When leaders were fuelled with a head full of ideas, their ragged armies would tag along on energy supplied by an empty stomach and a light head. Hunger and political idealism (reform and peace campaigns during the Napoleonic Wars) made a heady brew. Working men's groups, dedicated to both economic and political reform when not reacting with force to local negotiations over wages, could prove more powerful than any law to contain them. A magistrate called Fletcher in Bolton, himself a coal owner, could do little on his own behalf to protect himself or his property. On 4 September 1818 he sent this letter to the Home Office: 'the masters have not the courage to proceed against [the workers] for combination or neglect – although the workmen's committee sits on stated days at a public house in Manchester as if on legal business.'[6]

Miners and weavers had 'clout' and used it, the manufacturers often left with little option but to arm themselves, barricade their homes and wait for the magistrate (one of the local family squirearchy) to fetch the militia for them. As late as 1839, a police report on Oldham was reduced to the alarming conclusion that, 'if the principle of self protection were thus generally adopted which appears inevitable where due protection is not publicly provided, we need scarcely specify the serious inconveniences which are to be apprehended from each manufacturing town being rendered a fortress held by undisciplined troops'.[7]

Billhooks and banners may prove potent symbols but they are mostly sterile as military weapons against bullets, sabres and bayonets. Nevertheless, if workers could combine with sufficient muskets, under reasonable drill and with disciplined courage, they might hold their own against yeomanry or militia. A colliery owner from Bury, during 1807, reported on a meeting of local working people who had gone to listen to radicals calling for an immediate ceasefire with Napoleon, a meeting the coal owner thought was entirely down to troublemaking 'agitators' bent on 'revolutionary designs'. In Oldham, some months later, there was a 'minimum wage petition, a political strike and a full scale attack on the yeomanry'. General aggression, machine-breaking, arson, threatening letters, strikes, intimidation and secret drilling tied down 12,000 troops in the north and Midlands during 1811–12, and indeed Luddite machine-breaking continued throughout (it began on 4 November 1811 at Bulwell in Nottinghamshire). At Middleton, near Oldham, during this period there was full-scale guerrilla warfare (a tactic adopted by the Spanish during the Peninsular campaign being waged during the same years). One newspaper from Oldham reported, 'A body of men consisting of from one to two hundred, some armed with muskets with fixed bayonets, and others with colliers picks, marched into the village in procession [headed by a man who] waved a sort of red flag.'[8] The same men also fired two volleys at a cavalry detachment and began reloading for a third before fleeing. They left four local men dead.[9]

The situation was not made any better when, on the evening of 11 May 1812, John Bellingham walked into the lobby of the House of Commons and shot dead the Prime Minister, Spencer Perceval. The agitation in the country being what it was, MPs immediately jumped to the conclusion that a full-scale revolution was about to take place. As it turned out, Bellingham had only a personal axe to grind, but even so the Prince of Wales (then in the doldrums in public opinion) received a volume of hate mail. One from 'Vox Populi' was addressed to his secretary, John McMahon, and read: 'tell your master he is a Damn'd unfeeling scoundrel, and if he don't attend to the above, *Death* shall be his portion, & that soon, it's come to the point now, & we are determined to strike the decisive blow.'[10] A second letter read, 'George Prince of Wales. Take care of yourself, for your life is in danger, you shall meet the same fate as Mr Perceval if Billenghall [Bellingham] is hung before this reach you. You blackguard you shall be shot before three months is elapsed if Billenghall is hung you shall be shot as sure as I remain an enemy of all the damned Royal Family.'[11]

Without local consensus, Britain was almost ungovernable from the centre. Civilian disturbances by local malcontents could nevertheless be dealt with, if either anticipated by spies (as agents provocateurs or reporting agents) or if sufficient muscle, both local volunteer and governmental, could be brought to bear. The end of the Napoleonic Wars saw inflation, deflated wages and increasing poverty that could not be handled by the parish and evictions from failed farms. It was a time of heightened tension and sporadic outbreaks of anger and frustration could break out without warning. Such was the case in the small and isolated town of Littleport, situated in the Fens between Cambridge and the cathedral city of Ely. Here, poverty and distress had risen to such levels that an outbreak of violence was perhaps just waiting to happen. Nevertheless, when it did it was a surprise to the local inhabitants.

Events began when a large number of labourers gathered at the Globe public house for their regular meeting of the benefit club (on club nights, each member paid a shilling and got a quart of beer). On the night of Wednesday 22 May 1816, between fifty and sixty members were gathered, discussing the possibility that men from a local village might come to Littleport and cause disturbances. A man named Cornwall suggested that Littleport men could just as easily have their own riot as invite strangers, and the others seem to have agreed. By this time, many of the club members were tipsy or drunk and Cornwall went off and found a horn, which he blew as a signal to the village that something was occurring. Despite the fact that the local vicar, who was a magistrate, read the Riot Act, he was simply pushed aside as the rioters entered the homes of wealthier inhabitants, or inhabitants against whom they had a grudge. Considerable destruction occurred when the rioters (who numbered about 100) decided to wreck many of the homes in the village and to steal their contents. Help from Ely was called for, but all that could be mustered were sixteen men, the officer in charge humorously remarking, 'Last year we were in the battle of Waterloo, and now we think we are going to fight the battle of "Hullaballoo".'

While the soldiers prepared, the rioters arrived in Ely and started to break windows and cause problems. The cavalry was then called out and, after some time, the troubles in both Ely and Littleport were quelled. The only fatality occurred when a dragoon stationed in Littleport shot dead a rioter. As he did so, the local mail coach arrived, with the body lying still warm in the street. It was reported that one of the passengers on the coach went mad on seeing it.

The result of the riots, which had evidently been simmering for a long time but which were nevertheless spontaneous, was the execution of five men. One man, called William Gotobed, escaped across country and was sentenced in his absence. He seems to have made his way to America and only returned after a general amnesty, but lost his money in a card game and returned to America, where he died.

Most radicals felt that reform of the political system would cure much of the economic and social situation, and activity rose as problems worsened. The London branch of the reform clubs met at the Crown and Anchor tavern in the Strand and it was here that all the major radicals came to demand reform, including Cartwright, Hunt and Cobbett. This was the centre of parliamentary lobbying. Parliament was long overdue for reform. Many seats were under the control of the aristocracy and Members of Parliament often voted as instructed from on high. There were few voters, and those who did vote were often under the control or the patronage of the local MP and therefore beholden to them. Of the 558 members of the House of Commons, 405 were elected by 203 boroughs, most with electorates under 500. The county franchise had not changed since the fifteenth century; Cornwall sent forty-four members to the House of Commons, while Leeds and Manchester had no MPs. The system was supposed to support as many MPs as were required to perform the functions and duties assigned to them, and *not* represent the people. The Report of the Friends of the People had shown as early as 1793 (delivered 9 February) that only a 170th part of the kingdom voted for 256 MPs, and things had not changed since then. The Crown and Anchor meeting was to agree a form of wording for a petition for parliamentary reform. Burdett was meant to chair, but absented himself as he objected to universal male franchise and was replaced by the veteran reformer Cartwright. Burdett had already failed once to put reform to parliament, and his more liberal attitudes when he defended Despard in 1802 seemed to have evaporated with time.[12]

Meanwhile, no more dangerous and extreme group existed than those who called a meeting at Spa Fields in London's Clerkenwell area during 1816. Hunt was to speak on the necessity of universal political enfranchisement as the only cure for the economic slump following the war. The organising committee consisted of dedicated Spencean reformers, primitive agrarian communists, who met at various public houses to discuss their ideas; 'The Land is the People's Farm' was an indicative slogan. The leading lights of this little group of some forty or fifty committed republicans were a tight-knit cell consisting of 'Dr' James Watson, his son James (Jem) Watson, Thomas Preston (an alcoholic), John Castle, John Hooper (a labourer) and John Keens. Alongside Dr Watson, there was another leading member, Arthur Thistlewood, the illegitimate son of a Lincolnshire farmer. He had come into money and lost it, tried farming and failed, joined the British army, gone to Paris during the Revolution, become a soldier of fortune in a number of uprisings, was an expert swordsman and liked women too much. Information linked him to Despard's attempted republican coup of 1802. Thistlewood had spoken at Peterloo but an acquaintance described him as only 'fit for a straightjacket'.

On 15 November 1816 John Castle carried the black revolutionary banner into the first of two meetings at Spa Fields, London. The area was notorious for its seditious meetings and violence seemed likely. A second meeting was called for 2 December. Surrounding this demonstration were large numbers of police directed by the chief magistrate of Bow Street, Sir Nathaniel Conant. He had been warned in advance of serious trouble by one of his many spies. Conant's position effectively made him chief police officer in the capital, and, as a police magistrate, his own judge and jury. He could also call on the help of the Guards battalions stationed in the capital. An anonymous note to the Home Office declared, 'The meeting in Spa Fields is aware of the collection of soldiers in this vicinity. The appearance of troops will occasion the destruction of London. Twenty thousand Englishmen can set any city in such flames as no engines can extinguish.'[13]

The authorities were not prepared and the crowd was swelled by passers-by returning from a hanging who stopped to listen to Hunt as he gave a speech from the window of the Merlin's Cave pub. Jem Watson spoke from a wagon outside. The magistrates and Bow Street Runners who were mingling with the crowd finally decided to act and a general tussle began in order to arrest the leaders of the meeting and seize their flags and banners. Nevertheless, the rioters marched towards Newgate and it was said they were on their way to capture the Tower of London. Here Hooper was arrested; he was armed with two loaded pistols. As the crowd marched towards the Tower, they broke into gunsmiths and looted their shops. When one looter argued with the younger Watson, he was shot in the stomach at point-blank range. At the Tower, Preston climbed the railings and waved a cutlass while calling on the troops to join the revolution. They ignored him and he vanished, and the crowd, now bored, dispersed. The authorities were, of course, quick to act and arrested most of the leaders shortly afterwards. Although the elder Watson was put on trial, his son made his escape to America, after a final shoot-out when he was recognised by a police patrol in Highgate. Thistlewood remained at liberty for longer but he, too, was eventually captured. Despite the court's best efforts at a conviction, and despite a mountain of evidence, the elder Watson was acquitted and all of the conspirators walked free.

Another date to meet at Spa Fields was set in March the following year to coincide with the supposed arrival of the 'Blanketeers'. Devised during 1817 by the radicals John Johnson, John Bagguley and Samuel Drummond, this was an idea to get the hand-loom weavers to march to London to present the Prince Regent with a petition to plead for the alleviation of their poverty. They were called Blanketeers because of the blankets they carried, in which to sleep at night. It was believed that 100,000 would take part and many made their way to start the march at St Peter's Field, the scene of Peterloo. However, only one man actually made it to London.

Into this world came a spy called W.J. Richards (variously a carpenter, bookkeeper and possibly a surveyor), who may also have been a bigamist, Freemason and one-time volunteer soldier. He possibly hailed from Shropshire, a tall, slender man with a rich, almost Walter Mitty-like imagination. Richards began his life as 'William Oliver' after getting to know the activist Charles Pendrill in 1811. Pendrill had apparently helped him get out of the Fleet prison, where he was incarcerated for debt. Pendrill, a shoemaker, was also a former Spencean, a one-time colleague of Despard, and had good contacts with extreme groups, into which Oliver was introduced. A hunted man, Pendrill finally fled to America. At one meeting at the Cock Inn in Grafton Street, London, Oliver was introduced to most of the extreme radicals, such as Thistlewood, Watson and all those who would participate in the Spa Fields rising. Also present was Joseph Mitchell, a jouneyman printer from Liverpool, who would later travel the north as a self-appointed 'missionary' of reform. Oliver demanded of Mitchell that he help him join one of these radical groups.

Having got to the heart of the London organisation with relative ease, Oliver again made contact with Mitchell, telling him that connections should be built between London and the rest of the country. Mitchell, without consulting the London Committee, invited Oliver to travel with him to the north during 1817. Oliver represented himself as the 'London Delegate' speaking for that 'great leading body of revolutionists'. Many noticed that he dressed like a gentleman rather than like his audiences, who were all working men. Yet he carried a tradesman's 'chit' printed with the rather cryptic message, 'Dear sir, the bearer Mr Oliver is a good friend of reform and a man in whom you may place implicit confidence on the subject of repairing the old building or pulling it down and erecting a new one; as he is a skilled architect you may speak freely.' It seemed vaguely Masonic, vaguely revolutionary – ultimately to mean nothing.[14] The pair visited Leeds, Birmingham, Derby, Nottingham, Manchester and places in between throughout April and May, organising a national rising and making promises of mutual aid from London. In Nottingham, 'Oliver' became 'Hollis' and still no one questioned him, although by now he was regularly corresponding with the Home Office.

Things seemed to be coming to a head. It was rumoured that the Hampden Clubs had gone underground and had gathered arms and were drilling at night. It was rumoured that the whole of the north was about to rise and 200,000 men were to capture Nottingham, march on the Trent to Newark and take boats to London, where the black flag would be raised and the provisional government installed. Burdett would be president (some said 'king') and Lord Cochrane (a liberal) head of the (no longer) *Royal* Navy. It was rumoured that London had risen. There was much rumour, but no action. The rising was set to start at 10 p.m. on 9 June. Four hundred thousand were said to be under arms. A short skirmish at Huddersfield was the result of all the secrecy and planning. Almost nothing else happened, but many people were now caught in a web of intrigue.

Needless to say, much of the trouble was devised in Oliver's brain,[15] but there was substance enough in what was left. Oliver reported that 'conduct far surpasses my expectations' and that it was 'long since determined', as if he had stumbled on the facts rather than help frame them. Yet, to his surprise, the whole thing had been concocted by men of 'apparent moral and sober habits'. Mitchell was arrested (he was later acquitted); no wonder, as his companion had been a spy all along – 'Oliver the Spy', as he became known. From now on, Oliver would concentrate on the fertile area of Yorkshire and Nottingham. It was his plan to cook up a revolution in the north and then wait to see who mustered and have them arrested. He found one ready-made. It was after his fortuitous escape from a meeting near Dewsbury and after a difficult meeting with Nottingham delegates, explaining how he escaped, that he finally met Jeremiah 'Jerry' Brandreth, who had no knowledge of the cancellation of the national rising.

Brandreth was recruited not by Oliver, but by the ageing Jacobin Tommy Bacon, 'a zealous disciple of Thomas Paine' and a supporter of Bonaparte who came from Pentrich in Derbyshire and, it was said, 'had been thirty years trying to bring about a revolution'. Bacon had been watched for some time by the authorities, but seemed to slip away to Nottingham, where he met the man who would lead the Derbyshire end of the coming revolution (during which Bacon himself, thinking better of it all, went into hiding). Brandreth was a dark man with a mop of hair and a beard, whose looks made him appear to be of gypsy origin, but who was actually a framework knitter from Sutton in Ashfield (but originally from Wilford), near Nottingham. Born in 1786 or 1790, he had married in 1811 and already had two children and one on the way at the time that he was effectively made redundant when the style of stocking he specialised in went out of fashion. It is probable that he was a Luddite from 1811 and had become politicised from that date. Bacon brought him back to Pentrich as a substitute for a rather mysterious man named 'Waine', the chief of the 'people in Derbyshire', a man of whom we know nothing, but who apparently was too ill to lead the rebellion.

In Pentrich, Brandreth was known as the 'captain', a sobriquet given to all civilian leaders, especially brigands. He made a mixed impression on the locals who gathered to hear him at a secret meeting held in a barn on 5 June, where he was introduced by Bacon. It was the first of several meetings where Brandreth and Bacon explained their plan, including the inducement that every man was to receive 100 guineas, and bread and ale was to be plentiful. They would join the men of Nottingham in the revolution and 'raise the black flag' (here meaning no quarter) if the garrison there refused to surrender. Then they would all march along the Trent to seize Newark. Another meeting was held at the White Horse pub, which was owned by Bacon's sister. The Bradford and Leeds delegate was present. Where were the arms to come from? The contingent from Wolverhampton would supply them. It all seemed so easy. Brandreth produced a card map and even had a battle song for his followers, an anthem compared to the 'Marseillaise' at his trial.

Believing that Nottingham had risen and that 100,000 pike-bearing rebels were expecting the men from Derbyshire,

Brandreth gathered his band from the local area on the evening of 8 June and led between 50 and 300 men on a trek across the village to the Butterley Ironworks to gather men and weapons; but neither were forthcoming. Frustration built up as the rain increased and more men refused to leave their beds for a scheme that could only lead to the gallows. The band trudged on, stopping at inns to take drink and at local farms to order the men out. At one such farm owned by 'the Widow Hepworth', Brandreth fired a gun through a window and killed a servant; the whole enterprise was becoming desperate. The later depositions talk of threats and pointed pistols to persuade recalcitrants of the righteousness of the cause, but few gave in to such threats and so the little army trudged on towards Nottingham, only to be routed the next day at dawn by a party of yeomanry. There was a brief resistance and then flight.

Nowadays, Pentrich is a sleepy backwater, but in 1817 it was at the heart of Derbyshire's Industrial Revolution, with a colliery and Butterley Ironworks, which employed 700 men (and later made the ironwork for St Pancras station in London). There was also the Cromford Canal, and down the road was Richard Arkwright's Cromford Mill, one of the wonders of the industrial age. Those not employed hauling coal or working iron were farmers or framework knitters. The village itself had two pubs, one of which was the White Horse, and a church going back to 1150, while the nonconformists had their own chapel. The whole village was owned by the Duke of Devonshire, who systematically set about demolishing the homes of those who were transported, as well as levelling the White Horse. In 1818 the Duke built a new school and church, believing that it had been ignorance and ungodliness that had caused the trouble. In so doing, he deliberately destroyed the industrial growth of the village and reduced it to the backwater that it remains today. All memory of the great northern rebellion had to be erased from history.

All sorts of men were rounded up: framework knitters, stonegetters and stonemasons, labourers and shoemakers, colliers, miners and sawyers. Fourteen were transported to Australia and never returned, their cottages demolished. Three were jailed for two years, two men for one year, three men for six months. Twenty-three men went free. Bacon was dragged from a local squatter's hovel where he had been hiding during the disturbances and sentenced to transportation for life. He was 64. Brandreth and two others were to be hanged and beheaded as traitors. He was condemned by Sir Samuel Shepherd, the Attorney General, as the 'belted generalissimo of a hostile force' and sentenced at Derby Assizes to die on 7 November. The day of the executions became like a holiday and Derby soon bustled with the throng. The last words of the condemned were ambiguous: 'God bless you,' he said to the crowd, 'and Lord Castlereagh too' (alternatively he may have refused to bless Castlereagh). The others blessed the King and blamed Oliver. It was not exactly a defiant statement of republican views and other radicals were worried that these words would do their cause no good. Questions were raised in parliament about Oliver, of whom Liverpool complained on 17 June:

> There certainly prevails very generally in the country a strong and decided opinion that most of the events that have recently occurred in the country are to be attributed to the presence and active agitation of Mr Oliver. He is considered as the *main spring* from which every movement has taken its rise. All the mischievous in the country have considered themselves as subordinate members of a great leading body of revolutionists in London, as co-operating with that body for one general purpose, and in this view to be under its instructions and directions ... had not then a person pretending to come from that body and for that purpose made his appearance in the country, it is not assuming too much to say that probably no movement whatever would have occurred.[16]

It was all most un-English.

After each man was hanged and left for an hour they were cut down and beheaded by a 'muscular Derbyshire miner', who held up each head with the cry, 'Behold the head of the traitor'. The crowd, who had waited for the moment, let out a groan and were ready to riot but order was restored. It was said, long after, that the block would not dry and many witnesses were horrified at the barbarity of the occasion – but apparently not so horrified, as a commemorative china set soon appeared and one local barber produced a short-lived stir by pretending to be the ghost of the headless Brandreth![17]

Shelley was appalled by Brandreth's death (and by the sleazy means of its accomplishment). The execution of Brandreth may have been disgusting, and certainly attracted the ire of men like Shelley, but it was also a measure of the general traditionalism of English life that a headsman might still find employment with an axe. France had long since adopted machinery for the purpose, ever since the official headsman, Charles Henri Sanson, had pointed out that mass execution required accuracy and efficiency, somewhat unlikely if you overworked the state axeman. Joseph Guillotin's solution, proposed on 10 October 1789, that all capital offences should be dealt with by beheading, was adopted by the French Assembly and passed into law on 25 March 1792. Named after its proposer, the guillotine was intended as a symbol of the Republic's egalitarianism and humane intentions. Indeed, the axe was not only clumsy, it was also the embodiment of a tyrannous state, wielded on behalf of a tyrannical court and in the name of a tyrant monarch, all spiritually and physically channelled through the executioner's burly arm. In contrast, the guillotine was anonymous and democratic, the murder-machine of every man, and every man as equal citizen under the law – Louis XVI had been executed as plain citizen 'Louis Capet'.[18]

Chapter Ten

Killing the Cabinet

The years following the end of the Napoleonic Wars were frantic ones for would-be British revolutionaries. The day of insurrection seemed tantalisingly near, and plans, plots and counterplots marked the actions of rebels and authorities alike. On 16 August 1819 huge crowds gathered at St Peter's Fields in Manchester to hear radical speakers, but were charged by local yeomanry, with many fatalities and injuries. The day became infamous and 'Peterloo'[1] was taken up as the rallying cry for radicals. Henry Hunt had been at the centre of troubles at Peterloo and was arrested soon after. His trial followed others in which desperate men or radical Members of Parliament found themselves indicted for 'seditious libel' or, worse, treason. Revolutionary cliques seemed to lurk in every country tavern and assassins seemed to hide down every alley in Whitehall. Nevertheless, such groups were not a mere figment of a frantic government's imagination.

If the secret manufacture of pike-heads was a threat, then the carrying of flags by rioters and insurrectionists proved an irritating provocation. While police and army attempted to seize banners and flags, preventing the rallying of radicals around symbols of defiance, the courts were always willing to spend inordinate time establishing the meaning of captured standards and such evidence was regularly paraded into courtrooms as proof of revolutionary purpose. Indeed, the use of flags as a form of defiance by civilian rioters had been noted in 1780 during the street battles between the London mob and the regulars outside the Bank of England. Here, rioters flew the black flag of rebellion alongside flags representing the United States as the world's first republic. The American flag would be paraded at many radical meetings thereafter.

The flag that infuriated the authorities the most was the tricolour of Revolutionary France, adapted across England, Wales and Ireland as the flag of rebellion, its colours changed to local needs. The tricolour *was* revolution, symbolic of everything Jacobinical, and therefore prime evidence of nefarious intent. Such flags had to be seized at all costs. At the trial of Watson, much was made of the flags and banners displayed on the day of the Spa Fields Riot. What indeed was the intent in displaying a 'green, white and red' tricolour other than provocation and incitement, especially when the banners declared 'Justice, Humanity and Truth' or 'Nature, Truth and Justice', as John Stafford, chief clerk at Bow Street attested when acting as prosecution witness? Stafford's opinion under questioning was that these flags stood for a call to 'insurrection'. John Limbrick, an officer from Hatton Garden, had certainly seized one banner, which was brought into court. Its message was more equivocal: 'The Brave Soldiers are our Brothers, treat them kindly,' it said. Three flagpoles were also duly produced in court. Alderman Sir James Shaw had accompanied the lord mayor to the Royal Exchange entrance to Threadneedle Street and had also apparently seized a banner, after which the crowd had seemingly dispersed. The banner was not forthcoming as evidence and, as it turned out, Watson was eventually acquitted, without, presumably, the return of his flags.

The flag of the English Republic was red, white and green in horizontal bars. It is possible that the same colours were displayed at Peterloo. At the time of Brandreth's revolution, Oliver had spoken of 'Sir Francis Burdett waiting in the wings to lead the new British Republic with its red, white and green tricolour'. The Chartists also adopted the tricolour and its colouring from the late 1830s onwards. Claims that they made horizontal the vertical form of the French flag are unlikely, as the horizontal version existed to allow for slogans, which they certainly employed. The Chartists did, however, sometimes use the French version of the tricolour. James Linton's Chartist journal, *The Cause of the People*, carried the flag with the wording 'Fraternity–Liberty–Humanity'. The importance of flags and banners was most significant during the Chartist disturbances. The *Northern Star* reported on 17 November 1838 a meeting held near Stoke-on-Trent which included the following slogans on flags and banners: 'Universal Liberty', 'Universal Tax', 'No Tax-Hunting Parsons', 'May our actions be guided by peace, truth, justice and love', 'These are the weapons we use to gain our rights', 'Peace on earth; good will towards men', 'Glory to God in the highest', 'No Statecraft. No Priestcraft', 'Liberty or Death', 'United we stand, divided we fall', 'By Union we conquer', 'Divided we perish', 'Reform in Church and State', 'We die to live', 'No New Poor Law', 'No separation of man from wife, nor mother from children', 'No tax upon bread', 'Support our labour; not tax our industry', 'Plenty of food for eight hours' labour'. This tradition of flags and banners continued until quite recently in the trade union movement. The English tricolour and its colours were still being carried as late as George V's jubilee in 1935, where two maverick households spoiled the celebrations by flying the red, white and green of the revolution.

Occasionally other flags were carried on behalf of the cause of the revolution. The farm labourers who traipsed to disaster behind 'Sir' William Courtenay at Bossenden Wood during June 1839 carried a rectangular banner sporting the heraldic device of a lion rampant in gold (or faded red), surrounded by a triumphal wreath of laurel leaves on a background of white with a border of blue. The heraldic device on the flag suggests more an aristocratic whim by the eccentric Courtenay, rather than anything radical, but its odd shape (16in by 32in) also suggests it had been cut down from a larger processional banner. Another explanation is that the lion actually represented the Lion of Judah, a reference back to the Fifth Monarchists of the seventeenth century.

Welsh insurrectionists at Merthyr Tydfil in 1831 used a sheet covered with calf's blood that they had ritually slaughtered and although this may be the first understood use of a red flag for overtly political purposes, red flags had been signs of rebellion since the Nore Mutiny. Wild heartsease, a violet flower worn in buttonholes, may also have had secret revolutionary connotations during the 1830s. In Wales, the tricolour colours of red, white and green were associated with the revival of druidism at the end of the eighteenth century, with radicals such as Richard Price mixing in druid circles. After the Chartist uprising in Newport in 1839, the Welsh language and its symbols fell under suspicion, but this only gave rise to a mythology of Welshness whose symbolic (and considered ancient) colours conveniently matched those of the French Republic. Welsh Chartists also carried tricolours in horizontal stripes of blue, white and purple, or white and green, adorned with the motto 'Universal Liberty'.

All tricolours, however, owe their origin not to heraldry or conquest but to the rationalist and deist principles of the Enlightenment, where proportion and colour stood for equality of relationship and the symbolic unification of people, nation and principle. The suffragettes adopted the tricolour to the green, white and violet of 'Give Women Votes'. The Irish revolutionaries of 1798 adopted numerous home-grown designs for flags, but most were green, the colour of Irishness and of the common people, with yellow-gold harps or crosses and various mottoes or abbreviations. Scottish revolutionaries, meanwhile, needed no invented tricolour. They already had the white

St Andrew saltire on a blue background, or even the royal standard of the old Scottish monarchy.

Last, but not least, all radicals embraced the symbolism of the 'liberty tree' of America and the red Phrygian cap of the sans-culottes, which would be carried on a pole in any procession. Equally, too, labourers and farm hands would set a loaf of bread on a pike-head during rioting or insurrection, indicating the connection they made between political equality and social justice.

Among the many 'operatives' whose political imagination was fuelled by desire for both the political and economic reform that had begun in the 1790s, none was more articulate than Samuel Bamford, whose autobiographical writings create an unequalled picture of life as a subversive agitator in the poisonous political climate of the years 1816 to 1821. Samuel was born on 28 February 1788, the son of Daniel Bamford, a hand-loom weaver of muslin, and his wife Hannah, the daughter of a shoemaker. Both were strong Methodists and Daniel taught at Sunday school and wrote hymns. Nevertheless, having read Paine, Bamford senior seems to have gone through an almost religious conversion to the cause of reform, starting up a radical discussion group in his home town of Middleton, near Nottingham. Hounded out of Middleton as oddballs, the family settled in Manchester, where, in 1794, Daniel became a cotton factory manager. Tragically, Hannah and two of Samuel's siblings died there of smallpox and therefore, after a short stay at Manchester Grammar Free School, he was packed off back to his uncle in Middleton.

When he was 14, Bamford returned to Manchester in search of work. He swept floors, laboured on a farm and even joined a coal ship before saving enough money to set up as a weaver, living in near poverty, but still able to continue his self-improving education, which included producing his own poetry. Always politically aware from his early education, Bamford followed his father in championing Paine and the cause of reform, joining one of the Hampden Clubs. After a momentous few years in working-class politics, including being involved with the Blanketeers, constitutional clubs, and finally Peterloo, not to mention being arrested twice, Bamford eventually took to journalism, producing two works of autobiography, in 1843 and 1849, from which he left a picture of grass-roots radicalism.

From his visit to the famous meeting at the Crown and Anchor, which Bamford undertook during 1817 on behalf of his Hampden Club, he left a pen portrait of the reform leaders. The meeting was, for Bamford, 'an event in his life'. Here, in the flesh, he got to see the great reformer Hunt:

> Of Mr Hunt I had imbibed a high opinion; ... he was gentlemanly in his manner and attire; six feet and better in height, and extremely well formed... . He wore his own hair; it was in moderate quantity, and a little grey... . His lips were delicately thin, and receding... . His eyes were blue or light grey − not very clear ... but rather heavy; except as I afterwards had opportunities for observing, when he was excited in speaking; at which times they seemed to distend and protrude; and if he worked himself furious, as he sometimes would, they became blood-streaked, and almost started from their sockets. Then ... the kind smile was exchanged for the curl of scorn, or the curse of indignation.[2]

Next to Hunt was Cobbett, whom Bamford met on business at his offices in the Strand. 'That venerable patriot ... was far in years − I should suppose about seventy; rather above the common stature; straight for his age; thin, pale, and with an expression of countenance in which firmness and benignity were most predominant. I see him, as it were, in his long brown surtout and plain brown wig... . I should have taken him for a gentleman farming his own broad estate... . He was the perfect representation of what he always wished to be: an English gentleman farmer.'[3] When Bamford did meet his hero Burdett, he found him formal, his house cold and 'nothing in the shape of refreshment'; so much for professional politicians and for heroes, or perhaps, given the adulation accorded Burdett by people like Hazlitt, he merely caught him on a bad day.

Also of interest to Bamford on his visit to London were the many trades clubs of 'working men' who gathered in rooms 'dimmed by a suffocating vapour of tobacco' to discuss their concerns over a 'half-pint of porter'. To the rattle and clink of glasses and the 'hear, hear, hear' of resolutions could be added darker grumblings of incendiary intent. At one such meeting, Bamford witnessed the arrival of the Spa Fields insurrectionists, some of whom would later join Thistlewood's Cato Street gang. On enquiring who had arrived, he was told, 'that gentleman is Mr Watson the elder who was lately charged with high treason, and is now under bail to answer an indictment for a misdemeanour in consequence of his connection with the late meeting at Spa Fields'. Bamford then goes on to describe the others who had taken the initiative during the Spa Fields riot:

> [Watson's] son at this time was concealed in London, a large reward having been offered for his apprehension. The other man was Preston, a co-operator with Watson... . He was about middle age; of ordinary appearance; dressed as an operative, and walked with the help of a stick... . [Both Watson and Preston] narrated with seeming pride and satisfaction their several parts during the riots. Preston had mounted a wall of [the Tower of London] and summoned the guard to surrender. The men gazed at him – laughed; no one fired a shot – and soon after he fell down, or was pulled off by his companions who thought (no doubt) he had acted fool long enough.[4]

There were also local friends and colleagues in the reform movement who would share Bamford's adventures. One was Joseph Healey, an apothecary of sorts and an illiterate, who was nevertheless the local sawbones and therefore went by the honorarium of 'doctor'. Equipped with a political conscience, Healey formed the Oldham branch of the Hampden Clubs in 1816 and helped organise the meeting at St Peter's Fields, for which he was jailed along with Bamford. Such chance encounters would provide the warp and weft of Bamford's life as a radical, as well as creating the circumstances of his downfall.

After the defeat of the reformists and parliament's refusal to reform, the 'reform' movement largely went underground and in so doing became radicalised into a revolutionary movement. The Spa Fields rioters had now re-formed and intended business. Conspiracy was indeed back in the air and, as years went by after Spa Fields, Arthur Thistlewood became poorer and more determined, his fantasies taking flight, until at the head of a 'Committee of Public Safety' he saw himself master of London with an army of 40,000 armed workers at his side. He spent much time plotting how to undermine the London garrisons, how to work artillery pieces and how to make 'fireballs' and grenades. Finally, his opportunity arrived, as it was announced in the papers that the entire Cabinet would be eating together and it appeared that there would be little security. Both Sidmouth and Castlereagh would be there, between them responsible for the Gagging Acts and the carnage in Ireland twenty years previously. Wellington, too, would be present.

A new gang of revolutionaries soon formed, which included Richard Tidd, a shoemaker, William Davidson, the mulatto son of the Attorney General of Kingston, Jamaica, sent to Britain to study law but considered by some of his neighbours a man of psychotic tendencies with a plate in his head (by others as a popular and kind man), and James Ings, a butcher who thought all ministers were 'buggers'. However, the gang was riddled with spies and the Government knew their movements. There had already been leaks at the time of Spa Fields. John Castle, who had been active in the riot, had been reduced to penury and been approached by Government officers to spy on the group. This he had done. Of the conspirators, both Robert Adams and John Monument had turned King's evidence and Thomas

Dwyer, an Irishman, and George Edwards[5] were both paid spies, while Thomas Hidon, a cow keeper and milkman, had actually informed the Government of the goings-on in Marylebone. Indeed, the group had been watched one way or another since November of the previous year and it may be suggested that they were allowed to bring their plans as close as possible to fruition in order for the Government to crack down on all subversive groups.

The 'West End Job' needed a place to make and store weapons near the target in Grosvenor Square and a fake coffee shop was set up in order to hide the operations. Here, grenades, fireballs, musket powder and balls were stored. As the day approached, one conspirator boasted, 'We are going to kill His Majesty's ministers and will have blood and wine for supper!'[6] Premises in a run-down alley called Cato Street (just off the Edgware Road) were also taken and here, armed and in their great coats, the gang was surprised by Bow Street Runners and soldiers and, after a short, violent fight, captured.

There could hardly be any expected mercy, especially with the disturbances that had rocked the country in the previous three years. It was time for the authorities finally to end the radical threat. At the trial the accused made brave and eloquent speeches. These availed them nothing. Thistlewood, Davidson, Ings, Tidd and their gang were all hanged, beheaded and declared traitors to the crowd that watched them die on 1 May 1820. It was said that while Thistlewood died quickly, Davidson required three or four heaves before becoming 'motionless'. Thus ended the lives of those 'infatuated men' who had fully persuaded themselves of their competency to rule the nation.

Standing on the scaffold, Thistlewood and his companions might have taken some comfort from the fact that their most hated enemy, Castlereagh, would fall from office within two years, a victim of clinical depression who cut his own throat on 12 August 1822, while at home in Kent. Byron wrote a radical's epitaph:

> Posterity will ne'er survey
> A Nobler scene than this.
> Here lie the bones of Castlereagh.
> Stop traveller, and piss.

The Cato Street affair gave the Government what it needed in order to crack down on all the leading subversives and thirty-three were jailed immediately. One was already in jail for blasphemous libel. Robert Wedderburn was the illegitimate son of a Scottish plantation owner and an unwilling slave. He rose to become one of the leaders of the Spenceans in London and therefore a likely candidate to have been involved with the conspirators. Having been a tailor, Wedderburn opened his own Unitarian chapel in a hay loft in Soho, from where he seemed to be making seditious and anti-Christian speeches to large mixed-race and working-class audiences, who paid to hear him talk and debate. An emancipationist, Wedderburn was also credited with arguing one August day in 1819 that a slave had the right to kill his master, comments that were reported to Lord Sidmouth by the Revd Chetwode Eustace.

It is hardly surprising that Wedderburn came to the attention of the authorities, who were already twitchy after Peterloo and would become more so after the unearthing of the Cato Street plot. Wedderburn, like Spence, was a small man with a big and eloquent voice. He had met Spence and been converted to his way of thinking as they sold pamphlets on their stalls; he had been a Methodist and become a Unitarian. Where the altar would normally have been in a church, there were pictures of Tom Paine, Toussaint L'Ouverture, a skull and crossbones, a red flag and the red, white and green flag of the British Republic. Fiercely passionate about his origins, he wrote to the slaves in Jamaica urging them on to rebellion and the setting-up of a republic, by implication arguing for revolution at home. Having rejected William Wilberforce's quietism, he preached armed resistance both at home and abroad and called Peterloo a 'massacre'. Yet his worst crime, as it emerged during his trial in 1820 for blasphemous sedition (attacking the literalness of the Bible), was to preach in plain language to the labouring classes who packed his little chapel in the hayloft in Soho. He was not to remain free for long and was imprisoned in Dorchester jail, where he remained an unrepentant advocate of liberty, universal suffrage and republicanism, a victim of colour prejudice, class division and the judicial hatred of a clever working man whose words might turn the 'lower orders' to sedition and Jacobinism.

Spies, flight and imprisonment became the narrative of every self-respecting radical. In 1842, as an older man, Samuel Bamford reminisced about his own lucky escape from the clutches of revolutionary plotters some thirty years before, recognising in one incident in which he was caught up 'Oliver's first demonstration on his "professional tour"'. Bamford also recalled that, having returned from his excursion to London, he was awakened at home by a midnight visitor. Still sleepy, Bamford did not recognise the man at first, but soon realised it was one of his friends who had accompanied him south as a 'co-delegate'. It appeared that there was to be a secret meeting of reformers the following morning and that Bamford was expected to attend. Next morning, Bamford and half a dozen other 'best friends to reform' met an anonymous stranger (unnamed in Bamford's memoirs but possibly Thistlewood himself), who told them a tale of business failure and self-imposed wanderings (to avoid debtors' prison) that had finally taken him to London and meetings with a core of hard-line republicans. This strange semi-personal pilgrimage seems to have led by circuitous reasoning to 'a determination to strike a decisive blow at once'. The stranger outlined the plan: 'Some ten or a dozen of our best men were to provide themselves with arms, and march to London, where they would be joined by others, and ... were to rush upon the ministers at a cabinet council, or a dinner, and assassinate the whole of them. All London would then rise.... . Our arms were to consist of a stout walking staff, with a socket at one end for the reception of a dagger … [and] pistols might also be carried by those who could procure them.'[7]

Horrified by the absurdity of what was proposed, shocked to be included as a sympathiser and fearful of being associated with such desperation, Bamford and his local friends made it quite clear that the plan 'was far wide of [their] code of reform'; the 'project' was too dangerous and too politically extreme. Somehow, this 'egregious dupe' had been convinced by Oliver (or so Bamford thought) that a revolution was feasible. Was his meeting with the unnamed visitor an act of Government entrapment? Bamford certainly believed it to be the case. Was his visitor a spy or a foolish enthusiast? The answer seemed clear, 'had he been a spy, he would not have been left to struggle with poverty and disgrace in England, but would have been removed, and provided for, as Oliver was. Had he been a spy he would have betrayed those who never were betrayed.'[8] Fools, however, were prone to drag others to their doom and Bamford was already a marked man for attending, against his better judgement, a 'private meeting' – a euphemism for conspiratorial plotting.

Not long afterwards, arrests began around Middleton, Manchester and Oldham, and across the countryside between. Local magistrates had already arrested some men, and local radicals, fearful of their safety, began to meet to discuss plans to escape from the area. One of the arrested was a friend of Bamford's from Middleton. John Lancashire was ready for the revolution and had already hidden a pike in his house. Bamford went round and destroyed the incriminating evidence, before he and his friend set out across country to avoid capture. It was in vain, as the local police were already looking for them.

Bamford was arrested by Joseph Scott, the Middleton deputy constable, who had marched him a few yards back towards the town he had just left when they met Joseph Nadin, the deputy constable of Manchester. Nadin was a tall, sallow-faced man, strongly built but 'non-intellectual' with a 'rude and over bearing' manner and a 'coarse and illiterate' turn of phrase. He was, thought Bamford, 'a remarkable person in uncommon times' and in his pugnacious crudity the epitome of an age still possessing that vulgarity and earthiness that had not yet been tamed by Victorian reforms.

Born in 1765, the son a spinner, Nadin had turned himself into Manchester's leading thief-taker and climbed his way to power by an iron will and a penchant for bribery and blackmail which included rake-offs from brothels and pay-offs from those for whom he could do a favour. He had, Bamford ironically remarks, 'the tact to take care of his own interests', which allowed him 'to spend his evenings in ease and plenty'. By any standard, Nadin was a thug whose sideline was 'protection', but he also knew whom to serve and in 1803 had finally risen to his present position, a post he continued to hold up to 16 August 1819, when he took part in the suppression of the St Peter's Fields meeting. An uncouth and vulgar man Nadin may have been, but he was still a wily law enforcer when Bamford was arrested, handcuffed and taken to await a coach, protected by 'six or eight police officers, all well armed with staves, pistols, and blunderbusses'.

A crowd now gathered to boo and hiss the police and, having grown more bold, began throwing things. A brick just missed Nadin, who cowed the crowd by seizing a blunderbuss and threatening them all if another stone was thrown. Bamford's neighbours sensibly retreated and he was taken by coach and dragoon escort towards Manchester, stopping now and again to allow Nadin to search for other radicals. The alarm being given, most of the suspects had fled across the moors, a situation so surprising and un-English that the dragoon officer accompanying Bamford remarked he had only seen the like in Ireland.

An unsuccessful search for a man named Mellor led Nadin's 'runners' down an alley, where they came across a gangly and extremely tall (6ft 4in) wall repairer called George Howarth ('a decent, labouring, married man'). Howarth brandished a walling hammer in self-defence and was promptly arrested as a radical.

Over a meal of bread, cheese and ale at the Spread Eagle public house in Manchester Street, Oldham, Nadin explained to the forlorn Howarth exactly what he thought of him:

'Aye, an' I'll make thee into a graidley felley too, afore I ha'dun wi' thee. Theaw'rt a moderate length to being wi', but theaw'll be lunger afore theaw comes back to Reighton: ween ha' thee hang'd.'

'Nay, Mesthur Nadin,' said George, 'dunno' say so: they axt wot I had I mi' hont, an' I shode 'em: it wur nobbut a bit ov a walling hommer 'at I'd bin a borroin'.'

'Aye,' said Mr Nadin, 'an' theaw sed theawd knock their brains eawt wi' it. But ween larn thee, an' o' yo' Jacobins, heaw yo' threaten to kill th' king's officers.'[9]

Driven at last from Manchester to Salford's New Bailey jail, Bamford was greeted by the local magistrates and charged with high treason, to be sent as a prisoner to London for examination by the Secretary of State. Having written to his wife 'Mima' (to whom he was married for fifty-two years) for some clean clothes, Bamford settled down in his cell on the second floor of the jail, before being alerted to a noise in the courtyard. Stepping up to the barred window, Bamford saw a sight that was nothing short of Pickwickian. There was his friend Healey (who had been arrested after taking too long to get dressed ready for his escape) ranting his head off at the turnkeys to the effect that he was no common criminal, but a political prisoner: 'I am a reformer, and such will I live and die.' Despite everything, Bamford burst out laughing. Taken down to London for trial, Bamford was eventually acquitted for lack of evidence.

Many years later, when Bamford sat down to write his autobiography amid the 'physical force' of early Chartism, he rationalised what he considered to be the cause of his misfortunes during March 1817: 'Some of the nostrum mongers of the present day, would have been made short work of by the reformers of that time; they would not have been tolerated for more than one speech... . It was not until we became infested by spies, incendiaries, and their dupes ... that physical force was mentioned among us. After that our moral power waned; and what we gained by the accession of demagogues, we lost by their criminal violence.'[10] It was all too ironic. Government incitement, spies and incendiaries had robbed reform of its peaceful nature and actually handed over power to hard-line revolutionaries. The tragedy was too much for Bamford, who joined up as a special constable, having long abandoned the adventurous life of a political rebel. He died, a white-haired, grizzle-faced octogenarian, on 13 April 1872 at Harpurhey in Lancashire.

Brandreth was an overt revolutionary and he paid the price for his audacity. Bamford, caught up in the same political circles and in the same sea of political intrigue, spent the last half of his life telling people that he was not. Nevertheless, he had got too near for comfort to the inner cells of the reform clubs, whose idealism shocked the more conservative morality of this son of a former Methodist. Bamford, too, was quite capable of being carried away in his own dedication to the rights of man, as the spy known as 'Y' reported after one reform club meeting following Peterloo, where a collection of pikes had been discussed: 'We had plenty to drink ... [Bamford] gave a toast, which was "may the tree of liberty be planted in Hell, and may the bloody butchers of Manchester be the fruit on it", or very like that.'[11]

It seems quite clear from his own reminiscences that Bamford knew and mixed with men who not only contemplated armed uprisings, but who, thwarted in carrying out plans discussed at 'private meetings', went on to plot the overthrow of the Government and the execution of its ministers. So close was Bamford to the revolutionary cadres that agitators from London and Manchester sought his advice and looked to his attendance at their deliberations, while the Government worked to have him shadowed by spies (such as Oliver) until such time as they could arrange to have him arrested for criminal conspiracy.

The contingent Bamford led to Peterloo seemed to confirm Government concerns, Bamford's imprisonment in Lincoln jail finally to cool his radicalism. His reformism constantly touched the revolutionary republicanism of his friends and political allies, making his own political position untenable and his personal safety uncertain. A thoroughly respectable working man, intelligent, traditionally minded and reasonable in his pursuit of a political rapprochement between the rulers and ruled, Bamford may have been genuinely frightened by the revolutionary hotheads whom his own attempts at organising reform clubs had nurtured. There was little he could do but retreat into conformism, the record he left a unique insight into the turbulence of northern radicalism in an age of transition, where the loss of the world of the past seemed not yet compensated for by the utopia of the future.

What were the world radicals fighting to retain and how was the world to be different in the future? The old reform arguments seemed to be defunct and yet no new or consistent theory had replaced them. All around was defeat and misery. The Cato Street conspiracy was merely the tip of a deep-seated disaffection: the north was breaking up under the pressure of industrialisation and the movement of populations; Wales and Scotland were fertile grounds for both nationalist politics and republican sentiments; Ireland seemed always on the brink of civil war, its leaders determined to gain independence by whatever means; London was an apparent hotbed of revolutionaries and infidels. Dissatisfaction seethed just below the surface, but it had little focus. Rebellion was likely to break out anywhere.

It did so in Scotland soon after Cato Street. Although the United Scotsmen had long since vanished, industrialisation and nationalism had created an atmosphere of intrigue that had been exacerbated by the visits of Cartwright and the reformists between 1812 and 1815, a series of conspiracy trials and the secret unionisation of the working population. By 1820, there was a committee for the establishment of a 'Provisional Government' whose activities were known to the authorities and whose conspirators were soon apprehended. The committee even produced a proclamation which may have had its origin in a gigantic entrapment operation by the Government. Fooled into a precipitate rising by English agents, Glaswegians nevertheless armed and took to the streets, only to be defeated by the local yeomanry at Bonnymuir. For two days there was unrest and then the round-ups began. It was the end of Scottish aspirations for the next 150 years. It was also almost the end of the old-style insurrectionary politics.

It was from Wales, however, that the politics of the future would come. Of all the one-man revolutionaries no one was as practically successful, influential or unlikely as Robert Owen, a man who, although not a republican himself, made the greatest changes to republican thinking in the nineteenth century. It was Owen who taught the factory hand the pragmatic virtues of self-help and combination and whose cooperative dream inspired both Marx and Engels with its message of working-class self-awareness. For Engels such a message was the first real stage in proletarian consciousness, the next stage up from the failure of the artisanal revolutionaries of the period leading up to the 1830s. Where their individualism had failed, Owen's collectivism must surely succeed. Owen himself preached the revolutionary creed quite openly, even if he was believed to be speaking symbolically by the middle-class sections of his audience. Indeed, how clear did his message regarding the evils of money need to be? 'By commercial competition, I mean the competition which exists in producing and distributing wealth. This competition necessarily creates a covered [covert] civil warfare between the individuals who are engaged in the same profession or business.'[12] At the same time he invented the concept of the 'social democrat', the name by which communists and anarchists labelled themselves right up until the First World War, the umbrella term under which socialism in Britain first took on its radical wing, and a name by which republicans and reformers acted to combat the excesses of capitalism, imperialism and parliamentary democracy.

Owen was born on 14 May 1771, in Newtown, Wales, the son of the local saddler, who also doubled as the blacksmith and postmaster. A precocious child, Owen concluded that Christianity was 'erroneous' but that somewhere a true religion might be found in a combination of nature and society. Ever restless, he was sent away as an apprentice to a draper in Stamford in Lincolnshire in 1781, where he took to dealing in cloth so successfully that he was able to move on to a better position in Manchester. He was already an acute entrepreneur, a wheeler and dealer, but nevertheless felt distaste for the whole business world in which he was so successful. By the age of 19, the young Owen had gained sufficient loans to employ a small group of journeymen to work the new cotton-spinning machines he had installed in his factory. He also acquired a philosophical polish and joined the Manchester Literary and Philosophical Society. He was both ambitious and in love.

Caroline Dale was the daughter of David Dale, a Glasgow merchant and mill builder, who was himself a benevolent cotton master. The mill he had built was called New Lanark and it stood on the banks of the Clyde. Owen married the daughter and acquired the mill in 1800. He was only 28. Ten years later, the mill had a workforce of 2,000, including 500 children from the local workhouses. New Lanark was not only a factory complex, it was also a place for social experimentation where 'new views' of social order and sobriety could be imposed by a paternalistic and benevolent master on his workers. Although Owen did not worry about child labour or long working hours, and although he worked to high profit margins, he did believe in a vision of a reasonable working environment and in the social welfare of his employees. In this, he anticipated others, especially Quaker employers such as Cadbury and Rowntree. Unlike his competitors, Owen believed in the power of social and environmental conditioning and by 1817 he had embraced a secular 'religiosity', after finally breaking with the Church for good.

With the end of the Napoleonic Wars, social distress and political unrest could no longer be ignored. Having lost various political battles to try to reform both factory legislation and the Poor Laws, Owen turned to a utopian vision based on his experiences at New Lanark. What was needed, he argued, was an 'emancipation of mankind' brought about by the end of cut-throat economic competition. He began his campaign in August 1817 at a meeting held in the City of London tavern. To his audience he outlined a plan for 'villages of union', where the inhabitants would work together through 'mutual and combined interest' towards a self-sustaining economy of cooperative self-help based upon a combination of agriculture and industry. Much of it seemed to smack of the old Spenceanism. The villages would be rebuilt in grid-like patterns, with public buildings at their centre. The whole structure he called the 'social system', but shortened it later to 'socialism'.

Despite his friendship with Queen Victoria's father, the Duke of Kent, Owen's 'new moral world' convinced only dreamers, radicals and capitalist-hating aristocrats. If Owen wanted to show the world how his plans would transform things, he would need to finance his own experiment in living. Thus was formed the British and Foreign Philanthropic Society, which acquired 20,000 acres in Indiana. Here, at New Harmony, 800 radicals and free-thinking utopians began the first socialist experiment that would ultimately attract romantics from Samuel Taylor Coleridge to Walt Whitman. Not surprisingly, radicals made poor frontiersmen and the dream of collective farming and simple manufacture soon failed, sucking 80 per cent of Owen's fortune into the wilderness. After lecturing to Congress during 1825, Owen inspired another rash of failed homesteaders, but experiments dribbled on, more or less unsuccessfully, until the end of the 1840s.

Yet Owen inspired others to band together for mutual support based on principles of non-exploitation and sharing. In the late 1820s, Owen discovered a cooperative society that had been set up in Edinburgh based on his ideas. Another cooperative society was begun in London (the London Co-operative Society) and by the 1830s, over 300 such organisations had appeared across the British Isles. The vitality of the movement impressed the young men who would lead the Chartists, and the vision inspired key points in Marx's development. Nevertheless, Owen was far from delighted. The pace of change was too slow and, despite all his hard work, he was not acknowledged as the leader of this new movement. Frustrated, Owen next turned to organising a 'labour exchange' or cooperative organisation for mutual trade between the poor. A thousand artisans joined between 1832 and 1833, but all sorts of troubles, including unfair trading and a lack of variety in the goods, destroyed the effort. Undismayed, Owen next joined the Grand National Consolidated Union and campaigned for an eight-hour day, but he had no real love for working people and his paternalistic and aggressive hauteur needled his colleagues. Indeed, Owen was a visionary at heart and an experimental entrepreneur, not a communist or a saint.

At 65, defeated in his plans but inspirational in his very failure, Owen still had one last throw of the dice. In 1835 he formed the Association of All Classes of All Nations, or the Rational Society as it later became known, to take forward the message of communitarianism. The society's newspaper, *A New Moral World*, was published for eleven years and read by many more than the 40,000–50,000 members who attended the weekly lectures at over sixty branches. Speakers talked on issues of the day – economics and politics, history and even the craze for mesmerism – while Owen himself undertook tours in Ireland, the United States and France. A new community was even begun in Hampshire in 1839. Named Queenswood, it was designed for 700 people, many of whom were Chartists who joined after the abortive rebellion in Newport in the same year. Queenswood was lavish in style and expense and inevitably went bankrupt, but not before some of its intended funds had been used to build 'halls of science', where 'the branches met, attended lectures, held soirées, conducted services' and where 'social hymns' were sung praising the virtues of 'community and sociability'. From these branches, 2 million pamphlets on economic and social reform also came.

Owen may have been defeated one final time but Owenism went from strength to strength. At the age of 82 Owen was beguiled by the spiritualist movement that arrived from America. In it he saw the new holistic religion he had sought as a child. Many in the new labour movement followed him (spiritualism and labourism existed in harmony until the late 1880s), but many saw him only as a superstitious old man who had lost his way. In 1858 he finally revisited his Welsh hometown, where he died on 17 November. Owen may have been buried near his parents and his beginnings but Owenism went on to inspire the new generation of Chartists, trade union leaders, Fabians and a group of weavers, the Rochdale pioneers who formed the first modern cooperative in 1844. His legacy of secularism and socialism, however, formed the vital link between revolutionary artisans such as Spence, Bamford and Watson, and the new 'socialists' and 'social democrats'. Marx and Engels acknowledged their debt to Owen in the *Communist Manifesto*.

Chapter Eleven

A Maniac in Velvet

The violence that preceded the passing of the Great Reform Act,[1] both in Bristol and in Merthyr Tydfil, gave notice of the strength of feeling regarding political reform. Grey attempted to steer the bill through the House of Commons during 22 September, but it was defeated by the Lords. On 10 October rioting broke out in London. Wellington thought that 'we shall have a revolution' instigated by the 'lower orders', whom he considered 'rotten to the core'. In Nottingham, rioters set fire to the castle, and in Bristol, the Recorder, Charles Wetherell, a dedicated anti-reformist, became the unwitting focus of one of Britain's most violent riots. Widespread destruction led to cavalry charges, and at least a hundred killed – forty-eight by sword wounds and ten by gunshot. Four men were hanged and eighty-eight imprisoned or transported. Lord Melbourne placed London under virtual martial law.

Martial law was all well and good in the cities, but of little use in the countryside, where lawlessness was endemic. In 1830 it got worse as rural economic depression, unfair tithes and steam machines threatened poor farm labourers, especially in the south-east. To some extent, the crisis had been brought about by the collapse of the old (and trusted) parish poor relief and the introduction of the hated new Poor Law. Anything was better than the humiliation of the workhouse. The result was the 'Swing Riots', a sustained campaign of rural aggression, including hayrick-burning, machine-smashing, intimidation and sometimes even murder. The disturbances, named after a mythical 'Captain Swing', went on in varying degrees of intensity throughout the period of reform demands, and mingled with them. It took the transportation of 476 people (including one woman) before a semblance of calm was restored.

Things were not going better in industrialised areas. The ironstone miners of Merthyr, already disgruntled over pay and conditions, and without parliamentary representation, finally turned to rioting on 2 June 1831 and succeeded in defeating a detachment of the 93rd Highlanders, which was forced to retreat to a large mansion in the town, where it was besieged for eight days. Further Government forces were defeated by well armed and drilled insurgents, who seemed to have been organised with 'full revolutionary ritual', with banners, flag-bearers and torch-bearers. The miners set up road blocks; they had large amounts of captured ammunition and guns, and took to guerrilla warfare. Amazingly, no main attack followed the initial victories against the troops, and negotiations took the heat out of the situation. One man was hanged for his part in the uprising and that was that. Yet what occurred represented the first true rising of the industrial working class and of the power of that class with muskets in their hands.

A new Reform Bill was presented to parliament during 1832 and, again, the Lords threatened to reject it. Grey counter-threatened to create new and sympathetic peers and the opposition collapsed. The bill passed into law on 7 June 1832. The Act disenfranchised 56 rotten boroughs, and 111 members of parliament lost their seats; 30 boroughs with less than 4,000 inhabitants lost one member, and two boroughs gave up two of their four members; 65 new seats went to the counties and 44 seats were distributed among the 22 largest towns (including Birmingham, Leeds, Manchester and Sheffield), as well as giving London extra metropolitan districts; 21 other towns gained an MP, Scotland being awarded 8 extra seats and Ireland 5 extra seats. The right of voting was now vested in householders paying at least £10, and subject to a one-year residence, and the franchise was widened to the counties, with different rules for freeholders, copyholders and tenants. The 1832 Reform Act was meant to be the final revision of the British constitution. Robert Peel considered the Act an 'irrevocable settlement of a great constitutional question', as he told the constituents of Tamworth on 18 December 1834. The Tamworth Manifesto, as it became known, was the first full statement of modern conservatism. It was a reform Act for the new middle classes; it gave nothing to the mass of workers.

For some, the passing of the Act was the culmination of all their efforts and the terminus for their struggles (the middle class finally achieved the vote), but for others it was just the beginning of their struggle, and for those traditionalists who had predicted disaster once the flood gates of democracy were opened, it appeared a vindication.

It stirred old wounds too. The Orange Order was already at a low ebb in the early 1830s, having lost the battle for Catholic emancipation, but it had established a Grand Lodge in Britain, presided over by William IV's brother the Duke of Cumberland. It was believed that William was about to die and that Wellington would attempt to become dictator by taking over the regency for the under-age Victoria. Orangemen wanted revenge on the Duke for his betrayal over the Catholics and as a calling-to-account for William for sanctioning parliamentary reform in the first place. Through their recruiting agent, William Fairman, a captain in the Royal Irish Infantry and Lieutenant-Colonel of the 4th Ceylon Foot, they began to sound out the possibility of a coup. Many peers were sympathetic and the army, where there were a number of lodges, was scouted for sympathisers, Fairman adding that '[the Orange Order] would be happy to supply physical force against radicals if the occasion arose'. The plot had begun in 1832 and was advanced by 1835, but Fairman had been forced into hiding to avoid answering parliamentary questions and there was no effective leadership for the 500 possible Orange recruits. The plot fizzled out and the Grand Lodge, having caught a fright (by plotting to become destroyers rather than upholders of the constitution), disbanded on 14 April 1836.

For the next twenty years, the struggle over parliamentary reform would become more violent and more partisan, with almost every town in England and Wales (especially those newly industrialised) suffering from riots. Times were becoming strange. The strangest of all revolutionaries stepped into the rural landscape of Kent almost from nowhere. He was born plain John Nichols Thom, the son of a farmer and maltster of St Columb in Cornwall, who worked for a time in a wine merchant's warehouse in Truro. When the firm closed, he started trading on his own as a wine merchant and hop dealer, but unfortunately his business burnt down in an 'accidental' fire, for which he claimed rather too much insurance. It was not long before he recovered from his loss and made a considerable success dealing in malt, which he seems to have disposed of in Liverpool.

For a couple of years, he vanishes from the records, only to return as Sir William Percy Honeywood Courtenay, Knight of Malta, no longer in Liverpool but now in Canterbury. His eccentric title was apparently borrowed from the real Sir William, who was abroad. Thom had gone about previously as Sir Moses Rothschild. During 1832 he stood as a parliamentary candidate in Canterbury and was able to gain many respectable admirers despite the eccentricity of his manners and the sheer peculiarity of his dress, which consisted of a braided red velvet suit topped with epaulettes, a short cloak and a floppy medieval-style cap crowned with a tassel. For armament he carried a curved Turkish-style sword which he called 'Excalibur'.

Although he did not win a parliamentary seat, Courtenay began inveighing against the Poor Laws and gained a following from the local farm labourers. Indeed, he started a number of publications and took issue with various social and political wrongs. In his publication *Liberty* (motto: 'the British lion will be free'), he addressed himself to the 'lower orders of society', so that they should have the 'opportunity to read on a Sunday', and in the issue of Saturday 27 April 1833, he attacked both the Church and the moneyed classes. Landlords, he insisted, lived off the backs of the 'working classes', 'the poor stands [*sic*] as it were upon a gibbet', and 'for a country to prosper, the working classes, can never have too good wages'. The consequence of a parliament 'not being the voice of the people' was that 'England must go to a revolution', but at the same time no country in 'Christendom' could stand 'upon a republican form of government'.

It was then that Courtenay became delusional. His next action was rather bizarre, as he gave perjured evidence in a smuggling case (for which he had no reason to appear) and was found guilty at Maidstone Assizes during 1833. By this time, his actions were becoming more outlandish and his friends, having by now discovered his whereabouts, persuaded the judge that he was not of his right mind and had him incarcerated in a local lunatic asylum. Falling into dispute with his guardian, however, Courtenay left the asylum to take up residence near the small village of Dunkirk, near Faversham in Kent. Sir William now metamorphosed again. It was his greatest impersonation, for by this time the locals had started to believe that he was the reincarnation of Christ, and certainly many of the women of the village were fearful that if their husbands did not do as he said, 'fire would come from heaven and burn them'.

Dunkirk and its surroundings were unlike those of Pentrich twenty years previously. The villages of Kent were rural and isolated, prone to rumour and superstition. Nevertheless, it would be wrong to imagine that Courtenay's little band were all ignorant farm labourers. There were many labourers, but there were also distressed farmers (with smallholdings of between 7 and 20 acres), brewers, a gardener, a shoemaker, a bailiff and a mole catcher. More than half could read and a number were noted for their strict attendance at church. A high proportion were also over 40 and so not likely to be hotheads, yet quite possibly cynical about their lot. In a word, these were not the rambunctious material of the industrial villages, although almost ten years of rural disturbance had made them disaffected and rebellious. These were older men, perhaps inclined to think that they had little or nothing to lose by their efforts. As for the area, it was relatively isolated, sitting some way from the nearest town of Faversham, at an angle to the old Roman road to Canterbury. The area was also heavily wooded and a good hiding place for smugglers or thieves, especially as there were few inhabitants. Dominating the area, then as now, is Mount Ephraim, a large country estate.

Courtenay led his followers out on 29 May 1838, riding a horse, armed with a brace of pistols and a sabre and looking like a mixture of pirate king and banditti leader. His followers carried his 'standard', a lion rampant, and held aloft a loaf of bread attached to a pole. They toured the local villages for two days, calling for volunteers and promising the return of better days. By the second day they had a little force of some thirty-six to forty-nine men, according to the estimates of Norton Knatchbull, a local gentleman and self-appointed snoop who shadowed them as they gathered. Enough was enough and the local magistrate, the Revd John Poore, issued warrants for the apprehension of Courtenay, who was being followed at this point by a large force of local gentry and special constables.

By now the rebels were at Dunkirk and Courtenay was ensconced in a farmhouse. When the special constables arrived, Courtenay pointed a gun at one of them and pulled the trigger. The constable was killed. Afterwards Courtney hacked the body and threw it in a ditch. No longer could his antics be ignored and a detachment of the 45th Infantry, newly returned at Canterbury barracks from India, was called up. The infantry marched to Bossenden Wood, where the rebels were camped. The two sides sized each other up, the one armed with muskets and the other with sticks. There was little time for thought as Courtenay threw himself at Lieutenant Henry Bennett, aged 29 and a veteran of the Burma campaign. Both fired, both dropped dead, Bennett being the last soldier to die on active service on British soil and the first to die during Victoria's reign. Then followed pandemonium: a volley, bayoneting, twenty dead. After the 'battle', the owner of Mount Ephraim collected souvenirs: the lion banner, an ivory whistle, a comb, two swords, a money pouch, some bullets and a broken watch.

The question remains as to what exactly happened at Bossenden. It was called a riot by contemporaries, but no rioting took place, and it was not an uprising in any straightforward sense. Was it a sort of mad holiday or a religious parade to bring on the millennium? Recruitment began on 29 May or Oak Apple Day, commemorating the restoration of Charles II, but also the traditional day for making a holiday in the ritual of the rural year. Courtenay's language and manner were suffused with apocalyptic imagery. Before the murder of the special constable, Courtenay had told his followers that this was 'the first day of the Millennium – and this day I will put the crown upon my own head'. After the murder, he exclaimed that he was only 'executing the justice of heaven in consequence of the power God has given me'. He had already delivered a sermon on nearby Boughton Hill about the inequities of the rich, which he had taken from the general epistle from St James, and he was known for his compassion for the poor and his hatred of the rich, which was couched in biblical terminology:

Witnesses attested to his claim that he was not like earthly men: 'I fell down from the clouds and nobody knew where I came from.' He said that all he had to do was to place his left hand on the muscle of his right arm and 10,000 would be slain. He pretended to shoot out the stars with tow steeped in oil with iron filings, so that when he fired his pistols the shots emitted sparkles of light. He convinced some of his followers that they were invulnerable to bullets. When Courtenay lay dead, his lover, Sarah Culver, attempted to revive him with water – he had told her that if he appeared dead he would only be sleeping... . William Wills [one of his followers] believed that Courtenay could hear everything that was said even though he was a mile away.[2]

Courtenay's followers believed him to be the Messiah and 'Christ come down from the Cross'; he offered to show them the nail-holes in his hands. At Bossenden, the apocalyptic tone became more strident, with two followers, Alexander Foad and a man called Blanchard, worshipping Courtenay on bended knees as Christ rerisen. After Courtenay's death he was laid out in the Red Lion at Dunkirk, his wounds showing prominently, but this did not prevent one local woman, Lydia Hadlow, expecting his resurrection. Many locals kept his portrait on their walls or treasured souvenirs of his life. A delusional fantasist and a serial liar Courtenay may have been, but he was also a man created in his own image who gave hope, however briefly, to those without anything who, to all intents and purposes, were still living in the seventeenth-century world of the Fifth Monarchists.[3] It was the final peasants' revolt.

The last real uprising of the old peasantry gave way to new worries. Frustrated, the working masses were becoming politically aware, especially after the failure of their hopes for reform and they began to agitate for themselves and for their own needs. They created the 'Charter', a bill of rights, which they presented to parliament. This was originally a mix of middle- and working-class demands inherited from the old Corresponding Societies, but it increasingly came to represent working people's political aspirations. It was reformist in outlook and called for manhood suffrage, annual parliaments, payment of Members of Parliament, equal electoral districts, abolition of property qualifications for MPs, and vote by secret ballot. This was not perhaps unreasonable, but the 1832 Act was a once-for-all settlement. There could be no other. The Charter was continually rejected by parliament over the next sixteen years, so that attitudes hardened and parliamentary intransigence bred revolutionaries where only reformists had been. The first Chartist Convention was held on 4 February 1839 at the British Coffee House, near Charing Cross, London. Harassed in London by the authorities, it moved to Birmingham, where there were riots as a consequence. The term 'Convention' was chosen to echo the Convention of 1789 during France's own revolution. Although Chartism continued into the 1850s, it was in an intense period in 1838, 1839 and 1842 that the worst outbreaks occurred, with magistrates, police and soldiers left running about the country attempting as best they could to keep order.

George Ryles was one of those policemen, who wrote in haste to the chief constable of Burslem, near Stoke-on-Trent in Staffordshire, on 23 July 1839, regarding a Chartist procession which looked to turn violent and revolutionary if threatened. 'The number of Chartists in Lane End is fifteen hundred,' wrote Ryles. 'They don't mean to shoot their own police if they don't interfere with them, but if the London or any other police come amongst them they will be shot, and especially the cavalry, if they come, they all swear vengeance against them.... There will be fifteen thousand from Manchester which will come through Newcastle and the Potteries.... If they are not allowed the Charter, they are sworn to blow up the Parliament House.' The Chartists were armed and had already made preparations to blow up the new railway if troops were moved by this means (troops and police were now regularly transported by train). Ryles continued in apocalyptic vein that 'they have laid down a plan to place a barrel of gunpowder near the railway with a slow match connected to it, so that if the soldiers come to Birmingham they will fire the match and blow them up'. Yet again there is talk of pikes ('spears') and guns: 'The spears are generally for big lads or youths to use; the object is to get them in the crowd amongst the police to stab them; if they are interfered with at Burslam [Burslem] they intend to barricade the ... inn and shoot the police or soldiers as they come up.' The letter was written at night and in haste, following information from a Chartist informer, but it was in response to another letter from Ryle's chief constable asking for proof of weaponry. Ryles forlornly told his chief that the informer had purchased to his knowledge two pistols, but it was impossible to 'get possession of a spear' at such short notice.

Such letters were regularly exchanged between magistrates and police chiefs during the early years of the Charter which had originated in the London Working Men's Association (LWMA) in May 1838, the brainchild of Francis Place, Henry Hetherington and others. Place (1771–1854), 'the radical tailor of Charing Cross', was the son of a bailiff. His tailoring business also included a reading room where radical material could be read by his visitors. Although a moderate, Place took over the leadership of the LCS from Hardy and became joint coordinator of the society with Despard. Unlike Despard, Place was an advocate of moral force only, which perhaps accounts for his long career in radical circles. Hetherington was another radical, who earned his living as a printer and publisher of illegal newspapers. Born in 1792 he was apprenticed to Luke Hansard, the parliamentary printer. He was also an enthusiast for working men's education and helped found the Mechanics' Institute in London, which later became Birkbeck College. For his work on behalf of political reform, Hetherington spent much time in jail and he finally died of cholera on 24 August 1849. It was Hetherington whose 'Circular for the Formation of Trades Unions' formed the basis of the National Union of the Working Classes, whose aims eventually led to Chartism.

The LWMA sought to correct some of the anomalies of the 1832 Act, while restating older libertarian beliefs, and, coming when it did at the height of industrial change, it seemed to connect the conditions of working-class life to political struggle. Although moderate in intention, it could therefore, under the right conditions, become a dangerous lever of revolutionary activity. It had itself grown out of struggle. In February 1834 the first great union had been formed, the Grand National Consolidated Trades Union, which sought to unite all working men in one body. Yet, two months later, six agricultural labourers from Tolpuddle had each been sentenced to seven years' transportation for administering an illegal oath after forming a branch of the union. In August of the same year the union collapsed. Nevertheless, there were triumphs in the early years of the 1830s. In September 1835 the Municipal Corporations Act was passed, which dramatically reformed local government, opening elections to all male ratepayers (including dissenters) and regulating the administration of local councils. The Act also required councils to form a police force. However, this was just another triumph for the middle class.

Further, in March 1836 the Newspaper Act reduced the hated stamp duty to a penny and brought an era of widespread publishing and reading of political issues, essentially making local political issues national issues for the first time. In June, Place and others started the LMWA, and in Scotland a similar organisation was begun called the National Radical Association. The spread of cheap reading and the growth of literacy, the radicalisation of industrial areas, the appearance of new political organisations and a sense that the 1832 Act had let ordinary people down meant that the stage was again set for a great political struggle with its agenda determined by the ghosts of Paine and Hunt (who died on 15 February 1835). Indeed, there was still a feeling that 'old corruption' ruled in parliament, that landed aristocracy still had too great a say, that factory reform and trade unionisation had not progressed and that the Poor Law (which introduced the dreaded workhouse) was a direct attack by the rich on the working people. The Charter merely formed the focus for this mixture of grievances, many of which were local and had little to do with the national politics that occurred far away in London.

Newport in Wales may have been far away from London, but since the late eighteenth century it had grown from a sleepy little place no bigger than a large village (of about 1,000 inhabitants) to a town (of 10,000 inhabitants) with connections to the outside world via canal and train. The coal and iron industries had prospered and the town soon grew as the Irish and English came. Although an ancient place, the town developed its own industrial blight, dirty little rows of houses, and settled in to the pattern of industrial growth that would mark South Wales until the twentieth century. The population were still mostly Welsh-speaking and, on the whole, nonconformist and highly politicised in their beliefs, so that international politics were debated and sermonised upon. David Williams, originally from Caerphilly, helped draft the First Constitution of the French Revolution, and Morgan John Rhys relinquished his ministry in Pontypool and left Wales to go and witness the troubles in France. He was present at the fall of the Bastille. By the 1830s this political awareness had hardened into demands for reform, and union clubs and lodges had been formed, all of which were secret. By the time the Chartists had got their message to Newport, it already had an organised, secretive and active base from which to mobilise its workers.[4] Indeed, these lodges had a history of industrial terrorism organised around gangs or 'herds' of 'Scotch Cattle' who would intimidate or murder those employers against whom they had a grudge. Any agitation for reform was therefore likely to be tinged with latent aggression.

The centre of Chartist agitation was the mayor of Newport, John Frost. He was born on 25 May 1784, at the Oak Inn in Newport. Having lost his father when young, he was taken care of by his grandfather, who attempted to force the young man to follow the trade of a shoemaker. Nevertheless, Frost decided instead to apprentice himself to a tailor and was so able that by the age of 20 he had moved to London to take up a tailoring position there. While in London, Frost started to attend political meetings and to read the radical pamphlets of the day. By the time he returned to Newport in 1811, he had become wealthy, but he had also taken up local politics, especially defending the rights of the town's burgesses against the agent of the main local aristocrat, a man named Thomas Prothero, who, through a number of court cases, soon proved himself not only the match for Frost but a hated enemy. By the time that Frost was the town clerk, he was regularly crossing swords with Prothero over local political issues, but the libel action brought by Prothero bankrupted Frost and he found himself in 1822 in Cold Bath Fields prison in London.

When discharged, he returned to Newport a local hero and this seems to have increased both his sense of injustice and his determination to be involved with national politics, his radical speeches getting him noticed by the Government but also making him more popular in the town. When the Municipal Corporation Act came into force he became a member of the borough council and by 1836 he was mayor of Newport, with a fierce sense of what constituted personal and political injustice. He was not mayor for long, but in the pubs of West Monmouthshire he plotted with others and helped drill local workers in the dead of night, ready for the day of action. It came when the fiery physical-force 'missionary' Henry Vincent was arrested while in Wales, first being shipped to England and then back to Newport.

Frost determined that the Welsh would free Vincent and began the preparations for a rising. The Chartists were well armed and organised and marched in three divisions towards Newport with Frost as their commander-in-chief. On the way, the population fled and those who stayed were forced to join the rebels. Heavy rain was now falling and they took shelter in each pub that they arrived at, becoming more drunk and disorderly as they progressed. What did impress Government witnesses was the fact that the working classes should have organised the action at all and in secret and in such numbers. The Government was rattled. They had cause to be, as 10,000 men were marching towards Newport. They might not have been so alarmed if they had realised that, despite the well-worked-out drill and the passwords, the Chartist army was degenerating into a milling and largely leaderless mob who were hungry, drunk and wet.

The military were already prepared and a Captain Stack with a small body of regular troops was waiting at the Westgate Hotel. Arriving at the Westgate, Frost led his men forward in drill formation: musketmen, pikemen, those with pitchforks and those with staves. A stand-off followed, in which the mayor asked the rebels what they wanted. This might have been the limit of the action, as many were losing their resolve, but a special constable tried to seize a pike, firing started and a general assault on the hotel immediately followed. The mayor was injured, and dead and wounded Chartists fell as the soldiers fired down corridors. One rebel recalled, 'We broke through and reached the passage.... The red coats were firing ... at the wild throng in the road, and we were in the midst of fire, smoke and awful cries. How I ... escaped I do not know. In the fight in the passage I happened to look down and saw my hand covered with blood, and my finger gone. It had been carried away by one of the bullets of the soldiers.' Nine died in a few minutes. The rebels fled, as did Frost.[5] One of the rebels was George Shell, an apprentice cabinet-maker and still in his teens. The day before the conflict he had written to his parents:

> Dear parents,
> I hope this will find you well, as I am myself at present. I shall this night be engaged in a struggle for freedom, and should it please God to spare my life, I shall see you soon; but if not, grieve not for me, I shall fall in a noble cause.

His body was found among the dead.

Execution of Charles I at the Banqueting Hall in London. (Courtesy of the Guildhall Library)

Apotheosis of Oliver Cromwell. (Courtesy of the Guildhall Library)

Jean-Paul Marat, who learned some of his ideas in England. (Author's collection)

Louis-Antoine-Léon Saint-Just, theoriser of revolution and Robespierre's right-hand man, known as the 'Angel of Death'. (Author's collection)

Thomas Paine, world citizen and the apostle of revolution. (Author's collection)

Coin celebrating the acquittal of Thomas Hardy of the London Corresponding Society. (Author's collection)

An Irish pike from the Rising of 1798.
(Author's collection)

RICHARD PARKER.

Richard Parker, leader of the 'Floating Republic', points to his means of execution. (Courtesy of the National Maritime Museum)

Edward Despard, before his term in jail, dressed and coiffured in the style of the old regime. (Courtesy of the Guildhall Library)

Edward Despard on the scaffold, dressed in revolutionary garb. (Courtesy of the Guildhall Library)

A reform meeting with Henry Hunt in Smithfield in 1819. (Courtesy of the Guildhall Library)

Arthur Thistlewood, leader of the Cato Street gang. (Courtesy of the City of Westminster Archives)

Cato Street off the Edgware Road in London, now an office, but a hayloft in 1820. (Author's collection. By permission of Howard Hyman Associates)

Jeremiah Brandreth: the execution block said still to run with his blood. (Courtesy of Derby City Museums)

Jeremiah Brandreth: part of a grisly commemorative china service. (Courtesy of Derby City Museums)

Sir William Courtenay's banner preserved at Mount Ephraim, Kent. (By permission of Sandys Dawes)

John Thom, known as Sir William Courtenay when he came to Kent. (By permission of Sandys Dawes)

Interior of the reformed House of Commons, 1834. (Author's collection)

A meeting of a republican club in the late 1850s. Such meetings were noted for their clouds of tobacco smoke, seen here floating above the debate. (Author's collection)

Above: *Karl Marx, inventor of the creed that bears his name, lived in poverty in Soho.* (Author's collection)

Above, right: *Friedrich Engels, gentleman, business man and revolutionary, lived in Manchester.* (Author's collection)

Fenian bombing of Scotland Yard. (Courtesy of the Guildhall Library)

The Scots Guards at the Siege of Sidney Street in 1911. (Courtesy of the Guildhall Library)

Soldiers pose on the streets of Dublin during the Easter rising of 1916. (Author's collection)

2 November 2019, Glasgow. Independence supports with flags at the IndyRef2020 rally.
(SOPA Images Limited/Alamy Stock Photo)

16 September 2022, Cardiff Castle. Anti-royalist protestors outside Cardiff Castle as
Charles III makes his first visit to Wales as king. (Steven May/Alamy Stock Photo)

10 September 2022, London. Protestors outside St James's Palace as Charles III is proclaimed monarch. (Horst Friedrichs/Alamy Stock Photo)

Chapter Twelve

Northern Star

James Bronterre O'Brien, son of a tobacco merchant of Dublin, lawyer and latterly the co-editor of the *Poor Man's Guardian*, voiced the feelings of many when he wrote of parliament in the *London Mercury* on 19 February 1837 that 'session after session is wasted in rubbishing motions.... It would seem as though both factions had ... conspired to render the unrepresented millions as dead in public interest, as they are dead in law. Their whole talk [affects] only the members themselves, or the rich plundering fraction of the country that elects them.' O'Brien outlined his own version of a reformist Chartist parliament in the *Northern Star*, on 25 May 1839. He suggested that 'at the next general election we must have Chartists as our representatives.... We shall have a parliament legally chosen under the Queen's writ, and we shall then soon show our tyrants the difference between the parliament nominated by nine or ten millions and one elected by three or four thousand monopolists. The people's Parliament will meet at Birmingham.' For O'Brien, the political aims of Chartism were also social and economic, a point he made in *The Operative* on 17 March 1839, as 'universal suffrage means meat and drink and clothing, good hours, and good beds, and good substantial furniture for every man and women and child who will do a fair day's work. Universal suffrage means a complete mastery, by all the people over all the laws and institutions in the country; and with that mastery the power of providing suitable employment for all.'

There is no doubt that, although Chartism was moderate and certainly not intended as a revolutionary cause, the hint of armed protection for the newly elected delegates meeting now in the heart of the country was enough to make many think that Chartism was another word for civil war. Such violence was confirmed by Feargus O'Connor, a bitter enemy of O'Brien, who wavered between pacifistic 'moral force' politics and a more aggressive 'physical force' variety, in which he liked to fantasise about himself on the barricades with 'the people': 'A great many blind horses have taken fright,' he said, 'because they have seen physical force on one side of the road in practice, and on the other side of the road in theory. Why do you pay taxes? Because there is physical force. You are cutting sticks to fight yourselves with. Blackstone[1] says it is right to take up arms when the laws do not protect you ... I have said that if there was to be fighting, I should be found fighting on the side of the people.'[2] As 1838 progressed, O'Connor began to sound more and more seditious. At a speech in Leicester, he proclaimed that 'a party of man have sprung up ... who speak of moral courage and denounce physical force.... They consider it moral force to write a strong article in the newspaper.... But if peace procure not the law, then I am for disorder. Peace to be valuable must procure that which will give the greatest amount of happiness to the people, but if the peace is to be all on one side, I care not for it; I am for peace being general or not at all.'[3]

O'Connor was always a difficult character, a prickly man who made enemies and was called 'the Dictator' by O'Brien (whom O'Connor called 'the School Master'), but who dominated the more working-class element in the movement and may be said

to have created the first real sense of a proletariat, a situation recognised by Engels in a speech given at Brussels on 17 July and
published in the *Northern Star* on 25 July 1846:

> When the middle classes have carried their chief measure,
> when they have only to replace the present weak go-between
> cabinet by an energetical, really middle-class ministry, in
> order to be the acknowledged ruling class of your country,
> that now the great struggle of capital and labour, of bourgeois
> and proletarian must come to a decision… . Middle class and
> working class are the only classes betwixt whom there can be
> a possible struggle… . The middle class – 'extension of com-
> merce by any means whatsoever, and a ministry of Lancashire
> cotton-lords to carry this out', – the working class – 'a demo-
> cratic reconstruction of the constitution upon the basis of the
> People's Charter' by which the working class will become the
> ruling class of England.

Despite the endorsement of class war, O'Connor was never
an advocate of socialism, unlike other Chartists, such as Ernest
Jones and George Harney.

O'Connor was the son of Roger O'Connor, a United
Irishman with an estate in County Cork which the son inherited
in 1820, and, although Protestant, he acted benignly towards
his Catholic tenants, participating in anti-tithe agitation and
advocating the repeal of the Act of Union. O'Connor was soon
in parliament, helped by Daniel O'Connell, leader of the Irish
radicals, whom O'Connor hoped soon to replace. The two men
fell out, the first of O'Connor's many partings with colleagues.
O'Connor was fêted by his European fellows for his aggressive
stance on reform, and looked upon suspiciously by his British
counterparts, who did not trust him. It was as a European
that Engels applauded O'Connor's position on Ireland (at the
expense of O'Connell, whom he referred to as a 'political jug-
gler') in an article he wrote for the *Deutsche-Brusseler-Zeitung* on

9 January 1848. In response to an Irish coercion bill, Engels suggested that English working men join with Irish patriots. Such a coalition would, in Engels's mind, become truly revolutionary, and O'Connor would be its leader:

> For ... O'Connor speaks ... not only as an Irishman but also, and primarily, as an English democrat, as a Chartist.... O'Connor shows that the Irish people must fight with all their might and in close association with the English working classes and the Chartists in order to win ... the People's Charter ... only after [this] is won will the achievement of the [1832] Repeal have any advantages for Ireland ... there can be no doubt that hence forth the mass of the Irish people will unite ever more closely with the English Chartists and will act with them according to a common plan. As a result the victory of the English democrats, and hence the liberation of Ireland, will be hastened by many years.

In 1835, O'Connor lost his parliamentary seat and tried to stand for Oldham (the former seat of William Cobbett), but lost. He toured the country, joined the LWMA and, after moving to Leeds, began the *Northern Star*, one of the great publishing successes of the era. In a speech in Manchester, he finally came down on the side of physical force, giving 29 September 1839 as the date for a general uprising. The speech split the Chartists, who excluded him from the LWMA. He then founded the East London Democratic Association, which was in favour of violent action but which took none itself. Jailed for seditious libel, he continued to edit the paper from his cell, finally claiming the leadership of the Chartist movement. Released in August 1841, O'Connor was again in trouble, for his part in the 1842 Plug Riots (the nominated series of national strikes), but was acquitted.

By the 1840s, O'Connor had a land scheme (the Chartist Land Plan4) to collectivise the land, but his plantation in

Gloucestershire failed after he had already collected £100,000 from 70,000 people. Nevertheless, O'Connor remained the people's hero, speaking at the 'monster' rally on Kennington Common on 10 April 1848, where he referred to the gathered masses as 'my children'. Yet O'Connor had alienated most of the leaders of Chartism and was also acting bizarrely (possibly from syphilis), finally attacking W. Crips (MP for Cirencester) in the House of Commons. Such behaviour got O'Connor committed to an asylum in Chiswick. Discharging himself in 1854, he went to live with his sister, where he died on 30 August 1855. It is said that 50,000 attended his funeral.

The political creed of respectable middle-class aspiration contended for the limelight with its own extremists and the lower orders, who were slowly turning into a recognisable working class and who were already suspicious of their entrepreneurial 'betters'. Nothing brings this to light more clearly than the fight between the Anti-Corn Law League, led by Richard Cobden, and the Chartists under O'Connor. Cobden was born on 3 June 1804 at Dunford Farmhouse, near Midhurst in Sussex. His father, a yeoman farmer, lost his money and his mother had to open a village shop to support the family. Having been employed by his uncle as a travelling salesman in the cloth trade, Cobden finally found prosperity as a calico dyer and printer in Manchester, the rapidly growing industrial heartland of Britain. With 'Bonapartist feeling' and the sense that Manchester was 'the place for money making business', Cobden was soon to come to the conclusion that only a repeal of restrictive trade practice, exemplified by the tariff against imported wheat (the notorious Corn Law), would create the prosperity vital to economic, social and political wellbeing among all classes. Laissez-faire would, once the Corn Laws were repealed, open up the possibility not only of widening markets but of feeding the labouring poor. Market-led know-how would create the basis for the political reforms the Chartists were already demanding. Cobden, a good Anglican, saw it as God's work and Christian duty.

The national Anti-Corn Law League was founded in March 1839 after being tried out in a trial in Manchester. Cobden became its leading voice. Yet at its heart was a problem that Cobden could never fully solve. This was the new conflict between the rapidly self-recognising working class and their suspicion of the new system where 'three thousand hands [worked] under one capitalist'. Radical capitalism was now in direct opposition to revolutionary working-class demands. These centred around the six demands of Cobden's contemporaries, working-class Chartists who were, under extreme pressure, willing to take to guns, as they did at Newport. Chartist demands sought to deal with parliamentary reform prior to economic adjustment, seeing in this a strategy that would stop power slipping into the hands of the new 'mountebank cosmopolites', as O'Connor called his Anti-Corn Law opponents in the *Northern Star*.

Chartists believed that any such victory would lower wages, create unemployment, make factories worse and destroy the rural economy that supported agricultural labourers. Cobden believed in laissez-faire (limited in bad times by state help) and the repeal of restrictive trade practices (the Corn Laws) as the key to a new British utopia. Cobden saw that without an alliance of the entrepreneurial middle class and the working hands, the only winners would be the aristocracy, for whom working people had too much 'reverence'. In short, Cobden saw the Chartists as a revolutionary force for reaction and their talk of democracy as so much sincere humbug to whip up the masses. Cobden's *bête noire* was the working-class mob leader O'Connor, with whom he debated in Northampton on 5 August 1844. O'Connor, Cobden felt, was attempting to hold back progress in order to return to 'gothic feudalism' and, worse, he was fomenting civil war:

> We must deal boldly with these leaders, and expose them, and we must deal frankly with their deluded followers by telling them on all occasions that they are powerless without the aid

of the middle class. The working class, as a class, have been
flattered too much. They must be made acquainted with their
weakness. At no time in our history was the multitude so
powerless as at present in a physical point of view. In barba-
rous ages, when men fought with clubs or battle axes, a rude
undisciplined mob had a good chance if they outnumbered
their oppressors. But now, when the refinements of science
have been applied to the art of war, mere numbers are as
nothing in opposition to a disciplined force.[5]

For his part, O'Connor could point out that Cobden was
opposed to any factory reform, including limitation of working
hours, and he could take satisfaction in the fact that Cobden was
destroyed by laissez-faire, went bankrupt and had to retire to
his old house at Dunford. O'Connor, who championed primitive land-sharing communism, could not seem more different
from Cobden, the mill owner and self-made gentleman. Yet
both emerged from the two sides of the new social order that
ever so gradually (for there was often more noise than action)
was sweeping aside the old England of feudal respect, small artisans and landed interest. Cobden and his colleagues heralded in
their persons as well as in their actions a new capitalism and new
liberal democracy; O'Connor epitomised the new politicised
conscience of an emerging working-class movement at war with
both. Cobden's hopes of reconciliation were never to be fulfilled
and both O'Connor's and Cobden's dreams of a new utopia were
to become distant memories within one generation, as capitalists
and socialists began their struggle.

The utopian impulse epitomised by Cobden's economic
vision and O'Connor's political agenda illustrates the way revolutionary actions by the middle classes prompted the creation of
counteractions equally revolutionary but antithetical by their
opponents in the rising working class. The pre-industrial legacy
brought about new circumstances for revolutionary change but
it would remain a struggle for the labour movement to harness

the raw energy of traditional vigilantism and turn it into a parliamentary force.

During the months following Newport, Chartists still hoped for a rising. In Newcastle, where the *Northern Liberator* was published, a number of big meetings were held, where Harney and Dr John Taylor advocated physical force. Rumours circulated that pikes could be bought in the town for 1s 6d and that 10,000 had been ordered. On 20 August 1839 rioting finally broke out and soldiers had to be called.[6] The troops were led by Colin Campbell, later known as the officer in charge of the 'thin red line' in the Crimea.[7] The fury of the fight is well conveyed in the *Newcastle Leader* of December 1897, which reprinted an article written at the time:

> A tailor from Whittingham received a wound from a sword in the abdomen, and was instantly conveyed to the infirmary. [Three gentlemen] came up and assisted ... but [were] overpowered.... The mayor ... made another attempt to disperse the mob, the only effect of which was to cause a cowardly assault ... with stones. The Riot Act having been read four times without success, the police were ordered to march forward, which they did with great effect, seizing upon all the banners of the mob, and capturing several of the most active amongst them. The rioters next attacked the police with repeated volleys of stones.... But about this time, a troop of dragoons and some infantry ... which had been sent from the barracks, speedily put an end to the affray. The cavalry galloped along the streets, up passages and lanes, the affrighted people rushing in all directions to find shelter.

Revolution was in the air and in 1840 there were plans for general uprisings in Sheffield, Barnsley, Dewsbury, Bradford and Nottingham. Sheffield had long had a militant strain. This went back to the reforming Constitutional Society, which was active between 1791 and 1796 and was one of the strongest reform clubs in the country. During 1830 this became the

Friends of Parliamentary Reform, and in 1831 the Sheffield Political Union. During 1832, when elections were held under the new franchise, violent rioting left three men and two boys dead. Indeed, it has been suggested that if a revolution were to have occurred in these years, it was more likely to have been in Sheffield than in Manchester or London.

Between 1821 and 1831, the population grew from 65,000 to 91,000 and many strangers were now in Sheffield. There had already been much agitation for the Charter prior to Samuel Holberry's arrival in the town. 'Monster' rallies had gathered and been addressed by both O'Connor and Harney. Militant Chartism was in the ascendant once moderate middle-class reformers had deserted to the Anti-Corn Law League. Holberry came from Nottinghamshire, a former agricultural worker turned soldier in Ireland. Like many at this time, Holberry was a drifter making his way to London and then to Sheffield as a distiller. Meetings had been banned since the aborted 'national holiday' (a general strike) of 12 August 1839, but they continued, nevertheless, with clashes with police and soldiers. Holberry and others planned an insurrection with the gathered Chartists of the northern towns for the night of 12/13 January 1840. Holberry's plan was to seize Sheffield town hall and the Tontine Inn opposite, stop the mail and thereby alert the other towns, which would spontaneously rise too. Holberry had certainly convinced several hundred men that a fight might be worthwhile and that contingents from nearby towns would march to the aid of the Sheffield fighters. Indeed the whole plan was decidedly 'Irish' in its secret execution and planning. The Chartists planned in secret 'classes' adopted from the Wesleyan model and they had a general assembly room where the ammunition was stockpiled. They also had a general council of war. As well as guns and grenades, a number of caltrops (spiked stars) were provided for hobbling the cavalry horses. The plans included seizing the barracks and burning the homes of magistrates and 'gentlemen'. All police were to be killed.

Holberry and his confederates were betrayed by a Rotherham man called James Allen, and all were arrested on 11 January. Allen was the keeper of the Station Inn in Rotherham and passed on the information about the insurrection to John Bland, the chief constable of Sheffield. Allen regularly reported to Bland, who passed on the messages to Lord Howard. Allen alleged that delegates from Sheffield, Rotherham and Huddersfield had met at his beer house and that all had pledged support for a revolt. It appears that the Chartists grew suspicious of Allen and, under police advice, he declared himself for physical force at a meeting, in which confidence in him was restored. Nevertheless, fearing for his life, Allen finally escaped. Holberry was taken at his home at Eyre Lane and much ammunition was found there. When he was arrested, the police superintendent reported that

> [he] ... found twelve hand grenades, one and a half dozen of fire-balls, made of pitch and tar, three dozen of tin cases ... forty pieces of ball cartridge, one hundred or two of iron bullets, fuse conductors, and an iron pot with pitch in it.... I have seen a grenade opened ... and found first a coat of hards, then pitch covered with small pebble stones, and a bullet, in the centre a blacking bottle stopped up with a bit of wood, with a hole through it, and a quill through the hole filled with gun powder; the bottle was filled with blasting powder and slugs.[8]

Fighting continued to break out in the town despite the failure of the plot. The *Leeds Intelligencer* reported on 18 January 1840:

> In the outskirts of the town some of the policemen were fired upon, and others attacked with pikes and bayonets, and we regret to add that some of the wounds inflicted are of a serious nature. One man, who, from being dressed in a rough coat, it is supposed was mistaken for a policeman, was fired at, and so dangerously wounded that he was conveyed to the infirmary, and twenty seven slugs had been extracted ... from his neck

and shoulders... . In the course of the night several persons were taken prisoners, and a great quantity of muskets, pikes, daggers [caltrops], powder, balls, grenades ... were seized.

On 16 March, Holberry was brought to trial and

the court presented from the outset a very animated appearance; the gentlemen of the legal profession attending in large numbers both for and against the prisoners. Holberry [was] first indicted for conspiracy and riot. By way of supporting the evidence against the prisoners, a large basket full of hand-grenades, and other combustible materials, was placed upon the table, and a great number of pikes and daggers were also produced. The evidence went to prove that these were found in possession of the prisoners at the time of their arrest. The charges appeared to weigh most heavily against Holberry, who did not, when arrested, deny, but on the contrary, admitted, that his object was to upset the government and he professed his willingness to die for the Charter.

Holberry and John Clayton, a grinder, each received four years. Clayton died in jail in 1841 and, after bouts of solitary and on the treadmill, Holberry was so exhausted that he, too, died on 21 June 1842. He was only 29. It was a sign of social progress that Holberry was tried under the same statute as the Cato Street conspirators but did not suffer execution – only the 'execution' of a short prison sentence.[9]

Passions were high. In Dewsbury, fears mounted until the night of 11 January 1840, when Bradford Chartists were said to be planning on marching to the town, seizing cannon from the Low Moor Cannon Foundry and thereafter marching to London to demand the setting free of John Frost of Newport. Guns were fired as a signal and a fire balloon flown. Unfortunately the fire balloon ignited too quickly, ruining the Chartists' coordination of events. Nevertheless, 300–400 people entered Dewsbury firing pistols and generally making a row, but the pistols were not loaded and the only damage was some broken windows and the destruction of some wine bottles in a local warehouse.[10] One Joseph Page was arrested for inciting the rioters, but acquitted when it was realised he was too drunk on the night to have done anything. Despite the fact that the inhabitants of Dewsbury had requested troops to put down any disturbances, when they did arrive their billeting was thought too costly and they were asked to leave. Chartist disturbances, with broken windows and wine bottles or not, were preferable to the expense of the army.

The rioting and violence of 1839–40 again came to a head in 1842, with widespread disorder, especially in Leicester (the Battle of Mownacre Field), Hyde, Ashton-under-Lyne, Burslem, Dudley, Stockport, Salford, Manchester and elsewhere. The yeomanry, having fallen into redundancy, were revived to deal with the trouble, being often called out; new barracks were established for regular troops where problems might occur. With no national police force, the Metropolitan Police were taken by train around the country and special constables regularly sworn in. In charge of this force was Sir Charles Napier.

Napier was the eldest son of George Napier, a Scot, and Sarah Lennox, fourth daughter of the Duke of Richmond. He was a cousin of Charles Fox and Edward Fitzgerald. The family moved to Ireland and, at 16, he found himself fighting the 1798 rebels; in 1803 he was in action during Emmet's Rising. Napier went with Wellington to Spain, and thence to America, the Mediterranean and Greece. By 1839, he had given up military service and wanted to return to Ireland. He was an 'advocate for annual parliament, universal suffrage and the vote by ballot'. Described as a 'great radical', he believed that 'Chartism cannot be stopped, God forbid that it should'. Thus at the age of 56 and an unlikely candidate for keeping order, Napier, with his leonine locks (he had an under-chin beard of 1ft in length), was sent up north. The general, though strict himself, realised that the overenthusiasm of some magistrates caused more problems and he often had to restrain the yeomanry, whom he considered too fond of 'cutting and slashing'.[11] At the same time, he realised that a policeman with a wooden stave was a sitting target for armed insurrectionists – a man 'with a stick, surrounded by all sorts of rogues'. Napier did his best with a series of uncoordinated and essentially local forces to keep things in hand.

Meanwhile, the Chartists themselves, though ill organised, were probably the best-armed force of civilians that Britain had seen. They were certainly better armed than the Irish insurgents of 1798 and the rebels of Pentrich, and certainly better organised and equipped than the fanatics of Cato Street. The Government filled their ranks with spies, considered the leaders windbags, and worked on the assumption that, despite everything, any coordination between such rabble would be impossible. Yet a fundamental tenet of Chartism was the right to bear arms – an ancient liberty that it was felt the appearance of a police force might remove. Again and again, it was reiterated that an Englishman had the right to defend himself. On 12 May 1839 *The Operative*, O'Brien's newspaper, reprinted the following speech from the first Convention of 17 February:

> Aware of our position, your oppressors are moving heaven and earth to bring us into collision with the enemy. They are pouring spies and traitors into your ranks … and by brutal and unconstitutional treatment, seek to exasperate the people to madness and rebellion.
>
> […] Yes, countrymen, they are actually encouraging a project, of arming the enemies of the country at the expense of the state, whilst at the same time they are hunting out pretexts … for dispossessing the Chartists of their rightful arms… . You have the same right to arm that your enemies have, and that if you abandon that right your liberties are gone forever… . Parade not your arms at public meetings but keep them bright and ready at home… . This convention is of opinion, that wherever and whenever persons assembled for

> just and legal purposes ... are assailed by the police ... they
> are justified ... in meeting force by force.

The Metropolitan Police, especially, were seen not as protectors but as oppressors, roaming the country at will, their activities out of control. The Chartists on the whole believed them to be an 'unconstitutional and obnoxious force'. In 1848 George Brown, in his paper 'Physical Force', was urging his readers to 'get arms' to defend themselves against the police and yeomanry, and, as late as the 1880s, two bills to restrict the carrying of arms for personal use (1881 and 1883) failed as being against the principles of English liberty.

Republican sentiment flourished elsewhere, as well. In Canada, two rebellions broke out during 1837. For a time the future of Canada was at stake. The first rebellion, in Lower Canada, grew from French resentment at anglophone control, not made better by the arrival of Irish immigrants, who carried cholera to the country. Led by Louis-Joseph Papineau, the French formed a Parti patriote, and then a more militant wing, the Fils de la Liberté. On 23 November 1837 British troops suffered a minor defeat, but at the Battle of Saint-Denis and the Battle of Saint-Charles, the rebels were crushed. Papineau went into exile in Paris, while twelve men were executed and fifty-eight transported to Australia.

The second revolt was more serious and was an attempt to set up an independent Canadian constitution on American lines. The mainly American- or British-born inhabitants of Upper Canada, who were largely nonconformist and republican in their views, were increasingly annoyed about being excluded from political power. The Reform Party won an increasing number of seats in the elections of 1828 and 1834. Despite reasonable reform requests, the new governor, Sir Francis Bond Head, took a tough stance, which eventually pushed aside the moderates, and William Lyon Mackenzie (originally from Dundee) took control of the 'physical force' faction; this persuaded the radicals to draught a constitution modelled on that of the United States. There was an attempted coup in December and Mackenzie found himself in charge of a full-scale rebellion for five days. Defeated in a number of skirmishes, Mackenzie fled to the United States, but returned to seize Navy Island in the Niagara river and declare a republic. Finally he was defeated on 14 January 1838, and forced back over the border. This was not the end of the matter, as raids of a substantial nature continued, but all were defeated. Arriving in New York, Mackenzie ran a republican newspaper, *Mackenzie's Gazette*, but the 'neutrality laws' put him in prison for a year. Out of love with American ways, he returned to Canada after the general amnesty of 1850 and was promptly elected mayor of Toronto. Things had indeed changed and the British had learned their lesson. In 1840 the Act of Union joined Upper and Lower Canada into the Province of Canada. Mackenzie died on 28 August 1861 in Toronto.

Defeated at home, Chartists looked overseas. America beckoned. Hundreds of Chartists took their chances with icebergs and cliff-high waves when the Great Charter finally failed in 1848. Disappointment at home always allowed for possible success abroad. Paine turned going to America into a spiritual destiny; Cobbett used it as a bolt-hole between 1816 and 1817; Owen hoped to create his ideal society at New Harmony in southern Indiana during 1826; Cobden bought shares in railway projects that crossed the Midwestern territories; Coleridge and Southey dreamed of living the 'Pantisocratic' lifestyle on a little farm in the backwoods, but never quite made it; Dickens toured in 1843, preceded by Fanny Trollope, who braved the Atlantic in 1827. America called to the brave and the free, as well as to the starving and desperate.

The enthusiasm for America reached back into the 1790s, when men like Thomas Cooper, a Bolton merchant and Unitarian read Paine's *Rights of Man* and became so 'politically mad' that he travelled to the United States to fulfil his dream. Other British Jacobins joined him, such as 'Citizen Lee', John

Binns, John Gales, Daniel Isaac Eaton and many others, as well as Charles Pendrill, the shoemaker associate of Despard, who fled to the United States in 1817 to avoid capture by the authorities. For the LWMA, in Westminster, America represented 'a beacon of freedom for all mankind'. The *Poor Man's Guardian*, on 22 October 1831, represented America as the promised land, as somewhere English aspirations could flourish: 'For those Atlantic republicans have shown us that men can eat, and drink, and sleep, and have children and homes, and firesides and trade, and commerce, and agriculture, and great moral and intellectual, as well as political, weight in the world ... and yet have no national debt and no king.' The *Illustrated News*, in 1849, concluded that the exodus to the United States was the millennial fulfilment of the Anglo-Saxon race: 'The civilisation that is removed is not destroyed; and the genius of our people can exert itself as well on the banks of the Ohio, or the Mississippi, as on the banks of the Thames; and rule the world from the White House at Washington, with as much propriety as from the Palace of St James.'

Some were too enamoured of American liberty. Thomas Parkin actually invited the Americans to invade Britain in order to save the Charter, but such lunatics alienated those who had advocated emigration and who now increasingly turned to the land schemes that flourished in the period in order to encourage people to stay. Nevertheless, large numbers of Chartists left England. These were mostly 'physical force' men who were on the run from the authorities. In all, approximately 500 Chartists left England, of whom seventy were prominent leaders of the movement. Not all were 'hunted like wild beasts for being Chartists', as *The Times* reported on 4 October 1839, and some went either as 'missionaries' or as 'moral force' Chartists who, fed up with O'Connor, decided to make a new life in the new states with the most liberal constitutions, such as Iowa and Wisconsin. Indeed Wisconsin's constitution incorporated all the Chartist demands.

Harney invented the term 'political emigration' as a euphemism for being wanted by the law. One such group from Sheffield moved en masse to America and settled in Bridgeport and Waterbury in Connecticut. Most Chartists escaped through Liverpool and on to Waterford in Ireland and thence to New York or Boston, thereafter making their way into the newly settled West. In this they were often helped by the secret service, who wished to avoid expensive trials and were happy to see the back of troublemakers. During May 1852 the sum of £1,380 was used to help such people as George White, O'Connor's lieutenant, and others who were 'marked' to slip out of the country. Indeed, John Rees, who took part in the Newport rising, seems to have done just that, arriving in Virginia and becoming part of the Texican army, despite the fact that rewards had been posted all over Monmouth for his capture. When O'Connor went as a missionary to America (or skipped England for New York, in order to avoid being put into an asylum) he was given a civic reception, but had to leave again hurriedly when he acted inappropriately towards a female shop-worker. Yet it continued to be a secret policy of the Government to encourage or 'allow' as many members of the National Charter Association to escape abroad as possible, by which means they broke up the organisation without having to make expensive arrests or face trials that ended in acquittal. Despite this, 1,400 Chartists went to jail during the period, even though in 1842 there were only 2,000 members of the association, and by 1850 only 500 were still committed to the cause sufficiently to pay their dues.

The British government was certainly not inclined to stem the flow of those willingly leaving British and Irish shores. Malthusian visions of a population explosion in the United Kingdom followed by poverty and starvation gave added impetus to Government indifference. How convenient if troublemakers, Irish peasants and Highland crofters simply went a long way away and never returned. In London, three commissioners were in charge of regulating emigration along with some clerks representing the Colonial Land and Emigration Board. At ports where emigrants gathered, semi-retired naval officers on half-pay looked after paperwork. There was little point: the Tories and Whigs were happy to see human exports as part of the drive towards free trade. More importantly the numbers involved precluded much interference. From the first weeks of an independent United States until the mid-1850s, nearly 3½ million British and Irish left for Boston, New York and Philadelphia. And nearly 2 million of those left during 1846–55. A comparison with other nationals shows the enormity of the exodus. In 1846 only four Poles and three Greeks were registered as entering America, and in 1851 there was only one Russian and just over 400 Italians. During the 1840s, most of the emigrants were poor Irish crossing the Atlantic in American steamers and sailing ships outbound from Liverpool.

The journey was only one of the perils of emigration, which included being rooked while waiting in lodgings ready to embark, having your savings stolen or exchanged for useless currency or at a crippling exchange rate, or finding your belongings shanghaied before your eyes. The worst experience of all was seasickness, which all classes suffered and for which rest, cayenne pepper, good beef tea, ginger root and prayer were prescribed. If families were too poor for anything but steerage, the journey was almost equivalent to that on slave ships. Dysentery and seasickness made the human cargo holds little more than floating sewers. Nevertheless, observers noted that those leaving British shores were happy and forward-looking and certainly not crying and lamenting their former lives. It could not be denied, however, that the voyage had implications wider than a mere change of address. The Irish Emigrant Society of New York cautioned those thinking of leaving Ireland in 1849 'that you must never forget that when you emigrate, you leave home'. It was a truism, perhaps, but nevertheless profound.

Arrival in New York or any of the other east-coast cities was little more than a lottery and many poorer immigrants died before they had raised money to pay for their loved ones (usually wives) to follow. Worse, those who had no experience of manual labouring or a craft found getting a job almost an impossibility. For many of the radicals who travelled to America, the truth slowly dawned that this was not the democratic utopia they had dreamed about and fought for back in Britain. Radicals and others complained that the Americans, although strong and healthy, were also brash, dirty-mannered (especially the women) and uncivil. Fanny Trollope, in *Domestic Manners of the Americans*, a book she wrote after a visit to Cincinnati in 1827 (where she hoped to set up a 'bazaar'), expressed the view of many when she concluded that 'I do not like them. I do not like their principles. I do not like their manners. I do not like their opinions.' Her son Anthony could only agree with his mother when he found himself on an American train and discovered that his favourite writing desk had been dropped and broken by a careless porter. Owen's utopian New Harmony soon fell apart, ridiculed by Dickens in *Martin Chuzzlewit* when the hero buys a tract of useless swamp land in Illinois, called Eden. Cobden's railway dreams also failed when no one wanted to travel on his lines.

One who made his way to America was William Linton. The friend of Giuseppe Mazzini, Lajos Kossuth and every revolutionary nationalist in Europe, he was a deeply religious man who yet belonged to no church. His passions, nationalism and feeling for democracy were themselves part of his personal religious outlook, at their centre the idea of the working classes. In the year of Reform, 1832, Linton decided that his beliefs precluded his being a Christian. Instead, his religion was that of the individual priest – a believer in a private ethical deism. Linton accepted the historical reality of Jesus but only as a son of the working class, whose message was social and ethical. In this respect, Linton's own profession of a wood-engraver (of some talent) seemed apposite.

In his early publications, Linton had called himself 'one of the people', but in 1840 he changed his writing name to

'Spartacus', the hero-martyr of the enslaved. Spartacus was one of the people and the very one to overthrow the slavery of his fellows. Linton's entire personal outlook, with its emphasis on the people, enslavement, personal destiny and apocalyptic show-down with authority (Spartacus versus Rome), formed the same mould as his other heroes from the English Civil War. One of his most beloved possessions, pored over endlessly, was *A Retired Man's Meditations* by the mystical republican regicide Sir Henry Vane. In it, he underlined the passages relating to personal election and the tasks of the righteous. Everywhere, the righteous (the people) had been cheated, first by aristocracy and then by the middle-class coup that produced the electoral reforms of 1832. Linton, however, wanted nothing less than universal suffrage which rested upon the 'inherent right of humanity'. To succeed, one needed 'revolutionary virtue [and] energy', which would finally 'prostrate the aristocratic and shopocratic factions in the dust' and allow the workers to triumph; socialism was a religious duty but enacted in social space. This was religion devoid of supernaturalism, or the superstition associated with the Catholicism that Linton distrusted and which he believed was attached to the monarchy he hated.

The heroes of the revolution were certainly not men like Cobden, whom Linton thought a selfish traitor. In November 1853 Linton chastised Cobden in front of a gathering of European exiles. Cobden had opposed a war with Russia in the Crimea but Linton saw the action as an English duty determined by national destiny in the fight against European despotism. To great applause, Linton argued that 'the English [*sic*] must fight ... because while there were men in England who held the faith of Milton and Cromwell, England would not be divorced from Europe'. What was needed was the return to the austere republican virtues of the seventeenth century. Writing to Leigh Hunt in 1849, Linton reiterated his political creed in words that harped back to the 1640s and 1650s and would have been rec-ognised by Lilburne and Winstanley: 'I am content to give up a certain achievement in art … for the hope of creating a party – a religious party… . We … will lay the first stone of an England, noble as ever Milton dreamed, strong as if every Englishman was himself a Cromwell.'[12] In espousing the cause of liberty, equality and fraternity, Linton returned again and again to Milton and Cromwell. The basic foundation of society was to be a hard-working and virtuous (Protestant) family, with children and wives given freedom to develop in loving relationships. Not surprisingly, Linton looked to the happy childhoods of his heroes as models. The new 'English Republic' was Linton's socialist programme, aimed not only at righting social injustice but also in elevating the spirituality of the individual. Such socialism was already on the wane. Linton published his views in the *Red Republican*, the same paper that would publish Helen MacFarlane's translation of the *Communist Manifesto* (writing as 'Howard Morton').

Linton sailed for America after his dreams of a Chartist England came to nothing. He travelled to New York in 1866 at the age of 54 with the intention of setting up a British republican colony in Montana, but was, he claimed, frustrated by the financial failure of the North Pacific Railroad. By the time that he left England, Linton was forgotten and broke. Leaving his estranged wife, Eliza, and one mentally ill child back at home, he travelled, an unwilling exile to Manhattan. He had no great expectation of the American mentality; after all, this was not the place he originally hoped to set up his New Jerusalem. He was soon attacking the Anti-Slavery Society as weak-kneed, and critical of the cotton trade as heading for disaster. As for his fellow New Yorkers, he saw 'lack of reverence, and credulity, civilisation and yet existent savagery … a strange young people here; not yet settled … [a] tadpole state'.[13]

One or two old Chartists and reformers joined up with Linton but, for the most part, he gave up his old radical life, relinquishing the public plaudits to Eliza, who was now a famous author and virulent anti-feminist who fought all forms of liberation, despite (or even because of) her own not wholly repressed lesbianism. One area he would not relinquish was the support of revolutionary nationalism in Italy and Poland, and he continued to coordinate the American end of the Italian revolutionary Mazzini's network. Such aspirations did not apply to the Irish. Linton was contemptuous of their revolutionaries, who he believed had neglected the fundamentals of universal suffrage and land reform in favour of a vacuous republicanism. Indeed, Linton always stood by the fact that Ireland could have no existence outside the brotherhood of English-speaking peoples who formed the British Isles.

Linton could hardly stand the wishy-washy revolutionaries among his American colleagues, preferring instead to throw in his lot with those who had 'European revolutionary aspirations'. In so doing, he agreed to help General Gustave-Paul Cluseret and a Dr Basora, who were trying to raise an army to invade Cuba and help the revolutionaries there overthrow Spanish rule. Cluseret was a hero in revolutionary eyes, for although he had put down the French insurrection of 1848, he had subsequently volunteered to fight despotic Russia in the Crimea, joined Garibaldi in Italy, fought in America and then had gone on to support the Paris Commune of 1871. The Commune had been set up after the French under Napoleon III had been humiliatingly defeated by Bismarck's new Germany. In defiance of French government orders, the Paris National Guard had created the very first workers' republic on socialist lines. After days of extraordinary violence, and after 20,000 Communards had lost their lives, Paris was finally retaken by *French* troops. In the 1870s and 1880s the Commune became the legendary centre of republican ideology, just as the French Republic had been in the 1790s.

Cluseret was a black-bearded, white-faced, international freedom fighter – a nineteenth-century Che Guevara. Cluseret had, in fact, set up revolutionary communes in Marseilles and Lyons. During October 1870 he was appointed Minister for War by the Paris Commune and by a miracle he had escaped execution, primarily because he had been arrested and cashiered for negligence and could therefore claim, with some justification, that he was on the Government's side all along. Before all this, he had got a commission as a brigadier-general in the Union army during the Civil War, after which it was widely rumoured that he had become involved with the Fenians plotting to invade Canada. He travelled to England in 1867, where it was said that he had been involved with the bloody Fenian attack on Chester jail and got away by pleading American citizenship. He had been deported and taken himself off to proclaim the revolution in France.

Linton was to be Cluseret and Basora's front man in contacting the ex-Union general Ben Butler to lead the invasion. Butler, in turn, nominated Brigadier General Sumner Currutt as a more suitable candidate. Meanwhile, Linton wrote angry letters to President Garfield calling for urgent support for Cuba's revolutionary leader, Carlos Manuel de Céspedes. Garfield ignored the letters, and after the president's assassination Linton dismissed him as 'of little use to the people'. The Anti-Slavery Society also proved disappointing, refusing to support the Cuban anti-slavery campaign as being an irrelevance to its own aims. Linton was incensed but helpless, yet again let down because 'the real object of society [was] not the pursuit of happiness, but the close following of righteousness'; the United States was no longer a 'moral republic' but simply an 'assemblage of the free'. This was all little better than the England he had left behind in self-imposed exile, and exile is the bitterest pill to the lonely revolutionary planning his plots and coups in the vacuum of a foreign land.

Between November 1872 and June 1873, Linton travelled back to England. It was not a return but an extended holiday. He came again in 1882, 1887 and 1888, but his home was now New York and, anyway, London had changed beyond recognition. In New York, he was respected as the leading woodcut artist, and had become a member of the Century Club and the American

Academy of Design. It continued to rankle that he was never recognised by Britain's Royal Academy. Linton died in 1897, his family reconciled to an American destiny which was never quite settled upon. As late as 1924, his daughter Nelly continued to talk of returning 'home' to England.

Chapter Thirteen

Red Republicans

It was in Manchester that 'class' first raised its head. Men and masters had quickly separated here into an owning class and a working class, and class differences were the very mark of Manchester's society. It was, perhaps, no wonder, as Manchester had grown at a phenomenal rate alongside the industry that sustained it: cotton. From 1770 to 1831, the population had increased six times and by 1838 'flash' Manchester was one of Europe's most important cities, with a population virtually doubling each decade. The money-men of the city soon saw themselves as a class distinct from their workers, and the workers were quick to understand this gulf as a direct threat; the Peterloo massacre was long the symbol of this separation. In 1819 a local paper declared, 'Here there is no sympathy between the upper and lower classes of society.' Without a proper police force or civic government, the city was prone to riots and disorder. The result was that during the struggles for the Reform Bill, Manchester gained a reputation for rebelliousness. Indeed it was believed that the hand-loom weavers looked to revolution rather than reform. The cotton spinners, sophisticated in their thinking, demanded the rights of workmen and the 'whole fruits of their labour'.[1]

It was also in Manchester that the opposing creeds of the Anti-Corn Law League and the Chartists were first preached. Observers could witness the tyranny of the factory owner, as Engels did. Engels saw in the actions of the 'Norman baron mill owners' the 'snapping of the bands of devotion' and the creation (in Disraeli's words) of the 'two nations' – rich and poor. Here, in the slums of Manchester, Engels awaited the revolutionary zeal of the proletarian masses and the furious destruction of mill-owning capitalism. The capitalists included his own German compatriots who enlisted as special constables in 1842 to protect the city from the dangers of an increasingly Irish working class – the poorest 20 per cent of the factory population.

It was in Manchester that Marx and Engels cemented their friendship. The city was fast becoming a centre for a growing German community and, like the city itself, the Germans were also divided between merchants and revolutionaries. Engels was both a capitalist partner in an import–export business and a half-closet revolutionary dedicated to the overthrow of the system from which he made his money, and which paid for his riding to hounds with the Cheshire Hunt. Indeed his city connections did not prevent him from maintaining his revolutionary friend Marx and enjoying a secret life with two Irish proletarian sisters, Mary and Lydia Burns.

Engels was born on 22 November 1820 in the town of Barmen, in the Rhineland, the son of a wealthy businessman whose strict religious attitudes proved the ground against which the young Engels rebelled. A highly talented horse rider and swimmer, the teenager also wrote poetry and learned Latin and Greek, as well as French and English. In 1842 his father invited him to join the family firm of Ermen and Engels in Manchester. He jumped at the opportunity, less for the entrepreneurial possibilities than for his fascination with the Chartists, whose most militant, working-class component was centred on the English city. He spent the next twenty-seven years running the family firm while simultaneously plotting its overthrow (and all other capitalist enterprises). Engels was a man of humour and even temper, generous in money and time for his friends, and a keen military enthusiast, whose friends nicknamed him 'the general'. His book *The Condition of the Working Class in England*, which he first published in 1845 at the age of 24, launched a lifelong dedication to social equality and communistic revolution. Before the book's publication, Engels had written to Marx on 19 November 1844 that he intended 'to present the English with a fine bill of indictment at the bar of world opinion. I charge the middle class with mass murder, wholesale robbery and all the crimes in the calendar.'

Engels was helped in his research by Mary Burns, an Irish cotton-worker, who seems also to have sold oranges in the Manchester Hall of Science on the days when lectures were held. Here, 'ordinary workers' could be found, 'speaking with a clear understanding on political, religious and social affairs'. Mary and her sister Lydia were themselves women of considerable social awareness, Mary helping Engels in his research in the area known as 'Little Ireland'. By 1843, Mary and Engels were living together secretly, and later both Mary and Lydia ran a boarding house where Engels could meet his closest (often revolutionary) friends and where 'philistine' acquaintances were never allowed. Mary was not above taking personal risks for the revolution herself. An ardent patriot for the Irish cause, she was 'in continual touch with many Irishmen in Manchester and was always well informed of their conspiracies', recalled Marx's son-in-law Paul Lafargue. On 13 September 1867, the day before Marx published *Das Kapital* (1,000 copies in German), Lafargue had been taken by Engels to see where the daring rescue attempt had been made by American Fenian gunmen on a prison van taking other Irish republicans to jail at Bellevue. Engels had confided in Lafargue, who concluded, 'More than one Sinn Feiner found hospitality in Engels's house and it was thanks to his wife that the leader in the attempt to free condemned Sinn Feiners on the way to the scaffold was able to evade the police.'[2]

Engels was from the start a revolutionary at heart, for a time losing the support of his father because of it. It was only in 1850 that he was allowed to return to work for the firm in Manchester, becoming a clerk on £200 a year. From 1851, he took a cut in wages, but gained a percentage of the company profits, a large amount of which he donated to his impoverished friend Marx, then working on the 'scientific' basis of revolutionary analysis. In England, Engels was a keen supporter of the Chartists and in 1842 witnessed the 'general strike' and the pulling of the plugs on the steam boilers by the Plug Rioters. One Chartist visitor, John Campbell, was convinced that 'something must come of this, and something serious too'. Engels approved the 'insurrection' but diagnosed the problem as essentially social and economic. Nevertheless it was the first tentative move towards the rejection of parliamentary democracy and the embracing of the communist revolutionary position taken up in his book on the working class:

> The misfortune of the worker in the summer insurrection of 1842 was precisely that they did not know whom to fight against. The evil they suffered was social – and social evils cannot be abolished as the monarchy or privileges are abolished. Social evils cannot be cured by People's Charters, and the people sensed this – otherwise the People's Charter would today be the basic law of England. Social evils need to be studied and understood, and this the mass of the workers has not yet done… . The great achievement of the uprising was that England's most vital question … was raised.[3]

This was a considerable step beyond the Owenite utopianism that he and Marx had so admired. Just before his death in 1895, Engels suggested that the roots of 'modern international socialism' could be traced back to the heady days of the 1840s, when world revolution was a dream debated with aging Spenceans, enthusiastic Owenites, disillusioned Chartists, Irish revolutionaries and German republican émigrés in Salford and Manchester. It was in those years that he befriended the Chartist newsagent James Leach, a man Engels considered 'honest, trustworthy and capable', whose efforts towards factory reform and against free trade were central to Engels's thoughts in preparing *The Condition of the Working Class in England* and from whose newsagents, ten minutes from Engels's office, could be bought the *Northern Star*, the radical paper run by O'Connor. Engels met one of its journalists, George Harney, in 1843 during a trip to Leeds and was invited to become the German correspondent.

Engels's double life allowed him both to attend civic functions and mix with city dignitaries, as well as sit long into the night at the boarding house run by the Irish sisters, plotting revolution with his German friends. One was Georg Weerth, a writer and poet and a founder member of the Communist League, who lived in Bradford. Another was Wilhelm Wolff, nicknamed Lupus, a German teacher who spent ten years in Manchester and who also joined the Communist League and was the editor of *Neue Rheinische Zeitung*.[4] The three men became best friends, the glue holding them together the desire to rebuild society on socialist lines and the presence of Marx, the man who would describe Wolff as the 'noble protagonist of the proletariat' and who would offer the oration at his grave. Wolff in turn left Marx £800 to carry on the work of revolution.

Engels had met Marx in 1842 but it was in 1844, while in Paris, that the two became collaborators and best friends, Marx the swarthy 'bookworm' who had mastered philosophy and the classics, Engels the tall, educated gentleman with a social conscience and a penchant for military matters, horses, tobacco and alcohol. Engels happily played second fiddle to Marx, the two sitting for long hours in Manchester's ancient Chetham's Library and working on articles often written in the early years by Engels, because Marx was not yet fluent in English, and sent off to the *New York Daily Tribune*.

Marx remained incorrigibly impoverished all his life and Engels returned to his 'damned business', the better able to bank-roll Marx, who borrowed at least £4,000 during their friendship; Engels was always happy to help his friend. Hospitality, too, was not lacking and Marx made at least twenty-six visits to Manchester between 1851 and 1880, sometimes with his wife, Jenny, or with the family, to stay with the couple, who rented under the pseudonyms Frederick Mann Burns, Frederick Burns or Frederick Boardman – secrecy being a prerequisite of love affairs as well as revolutions.

Engels also helped out with money for short holidays when Marx felt ill. In January 1852 Marx complained to Engels that 'this time my piles have afflicted me more grievously than the French Revolution'. Later he worried about 'kicking the bucket', and always Marx suffered from vitamin deficiency, resulting in 'carbuncles' and other skin infections. It was disease resulting from extreme poverty that killed his 8-year-old son, Edgar, in 1855, when Marx was living on the edge of destitution in Dean Street, Soho (his home now recorded in a blue plaque above a fashionable West End restaurant).

Despite everything, Engels kept Marx financially afloat and provided a bedrock of friendship when their work seemed to reduce Marx to a physical wreck. Engels had already produced his great book in the 1840s, but Marx was to spend another twenty years before producing his masterpiece. The interim period saw both work on history and political economy, Marx borrowing books, meeting Chartists and Owenites, putting together the Communist League and learning English, long before he settled down to the unbending routine of work and study in the British Library for which he would became famous. Indeed, in the early years up to 1845, Marx was solely dependent on Engels for the books with which to continue his research, and the books he saw were such 'as were procurable in Manchester'.

When Marx was buried at Highgate Cemetery in London on 17 March 1883, it was Engels, his friend, who gave the funeral oration, best placed of all to recognise the spirit of revolution inherent in his friend: 'Marx was before all a revolutionist. His real mission in life was the overthrow of capitalist society, fighting was his element and he fought with a passion, a tenacity, and a success such as few could rival.' Above all, however, Engels knew that he had been a partner in this the most important partnership of his life and for which his business partnership had paid. He knew, too, that he played a subordinate part – the straight man in a revolutionary double act that had lasted almost half a century. Marx's daughter remembered Engels once saying that, 'in Marx's lifetime I played second fiddle, and I think I have attained virtuosity in it and I am damned glad that I had such a good first fiddle as Marx'.[5]

What motivated Engels to throw in his lot with the masses and live the double life of a revolutionary? His friend Marx, living a life of grinding poverty, unable to feed his family and irritated by his own intellectual quest that did not bring wealth, social change or personal closure, certainly had cause. Engels was rich, rode with the hounds, visited those of his class, both English and German, to whom he could talk wine, art or duelling, and could afford to keep a second, secret home away from his official life. Yet perhaps Engels was frustrated too. His mind, quick and restless, was also unanchored; in short, he was already an idealist in Germany but only in England could he find his 'objective correlative' to his intellectual and abstract longing. The working classes became the focus of an already vague frustration that came partially from innate kindness and altruism but also, and perhaps more importantly, from an inner void that German philosophy could not fill – a sense of unfulfilled passion that needed only direction. Engels *found* the English working class and by so doing found his own destiny, just as others years before had found the French Revolution. Engels's personal vision coincided with his times (he found the social circumstances he needed only afterwards) and this saved him from being another failed incendiary or a mere Victorian eccentric.

Yet his zeal always found itself frustrated by the very historical material he was dealing with – the lives of the working classes. Engels dedicated his life to understanding the 'sufferings and struggles' of working people and to acting as a 'witness ... against the social and political power of [their] oppressors', the 'brutally selfish ... ruling middle class'.[6] He was happy to forsake 'dinner-parties, port-wine and champagne' in order to get to the 'realities of life', where 'free-born Britons' were the victims of an 'indirect trade in human flesh'. 'Blue book' researchers and Home Office officials had, however, ignored the plight of their fellows, but Engels, fired with indignation, would not; the work had been 'left to a foreigner [that is Engels] to inform the civilized world of the degrading situation'. Engels was on a crusade to save the English from their own degradation, for things seemed as if they could only get better 'by force alone'. Nevertheless, the raw materials of revolution frustrated Engels as much as their oppressors. Could not those to whom self-help had been offered see its benefits? Why did the people not seize their opportunity? The answer seemed clear. It was because, cocooned in the history of the labouring poor, '[there] were men and women already intellectually dead ... not human beings [but] merely toiling machines in the service of the few aristocrats'.[7] A revolutionary life is one where personal inner vision (the belief in a type of rightness) is frustrated and blocked not only by the social and political enemy but also by those on whose behalf the revolutionary works: the stubborn refusal of the masses to act in their own best interests.

While working on their various publications, Marx and Engels came across the League of the Just, which had been founded in 1836 on utopian socialist and Christian communist ideas. Intrigued, Engels went to their conference in London in June 1847 and persuaded Marx to attend. Before long, the pair were the leading lights in the organisation, which had now changed its name to the Communist League and adopted Marx's slogan: 'Working men of all countries, unite!' At their second meeting, also held in London, during November and December 1847, Marx and Engels were given the go-ahead to draw up a manifesto for the group. This became the *Communist Manifesto*. In March 1850 both Marx and Engels addressed the League, calling for 'permanent revolution'.

The Communist League was small, divided and still apparently irrelevant when the people found themselves everywhere defeated and crushed on the barricades of Paris, Berlin and Vienna, and when, in Britain, the working classes were regimented into the factories against which they strove to gain only equal wages and fair working hours. Marx's famous rallying cry may have been prescient but it was hardly exact. In 1848 the most sophisticated of the working classes in revolt were French artisans, especially those from Paris. They still formed part of the people, as opposed to the proletariat, and their interest in socialism was attached to 'primitive' socialists like Louis Blanc. The last days of Chartism in 1848 took no notice of Marx or his colleagues.

Chartism was finished[8] and nothing gained; communist delegates to their first 'congress', as they called their pub meeting, spoke a dozen languages and were successful in making revolutions in none, living lives only as hopeful exiles. Other socialists, utopians, liberals, anarchists, revolutionary egoists, religious communitarians and secularists ignored or argued with these extremists and their message; the police spied upon them, as they did on all subversive groups; foreign governments complained about them and watched them. Yet the threat from Marx and Engels amounted to a rewriting of the virtue of the people, already (in their minds) the international movement of citizens of the world that stood against all national boundaries and preached unrestricted world revolution from below. Pretentiously, they declared that 'communism is already acknowledged by all European Powers to be itself a Power'.

Communism would, from now on, be the creed of the poor against all governments, and the Communist League the government in exile of the New World Order. This new and, as yet, invisible 'Power' stood as the ultimate anti-nation, declaring world war against 'all European Powers', its troops the international working classes, whose mission would be the overthrow of despotic government and exploitative capital.

How was such a victory to be won? George Harney thought that he knew. He had been born on 17 February 1817, the son of a Deptford seaman, and, after life in the navy and as a shop boy, he rose to prominence as a leader of the militant working-class wing of the Chartist movement. In January 1837 Harney helped found the East London Democratic Association, which preached solidarity among workers, revolution and republicanism. He also helped to produce the unstamped (and, at the time, untaxed and therefore illegal) *Poor Man's Guardian*, for which he suffered three jail sentences. Just as the Chartist convention had deliberately echoed the French Revolution, so newspapers made the connection explicit. Harney's own paper, the *Red Republican*, which ran between June and November 1850, sported a woodcut of the Liberty cap and the fasces of the French Republic, Harney himself taking the sobriquet 'l'Ami du Peuple', originally used by Marat. Alongside another revolutionary, William Benbow, Harney attended the Chartist convention of 1839 and argued for a Grand National Holiday – a general strike – to be held on 12 August. It was Benbow, Cobbett's old publisher, who first proposed the 'General National Holiday', a strike to bring down the Government. The strike or 'holy day' (like Spence, Benbow's ideas were saturated by the Biblical idea of a 'jubilee') was called off when he and others were arrested. Sentenced to serve sixteen months, Benbow was unable to endure the harsh prison regime and died in jail in 1841. In effect, Harney believed such a strike would be the first tactical move in a full-scale revolution. Unfortunately, his fellow conventioneers rejected his ideas and he was picked up by the authorities soon afterwards and imprisoned in Warwick jail. Luckily, Harney avoided trial and was released, moving temporarily to Scotland, where he married before moving back to Sheffield as its Chartist organiser. During the Plug Riots of 1842 he was again arrested and again allowed his freedom (after his sentence was overturned).[9] He worked for O'Connor on the *Northern Star* until becoming its editor.

It was through this editorship that Harney had met Marx and Engels, persuading them to contribute to the paper, as they persuaded him of the need for socialism. In 1848 he went to see the revolutions in Europe for himself and mixed with the provisional government in Paris. O'Connor did not like communism, and Harney therefore resigned as editor of the *Northern Star* to begin the *Red Republican*, in which he published the *Communist Manifesto*. Unfortunately, Harney's newspaper did not last long and he was forced to edit a further series of unsuccessful radical papers, the classic example of the marginal revolutionary journalist. Admitting defeat in England, he moved to the United States in May 1863 and worked as a clerk in the Massachusetts Statehouse. After fourteen years, he retired, finally returning to England and resuming his life as a journalist on the *Newcastle Chronicle*. Harney died on 9 December 1897, convinced, no doubt, that the manifesto he had published nearly fifty years before was about to be fulfilled.

Alongside socialism was a new craze. Spiritualism was an import from the United States. It began in 1848 and coincided with the wave of European revolutions and home-grown Chartist disturbances and rallies which so inspired Marx and Engels. The craze began in Hydesville, Rochester, New York state, in the home of the sisters Katherine and Margaret Fox, which had become the centre of mysterious knocking and rapping sounds. They claimed that by this means they could communicate with spirits. Buoyed up by their huge celebrity in America (where P.T. Barnam exhibited their skills at spirit communication), the two girls soon created a following for their activities in Britain.

The seance provided a quasi-spiritual activity for the manifestation of weird phenomena, ectoplasmic encounters and
levitation which seemed to prove that life existed after death.
The importance of this was grasped immediately by adherents.
If life and death were a continuum, then here was a rational
and material explanation for belief in the supernatural that did
not have to accept religious orthodoxy, but instead could syn-
thesise religion and science. 'Summerland' became the name
of an, as yet, unrealised utopian dream of social and spiritual
perfection, where benevolent (but deceased) elders taught the
wisdom needed to unite the community. Robert Owen saw his
own socialist doctrines fulfilled in the discovery of the spir-
itualists, as did other socialists whose dreams of political and
social harmony had been shattered by the universal failure of
the revolutions in 1848. Indeed, spiritualism 'rapidly became
part of an "alternative" synthesis which included vegetarianism, feminism, dress reform, homeopathy and every variety of
social and religious dissent'.[10] The force of spiritualism was in
its reconciling opposites: life and death; community and individualism; capitalist and worker. Social campaigners such as
Annie Besant (who led the Match Girls' Strike of 1889) took to
spiritualism as the complement to socialism, not least because
of its egalitarian nature.

By the 1860s and 1870s, old Chartists could still talk of 'the
people' as a rallying cry for the masses, but the term had passed
imperceptibly into the language of civic pride that had taken
root in the new Liberal municipal government of Birmingham.
Here, a new party had formed which sought to unite those
classes that in Manchester seemed ready to destroy each
other. Speaking as Birmingham's city mayor in 1873, Joseph
Chamberlain clearly defined the role of local government: 'I
have an abiding faith in municipal institutions, an abiding sense
of the value and importance of local government.... Our corporation represents the authority of *the people* [emphasis added].
Through them you obtain the full and direct expression of the

popular will.'[11] Somehow the language of revolution had passed into the pronouncements of plutocrats. Pillar of Victorian liberalism, upholder of empire and eventual demon of protectionism, Chamberlain seems the unlikely inheritor of the strict justice of Saint-Just, but his language lacks nothing of the revolutionary authoritarianism that marked the Jacobin cause.

Where the Government could not suppress revolution, they exported it, and, again, Australia was high on the agenda for human cargo. Nevertheless, Australia was changing and people were settling there of their own free will, while the families of ex-convicts became administrators, farmers, policemen and even magistrates. Indeed, a remarkable number of Irish actually entered the police after they had served their sentence. The most extreme change was to come when gold was found and a gold rush began; transportees actually demanded to be sent to the gold-rich colony. New divisions were also coming about in the colonies, and Victoria separated from New South Wales on 1 January 1851. By 1854, an estimated 25,000 miners had started digging around Ballarat. 'Money, lucre, profit – these are thy Gods, O Australia!' intoned the *Sydney Morning Herald* as early as 1838. The miners came from all parts of the world, especially Germany and America, although half were Irish – with the indignation of the Irish – and some were Chartists of the 'moral' and 'physical force' persuasions.

To cash in on the gold rush, the government of Victoria imposed licences, the enforcement of which was considered brutal and unnecessary. To make matters worse, the 'squatters' of Victoria (the landed conservatives who had settled down on 'illegal' land anyway) objected to 212 pardoned 'exiles' (actually convicts) coming over in 1849 to a colony that had never had convict labour. The gold rush exacerbated these worries and a tax was imposed on free labour, which itself was considered unfair. By this time, a flood of immigrants were arriving (in 1854 there were nearly 300,000 arrivals) and by the 1850s, 100,000 people were 'diggers' in the gold fields.

Some of these diggers were members of Young Ireland transported after 1848, and some came because of the Irish Potato
Famine. There were also Germans and Italians who had fled
after the failed 1848 revolutions in Europe. Some, such as J.B.
Humffray, Tom Kennedy and George Black, were Chartists. It
was quite clear: if the Government was to tax the diggers, then
they should have representation. It was the Boston Tea Party all
over again. The miners' demands were encapsulated in the 'Gold
Digger's Advocate', but despite the placards that proclaimed 'no
chains for free Englishmen' and the fact that German colleagues
were willing to take up arms, and even despite the founding of
the Ballarat Reform League, the Government took no notice.
The diggers did not want to separate from Britain, but talk of
revolution became more prominent as the Government became
less flexible.

Moral force had failed; Kennedy's physical force must now
prevail. The Ballarat Reform League had already resolved on a
seven-point plan for peace. It consisted of disbanding the office
of Gold Commissioners, abolishing the miners' licence tax,
full and fair representation, manhood suffrage, no property
qualifications for legislative council candidates, payment of such
candidates and short parliaments. The Chartists' demands had
bizarrely re-emerged in the gold fields of Victoria. The declaration went on: 'That is the inalienable right of every citizen to
have a voice in the making of laws he is called upon to obey.
That taxation without representation [is] tyranny... . If Queen
Victoria continues to act upon the ill advice of dishonest ministers ... the Reform League will endeavour to supersede such
royal prerogatives by asserting that of the people ... as the people
are the only legitimate source of all political power.'[12]

It was a call for democracy, but it was also a threat of republicanism. It could not be ignored for long, especially as the
diggers now had a flag: a white cross on a blue background, with
five stars representing the Southern Cross. It was designed by
a Canadian, 'Lieutenant' Charles Ross, and, like the flag sewn

for the new American republic by Betsy Ross, it would come
to symbolise Australian democracy.[13] On 28 November miners
attacked a column of troops, killing some and taking their
weapons. On 29 November a meeting boiled over and 'physical force' Chartists linked up with the disaffected Irishmen. The
leader of the Irish was Peter Lalor, who was the son of an Irish
MP and the brother of James Lalor, the Young Ireland advocate
who was broken in jail. Humffray had recommended caution
but the others did not and the burning of licences followed. The
chair of the meeting, an Irishman named Timothy Hayes, put
the motion that if anyone was arrested for burning the licences,
they should be rescued. The response was overwhelming, as
Raffaello Carboni, the Italian revolutionary, recalled: 'No one
was who was not present at that monster meeting, or never saw
any Chartist meeting in Copenhagen-Fields, London, can possibly form any idea of the enthusiasm of the miners of Ballarat
on that 29 November. A regular volley of revolvers and other
pistols now took place, and a good blazing up of gold licences.'[14]
The Southern Cross was raised and the miners swore 'by the
[flag] to stand truly by each other, and fight to defend [their]
rights and liberties'. It was a turning point.

The diggers were tough men and soon began to arm them-
selves. There were to be two 'pike divisions', led by Irishman
Patrick Curtain and the German Edward Thonen. The tradi-
tional Irish weapon was to make almost its last appearance. A
German blacksmith made the pike-heads. There were, however,
plenty of armed men, especially Americans and Canadians, and
these were organised into 'regiments': Captain or Lieutenant
Ross's Rifle Brigade, Captain Nelson's American First Rifles,
James Magill's Californian Rangers Revolver Brigade and
Captain Nealson's Regiment. A council of war was formed, with
Lalor in charge. The decision was that only defensive measures
were to be taken. The Government had redcoats on the scene and
on Friday 1 December and Saturday 2 December the two sides
weighed each other up. Government troops consisted of the 12th

and 40th regiments with howitzers and field guns. They were led by Sir Robert Nickle, commander-in-chief in Australia.

The diggings on Eureka Hill were reinforced with pit props ready for the assault by the troops. The stockade was fortified and the password among the rebels was 'Vinegar Hill', in memory of the Castle Bar revolt of 1804 at Parramatta. On Friday, 300 more volunteers arrived, led by Kennedy and said to have been singing 'La Marseillaise'. On Saturday the American rifle 'regiment' finally arrived. About 1,500–2,000 miners were ready to fight, although desertions were rife and there was agitation for more aggressive action. Yet the defensive posture was maintained, because the miners could not win an assault against artillery and, more importantly, because they did not want their attitude to be regarded as an insurrection, but rather as a defence of lost liberties. To the Government, things seemed a little different. Here were armed men, who refused to pay taxes and whose ranks were led by Irishmen and Chartists, dug in in a fortified camp, with a rebel flag and having taken a possibly republican oath. Governor Hotham concluded that 'a riot was rapidly growing into a revolution, and the professional agitator giving place to the man of physical force'. With all their bluster and parading, on 3 December at 4 a.m., the miners could muster only about 120 men against an assault by nearly 300 police and troops. Pikes and guns went into action, but after ten minutes the stockade was overrun, with twenty-nine miners and four soldiers dead. John Hafele, who made the pikes, and Thonen, who led the pikemen, were shot down. Lalor was wounded and lost an arm.

Three days later, the mayor of Melbourne held an open-air meeting to support the Government, but it was highjacked by those who supported the miners. Another mass meeting was held, with Humffray in the chair, pressure building up for the Colonial Secretary to resign. He was finally forced to do so. Meanwhile, the trials began during February 1855, but such was public sympathy for the miners that there were no convictions.

Marx commented on the trials that there were 'essentially similar reasons to those which led to the Declaration of Independence of the United States'.[15] The trials proved a gigantic Government flop, with Lalor and Humffray both being elected to parliament in October 1856. Universal male suffrage (without property qualification) was granted in November 1857. In February 1858 stonemasons gained the eight-hour day. The fruits of Chartism were finally ripening in the sunshine of Australia. Mark Twain visited the area in 1895 and commented, 'It was the Barons and John, over again; it was Hampden and Ship-Money; it was Concord and Lexington; small beginnings, all of them, but all of them great in political results, all of them epoch-making. It is another instance of a victory won by a lost battle.' It was the last flash of Chartism and the final battle of 1798. This time, victory was snatched from defeat.

By the 1860s, no more prisoners could be sent to Australia and the system closed. The end of transportation created a crisis in England and was replaced by 'penal servitude' with tickets-of-leave facilities for early release. Many felt that England would be overrun with criminals. The 'crisis' led to a select committee in 1856 and demands for a nationwide police force before England itself became one gigantic penal colony.

Chapter Fourteen

Blood on Niagara

It is a curious fact that throughout the period of the Chartist disturbances, England and Wales were unpoliced. That is, from 1837 to 1848 there was no effective countrywide police force, nor any system of secret police or useful detectives that the Government could call upon to combat the Chartists. Instead, the Government relied on the regular army, special constables and, during occasional emergencies, the calling-out of the Chelsea out-pensioners, ex-soldiers usually of middle age, who could be called up. The Government still used spies when needed, but the Home Office would pay them only erratically. Spies earned what living they could from local sources, especially the magistrates and, where available, the chief constables of the area. Thus, Joseph Fussell, a 'physical force' Chartist, nevertheless earned £2 per week, and was described as a 'bad one' by his spymaster.

The yeomanry was still in evidence, but its numbers had been cut by 25 per cent during 1838, and Napier, in charge of the almost ungovernable north of England, was without any effective local police help. Police were overwhelmed or stood aside during troubles and there was almost a non-existent county force. Thus, the general was reliant on the regular army, which grew to 8,200 troops in the north by May 1840 and subsided again just as the Plug Riots got going, leaving only 4,750 men to deal with overwhelming numbers of marchers, rioters and disturbances. Ireland was to be called upon to play its part too: 'Between December 1838 and August 1839 six regiments – three infantry, three cavalry – were moved from Ireland to the Northern District... . The importation of these 3,600 men, nearly half of the total military presence in the north, meant that Ireland played a critical role in the suppression of English Chartism.'[1]

With these forces in place, Napier was ready to confront Chartism. As for physical force and talk of revolution, he was sanguine:

Poor people! ... they will suffer. They have set all England against them and their physical force: fools! fools! We have the physical force not they. They talk of their hundred thousands of men. Who is to move them when I am dancing round them with cavalry, and pelting them with cannon-shot? What would their hundred thousand men do with my hundred rockets wriggling their fiery tails among them, roaring, scorching, tearing, smashing all that came near? And when in desperation and despair they broke to fly, how would they bear five regiments of cavalry careering through them? Poor men! How little they know of physical force.[2]

The railway network, which could whisk troops across country in hours rather than days, and the electric telegraph meant that orders could be sent quickly and effectively (thus uniting the country for the first time); England was governed as a totality but rarely controlled, and rioting continued. The police were too weak, except in London and Ireland, or non-existent to interfere. In Manchester, during disturbances, it was said that 'the people would rather be kept in order by an army in red than by those clothed in blue'.[3]

Yet, just a little over forty years later, British disturbances would be dealt with by the police and there would be a secret political police in place: the Irish Special Branch, later just 'Special Branch'. In 1841 there were only three forces outside London: Bolton, with forty men to cover 51,000 inhabitants; Manchester, with sixty-four officers and 319 men; and that in Birmingham, where there were thirty officers and 340 men. The Bolton force soon joined with the Manchester force, leaving only two police establishments outside the Metropolis. On the whole, these forces proved to be riddled with drunkenness and corruption and therefore were useless either as thief-takers or keepers of public order. Even such provision as existed was to lapse in 1841, and by 1842, when the boroughs were incorporated, the police were handed over to the local Watch Committees as laid down in the Municipal Corporations Act of 1835.

The rural counties were effectively without a police presence until the 1850s and 1860s, and the boroughs, deeply suspicious of London, refused to do any more about the police, relying on the local watch or the troops to catch thieves or keep order. Old liberties were at stake and local independence was jealously guarded. Indeed, the ancient title 'chief constable' was usually used, rather than the foreign-sounding (and therefore politically suspect) 'commissioner', for the new heads of borough or county forces. More than this, the local police, when established, were to be a civilian force in uniform and for the most part only carried staves or truncheons. The stipulation regarding the physical height of policemen and other qualifications did exist, as laid down by Government for the Irish police, which was older, centralised and fully professional, all things stubbornly resisted outside London. By a fluke, with the decline of Chartism between 1841 and 1842, and the Plug Riots having not yet begun, magistrates in Lancashire and elsewhere *reduced* the number of constables, considering them an unnecessary expense. In most places where Chartist disturbances continued, the police often acted with vigour when backed by regular troops facing the 'enemy' (as Napier put it). At the parish level, there were still the faithful 'Charleys' or watchmen, totally useless for keeping order or for catching thieves, but retained through tradition or bloody-mindedness. Nevertheless, these persisted into the 1860s.

Magistrates frustrated by the lack of regular police might call upon special constables who were sworn in locally. Often in rural areas where no police existed, such specials could be brought out at short notice during an emergency or panic. Such was the case in the ancient town of Winchelsea, near Rye in Sussex, following the Irish bombing campaign of December 1867, when forty-nine specials were enrolled and thirty stout wooden batons manufactured to defer 'riot and tumult' by Fenian conspirators, a belief as wild as it was pointless, the Irish being armed with revolvers and bombs and nowhere near East Sussex.

There remained three areas of suspicion and resentment that had to be overcome before a nationwide police force could be formed. These were that the police were an unnecessary expense, that a uniformed police would encourage strangers into an area, and finally that the police were actually a moral force, intended to monitor working-class behaviour and create 'diligent workers'. There was truth in each of these accusations. Nevertheless, the idea of a police force grew, as did the railway network, which had doubled between 1846 and 1848 (and created a national timetable as a consequence – clocks had to be coordinated). England was shrinking.

Despite this, England was still considered a country not ready for a police force. The continual disturbances of 1848 did not shake that conviction and 4,000 unarmed police were spread between London, Liverpool, Manchester, Bristol and Birmingham, with no police in some cities and two-thirds of counties refusing to set up a constabulary. Yet it was a comfort to English men and women that the revolutions then rocking Europe had been prevented by 'moral strength alone', as *Blackwood's Magazine* noted in October 1848, and that, on the whole, the camaraderie of the special constabulary (which anyone with some property joined) had united the nation to defeat the threat:

> Noblemen, tradesmen, and workmen thoroughly intermingled. No class stood apart. Grey-haired men and slim youths went side by side; coal-whippers and young dandies; literary men and those to whom books were unknown.... There was more grumbling ... regarding the defective arrangements for making special constables, from those who were impatient to be sworn in than there was from the Chartists themselves against the government.[4]

So the situation might have remained, with soldiers and specials called out as needed, but things were changing. The Crimean War had alienated the regular army from home duties, the railway network had joined the country, so that men could be moved in hours not days, and communication, by telegraph and by letter, was much improved. The police, when encountered, also proved better than expected. Instead of this 'disjointed, and absurdly anomalous system', a united one was suggested, run by the Home Office, but it smacked of centralisation and the curtailing of liberty, so that when a bill was introduced in 1854 to regularise policing, it was heavily rejected. Two years later, with Home Office control and all hint of centralisation removed, the bill passed and the modern police force came into being. It produced a 'little army of truncheon bearers', which (being accepted as constitutional) even radical MPs supported by 56 per cent. Just as O'Connor, years before, had endorsed the need for working in the factory system ('none but fools could object to its use ... but it must be regulated'), so now a regular police force keeping civil order was generally accepted as part of Britishness, and the centralisation and loss of local rights was to be a new, but inevitable, feature of British life.

The police experiment in London was predated in Ireland by forty years. The elder Pitt had already failed with his police bill of 1785, and the 1786 Dublin Act was not tried in England for fear of the consequences. As in England, so in Ireland there was much disquiet and concern, especially as the police were seen to be political from their creation, and they were armed with a musket and bayonet from the outset. Dubliners soon complained that the police, drilling and marching like soldiers, thought and acted as regular troops, behaving with 'flippancy and insolence'. It was the sort of police that Englishmen thought they needed for a colony held by military force. In 1795 the Dublin Police Act restored local Protestant control to a force already mistrusted. Between 1792 and 1793, Catholic 'Defenders' were agitating for agrarian reforms and hoping for a French invasion, and the growing troubles saw the suspension of habeas corpus, the introduction of an 'Insurrection Act' and the establishment of the Protestant yeomanry. With the Irish rebellion and then the plots of Despard and Emmet, the Government needed more, not less, control and the police were handed over to direct control from Dublin Castle, Dublin itself becoming the 'garrison headquarters of a conquered colony'. Although the police in Ireland were ineffectual compared with the yeomanry or regular army, they continued to function and a further Act of 1808 was passed by 'English gentlemen' to increase the force, with military barracks sprouting up all over the country.

In 1813, 12,000 soldiers held down Ireland, but by 1815, with the end of the Napoleonic Wars and the disbandment of the regular army, this number was untenable. Yet it was also clear that the yeomanry could not continue to act in the unlawful, disruptive and partisan way that it had in the past. Nevertheless, the police were always at a disadvantage, especially when it came to the secret gangs that ruled the countryside. Indeed these had been increasing with the appearance of the Whiteboys, Thrashers, Caravats and Shanavests, who terrorised large areas of the south-east. Another rising was felt very near and the viceroy protested of the running-down of the army that 'a peace establishment may do in England, *but here we are not at peace*'.[5]

Peel now brought in the 'Peace Preservation Police', a mobile force to be sent anywhere violence lurked. These 'Peelers' were largely employed against widespread assassinations and rape and were often subject to attack themselves from gangs of Whiteboys. Magistrates were killed publicly by the Whiteboys, against whom witnesses were difficult to find and the Peelers had only limited success in combating the gangs. The reduction of regular regiments in Ireland and the downgrading of the troublesome yeomanry meant that a better police force was needed, especially after Peterloo, when Arthur Thistlewood was rumoured to be in Ireland and Catholic Ribbonism (against the Protestant 'heresy') was growing. By 1821, Ireland appeared to be again heading for civil war, with rumours of arms caches. In 1822 the few Peelers had grown to 2,300 men, all armed and all ex-army. Two years later, about 4,000 people would be arrested in the open warfare that had broken out between the Peelers and Whiteboys. There was a need not only for a national police force but for one that could curb Orangeism and Whiteboy outrages and replace the ill-disciplined yeomanry with a properly trained force. In 1822 a constabulary was established: 'The constables were heavily armed. Each man had to carry a sabre, a pistol, and … a short carbine with an attached bayonet.'[6]

Again, there went up the cry that this was a 'gendarmerie' on the French model, armed against the population. During the 'Tithe War' of 1830 to 1833, patrols were sent out only to be attacked with extreme violence. Indeed, in one ambush, a chief constable and fourteen policemen were killed. Forty-four policemen were killed between 1824 and 1844. This was in comparison to one police constable, a PC Culley, killed during 1833 in England at the Cold Bath Fields riot. Such outrages would continue into the 1830s, with revenge leaving four or five civilians dead for every policeman slaughtered. By 1836 there were already 7,400 constables in Ireland, centrally organised, highly professional and armed. In England, there were none outside London.

Nevertheless, a more oddly disturbing form of Irish protest came with Daniel O'Connell, who led a widespread independence movement which was entirely peaceful (and therefore a form of disturbance unknown and sinister in English eyes) and who encouraged Catholics to join the police because it would give them a job and reduce prejudice. O'Connell fought for Catholic emancipation and was returned to a parliament he could not attend. During the Chartist disturbances in England, as O'Connor gathered crowds in the north, so O'Connell was gathering large crowds in Ireland to hear about independence. The two causes were not yet united.

O'Connell's bid for independence failed in 1843 and politics took a darker hue. The 1840s had already seen famine and emigration on a large scale, scattering Irish resentment across the globe. A new revolutionary group was formed, called the Irish Confederates, from January 1847; O'Connell died in the same year in Genoa, aged 71. The group quickly declared its allegiance to the Parisian Republicans, then in the middle of a revolution, and finally to the Chartists. They turned away from the language of O'Connell and instead returned to that of violence, talking the language of physical force, though they hardly dared contemplate it. Moreover, the leaders of Young Ireland (as the movement came to be known) were idealistic and educated and had too little in common with the peasantry, who anyway were starving and ill organised and to whom O'Connell had offered a path no longer strewn with the dead martyrs of failed plots.

The leaders of this latest plot to free Ireland were Thomas Francis Meagher, a merchant's son, handsome and eloquent, and William Smith O'Brien, descendant of an aristocratic family, but a man of liberal feelings and dedicated to the relief of the Poor Law and to educational reform. Around these two men formed the idea for a rising, to take place during July 1848. In mid-March both men were able to hold mass meetings in Dublin and around the country, and although the Government brought charges of sedition, the men were released on bail. Thereafter O'Brien and Meagher travelled to France to make an alliance with the new French Republic. While in Paris they met the acting president, Alphonse de Lamartine, who presented them with a green, white and orange tricolour, based on the French design.[7] It had been designed by Meagher and eventually became the flag of 1916 – the flag of the republic in 1922. Unfortunately for the rebels, the intervention of Foreign Secretary Palmerston brought this adventure to nothing. At the same time, it was reported that arms were being gathered around the country and the police and military were put on alert.

Meanwhile, the Government was thinking of ways to tighten security and, with this in mind, parliament debated the Crown and Government Security Bill, which had its second reading on the very same day as the 'monster' Chartist meeting was taking place on Kennington Common. The Act, which was finally passed on 22 April, made treason an offence punishable by transportation. The Government also put a number of cities under the 1847 Coercion Act, virtually marshal law. Furthermore, habeas corpus was again suspended and preventive arrests began. One of the measures was immediately to dissolve the 'Confederate' clubs and amass troops on the west coast of England and Scotland (finally dispatching 9,000 extra infantry to Ireland), as well as to prepare a fleet and send it to Waterford and Cork. It was clear that the Government was almost precipitating the revolution that it was trying to avoid.

As for the revolutionaries, they had little understanding of planning and no sense of how they would proceed. Indeed, there were no evident signs of mustering nor any sense of where a blow should fall. In the minds of Meagher and O'Brien, this had become a purely symbolic rebellion with the idea of taking one or two key points and holding them until troops massacred the defenders. Thus this would be the first 'blood sacrifice' – an emblematic uprising to stir the people.

Dublin became an armed city and the rebels looked for a favourable place to begin. They thought they had found such a place in Tipperary, which had a long history of lawlessness and of opposition to the Government. Although volunteers came from Liverpool and Glasgow, they nevertheless came in single numbers and no great enthusiasm for the rebels was to be found. Tipperary did not rise and only a few hundred men, mostly without weapons, joined the rebellion, despite enthusiastic receptions wherever O'Brien and Meagher had gone. It was decided that the rising would take place at Kilkenny, but that failed and so they decided to rise at Carrick, which also failed. Finally, O'Brien decided that they should declare an Irish republic at Cashel, but again, apart from the tearing-up of a few railway tracks, nothing happened. By this time the Confederates had an army of about 2,000 men, most of whom were ill armed and certainly unable to face regular troops. Indecision meant that this number dropped to about 600, and encounters with the 8th Hussars, who were patrolling the area, ended without bloodshed. Indeed, these were the only encounters with regular troops.

The final episode was inglorious. A number of policemen were trapped in a smallholding when one of the rebels started throwing stones and the police opened fire. The so-called battle at the widow McCormick's farmhouse ended in negotiations and two dead. O'Brien and his associates fled, hoping to get to the United States. O'Brien and Meagher were both arrested at railway stations and sentenced to be transported to Australia.

Young Ireland had been a nationalist organisation only, and there were others who favoured a more class-based approach: a republic founded on the emancipation of the agrarian masses. Thus, as one group declined, another began to take shape around James Fintan Lalor (brother of the Australian hero of Ballarat) the 40-year-old hunchback who edited the *Irish Felon*, a newspaper that was also sold in England. Lalor started Felon clubs, dedicated to a 'socialist' approach which even found a home among Chartists in the north of England. He was inclined to oppose Young Ireland on the principle that Meager, O'Brien and their associates ignored the plight of rural peasants. In that respect, he was taken up by Marx and Engels as a proto-socialist.

Equally important was a young man making his way in the Young Ireland movement as the lieutenant of O'Brien. James Stephens had been wounded at the widow McCormick's farmhouse. At the time he was 24 and a civil engineer on the Waterford–Limerick railway. After the defeat of the movement, Stephens escaped to France and began to conspire to create a new organisation to carry on the revolutionary struggle. He could speak numerous languages and his sophistication opened many doors. Stephens himself was inclined towards socialism and indeed claimed he was a member of the 'communist' party. He was certainly a member of the International Workingmen's Association (the first International) alongside many other Fenians. His time in France brought him into contact with republicans and socialists, and a number of Bohemians who floated between the various secret societies then active in Paris.

While the Fenian Brotherhood was being created in America to serve American needs, Stephens had begun to put together the Irish Republican (or Revolutionary) Brotherhood (IRB) in order to overthrow English rule by fighting a revolutionary war in Ireland itself. This organisation was founded on St Patrick's Day 1858 in a Dublin timber yard. Stephens was small, only 5ft 3in tall, described as thick-set, with a florid complexion and quite bald. He had already visited America under the name 'Daly'. Rumours soon spread around this charismatic figure and it was said that he had fought on the barricades of the Paris Commune. He certainly found time to translate two of Dickens's books into French. Following the creation of the IRB, Stephens

toured Ireland between 1858 and 1859 and became known as
'*An Seabhac Siulach*' (the Wandering Hawk) a name used by the
peasantry to embody the spirit which preceded the coming of
invincible armies; by his followers, he was also known simply as
'the Boss' or 'the Captain'.

Soon an organisation was forming and it was expected that
Irishmen from America would flock to liberate their country.
Stephens took the title 'Chief Organiser, Irish Republic'. He
appointed James Devoy to subvert the British army in Ireland,
of whom 1,600 were meant to have sworn the Fenian oath.
From the United States he recruited Francis Millen, a Catholic
from County Tyrone, a former soldier of fortune and one of
the 'Irish Geese', who had fought in Mexico for Benito Juárez.
He found ill-trained peasants and too few guns. Stephens
annoyed him, too, with silly requests for a plan of a *corps d'armée*
of 50,000 troops. Millen did not think one of the Fenians a
'gentleman', but he could hardly comment, having already
turned informer. Unfortunately, Stephens seems to have been
another incompetent and, for all his boasts, the 'troops' did not
arrive, nor were enough guns gathered. Worse still, the plans
for the rising were lost by a drunken courier and found their
way on to Superintendent Daniel Ryans's desk at police headquarters in Dublin.

With this information, the authorities began a mass round-up
of the IRB, the leftovers of Young Ireland and Lalor's splinter
group on 15 September 1865. So unexpected were these raids
by the police and army that the usual Fenian tactic of escaping to France or the United States was impossible and most
were imprisoned. Many were American and some were from
the British army, having been subverted by Devoy. Millen,
however, took a ship to New York, having briefly been commander-in-chief. On 24 November 1865 an Irish-American
officer called Thomas Kelly actually succeeded in breaking
Stephens out from Dublin jail with the help of a prison hospital
orderly called John Breslin, and, on 12 March 1866, after some

time in hiding, the rebel leader took a boat to France and then made his own way to America.

A year after Stephens had set up the IRB, his friend John O'Mahoney had travelled to America in order to create a powerful organisation to support Irishmen abroad, providing the money for revolutionary activity. It would be his organisation that would begin the fight that Stephens could now only dream about. The scene now shifts politically to the United States. Emigration had forced Irishmen into exile since the 1830s, and the potato famine of the late 1840s forced more abroad. For many who had been involved with political activities in Ireland, exile had always been an option that had to be considered.

In the 1850s there were thousands of Irishmen in America, and here they took their grievances and nursed them in relative security. Moreover, they rebuilt the secret societies and support systems that had existed in the old country. Thus it was that the American wing of the IRB became the Fenian Brotherhood, led by O'Mahoney, a veteran of the 1848 rebellion and a man still dedicated to the desire for an Irish republic. It had been O'Mahoney who had recruited Millen, and he was soon building a nationwide organisation. O'Mahoney was said to look like a ruffian and wear threadbare suits, not what Millen would call a gentleman.

Veterans of 1848 came together secretly at the elegant New York townhouse of lawyer Michael Doheny during 1858 to form Fianna Éireann, named after the ancient warriors of Ireland. The organisation was based around 'centres', a structure O'Mahoney and Stephens had seen in France while in exile among the revolutionaries. The Fenian Brotherhood soon became a militant and military-style organisation. As such, it was dedicated to continuing the fight against England on foreign soil.

Although O'Mahoney was the president of the organisation, real power lay with William Randall Roberts and 'the Senate' wing, who wished to attack the British Empire wherever it was found. The two wings of the organisation began to split apart as the more militant of the Fenians gained power. Important to the success of the American Fenians would be an attack on Canada, but this needed the acquiescence of the United States government. This was easier to find than was expected, as the years of the American Civil War saw British support for the Southern Confederacy, and Canadian spies in the north. The American government was therefore not overly inclined to curb the actions of the Fenians or to warn the Canadian government.[8]

The American Civil War saw Irishmen fight on both sides and, when the war concluded, a large number of trained, armed and resolute men (between 190,000 and 200,000 men, mostly in their mid- to late twenties) were discharged; some were prepared to fight for the independence of Ireland, but were stranded in the United States. For some time, Canadian reports of a build-up of arms and ammunition and of a threat from a volunteer Fenian army filtered through to the provincial government. Queen Victoria confided to her diary on 12 February 1865 of the prospect of a war and of the impossibility of holding Canada. Yet no preparations were made.

Eventually, O'Mahoney, desperate to unite the two sides of his splintering movement, bought an old Confederate blockade-runner and attempted an abortive invasion of Campo Bello Island in New Brunswick, but, apart from burning a few cabins, nothing happened and the whole expedition ended in failure when the United States government confiscated the boat. O'Mahoney was financially ruined and even dismissed from his own organisation. This gave the Canadians the idea that the Fenians were a spent force.

Meanwhile, Roberts was more determined than ever to try for a full invasion of Canada and hold the eastern area around the Great Lakes as a surrogate free Ireland. To this effect, he purchased 10,000 rifles and 2½ million rounds of ammunition to arm his volunteers. The stockpiling did not go unnoticed in Canada, but it was again ignored. It was not long before Roberts started to gather the Irish elements left over from the

Civil War and, in May 1866, a large number of 'strange military men' started to arrive in Buffalo, New York state. They called themselves the Irish Republican Army, a name not revived until after 1916. Eventually there would be 1,500 well-armed, dedicated and battle-hardened Irishmen prepared to invade Canada via Niagara, but desertions and mistakes reduced this number to 800, of whom 600 were finally in John O'Neill's battle line.

Lieutenant-Colonel O'Neill had moved to America in 1848 and enlisted in the American army in 1857. Having fought with Custer in the Union cavalry, he had eventually been wounded at the Battle of Nashville in 1864, and thereafter left the army to become a land claims agent. He had not been intended as the commanding officer of the Irish but the original commander had fallen ill and, armed with scant knowledge of how to organise a campaign, he found himself in charge of this little force at short notice.

By this time, the Canadians had woken up to the danger and organised three small columns of troops to cut off the enemy. The commander of the main column was Lieutenant-Colonel Arthur Booker, originally from Nottingham and a wealthy, self-made merchant who enjoyed entertaining guests by performances of puppet shows and ventriloquism. Unfortunately, he was unused to command and, armed only with a cheap post office map, was not up to the task of defending the Niagara area against such a formidable enemy. To make matters worse, his command was made up of militia, of whom none had active experience and many were teenagers. There were no regular British troops near enough to come to his aid.

O'Neill, using his war experience, decided to set up a skirmishing line and draw the Canadians towards him, where they might be destroyed by the massed fire of his 'regiments'. The Battle of Ridgeway began at 8 a.m. on 2 June 1866. Booker had no plan of attack but nevertheless advanced and soon took casualties. At a critical moment, someone shouted that cavalry were coming and Booker ordered his Canadian troops to form a square (a formation not used for sixty years and revived only later against spear-armed native troops). Realising that no cavalry were attacking, Booker reversed the order, causing utter chaos. Meanwhile, the Fenians themselves, although taking virtually no casualties, seemed to become undecided as to what to do next, and pressed the advantage only when the militia began to break and run.

Although he had inflicted casualties on the Canadians, O'Neill soon realised that his position would become rapidly untenable when the other British columns tightened their grip. He therefore decided that it might be a good idea to retreat to an old fort that had been used during the war of 1812. He hoped that the large population of Frenchmen and Irishmen in Canada would spontaneously rise up and help him. Unfortunately, no more reinforcements arrived and no spontaneous uprising occurred. Eventually hemmed in, O'Neill conceded defeat and, at 2 a.m. on 3 June, fourteen hours after the final skirmish, the Fenians were evacuated by the USS *Harrison*. Temporarily jailed, O'Neill and his volunteers were soon released. The mayor of New York paid their train fares home and Stephens spoke to a large crowd in the city, still boasting of 'the Irish flag floating in an Irish breeze by New Year's Day, 1867'.

The Battle of Ridgeway was the only victory for Irish independence that occurred between 1798 and 1919, and it happened a long way from Ireland. Booker took much of the blame for the disaster and died on 27 September 1871, still bitter. The Fenians were not so easily beaten and made several more abortive attempts to invade Canada; they finally gave up in 1870, having been defeated at Pigeon Hill and Eccles Hill. O'Mahoney died in poverty in New York, while O'Neill, now a hero, rose high in the Fenian Brotherhood until he took to drink, dying on 7 January 1878. The town of O'Neill in Nebraska is named after him.

The attacks on Canada continued and Stephens concocted a plan to pursue the war in Ireland. Others proposed an attack on Chester Castle in England as part of a series of raids which would finally lead to a rising in Ireland. Kelly planned a rising in Ireland but was in hiding in England. Unfortunately, the plan was betrayed and the usual round-up of suspects began, with special attention being paid to Irishmen returning from America. On 5 March 1867 the rising went ahead regardless in Dublin, Louth, Tipperary, Cork, Waterford, Limerick and Clare. Unlike the invasion of Canada, this whole affair was a simple disaster, with dreadful weather (it snowed), poorly armed peasants and the organisation riddled with spies.

As for the hapless Stephens (then in Paris), he was condemned by the Brotherhood in New York for planning a rising that was delayed (in 1864) and that failed (in 1865), and replaced as head 'centre' by his rescuer, Kelly, whose frustration at the man soon spilled into open hostility: 'Little Baldy [James Stephens] has finally given up the ghost and acknowledged that if he came to Ireland the people would be certain to make short work of him. The rascal is … taking his ease with his wife, whilst the destiny of Ireland is in the balance.'[9] Indeed, it had been Kelly who had finally made the effort to call the IRB to arms. Dispirited, Stephens had already returned to France, where he earned a living as a journalist until being expelled for supposedly fomenting a French insurrection. From France he travelled to Switzerland, and from there he petitioned the British government to allow him to return to Ireland. Amazingly, they did so and he died in poverty in Dublin in 1901.

With the disasters in Canada and at Chester behind them, it would be reasonable to believe that the IRB was finished. However, in August 1867 the remaining leaders held a secret convention in Manchester, where they were soon spotted by the police and arrested. Among those captured were Kelly and his aid Timothy Deasy, Kelly being picked up on a charge of vagrancy on 11 September 1867. On their way to Bellevue jail, however, they were rescued by Fenians commanded by a gunrunner called Richard Burke, one of the men who stood opposed to Stephens.

A police sergeant was shot, but both Kelly and Deasy made it to America. Burke slipped away to London. Ernest Jones, a leading Welsh Chartist, took the defence for those IRB men who remained to stand trial. Nevertheless, the outcome was never in doubt: seven men were sentenced to penal servitude and five condemned to death.

This immediately aroused indignation among the English working class and a number of mass demonstrations took place to protest. At this point, Marx and Engels became extremely interested in the Irish question, both believing that the English working class were starting to make allegiance on a class and anti-imperialist basis. The International Workingmen's Association passed a resolution supporting the Irish, which was published in *Reynolds's Newspaper* on 21 November 1869. Whatever the truth of this new alliance between English workers and Irish peasants, Engels travelled to Ireland to see for himself, and he even learned Gaelic (which he claimed was easy). Their efforts at support came to naught, unlikely ever to have registered with the Government.

Eventually, three men were hanged and two were reprieved. On 13 December 1867 an attempt was made to free Burke from Clerkenwell prison in London after he, too, had been captured. Captain James Murphy was put in charge and around fifteen men plotted Burke's escape. Things did not go to plan and the gunpowder pile was so big that it blew up a large section of the prison itself and killed twelve civilians, including a child. One man did escape, but Michael Barrett was finally hanged for his part in the explosion on 26 May 1868. He was the last person to be publicly hanged in Britain. Burke was sentenced to fifteen years' hard labour.

This episode quickly showed to Marx and Engels how fickle were the British public, who soon turned away from their allegiance with the Irish. On 17 September 1869, while in Ireland, Engels wrote to Marx, 'The country itself looks absolutely depopulated.... . The state of war strikes one everywhere. Bands of the Royal Irish Constabulary are to be seen everywhere, with cutlasses, and sometimes revolvers at their sides... . In Dublin a battery of field artillery drove right down the middle of the city... . There are soldiers everywhere, everywhere.'[10]

The defeat of the Fenian invasion of Canada did not persuade Irishmen in exile to desist from the war with the English. To all intents and purposes, the war was simply exported to America and continued there; wherever Englishmen were to be found, the Irish were expected to make war upon them or their prox- ies – Ulster Protestants and the Welsh and, in Canada, the Scots. So it was that, when the threat to Canada receded, another group arose, ostensibly an extension of labour conflict, but just as much a part of the vendetta, feud and revenge culture of the old country. This was the Molly Maguires, a secret organisation set up in the coalfields of Pennsylvania, the militant wing of the Ancient Order of Hibernians, itself set up to protect Irish inter- ests in the United States. The Mollies had offered support to the IRB, but nothing had come of it.

Supposedly named after a widow who was evicted in Ireland and the group set up to avenge her, the Mollies emerged in America as the protectors of Irish Catholic interests in the five counties of eastern Pennsylvania from 1865 to 1874, growing to control most of the town councils and official positions in the area. Nevertheless, they were also organised as a secret assassi- nation society, dedicated to the intimidation, harassment and murder of mining officials who did not toe the line, tricks they may have learned from the miners of Wales. With few excep- tions, such mining bosses were of English or (ironically) of Welsh extraction, with a sprinkling of Pennsylvania Dutch (German) policemen as protection. *McClure's Magazine* described the organisation as having 'a peculiar reciprocity system ... in opera- tion between the various "patches", in accordance with which, if the body-master of District No. 1 wanted a certain man killed, he would call upon the body-master of District No. 2 for men to do it; and in return for this favour, he was bound to furnish assassins for the body-master of District No. 2 whenever the latter found himself in a murderous mood'.[11]

After a period of these outrages, Franklin Gowen, a Protestant who was president of the Philadelphia and Reading Railroad and had extensive interest in the coalfields, called in Allan Pinkerton,[12] 'an intelligent and broadminded Scotchman', to break up the organisation and restore power to the mine bosses. Pinkerton chose James McParlan (or McParland) to act as his agent. McParlan had done a number of jobs before accepting this one as agent provocateur and spy for the Pinkerton agency. It would take McParlan five years under his alias, James McKenna, to get to the top of the Mollies and infiltrate their plans (often taking part in dubious proceedings himself). Although suspected of his police connections, McParlan kept his real identity secret long enough to bring all of the Mollies to trial, many for murder. Even John 'Black Jack' Kehoe, the so-called king of the Mollies, was brought to book and sentenced to fourteen years. The Mollies were effectively broken, but the justice was rough, administered by Cyrus L. Pershing, a man who had been beaten to the governorship of Pennsylvania by Irish votes and bore a grudge. In 1889, unable to break the unions as he had broken the Mollies, and suffering from depression, Gowen committed suicide. For his troubles, McParlan was rewarded with the Pinkerton office in Denver. He re-emerges in 1905, again engaged in labour disputes. He died in 1919. John Kehoe received a full posthumous pardon in 1979.

With the Mollies defeated and the old IRB and Fenian Brotherhood at each other's throats, and with no perceptible gains against the old foe, a new set of men with new ideas had to appear. By the 1870s, American politicians could not wait to press the eager flesh of potential Irish voters but, whether Democrat or Republican, they did nothing. Dr William Carroll, ex-Confederate army, one of the founders of Clan na Gael, wrote that 'this simply confirms the general opinion of our American friends, that while we are capable of brilliant, desperate disconnected personal effort, there is no hope of our ever rising to the level of successful revolutionaries'.[13] It was an expression of resigned despair, but within a decade the American Irish would come back to haunt the English with new money, a new organisation and deadly weaponry: Alfred Nobel had invented dynamite.

Chapter Fifteen

The Door of the Tomb

During the 1860s and early 1870s, Irish fortunes were at their lowest, with many Fenian prisoners languishing in Australian jails after the Government crackdown. Indeed, the last convict transport, the *Hougoumont*, sailed to Fremantle jail in 1866. On board were civilian insurrectionists and those subverted from the military by Devoy. These 'military' Fenians were closely guarded and any pardon for the civilians was not going to be accorded to them. After a perilous journey, they arrived on 10 January 1867 to be confronted with a harsh and unforgiving landscape. Most were dispersed to chain gangs, though a few were given jobs as jail librarians or couriers.

One who was 'lucky' in this respect was the ex-hussar John Boyle O'Reilly, who was determined to make good his escape. In this, he was helped by Father Patrick McCabe, who, although under threat of excommunication from the Catholic Church, nevertheless smuggled information into the jail and took poems and letters out. O'Reilly tried twice to escape on American whalers which regularly called in on Australia. The first time, he failed, and was reduced to such despair that he attempted suicide. The second time, he was successful, eventually getting to Boston and finding his forte as a journalist.

Fenian influence nevertheless spread across the globe during the 1860s, especially in the United States, leading to rising levels of frustration among British politicians, who watched impotently as funds accumulated in New York or Boston went towards guns or dynamite destined for Britain. Sir William Harcourt noted in the early 1880s that, 'in former Irish rebellions, the Irish were in Ireland... . Now there is an Irish nation in the United States, equally hostile, with plenty of money, absolutely beyond our reach and yet within ten days' sail of our shores.'[1] Nevertheless, nothing was done about the situation until the 1880s, and it was certainly not considered sufficiently threatening or important for the protection of Prince Alfred when he made his royal progress to Australia in 1868 – the first royal visitor to come to those shores. He was scheduled to visit Adelaide, Melbourne, Brisbane, Sydney and Tasmania, the Government blissfully ignorant of Catholic-Irish Australian feelings. On 12 March 1868, while on a beach at Clontarf, near Sydney, Alfred was approached by an Irishman called Henry James O'Farrell, who shot him in the back. As he did so, he shouted, 'I'm a Fenian – God save Ireland.' The bullet lodged in the Prince's extra-thick rubber braces and he survived. O'Farrell, meanwhile, had to be rescued from an angry mob who threatened to lynch him. O'Farrell's 'obsession with Fenianism and the ways of Ireland' did not save him from the gallows, which he mounted on 21 April 1868, even though he was pronounced deranged (as all assailants of the royal family have been).

The Australia of the Eureka Stockade had changed immensely in the ten years or so since that rebellion. Australians were loyal and wanted acceptance. The assassination attempt shocked them and 'indignation' rallies were held the day after, as an expression of amazement that Fenianism was in Australia. Anti-Catholicism rose and Orange lodges proliferated. Henry Parkes, then Colonial Secretary, conducted his own inquiry into the incident and he was said (although the evidence may have been planted) to have found such details in O'Farrell's rooms as to suggest a Fenian plot. Parkes, however, was anti-Catholic and anti-Irish, although his police force was predominantly both Catholic and Irish. Indeed, he called the Catholic Irish 'jabbering baboons', which hardly endeared him, except to the ultra-Protestant loyalists. He had soon passed the Treason and Felony Act to reinforce his position. He also used the incident as an excuse to shut down aid to Catholic schools. The outpouring of loyalist feeling was enough to make the Prince consider Australia still to be a 'colony of England' and not a country in its own right. As a parting present from the Australians, Alfred brought back a wombat and his broken braces. The nature of the crowd on Clontarf beach may have convinced Prince Alfred of the loyalty of Australians, but the smell of burnt braces should have convinced him otherwise. Despite the end of transportation, there were still plenty of people in Australia who certainly did not wish to become its citizens. Most of these were in Fremantle jail.

O'Reilly, now a famous journalist in America, was nevertheless only too well aware that his companions remained in British custody some 11,500 miles away. Things had changed in America and the Clan na Gael had been formed to complement the IRB; it raised funds for a war. Devoy also was pricked by conscience and decided to organise a rescue through the Clan's skirmishing fund, established by Jeremiah O'Donovan Rossa, which stood at $42,000. The Clan, however, wanted the money to use for an offensive against England and refused to help, so Devoy set up his own rescue committee, which was, nevertheless, monitored by his fellow Fenians.

The first job was to procure a boat suitable for the journey to Australia and this they found in an old whaling hulk, which they called the *Catalpa* and which they refitted. With whaling as an excuse for the rescue, Devoy could save his comrades and turn a profit. O'Reilly, meanwhile, worked on contacts and, after a false start, a Quaker whaling captain was hired, called

George Anthony. He had not been to sea for three years and had no attachment to anything Irish. He took the job because he felt it the 'right thing to do'. The crew had few Irishmen and Englishmen, to avoid rousing suspicions, so the boat was manned with Portuguese and Malays. The *Catalpa* sailed for Australia, its mission unknown to its crew, on 29 April 1875.

Meanwhile, Devoy had to find a man to become the land side of the operation and this he found in John Breslin, the man who had helped Stephens escape from prison in Dublin. Breslin was now living in New York and he met Devoy in Hoboken during April. He accepted the challenge and travelled separately to Australia, pretending to be a wealthy businessman looking for a new investment. His cover name was 'James Collins' and he was accompanied by Thomas Desmond, who also travelled under an assumed name. They arrived in Fremantle on 16 November and stayed at the Emerald Isle Hotel, where Devoy met the governor and had an affair with the maid.

Soon the two Fenians had made contact with Father McCabe; the password was to be 'the door of the Tomb is ajar' and the rescue attempt would be on Easter Monday, 18 April 1876. McCabe would be the conduit to the prisoners; other local Fenians would help cut telegraph wires and cause disruption. The *Catalpa*, after some months of successful whaling, prepared to pull into Australian waters, when it came across another ship captained by the former master of the *Hougoumont*. He lent Anthony his charts, not realising the irony of the situation, and with them Anthony completed his journey, arriving safely in March 1876.

The spring was sprung and six military Fenians were free, having fooled their guards by pretending that they were assigned to potato picking. They made their way to the beach, where a boat, guns and new clothes awaited them. Their rescuers were prepared for a fight and were heavily armed. As the longboat pulled away into the surf, Breslin read out a letter to the rowers: 'This is to certify that I have this day released from the clemency of Her Most Gracious Majesty Victoria ... six Irishmen, condemned to imprisonment for life by the enlightened and magnanimous government of Great Britain for having been guilty of the atrocious and unpardonable crimes known ... as "Love of Country" and "Hatred of Tyranny".'

An hour and a half passed and still they were not missed; then it dawned on the British. A gunboat was soon catching up with the *Catalpa*, but she was in international waters. The *Catalpa* ran up the Stars and Stripes. A shot went across her bows. The two ships were close enough now for a slanging match between their captains: 'You have escaped prisoners aboard,' shouted the captain of the gunboat *Georgette*. 'You are mistaken,' roared Anthony. 'There are no prisoners aboard this ship. There are none but free men ... !'[2] The stand-off finished without conclusion and the *Georgette* withdrew. The rescue was a success. The British government was stung but in no position to start a war with the United States, and the affair was quickly and quietly glossed over. Back in America, Devoy had established a commanding position in Clan na Gael and was planning a final showdown with the English.

As always, the Fenians were looking for that secret solution, that one-off blow that would bring the English to their senses or to their knees. What better if that secret, invincible weapon was capable of actually being manufactured in America. So it was fortuitous when Breslin, fresh from his rescue, came across John Philip Holland. It was Michael Holland (John's brother) who told Breslin a story about a potential secret weapon that might reduce the Royal Navy to impotence. John Holland was born on 29 February 1841 in County Clare, Ireland, the son of a coastguard. After his father's early death and the death of his brother Robert of cholera in 1847, John's mother moved the family to Limerick, where he joined the Christian Brothers and became a teacher. Nevertheless, John had a passion for a special type of boat, an underwater boat, even though he himself was 'a civilian landsman'. In 1873, because of ill health, he moved to Boston, where his mother already lived, and then to Patterson in New Jersey, still nursing dreams of his submersible.

The Fenians had a 'navy' in America, three ships including a tug, but they soon realised that a submarine might be able to be taken close to a Royal Navy warship by one of these old boats and then launched into the attack. The plan was audacious and the skirmishing fund was put at Holland's disposal. In May 1878 the first submersible boat (powered by petrol and electric) was launched on the Passaic river near Patterson. It remained submerged for an hour, but was scuttled.

The next project was the *Fenian Ram*, launched in 1881. Known as a 'wrecking boat', it carried a crew of three and a pneumatic gun to fire its torpedoes. It was shaped like a porpoise and worked well in trials around New York harbour. Yet this revolutionary vessel was short-lived as it was taken away (or simply stolen, according to other sources) by Breslin during a dispute over the use of the skirmishing fund. Taken to New Haven, she remained there until 1916, when she was trotted out to raise funds for the victims of the aborted Dublin Rising.[3]

The 1880s and 1890s were difficult times for the exiled Irish waiting impotently in New York with funds but little opportunity, and their organisations fell to bickering. At home, the aggression against landlords (the Land War) was having great effect and Charles Parnell had already stepped up to lead the parliamentary party, a move with more likelihood of gaining some form of independence than all the others put together. In America, however, the Clan were willing to exploit any crisis that hit the British Empire; they were in Russia touting for help when the Balkan War broke out; they were in Afghanistan, Guatemala and even India drumming up support. They were often heard sympathetically, but never sponsored.

In 1880 Rossa began to take a harder line about action and formed the breakaway reformed 'United Irishmen' with a remit to take things to the mainland of England. In 1881 bombers or 'missioners' entered England, armed with dynamite. They bombed the Mansion House and locations in Liverpool. With Parnell now in jail for 'incitement' and the Land League declared illegal, the revolutionary situation in Ireland seemed again to be leaderless and to calm down. The calm was broken when a terrorist group known as the 'Invincibles' stabbed to death the newly appointed Chief Secretary, Lord Frederick Cavendish and his Under-secretary, Thomas Burke, as they walked in Phoenix Park, Dublin.[4] The murders were savage, using long, surgical knives. Parnell offered to resign his leadership of the parliamentary party, but Gladstone persuaded him otherwise.[5] The general outrage, even among Fenians, did not stop Rossa despatching bomb teams to Liverpool and to London, where the underground was attacked. Rossa had changed the rules of engagement, as civilians were now targets. There was considerable loss of life. Scotland Yard was the next target; almost the whole of the newly formed Special Branch was wiped out.

By 1885, dynamite 'outrages' in London were a regular occurrence, with attacks on both the Tower and the House of Commons. The authorities floundered; men were sacked and replaced, but to no avail as the attacks continued. By 1886, Gladstone was in secret talks with Parnell and had been convinced that Home Rule was the only solution to the bloodshed. By the start of the 1890s, things were again falling apart. The Clan was riven with dissension and broken by financial scandal, and the British secret service was cooking up a plot to entangle Parnell with the bombing campaign and a supposed attempt to assassinate Victoria. The evidence was forged, but Parnell's famous affair with Kitty O'Shea broke him instead.

Behind much of the anxiety in the late nineteenth century was the fear of terrorism, the ultimate tool of revolution. By the 1860s, the word 'terrorist' had begun to be used to describe members of clandestine groups, applied initially to the Fenian Brotherhood and their more extreme national liberation squads, which had begun to bomb England. The term was also applied retrospectively to describe those who had been involved in the

Irish Civil War of 1798. The word had taken on its modern meaning, with *Century Magazine* referring in its November 1887 issue to those who were 'the leaders of the "terroristic" or extreme revolutionary party'. Until very recently terrorism has consistently been associated with the Irish.[6]

Britain was entirely bereft of any home-based organised secret service to deal with the Irish onslaught. The Foreign Office continued with imperial intrigues in India, Egypt, Persia and the Sudan, but spent diminishing resources on intelligence, even as it consolidated its bureaucracy in its Whitehall offices from 1868. The army had an intelligence department that had hardly any effect on military thinking and was often left with little to do except catalogue maps and read through foreign newspapers for clippings. Only in 1871 did the 'Topographical and Statistical' Department get a definition of its mission, which was 'to collect and classify all possible information relating to the strength, organisation, etc of foreign armies: to keep themselves acquainted with the progress made by foreign countries in military art and science and to preserve the information in such a form that it can be readily consulted'.[7] The department was transformed into the Intelligence Branch in 1873, but the army made little use of its services, with Victoria's cousin, the Duke of Cambridge, commander-in-chief between 1856 and 1895, remarking sourly on the pursuit of 'progress'. Ten years later, the Admiralty set up its own Foreign Intelligence Committee, with a minuscule staff of four. Sir George Ashton, in charge of the department, admitted to ignorance of geography, foreign affairs and foreign languages.

With all its drawbacks, spying appealed to the late-Victorian spirit of adventure and (when not directed at Irish affairs) was no longer seen as a 'dirty job' for a working-class man but as a holiday with a purpose for a rather richer sort. Baden-Powell called it 'glorified detective work', a game for enthusiastic and patriotic amateurs with the love of a sporting chance who did the work for the 'love of the thing' and of 'great sporting value', a feeling encapsulated in John Buchan's *Thirty-Nine Steps* (1915). Baden-Powell enthused, 'For anyone who is tired of life, the thrilling life of a spy should be the very finest recuperator.' Baden-Powell, Sidney Reilly and Paul Dukes all enjoyed the fun of disguise and the frisson of going under cover, lovingly recreated in a domestic setting by Arthur Conan Doyle in his short story 'A Scandal in Bohemia' (1891), in which Sherlock Holmes donned the disguise of a 'drunken-looking groom' in order to spy on the 'well known adventuress, Irene Adler'. If a spy was caught, the consequences of such meddling in real life were, in the words of George Ashton of the Foreign Intelligence Committee, merely 'unpopularity' brought on by the effect of the exposure of a necessary vulgarity in taste.

Only in one area did spying cease to be a game, and that was at home. Political order and communal acquiescence could be disturbed by radical pamphlets and speeches, republican plots and attempted coups, food rioting and industrial sabotage and, worst of all, the continuing threat of Irish dissent. Effective government was undermined by its amateurish and haphazard attitude to secrecy and its ad hoc approach to surveillance.

Interception and bribery went hand in hand. The deciphering branch was created in 1703, with the Oxford don the Revd Edward Willes in charge, and his entire family as employees, so that by the time he became Bishop of Bath and Wells during the 1750s, he had three sons in the deciphering business. All worked part time for the state and passed on their expertise to the following generations of Willes until, in 1844, their clandestine letter-opening business was exposed amid the scandal of the surveillance on Mazzini. Secret service money paid for the family's retirement from the game of spying.[8]

Mazzini's cause was taken up by most of the British Establishment, who considered tampering with mail, especially that of a nationalist exile who was a guest in Britain, to be quite against the spirit of gentlemanly behaviour. The case defined political attitudes in mid-century and reaffirmed the consensus regarding privacy, private property and honourable behaviour among leading thinkers and politicians. Jeremy Bentham's dictum was unequivocal, for 'secrecy is an instrument of conspiracy; it ought not … to be the system of a regular government'. Most contemporaries agreed that government by secrecy was the way of foreigners and not at all British. Peel's introduction of a modern style of cabinet government was itself chastised by a later Liberal prime minister, Lord Rosebery, as 'the spectacle of a secret council, on the Vatican model, and sworn to absolute silence… . Whether the system of cabinet government be an efficient one or not is not now the question… . In an Anglo-Saxon community, during the present epoch … the strangest is the government of the British Empire by a secret committee.'[9] Nothing could be less British in a country with 'so much of democracy about it'.

With a conviction that only openness and ease of communication could create an orderly society, mid-Victorian governments moved cautiously towards fuller democratic participation, inevitable steps towards parliamentary reform. Following the Reform Act of 1832, the Government had committed itself to the creation of a literate population in which secrecy was anathema.

Privacy and the sacredness of private property went together with a sense that those who ruled should do so with honour and that a free society was one in which a benevolent hierarchy acted honestly and openly. Gladstone was convinced that, along with the growth of a civil service, there had to be a place for 'those who may be called gentlemen by birth and training'. Frederick Wills defined the new gentlemanly vocation in 1844: 'The essence then of a gentleman is unselfishness, and the laws by which a gentleman was governed are the laws of honour. Honour implies perfect courage, honesty, truth and good faith. It forbids anything underhanded … such as listening at doors or opening other people's letters, reading their correspondence, or breaking confidence.'[10]

Set against the actual power of the Government (who were mostly aristocrats) and their servants, the gentlemen of the civil service, was the opaque world of the working classes. Faced with the growth of unions among artisans, successive governments had first tried force and then more liberalising legislation in 1824 and 1825. Having repealed the Combination Acts, Government may have hoped the emergent coherence of working-class demands could be curbed and the bad old days of the revolution-ary period forgotten.[11]

The making of oaths to bind working-class aspiration to industrial or political ambition smacked not only of dishon-ourable and ungentlemanly behaviour, but also of a traitorous refusal to except the decisions of one's superiors. It was felt that 'the objection to voluntary oaths acquires much greater weight, when they are not only voluntary but secret, and used as a bond of union by large bodies of men, deriving ... an additional force ... from the cunningly devised terms of a superstitious ritual'.[12] For the writer and traveller Harriet Martineau, such oath-taking was foreign to British thought and an import from the continent of Europe, 'honeycombed with secret societies'. Legislation and negotiation with Government seemed the only way forward, even if the whole process would be dogged by suspicion, and legislation passed only begrudgingly. *Blackwood's Magazine* in 1867 concluded with reluctance that, 'if the law would try to prohibit trades-unions, they would, in spite of the law, continue to exist, as long as the working man consid-ered them necessary ... with this difference, that they would be organised as secret societies with secret oaths and passwords, and that, being secret and illegal, they would be more blood-thirsty'. The article was ominously entitled 'Work and Murder'. Ireland remained intractable.

Secrecy may not have been pleasant, but by the 1880s it was considered absolutely necessary when it came to combating the Fenians. By 1883, there was a system of secret police in Ireland and a network of spies that kept watch across the Atlantic. There was no such system of security in Britain, apart from the sixteen Royal Irish Constabulary police stationed at the ports. 'Nothing is known of what is going on in England,' lamented Edward Jenkinson, the man in charge of counter-intelligence against the Fenians and unofficially known as the 'Spymaster-General'. After the 1880s bombing campaign, an 'Irish Bureau' was set up at Scotland Yard, specialising in Fenian affairs, but things were becoming chaotic, with enforcement agencies in London, Ireland and the rest of Great Britain, each with a budget, each running its own spy network and each not talking to its fellow agencies. There was also a belated Explosives Act passed on 9 April 1883, in just half an hour. The bombing campaign of 1884 showed that there was much still to do. The apparent solution was to amalgamate all three services. By a secret deal, Jenkinson assumed control of operations from London, but tensions arose with subordinates, and the system carried on as before. Indeed, he became so disenchanted with the system and the way he had been treated that he actually fed information to Davitt (the lead figure in the 'Land War'). The different security agencies continued to stumble across each other (even to running spies in each other's networks) for another few years.

Finally, in January 1887, the Metropolitan Special Branch came into existence, having gestated in the Government's mind since 1881. At this juncture, five agencies, including uniformed police on protection duty and port police, not to mention the 'Special Irish Branch' officers at Central Office, were charged with protecting Britain against the Irish 'dynamitards'. The formation of Special Branch was complex.[13] It was now officially part of the Metropolitan Police and consisted of special-duty CID men who had been seconded to the job. It was known as Section D, as distinct from the Irish Branch, which was Section B, or the port police, who were Section C, and for some years even its name was doubtful. Its formation was highly secret, being effectively a semi-legal national police force which had never been sanctioned by parliament;

moreover it was tasked with watching not only Fenians but also anarchists. Section D answered to the Home Office and not the Metropolitan Police Commissioner, a source of much future trouble. Britain finally had a secret political police, like its continental neighbours. Partially in charge of this unwieldy organisation was James Monro, who headed both the CID and the 'Secret Department', being known as the 'Secret Agent'. He resigned after a number of disputes with the Commissioner and retired to Bengal to do missionary work and complete his book, *Preparing for the Second Coming*.

It is said that the idea for Home Rule for Ireland came to Gladstone while he was taking a holiday on board a friend's yacht around the coast of Norway, but perhaps the secret talks with Parnell or the evident success of the 'Land War' or even Gladstone's own moral uprightness had already persuaded him. Whatever the truth, it was a wake-up call to the men of Ulster. The Orange Order had recovered from its embarrassment in the 1830s and the lodges again thrived, although with little to get hot under the collar about. On the whole they were working class now, with fewer aristocrats being bothered to join. Home Rule changed all that and again united peers with proletarians and reminded politicians just how difficult it was dealing with the Protestant Irish. It was also proof of the 'traitorous' nature of the Liberal Party and just how much influence Parnell had over its leaders. It was a perfect time for the Conservatives to play their hand, and soon Randolph Churchill (possibly already suffering from the dementia that would kill him) took himself to Ulster to stir trouble. His dementia would be catching. With his slogan of 'Ulster will fight and Ulster will be right', Churchill visited Belfast to speak and started three days of violent rioting. Whatever his purpose in going, Churchill's rhetoric was wilfully inflammatory, inciting the lodges to armed insurrection. In February 1886 in the Ulster Hall he openly challenged the Orangemen to show what they were made of: 'Now may be the time to show whether all those ceremonies and forms which are practised in Orange Lodges are really living symbols or idle meaningless ceremonies.'[14]

Gladstone introduced his bill on 8 April 1886, in which he proposed to restore the Irish parliament in Dublin and give it limited powers. It was the slippery slope to Catholic rule, and parliament would have none of it. Gladstone had to wait until 1893 to try again and it was debated over eighty-five sittings, but to no avail: the bill was outvoted by thirty-four votes and Belfast went wild. In the meantime, sniffing the winds of change, Major Fred Crawford had founded 'Young Ireland', membership of which required either ownership of a Winchester rifle or a pistol. Things were getting serious again in Ireland. The Magheramorne Manifesto, drawn up to unite the two religions, died at birth and Ireland again set sail for disaster. Gladstone and Parnell had left the fight long since and so a third Home Rule Bill was introduced by Campbell Bannerman, supported by John Redmond, Parnell's successor in parliament.

The bill was to be introduced in 1912, but for the intervention of Sir Edward Carson, a Dublin barrister who was nevertheless invited to take over the running of the Unionist wing of the Conservatives in February 1910. Carson got to work quickly and travelled to Craigavon to hold a military-style review of the lodges. Here, in front of 100,000 people, he announced that should Home Rule pass then he would immediately set up a provisional government: the Protestant Province of Ulster. He was cheered; the Protestants would remain loyal to the Crown and the union with Great Britain by *breaking away* from them. This was a strange logic but the Ulstermen felt betrayed and abandoned. It was also treason, but no one seemed to be listening. Soon Carson and Crawford were drilling a private army, the legality of which was justified by a loophole in the law which allowed magistrates to sanction local militias as long as they were upholding the 'constitution'. There was no holding the Carsonites once they realised their strength and Carson himself was now able to address rallies of 200,000. He was now quite open and assured in his threats to the Government and his appeal to the people: 'I know that force has been used to compel retention to government against the will of the people. But a precedent has yet to be created to drive out by force loyal and contented citizens from a community to which by birth they belong.... Assume for the sake of argument – what I do not believe – that the people of this country would condone the coercion of their kith and kin, what would be the effect on the army? Many officers would resign; no army could stand such a strain.'[15]

It was a call to mutiny. Yet nothing was done as unstoppable forces gathered. On 28 September 1912 a Solemn League and Covenant was signed by all but 3,000 of the half-million Protestant adults in Ulster, some in blood. In July 1913 the Provisional Government was secretly formed and Carson and Crawford landed between 30,000 and 40,000 rifles, with several million rounds of ammunition, taken off the boats unopposed by any law. Carson was now the law in Northern Ireland and his army, the Ulster Volunteer Force (UVF), consisted of over 100,000 well-armed men regularly drilled in public. Protestants had no need of pikes. This loyalist rebellion, organised to bully Westminster into abandoning the bill but not abandoning Ulster, would be impossible to suppress without the army; but even they had refused to implement the bill by force if it became law, and fifty-eight out of seventy officers at the Curragh barracks were ready to resign. The Conservatives had brought Britain to the brink of a crisis that only the declaration of war on Germany could avert. The Home Rule Bill included an exclusion clause for Ulster, but it was a moot point, as, on 15 September 1914, further debate was suspended for the duration of the war. On this, at least, Carson and Redmond were agreed. Redmond went further and pledged the loyalty of the Catholics. Fifty-nine thousand troops of all denominations were called up immediately.

Catholics were slow at first to react to the activities in Ulster. It was true that they had organisations with nationalist political and religious leanings: Sinn Féin had been founded in 1903 by Arthur Griffith, the Catholic Boy's Brigade was active as the century turned, and Fianna Éireann, the republican version of the boy scouts, began in 1902. All these organisations had caught the spirit of militarism and existed to inculcate 'manliness', 'discipline and obedience'. Despite its revival in 1909 under the leadership of the gun-toting Constance Gore-Booth Countess Markievicz, Fianna Éireann was dedicated to producing a military spirit in its children. Uniforms were everywhere and private armies drilled. Militarism had taken hold. In 1913 the trade union leader James Connolly, after a long and exhaustive strike in which Catholics had been intimidated, formed the Irish Citizen Army in Dublin; Markievicz joined. There were also the Hibernian Rifles, which were formed, as were all the other organisations, because of a lapse in the law that now made gun clubs legal. Biggest of all were the Irish National Volunteers (Oglaigh na hÉireann), which formed in 1913 in Dublin under Eoin MacNeill. Priests joined in the Catholic equivalent of the UVF in Belfast.

The Catholics also began gunrunning. The author Erskine Childers and his American wife, Mollie, brought in rifles on their yacht *Asgard* in July 1914 and these were distributed in readiness for some sort of defence against Protestant aggression. In 1914 Sir Roger Casement, the diplomat, humanitarian and organiser of the Volunteers, travelled to Germany to argue for an invasion and to raise an Irish Legion among prisoners of war, but, unsuccessful in his attempts, he returned to Ireland on 12 April 1916 to warn against the planned rising. He was arrested and charged with treason. The Catholics now had guns and uniforms and, although there were only 20,000 recruits compared with 85,000 well-armed Ulstermen, and although the Catholics were ill armed, untrained and largely incompetent, nevertheless they thought that they were ready for action.

The Volunteers were cheered on by Patrick Pearse (Pádraig Mac Piarais), who saw the makings of a revolution. He had been born in Dublin on 10 November 1879 and educated as a lawyer, before becoming a journalist and finally president of the Gaelic League. Obsessed with the vision of Ireland that was known as the 'Celtic Twilight', Pearse founded a bilingual school and took to poetry. In 1913 he joined the Irish Volunteers and in 1914 was on the supreme council; by 1915 he had also joined the IRB, which was secretly guiding the machinations of the Volunteers. Pearse was a romantic dreamer with a Wagnerian line in 'Liebestod'; for him, everything boiled down to sacrifice and crucifixion, to bloodshed, a 'blood sacrifice' and the idea of bloodshed as a 'cleansing and sanctifying thing'. He was obsessed with Christ-like fantasies of death and regeneration. This was a Catholic dream of martyrdom, not of victory, a perverse form of victory-in-defeat designed to awaken the people, and it would soon have dreadful consequences. The wonder is that others listened and were convinced. Connolly thought that Pearse was a 'blithering idiot', but still joined him, though the odds were 'a thousand to one against us'.[16]

The idea of a rising was discussed early in 1916 by Pearse and others of the IRB. It was to take place symbolically on Easter Sunday (23 April) in Dublin, when a number of strong points were to be seized and the republic declared. At the last minute, MacNeill called off most of his Volunteers and left the rebels short-handed but still with a core of well-trained IRB men and women. The revolution went ahead on Easter Monday regardless, with the main body of troops under Pearse commandeering the General Post Office, and others scattered around the city in places sometimes sensible and sometimes downright suicidal: Trinity College was successfully defended against the rebels by its porters, Dublin Castle was virtually ignored when it could have been captured and St Stephen's Green was defended although nothing more than railings stood between the defenders and machine guns. Some, like Michael Collins, wore their green uniforms as if on parade; others were in civilian clothes. There was no system of communicating with the outside world, no stockpile of food, no real thought to any wounded and no real plan. The whole thing was a gigantic act of bravado – a 'blood sacrifice'. Needless to say, busy shoppers and passers-by were bemused when the post office was taken over, and more bemused when the tricolour and the green flag of the United Irishmen were raised and the union flag lowered. Then Pearse read the Proclamation of the Provisional Government of the Irish Republic to the People of Ireland. It read in part:

> Irishmen and Irishwomen: In the name of God and of the dead generations from which she receives her old tradition of nationhood, Ireland ... summons her children to her flag and strikes for her freedom. Having organised and trained her manhood through her secret revolutionary organisation[s] ... having patiently perfected her discipline, having reso-lutely waited for the right moment to reveal itself she now seizes that moment, and, supported by her exiled children in America and by gallant allies in Europe, but relying in the first on her own strength she strikes in full confidence of victory.
>
> We declare the right of the people of Ireland to the own-ership of Ireland, and to the unfettered control of Irish destinies, to be sovereign and indefeasible. The long usurpa-tion of that right by foreign people and government has not extinguished the right, nor can it ever be extinguished except by the destruction of the Irish people. In every generation the Irish people have asserted their right to national freedom and sovereignty.... Standing on that fundamental right and again asserting it in arms ... we hereby proclaim the Irish republic as a sovereign independent state, and we pledge our lives ... to the cause of its freedom.[17]

And with that, the war had started and the rebels waited for the British to react.

The Government was taken by surprise, but soon brought thousands of troops, including six Irish battalions, into the city, equipped with machine guns and artillery. Pearse and the other thousand rebels were slowly being fought into a corner; they were amassing casualties, lacking sleep and food and running out of ammunition, but they held off 16,000 troops as the General Post Office and the surrounding streets of Dublin were reduced to a heap of rubble. After a week, the rebels surrendered. Those who came out of their defences included elements of the Irish Citizen Army, Hibernian Rifles, the Irish republican boy scouts and their sisters in the Cumann na mBan, as well as the Irish Volunteers. One hundred and thirty-two rebels had died, and exactly half that number of soldiers; there were also wounded civilians and a large number of wounded soldiers. The country was placed under martial law between April and November.

The streets of central Dublin were in ruins. The populace had not risen in disgust at English rule – too many had men at the Western Front – and no risings had occurred outside Dublin, whose shops were now being looted by an ungrateful population. The rebels were led off to prison and, one by one, the leaders were condemned and executed. Pearse was shot at Kilmainham jail on 3 May. In jail in Lewes in Sussex, Eamon de Valera, future president of Eire, and his confederates began rebuilding their organisations. Michael Collins worked within the IRB. A reckoning was coming.

The whole affair was going to destroy Home Rule, and Redmond condemned the business as 'wicked and insane'. The executions divided opinion. They were too obviously a vindictive response to men and women who seemed to have acted out of frustration and whose cause many in England could sympathise with. The harsh treatment of civilians galvanised an Irish population indifferent to the Volunteers. Indeed the rebels had acted with conspicuous care towards civilians and wounded British soldiers, and many had done so while wearing a uniform. In Ireland there was a campaign in the *Daily News* to avoid a British 'reign of terror', and the *Irish Independent* on 8 May argued for 'wise clemency'. John Dillon, a prominent Irish MP, warned the House on 11 May of the 'river of blood' that would be unleashed if the executions continued. The Government, in the middle of a desperate war, had no ears for such clemency, the papers were ignored and Dillon was ostracised.

The casualties and executions did not delay the war in France, nor much influence Irish loyalty to the Crown. Men flocked to the colours until there were no more men to take. There were to be three Irish divisions, Catholic and Protestant alike, a total of 191,000 recruits from north and south, of whom over 27,000 were to become casualties, the rate of attrition meaning that, in the end, English recruits filled the vacant places left by the dead and wounded of Ireland. A further 23,000 were to die as Englishmen in Irish regiments.

In 1917 de Valera became the president of Sinn Féin, which had stood aside from the rising but which now declared for a republic, and in 1918 they overwhelmingly won the 'khaki' elections in Ireland. On 21 January 1919, with the ghosts of Tone, Fitzgerald, Rossa and Pearse looking down, the Irish entered their penultimate bloody war for independence.

Chapter Sixteen

A Room Full of Bombs

While things brewed in Ireland, politics in England especially had already begun to change, especially as the century turned and left-wing ideas began to coalesce into recognisable socialism. With Engels in Manchester and Marx in Soho, it is indeed a wonder that the revolution that would swamp Russia did not take place in England. Nevertheless, in their own lifetimes they were never able to build up a mass organisation and did not, of course, have the idea of a 'party of the avant garde' that would inspire Lenin and the Bolsheviks. As late as 1864, after nearly twenty years of planning, few were interested in socialist ideas. On 21 October Marx addressed the newly formed International Workingmen's Association (founded 28 September) with an impassioned speech about economics and poverty, ending with the rallying cry, 'Proletarians of all countries, unite!' The speech, along with the rules of the association, was duly published on 27 October. The words sounded good, but the speech was delivered to a handful of listeners, some of whom were those ubiquitous police spies who seemed to attend all such meetings. The association (founded at St Martin's Hall) was the inheritor of a long tradition of working men's associations that went back to Cartwright and Place and that debated the current political situation in the country as well as schemes for setting up cooperatives.

As the nineteenth century progressed, these associations became political again, especially with the creation of the Social Democratic Foundation (SDF) by Henry Hyndman in 1883. Hyndman was a maverick conservative turned Marxist. Despite a Marxist programme, the SDF were not a dangerous revolutionary body (although they frightened the authorities). They were, however, the embryo of a whole set of socialist views from primitive communism to anarchism. It was the appearance of foreign exiles from France, Russia, Germany, Italy and Spain that began a new era of political debate among radicals and gained for Britain the sobriquet of the world centre for communism, the French and German authorities constantly complaining about Britain's liberal policy towards these dangerous revolutionaries. For the most part, the British government ignored these unwelcome complaints from foreign embassies and simply watched the terrorists. Thus Peter Kropotkin, Alexander Herzen, Johann Most, Mikhail Bakunin, Errico Malatesta, Lenin, Trotsky and Stalin all passed through London between the 1880s and the early 1900s. From clubs such as the Club Autonomie in Windmill Street, London, or the International Club in St Stephen's Mews, these men hoped to destabilise Europe with talk of 'propaganda by the deed' (a euphemism for bombing) or expropriation (a euphemism for burglary – usually from banks). By 1894, it was estimated that 1,400 foreign anarchists were in London; *The Times* calculated that there were 1,000 of these desperate men in Soho and Fitzrovia.

The most important of these anarchist clubs where exiles could dream of revolution and upheaval was the German Communist Workers' Club, situated in Rose Street, Soho, and known as the 'CABv'. The German Autonomie and the Jewish Berner Street Club later merged and there was even a British section (although speaking German) under Frank Kitz. On 14–19 July 1881 a congress was held in London to unite all sections of the anarchist movement. To this, Malatesta came, having been expelled from France, as did Kropotkin, having escaped from Tsarist Russia, and Nikolai Thaikovsky, leader of the Populist Group. In 1878 the Russian Populists had turned to terror to get radical change in Russia and by 1880 there was much agreement in radical circles over the need for the bullet and the bomb. The 23 December issue of *Le Révolté* argued for 'permanent revolt, by spoken and written words, by the dagger, the gun, [and] dynamite'. Kropotkin advocated a similar line by 1881.

Although aimed at continental systems, this violent language was international in tone, the first time internationalism had entered the argument since the French Revolution. As Most's trial in London showed, after he had been arrested for publishing an article in praise of the assassination of Alexander II, such international terrorist plots were considered 'brutal and un-English' and, although British anarchist groups were inspired by the fiery language of revolution, they never reached international proportions and only two home-grown anarchist bomb plots were ever discovered (the rest of the bombs stamped, as it were, 'made in England' were for export to France).

Indeed the most famous incident, the Greenwich Park explosion, in which Martial Bourdin blew himself up while transporting a bomb to the Royal Observatory, may have been an accident in which Bourdin was delivering the bomb to a third party for export to France. The incident of the Walsall bomb conspiracy of 1892 may have been the result of infiltration by the police and an entrapment operation by a spy. Little evidence was found. Home-grown anarchists:

> were much less revolutionary, as illustrated by an incident in London on 31 December 1891. On that occasion an Oxford educated man, aged thirty, fired a five-chamber revolver at the speaker's residence. This of course ... was merely a gesture.

When John Evelyn Barlas, former member of the SDF [and a friend of Oscar Wilde] was approached by a policeman, he handed him the revolver saying: 'I am an anarchist and intended shooting you, but then I thought it is a pity to shoot an honest man. What I have done is to show my contempt for the House of Commons.' He was not drunk and refused to give an address or occupation but he was described in court as 'highly connected'. The Holloway prison medical officer concluded that he was insane.[1]

Throughout the thirty years from 1880 to 1910, many international 'socialisms' were debated, from anarchism and anarcho-communism to 'pure' Marxism and Christian communitarianism. None took the field and each had its day in the arena of the 'International'; Marxism was for most of the nineteenth century only one choice among many. Even when the Socialist League split up, joined the SDF and proclaimed itself communist, the definition of such communism was always open to debate.

Lenin came to England in 1902 when things became too hot in Russia and, through his comrade Georgii Plekhanov, then a more important figure, he made contact with Harry Quelch, the printer for the SDF, who arranged for him to have the SDF print *Iskra* (Lenin's paper) from Clerkenwell Green. In 'disgusting weather', Lenin and his wife, Krupskaya, arrived in London on 12 April 1902 and were found rooms near King's Cross. The rest of the board of *Iskra* were either in London or in Switzerland and, with time on his hands and in order to improve his English, Lenin joined the British Museum Reading Room under the name of Dr Jacob Rachter. Lenin and Krupskaya also went to Speaker's Corner where, having not heard spoken English before, they found the accents difficult.

While in London, Lenin attended meetings and rallies, including meetings of the Russian Emigré Workers' Clubs in the East End, which Lenin addressed on 29 November 1902. On

21 March 1903 he gave a talk to the London Jewish branch of the SDF alongside Frederick Lessner, a close friend of Engels. His last appearance was at Alexandra Palace on May Day 1903, when he was accompanied by Hyndman and Keir Hardy and where he spoke this time in Russian. He also enjoyed the open-topped buses, and looked down on the trees and squares of the capital,[2] where he admired the beautiful homes of the well-off, but, noted Krupskaya, 'there were other places, too. Mean little streets tenanted by London's work people, with clothes lines stretched across the road and anaemic children playing on the doorsteps. To these places we used to go on foot. Observing these startling contrasts between wealth and poverty, [Lenin] would mutter in English through clenched teeth: "Two nations!"'

The second congress of the Russian Social Democrats was to be held in Brussels during 1903, but was broken up by police after only one day. The fifty delegates therefore decamped to London. It was Lenin's second visit: 'Here a succession of meeting rooms were hired ... the congress did not stay in any one place for longer than one day. The first meeting was called somewhere in Charlotte Street, near Tottenham Court Road, not far from the premises of the Communist Club [in] Charlotte Street. Apparently, it also met in an anglers' club, where there were trophies on the wall, and the landlord was told this was a meeting of Belgian trade unionists.'[3] Despite the divisions in the party organisation between the Mensheviks and the Bolsheviks, which forced Lenin to resign his position on *Iskra*, he took the whole delegation to the tomb of Karl Marx in Highgate Cemetery on 24 August.

The party met again in London during 1905, after the defeats in the Russo-Japanese War. This time the Mensheviks stayed in Switzerland for the congress and this split the party. The other thirty-four delegates drank German beer in a Pentonville pub, once the day's discussions had concluded. Lenin stayed again near King's Cross, in a house which was finally demolished in 1969. After the congress, which lasted from 25 April to 10 May, Lenin took the delegates to the Natural History Museum and London Zoo. Denied access to other countries, Lenin again chose London for the venue for the fourth congress in 1907, and 366 delegates (including Mensheviks) duly arrived. They met between 13 May and 1 June in a socialist church (the Brotherhood Church) on Southgate Road, which was run by the Revd F.R. Swan, later to be the cashier for the *Daily Herald*. Twelve detectives and two Tsarist spies also went, and participated in the fish and chips that Lenin provided for the many poor and hungry delegates. Again Lenin was welcomed by Hyndman and the SDF, and again he visited the British Library, where he whiled away the hours and found books that he was denied access to while on the move.

Lenin was back in London during 1908, where he spent a month formulating an argument against socialist 'revisionism'. His last visit was in November 1911, when he stayed near Mornington Crescent. Here he read Hyndman's *The Record of an Adventurous Life*, the first volume of Hyndman's autobiography. Lenin, never one to curry favour, was caustic, describing Hyndman as 'an English bourgeois philistine, [who] being [the] best of the best of his class, finally finds the road to socialism but never completely throws off bourgeois traditions, bourgeois views and bourgeois prejudices.' It was an unpleasant way to end a friendship but, perhaps not surprisingly, Lenin needed distance from those he felt were opportunists and hangers-on.

With the rising number of European monarchs and heads of police cut down by bullet and bomb, it was felt expedient to set up protection for the British monarch. Queen Victoria had had protection since the Irish crisis of the 1880s. Her guards were Patrick Quinn (later head of Special Branch, 1903–18) and John Sweeney. It was Sweeney who saved the Tsarevich from a kidnapping or assassination plot when the Russian royal family were staying at Osborne on the Isle of Wight. John Macarthy accompanied the Prince and Princess of Wales to Vienna in 1904 and Edward VII (as he became) took both Sweeney and George

Riley, who protected him from the feeble assassination attempt of a Belgian revolutionary called Spido.

Despite police surveillance, there was no internal intelligence network and things remained haphazard and amateurish, somehow exemplifying the British (rather than the professional French, German and Russian) approach to matters terroristic. This was not even really disturbed by the bungled anarchist burglary that led to the Tottenham Outrage of 23 January 1909, when a policemen was killed and several others injured in Walthamstow and Chingford in Essex. Nor did the situation change when three policemen were killed and two wounded in another bungled anarchist raid in Houndsditch in the East End of London, the consequence of which was the disastrous siege of Sidney Street on 3 January 1911, in which most of the perpetrators were burnt to death, escaped or, when captured, were acquitted at trial.

The ambivalent attitude shown towards anarchists by many before the First World War (at once comic and yet sinister) is best summed up in G.K. Chesterton's *The Man Who Was Thursday* (1908), in which a detective called Gabriel Syme infiltrates a notorious gang only to find that it is entirely made up of other detectives. Nevertheless, anarchists represented something un-English and something profoundly uncanny in which the normal laws of society ceased to exist. 'You want to abolish government?' asks one of Chesterton's protagonists. 'To abolish God!' is the reply. Syme concludes that 'they are under no illusions; they are too intellectual to think that man upon this earth can ever be quite free of original sin and struggle. And they mean death. When they say that mankind shall be free at last, they mean that mankind shall commit suicide.'

For the most part, the prosecution of a vigorous policy towards anarchists or communists before the formation of the Communist Party of Great Britain (CPGB) was neither followed nor desired. No particular provision was put in place to watch or prosecute anarchists. Marx lived in peaceful poverty in

England from 1849 to his death in 1883, laws expressly forbade the extradition of offenders deemed 'political' (even murderers were excluded) and guns were allowed to circulate freely and were unregulated. The right of asylum was considered sacred (especially regarding Russia) and, as no incident ruffled the feathers of the Establishment, the policy, with a bit of heightened security every now and again, seemed to suffice in all cases. *The Times* summed it up in April 1872 when it said that 'we have little [to] fear of the International', as working men were not supposed to be so stupid as to be duped by promises from anarchists or communists.

As anarchists shot or bombed their way across Europe between 1881 and 1910, it was left almost exclusively to novelists to imagine what might happen in Britain. The British remained 'unshaken, unseduced and unterrified' by it all, anarchism lacking any real native roots. In the late 1880s Special Branch had almost to resort to creating plots in order to justify its existence at all and, at the height of the European atrocities, Britain remained a haven for foreigners, with no alien act or extradition. In 1898 Lord Salisbury told his minister in Berne that 'great objection would be felt to any attempt to meet the dangers of the anarchist conspiracy by ... encroaching upon the liberties of the rest of the community'.[4]

There it remained, even after the 1898 anti-anarchist conference held in Rome, at which Britain managed to frustrate the Russian, Italian, German and French representatives. In any case, Lord Rosebery argued, 'the present law is quite adequate', and, despite the fact that most foreign outrages were 'organised on this soil', according to Lord Salisbury introducing his new Alien Bill of 1898, nothing except a general tightening of normal police security ever took place. Such security was itself vaguely risible. In 1905 Constable Herbert Fitch hid in a cupboard to hear Lenin preach 'bloodshed on a colossal scale', and, a little later, the same constable, this time disguised as a waiter at a meeting of the 'Foreign Barbers of London', smuggled out an agenda, which he claimed delayed the Russian Revolution for twelve years. Thus it continued, with Special Branch exclusively interested in anarchist and Fenian activity.

However, things were going to change. It was the campaigning journalist William Stead who thought he had the answer to revolution. The Old Age Pension Act of 1908 was the industrial legislation that made violent revolution unlikely, 'not with the bursting of bombs, nor with the click of the guillotine, but with the quiet handing out in innumerable post offices of a weekly couple of half-crowns'.[5] Baden-Powell might have thought the same, for in 1908 he founded that particular form of patriotic, muscular Christianity known as the scouts.

Nine years later and in far away Russia, Lenin declared once and for all the birth of communism. With the advent of world revolution (as opposed to merely Russian revolution), Special Branch had an active opposition and a specific group to target. The state would have to change its tactics to combat the new threat. By the 1860s, Britain had got used to a uniformed police force and, by the 1880s, to a *secret*, centralised Special Branch, but there had never been an acceptance of a paid home intelligence service. It smelled too much of the continental spy system. Nevertheless, the First World War made it clear that such a section would have to come into existence to complement spying abroad. By 1919, the Home Service was not only looking for German (or French or Russian) spies, but also homegrown trade unionists and a variety of anarchists, communists and pacifists.

The origins of the home secret service lay in a Government report of 1909, creating a Secret Service Bureau divided into military and naval divisions. By 1910 there was a home department for counter-espionage and a foreign department for spying. In 1911 the Government passed the second Official Secrets Act, thereby repealing a weaker Act from 1889. At the same time, they appointed a head of the Bureau's military section, a man called Vernon Kell,[6] later head of MI5. Kell was born to a British army officer and a Polish countess. He travelled on the continent and learned five foreign languages, after which he joined the army as an interpreter. Later, he was sent to Moscow and then to Shanghai, where the ability of the Boxers during the rebellion to 'poison' the minds of the villagers remained with him when later he found himself fighting communists. During the war, Kell remained in his office twenty-four hours a day, surrounded by telephones, the epitome of a spymaster, with nine officers, three assistants, four female clerks and three policemen to assist him.

In 1916 the department changed its name from MO5g to MI5. By the end of the war the department had over 800 operatives. More importantly, Kell had built up a filing system that needed 130 filing clerks and would later serve as the basis for work against other subversives. There was also cable and letter censorship. As his operational wing, Kell could call upon Basil Thomson's 114-officer Special Branch, but rivalry between the two wings of security meant that the system never worked well. Although counter-espionage went on throughout the war, it was on 11 April 1916 that the last German spy was executed in the Tower of London. This was Ludovico Hurwitz-y-Zender, caught for sending bogus orders of sardines! From 1916, Kell was watching home-grown pacifist organisations like the Independent Labour Party (ILP) and the Council for Civil Liberties. Kell regarded these people as 'peace cranks' and felt it was better to ignore them. Not so easily ignored were the Clyde Workers, whom Kell also began watching in spring 1916. To watch these industrial 'saboteurs', a short-lived department was set up under Colonel Labouchere, known as PMS2.

Labouchere's intelligence department in the Ministry of Munitions began the war in November 1915 inside two bar-rooms with a 'few kitchen chairs' and a trestle table, but within a year it had taken over two hotels and several buildings and employed many thousands of people. The Ministry of Munitions was vital to the war effort and Labouchere's

unit monitored industrial strife and pacifism as well as potential subversives. They also ran spies and agents provocateurs.
Labouchere employed two case officers, one of whom was
Major William Melville Lee, and he in turn ran two amateur
agents called Francis Vivian, who went under the name 'Alex
Gordon', and Herbert Booth. Vivian was a 'thin, cunning-look-
ing man of about thirty, with long black greasy hair',[7] who had
wandered into the spying game almost by accident, but who
was nevertheless put on the road as a fake deserter and pacifist
looking for refuge. Booth, Vivian's senior, was a former publi-
can who deserted his first wife, did some law work and finally
turned up as a spy. Although poorly and irregularly paid, Booth
and Vivian went sniffing for a plot. Eventually they found one
in Derby, where it appeared that a cell of revolutionary socialists was plotting to assassinate Lloyd George (whom they held
responsible for the war) by firing a poisoned dart from an air
rifle while he was playing golf on Walton Heath.

At the centre of this bizarre plot was Alice Wheeldon, a
second-hand-clothes dealer in Derby and a woman of 'extreme
anarchist opinions' who had been a militant suffragette and
was now a 'militant' pacifist running an underground railway
for deserters. There was also her daughter Hettie, a scripture
teacher, another daughter called Winnie, and her son-in-law
Alf, a chemist. All of this radical family had been brought up
in the politics of half a century of socialism and were part of a
milieu that imagined 'it could embrace vegetarianism, nudism,
the emancipation of women, sexual liberation, anti-pollution
campaigns, the design of furniture and dress, magnetism, spiritualism and progressive schooling'.[8]

In their 'war' against capitalism, the family declared themselves for the revolution of the workers and they were vocal
about it. It did not take long for Vivian to latch on to the underground railway and find his way into the Wheeldon household,
where he soon discovered a 'plot' to manufacture chemical
poisons and then carry out the assassination to rid the world of

the 'buggering Welsh sod'. Vivian believed he had uncovered a conspiracy (rather than an eccentric family simply bragging after too much drink), of which the Wheeldon family was the centre and which united all the dangerous elements in society opposed to the war.

Booth had sent Vivian to Derby on about 23 December, and Alice Wheeldon, unsuspectingly, had given him a refuge on 27 December. By 28 December, Vivian had telegraphed Booth and Melville Lee and on 29 December introduced 'Comrade' Booth to Alice. Booth was posing as a refugee from the army and a member of the International Workers of the World (IWW). On 4 January 1917 Winnie sent four phials of poison by post, but Derby post office was already alerted and opening the mail. The poison was tested on guinea pigs, which died. On 30 January the police arrested Alice and Alf, Hettie and Winnie.

At the trial the family were defended by an incompetent lawyer called Dr Riza, a Persian, who was treated contemptuously by the judge. No barrister could be found to take up the case. For the Government there was F.E. Smith, the Attorney General (later Lord Birkenhead), who was a notoriously right-wing politician. Smith found Alice's lower-class attitudes and lack of deference abhorrent:

> Mrs Wheeldon ... was in the habit of using language of the most obscene and disgusting character... . Her disgusting form of speech had spread to the two younger women [Winnie and Hettie] both of whom were engaged as teachers in the instruction of the young. Each of these young women was possessed of very considerable capacity, and yet in their correspondence they were in the habit of employing language which would be disgusting and obscene in the mouth of the lowest class of criminal.[9]

By the end, Riza was actually calling for 'trial by ordeal' and the whole affair was becoming a farce, with Vivian apparently unable to give evidence and Booth making mistakes in his. It turned to tragedy, however, with Alice getting ten years and her daughter and son-in-law five and seven years. Hettie was found to be innocent. As for Vivian, he left for South Africa, finally returning an odd schizophrenic paranoid, determined to tell his side of the story to anyone who would listen.

Alice went to Aylesbury prison. She was already 50 and poorly. Socialist friends came to the prison, including Sylvia Pankhurst and Arthur McManus, and she spent some of her confinement with the Countess Markiewicz, in prison after the 1916 rising in Dublin. Alice died in February 1919 of Spanish influenza and was buried with the red flag on her coffin. All her children were too ill to attend her funeral. In April 1917 Labouchere's unit was out of favour and reabsorbed into MI5, partly because of the poor publicity from the 'poison plot' and partly through a secret-service 'turf war'.

Hettie had long since lost her job as a scripture teacher to campaign for her mother's release and, oddly, she vanishes from the record soon afterwards. Nevertheless, she had already married McManus, one of the militant Clydeside shop stewards (see chapter 18) who had been internally exiled to Edinburgh alongside other members of the Clyde Workers' Council. He had lingered there for a little while, before looking for work in England. He travelled to Derby, where the Socialist Labour Party, of which he was a member, had a base around Wheeldon and her pacifist operations. McManus was born of Irish parents, his father and grandfather being Fenians, and through unemployment McManus was soon heading to become a 'professional revolutionary'. On the way, and while in Derby, he met and married Hettie, whom he later appears to have abandoned. McManus was a small, feisty Glaswegian who liked his booze and who, on his first trip to Russia, accused his 'minder' of spying on him: 'Spy! Spy! I am not going to stay here, I am going home Spy!' he shouted. The minder then hit and kicked McManus about the room, crying 'Go back and make your own revolution and don't stay in Russia to insult a real Communist.' McManus replied (rather oddly), 'I am not a communist. I am an anarchist, anarchist, anarchist.'[10] Perhaps McManus smelled policeman, smelled for a brief second the revolution going wrong. 'You can tell the Special Branch the whole world over – they are all the same, talk the same and act the same,' as his Communist Party colleague Harry Pollitt pointed out.[11] McManus died, worn out, aged only 38, on 27 February 1927.

During the war, the Government had already passed the Defence of the Realm Act (DORA) and it was from this beginning that a much higher level of state interference in private affairs began. From the end of the war until 1939, a series of laws were passed, tightening security and secrecy. These were the Police Act of 1919 (preventing affiliations to the trade union movement following two strikes), the Emergency Powers Act 1920, the Official Secrets Act 1920, the Trades Disputes Act 1927, the Civil Authorities (special powers) Act (Northern Ireland) 1922 and 1923, the Incitement to Disaffection Act 1934, the Public Order Act 1936 and the Prevention of Violence Act 1939. Brought in to defeat terrorism from Ireland, mutiny in the armed forces and a general strike leading to a revolution, these various acts curtailed the ancient freedoms of the British to a point that would have been unthinkable before 1914.

The Communist Party of Great Britain (CPGB) was formed in the summer of 1920 at the Cannon Street Hotel in the City of London, where 160 delegates (mainly from the British Socialist Party, the more extreme element of the SDF) met on 31 July. The chair was McManus. All in all, the party started with only a few thousand members from groups such as McManus's own SLP to the Workers' Socialist Federation led by Sylvia Pankhurst, to the small groups like the South Wales Socialist Society. Although non-existent during the revolutionary days on the Clyde and ineffectual during the General Strike, the CPGB nevertheless held itself ready for revolution. As Jack Murphy of the SLP put it, 'We had got to learn that a communist party was the general staff of a class marching to civil war, that it had to be disciplined, a party organised on military lines, ready for every emergency, an election, a strike, and insurrection.'[12] Trotsky, in his pamphlet 'Where is Britain going?', expected a showdown at any moment: 'Will a communist party be built in Britain in time with the strength and the links with the masses to be able to draw out at the right moment all the necessary practical conclusions from the sharpening crisis? It is in this question that Great Britain's fate is today contained.'

To provide aid to the new organisation, the Russians sent Mikhail Borodin (Mikhail Gruzenberg) to England to work under the name 'George Brown' and he helped McManus and the CPGB to affiliate to the Third International – the Comintern – dedicated to world revolution. The intention was the creation of a dictatorship of the proletariat and then full communism in Britain. Should armed revolution be necessary, one delegate to the Comintern proclaimed the importance of 'the historic and revolutionary value of a gun in the hands of a man of the working class'. Guns, however, were not deemed necessary as the fall of capitalism was thought to be only weeks away. Willie Gallacher and Sylvia Pankhurst travelled to Moscow to learn what to do, and Gallacher had an interview with Lenin, who assured the Scotsman that on his return to Britain he should forge ahead with the revolutionary Communist Party. Money also flowed secretly from Moscow, as did its directives, filtered through Comintern agents. The party could boast three Members of Parliament by the 1920s, Cecil L'Estrange Malone, an Anglo-Irishman with aristocratic connections, J. Walton Newbold and Shapurji Saklatvala. Phil Piratin and Gallacher followed, but no breakthrough was ever made and success in parliament (of all places) fell away, leaving hardliners like Albert Inkpin, Rajani Palme Dutt, an unswerving Moscow toady, and Harry Pollitt to carry on.

Pollitt was the son of Samuel and Mary Louisa (Charlesworth), the second child of six. The family lived in a modest terraced house in Manchester, his father working as blacksmith's assistant in a foundry and his mother at a cotton mill, after which she came home and often read socialist leaflets. Later, his mother joined the Openshaw Socialist Society. Pollitt started work as an apprentice plate-maker, becoming a skilled boilermaker, and by 1911 he was fully involved in local political life. When he was 21, his mother bought him *Das Kapital*; Pollitt was no longer a reformer but a revolutionary.

The CPGB had long looked to create disturbance in the armed forces. The mutinous state of the army in 1919[13] had come too quickly and, anyway, the party had not yet been formed. The authorities were also only too well aware of the potential for troublemaking in the army and navy, and MI5 had a special unit to watch this area. In 1921, for instance, Admiral Sir Walter Cowan warned that discipline in the navy 'hangs by a very slender thread' and that it was threatened by the 'mass of mischievous and revolutionary literature which floods the country'. With relationships with the Soviet Union degenerating and fear of revolution at home, the Government finally decided to act against what they considered were subversive activities. On Wednesday 14 October 1925 Pollitt and eleven other members of the British politburo, including McManus, were arrested and taken to Bow Street magistrates' court, where they were charged with three counts of sedition, including one under the Mutiny Act of 1797, under which they were accused of 'seducing the armed forces'. They were sent to the Old Bailey for trial, where Pollitt addressed the jury:

> There were newspaper articles, there were cartoons — [which] represented my comrades who were arrested and [depicted] us in a motor car with whiskers and bombs in our hands, labelled 'Mutiny and Sedition'... . After all you have read about the Reds, Communists, agitators and Bolshevists, you will naturally evince some sort of curiosity as to what the twelve dreadful people would look like when

they were marched into the dock.... You will notice that there is neither a suspicion of a red tie or a whisker amongst any of the twelve.[14]

The speech went on to talk about the political nature of the trial and reflected on the working-class nature of the army, the navy, the police force and the air force. Despite the fact that Pollitt and his comrades looked like everybody else and not like revolutionaries, the jury was not convinced. Pollitt still got twelve months, alongside his comrades.

In 1926 the 'Red Plot' eventually led to the banning of the film *Battleship Potemkin*. By 1930, MI5 believed communist efforts to tamper with 'HM Forces [to be] on the increase'. But despite exposure to communist propaganda, it still took a monumental mistake by the Government to create a problem similar to that at the Nore during the French Revolution.

In 1931 Britain had returned to the Gold Standard, but found itself under pressure, and was finally forced to look to reduce government wages where possible. The armed forces were thought an easy place for cuts and so a swingeing 25 per cent cut in naval ratings' pay was introduced. Such a cut was liable to reduce the lower ranks to penury. At the same time, the Atlantic Fleet was riding at anchor off Invergordon, in northeastern Scotland. When the news arrived of the cuts, the sailors decided to 'go on strike' rather than mutiny, a lesson they had learned from the miners, and one in which they showed their class-solidarity. It was certainly not a class uprising, more a wage strike, and no red flags or communist propaganda penetrated the workers. Yet the episode was long hailed as a victory for communist propaganda, as one able seaman, Len Wincott, eventually became a communist and went to live in Moscow, writing what was considered the definitive account of the 'Invergordon Mutiny'. The mutiny not only found the Government forced off the Gold Standard, but it also thoroughly alarmed the Establishment, and George V was all for conciliation for fear of revolution. Indeed, the King felt that the sailors had a valid claim. The leaving of the Gold Standard was another business altogether and, with its going, capitalism itself was threatened with free-fall. The triumph of communism seemed assured.

The disaster did not happen, but communists stepped up their infiltration of the ports and helped sailors like Wincott who could not find a job after leaving the navy. This was as close as the Communist Party ever came to creating a revolution in the armed forces of Great Britain. In 1936 Tom Wintringham, 'the Red Revolutionary', produced *Mutiny: a Survey of Mutinies from Spartacus to Invergordon*, which interpreted the navy unrest in the light of social upheaval and the rise of proletarian consciousness, effectively recruiting the actual events of Invergordon for a Marxist view of historical struggle. Nevertheless, the Establishment continued to believe in a communist plot for years afterwards – hardly surprising, as facts were either not known or distorted, and history was being rewritten from a communist perspective. The whole affair ended with 400 people being put in the already voluminous MI5 files.

The CPGB remained a revolutionary party until 1935, when, at the Thirteenth Congress, held on 2 February, it set out its blueprint 'For Soviet Britain'. The beginning of the struggle was class warfare, easily recognised when 'Britain ... is in the hands of millionaires – owners of the biggest trusts, the biggest banks, the biggest steamship companies; in short owners or controllers of the big monopolies... . These millionaires, these monopoly capitalists, not only own or control the chief means whereby we work and live, but, in fact control the whole governing machine. They pull the strings. And they use their power to make themselves richer and richer.'[15]

The consequence was that 'monopoly capitalism' would somehow move towards a crisis in which 'war [was] inevitable' and the workers would be the victims. At the same time the power of the state was seen to be growing. It was state dictatorship on behalf of capital and the prospects seemed dire, for 'in Britain … the fascist form of government … is also preparing the ground … [by] swelling the numbers of its secret police, to spy upon working-class organisations; it is organising concentration camps for the unemployed, suppressing still further the workers' right of free speech, and abolishing many other existing rights through the Sedition Act, and taking additional measures to concentrate control in the hands of central officials instead of elected local bodies.'[16] The way to change the system was not through parliamentary reform but by revolutionary action led by the Communist Party: 'A workers' revolution can do it.' 'Nor,' continues the manifesto, 'has the Communist Party ever denied that the overthrow must be a forceful one.' It was the capitalists themselves who advocated violence, and therefore the party's stance was merely self-defence. To establish a 'dictatorship over the defeated capitalist class', it would be necessary to set up a 'workers' dictatorship' in which local councils, or soviets, would work through a national council, with a 'red army' to protect the workers and 'punish' (a euphemism for 'kill') the capitalist enemy.

The Thirteenth Congress reaffirmed the revolutionary and insurrectionary idealism of the early years and made its plan quite explicit. The party therefore remained committed to some form of armed revolution from at least 1920 to 1935, although it was only in 1935 that the aim was so clearly stated. It might, of course, all have been empty rhetoric. There were no weapons or sources for weapons (certainly not the USSR), but the rhetoric coincided with the rise of fascism and the obvious potential for the spread of communism. Thus the situation was reminiscent of that during the French Revolutionary War, when a state actually existed to encourage revolutionaries abroad. Moreover, just as with France, Moscow encouraged change with agents and money. Despite the low risk of revolution and the retrospective ridicule of communist historians, it would have been most foolish if the state had ignored the party's activities.

From its inception, therefore, the party remained *overtly* tied to the overthrow of the British government and, with its secret agents, especially after the Second World War, *covertly* dedicated to the defeat of Britain. Lenin had long advocated two parties of revolution: one that was open and political, and another that was secret and subversive. The one should not know about the other. It was an idea he borrowed from the anarchist Kropotkin and it would remain Soviet policy until the fall of the Berlin Wall.

In the end, was the CPGB the threat that the security forces made out and that its attachment to Moscow in the early years would suggest? Certainly the question is hard to answer for a number of reasons. First, the party never led an organised armed rising. It was not around, of course, in the revolutionary years between 1916 and 1919, and moreover the party refused to set a date for such an uprising. In all of its existence, the time was never right and, of course, the party virtually abdicated responsibility during the General Strike of 1926. Furthermore, the party veered in its political policies (following those dictated by Moscow): its approval of parliamentary politics at the same time embraced 'entrism' and the voting procedure, and watered down its rejection of capitalist exploitation. Bending an ear to the whims of Moscow also meant a swing from 'class against class' to 'the popular front' and back, working with, and then sometimes against, the democratic left in parliament. Equally, the CPGB veered between trade-union shop stewardism and parliamentary tactics, at once fighting a local war with employers and a global war with imperialism and capitalism. The project was never clear. Pollitt's biography is laced with the need to 'call for the revolution', but it is never enough, and there were always more 'principles', 'struggles' and 'experiences' to follow. If 'every phase of revolutionary activity' needed planning and thought, then far better to form a committee, as he, Inkpin and Dutt did during 1922, than act with spontaneity when the time came (this smelled of anarchism); the 'world victory for the workers' would have to wait while the ink dried on yet another report. Even his meeting with Lenin, described as the 'greatest [day] of my life', only paralysed Pollitt in the great man's presence. Despite honestly believing himself to be a 'revolutionary worker', Pollitt and others did nothing much to turn other workers into revolutionaries, and neither Pollitt's autobiography nor John Mahon's biography so much as mention that the aim of the party was to turn Britain into a soviet republic. It is part of the disingenuousness of the party's literature that there is a veil drawn over this aspect of its politics.

The party was also the despair of the Comintern. Georgi Dimitrov (its general secretary) commented in 1932 that 'our British movement is in pain. It will not grow, neither will it die. Harry Pollitt and his crowd are as snobbish and as incapable of revolutionary mass work as they are English.'[17] Indeed, the party never really had a mass membership; in 1920 it was about 4,000, and by 1930 only around 2,500, rising above 12,000 during the worst of the depression, and finally peaking after the Second World War. Commentators have suggested, therefore, that 'one cannot criticise the [Communist Party] for what it could not seriously hope to have achieved', but this is an extremely problematic statement as the whole rationale of the party was revolutionary and their failure was a failure of nerve as much as a failure of practicality. The party was the only revolutionary group that failed to attempt a revolution. Trotsky concluded in 1926 that 'the English working class is not yet ready for a mass revolutionary party'.

The party would continue to play the waiting game and even when, in October 1935, the Revolutionary Policy Committee of the Independent Labour Party [ILP] went en bloc to join them, reasoning that consequently there could only be one revolutionary party, still nothing happened. The threat came from covert communists acting for Moscow as spies in the national interests of Russia, and occasionally from local difficulties brought about by trade unionists. The revolution was permanently abandoned almost as soon as the CPGB was formed, but rumour seeps deep and proved more corrosive than the actual threat.

Rumour may just have become fact if Tom Wintringham had had his way. With his bald head, glasses and 'academic stoop', Wintringham came to communism not through poverty, as had Pollitt and McManus, but through a conviction that something had to be done. He was one of a new breed of intellectual followers, university-educated, moneyed (at least in the family) and highly articulate. Such comrades were never trusted by the old guard, whose own working-class morals disapproved of Tom's sexual philandering. Too intelligent to toe the party line, and despite going to prison for the cause, Wintringham was never trusted.

It was, nevertheless, this easy-going intellectual who first thought up the idea of sending an 'international' brigade to fight in the Spanish Civil War, an idea that had grown out of a lifetime's interest in military matters, experience of the First World War, and a strong sense that warfare was changing towards guerrilla tactics undertaken by a citizen army fighting in a just cause. His model was Cromwell's ironsides: 'It's the first battalion put together by English speaking people – the first since Cromwell's day – to be part of a people's army. It's as important as the New Model Army.'[18] Only through such tactics could the working class wrest power from the bosses, and Spain would prove an important example. Things did not go as planned. At the Battle of Jarama, as 'Capitaine', he found himself in charge of his own 'model army', but the result was not as predicted in his military theory, for, despite excellent discipline, the battalion was pinned down and systematically destroyed. There were many casualties, including Wintringham (of 2,300 British volunteers, 526 were finally killed).

In the late 1930s the heady atmosphere of the early revolutionary days had receded, leaving instead bitterness and the party line. The purges went on in Russia and Britain, and Wintringham saw himself expelled from the party for deviation, both political and sexual. He earned his living by journalism on bourgeois newspapers, having lost his modest job on the *Daily Worker*. He was still dreaming of the English revolution when he wrote of the returning fighters from Spain that they had inherited 'directly from the buff-coated Independents and Levellers … liberty and England … words respected all over Europe'. This mixture of patriotism and revolution was not the repeated mantra of communist propaganda, but something which went deep into the roots of British radicalism. It was more, it was heartfelt, so that when war with Germany became inevitable, Wintringham's blend of patriotism and radicalism saw that, in defeating Hitler, the British working class would also open the way for a democratic socialist Britain. 'We are in a strange period of history,' wrote George Orwell, 'in which a revolutionary has to be a patriot and a patriot has to be a revolutionary.'[19]

With his understanding of guerrilla tactics, who else should come up with the idea of a 'home guard' in case of invasion? In a broadcast on 14 May 1940 Wintringham called for Local Defence Volunteers (LDV), and on 10 July the magazine *Picture Post* sponsored the 'quasi-revolutionary' defence school at Osterley Park, near London. Here at last could be trained the 'New Model Army' and even Orwell thought the 'red militias' were just a breath away. Ironically, although a member of the LDV, Wintringham was never allowed to join the Home Guard he helped found, being too distrusted by those in power. Perhaps they had a right to be suspicious, for he was fantasising during 1940 about a coup led by 'his' Spanish brigade if Britain made peace with Hitler.

Wintringham's notions on warfare did not in the end bear fruit in Britain. It was in Palestine that his writings regarding guerrilla tactics were read with interest and it was his ideas regarding a secret military organisation to fight imperialist oppression (partially learned from Mao Tse-tung) that were put into effect by the Jewish Defence Force, or Haganah. The highly secret Irgun (a secret force within Haganah) even had his

Picture Post articles translated into Hebrew. After the war, it was Wintringham's patriotic British tactics that blew up British soldiers and helped create Israel. This last revolutionary never gave up on the Communist Party that had expelled him, or on Russia that finally betrayed him, nor did he give up on England, where he died harvesting hay at the age of 51.

Chapter Seventeen

Scarface

We have tended in Britain to regard revolutionary movements as, on the whole, left wing in nature and therefore socialist in outlook. In the 1880s the rise of 'social democrat' parties of anarchists and communists had culminated in the founding of the CPGB, the victory of socialism assured. Fighting against the 'scientifically' proven tide of history, socialism's enemies were counter-revolutionaries, reactionaries and crackpot imperialists, themselves servants of the capitalist plutocracy that socialism would wash away. Loyalist groups dedicated to their own brand of 'king and country' soon formed to defend the British way of life against the international Bolshevik conspiracy (which oddly always seemed in cahoots with international finance). By their nature, such groups were considered incapable of revolutionary (that is utopian) ideology, being the super-patriotic ultra-Tories that they evidently were. This was a misassessment.

Ultra-rightism looked to a utopia (this time of homogenous nationhood) and also believed that those in charge had betrayed the nation. If for socialists this betrayal was inherent in capitalism, in loyalism such betrayal was the result of a conspiracy. For socialists, this betrayal robbed the working class of its rights; for loyalists, it robbed the English of their birthright. Both sides could point to the enemy: capitalists, plutocrats and the bourgeoisie, or foreigners, malcontents and communists. Both sides believed that their version of rights was the only version, and that only they had the correct interpretation of the betrayal and its perpetrators. Thus there grew up a revolutionary potential in right-wing politics. It had shown itself in the Curragh Rebellion of 20 July 1914 among the officers stationed in Ireland. It had shown itself in the recalcitrant Lords on Home Rule: it had shown itself as revolution from above, within loyalism itself. By the 1930s, that form of 'loyalism' known as British fascism was a 'patriotic' response to both British communism and the Labour Party, as well as an international political movement. It would produce at least one actual revolutionary: William Joyce, the national socialist, anti-Semitic broadcaster who became 'Lord Haw-Haw'.

All the fascist organisations of the 1920s and 1930s were anti-communist, part of the very rationale of their being, but as ultra-loyalists they were also at odds with any government which was seen to dabble in socialism or whose liberal tendencies they saw as the cause of economic chaos and communal disorder. Occasional secret dalliances with MI5 or Special Branch did not lead to a lasting partnership or a planned anti-communist crusade. Such connections fizzled out with the more highly organised (and therefore less palatable) fascism of Oswald Mosley's black-shirted British Union of Fascists (BUF), ending in the arrest and temporary imprisonment of most of the leading lights of the British extreme right during May 1940, under the Defence of the Realm Act – Emergency Regulation 18b.

Special Branch had been monitoring fascist meetings since at least 1934, when Detective P.C. Kay took notes at the fascist rally in Hyde Park on 9 September, while his fellow officer P.S. Coveney took notes at the communist counter-demonstration. More significantly, non-Jewish sympathisers belonging to the police infiltrated fascist groups and reported back to the Board of Deputies of British Jews. Thus one 'memorandum on the Nordic League and Allied Organisations' is prefaced by the following note: 'The source of this information is an ex-inspector, Special Branch, C.I.D., who is working on these cases on our instructions, but of course under conditions of strict secrecy. He is a person of the highest character, whose integrity and veracity can be implicitly relied on. Most careful enquiries were made before he was asked to undertake this service.'[1]

Fascists had long associated communism with Judaism. Arnold Leese, the veterinary surgeon, expert on camel diseases and violent anti-Semite, was self-publishing such arguments in pamphlets such as 'Bolshevism is Jewish', a publication still available from his home in Guildford as late as 1946 (priced at 3*d*): the alienation of loyalists from the state could only be the result of a secret Jewish conspiracy in government and beyond. The 'defensive' anti-Semitism of the early anti-immigrant Tories had now become a more highly developed ideological position and as such it deepened as Munich loomed. The potential for a revolutionary home-grown national socialism existed in the minds of those for whom Mosley was too much a pragmatist or collaborator, too much already infected with 'kosher' fascism,[2] as his opponents believed; Bolshevism had already corrupted government, and infiltrated unions and even the secret agencies of state, while the world Jewish conspiracy was heading to a war with Germany, whose leader alone had the vision to turn on the 'enemy within' and destroy them before taking the fight to Russia itself.

For Leese, the BUF was itself a Jewish conspiracy, as it was for William Joyce who finally broke with Mosley to form the National Socialist League in 1937, a hard-line anti-Semitic, anti-communist, anti-liberal, pro-Nazi revolutionary party. With his taste for brawls and bravado, Joyce was a prototypical stormtrooper in a political milieu where only self-discipline and acquiescent practicality might gain respectability and power.

In the end, a Nazi at heart, Joyce embraced the fate of his spiritual fatherland, his desire for martyrdom on behalf of the cause finally fulfilled on the gallows.

William Joyce was born to Anglo-Irish parents in Brooklyn on 24 April 1906. His father was Michael Joyce from County Mayo, who, in 1888 at the age of 20, had emigrated to Ireland, having fallen out of sympathy with republicanism. In 1894 Michael became an American citizen, thus making his son a citizen of the United States, a fact carefully glossed over during Joyce's trial for treason in 1946. Having got a passport from his new country, Joyce's father returned to England and met a Protestant girl from Lancashire called Gertrude Brooke, who travelled back to Brooklyn to become Michael's wife. Now better off, the family returned to Ireland. The Joyces lived first in County Mayo and then, after partition, in Galway. In 1917 the family travelled to England, registered as 'aliens' on a limited stay, lied and put down roots, only to be ordered (very politely, as this was a middle-class, respectable, property-owning 'British' family) back to Galway. Indeed, Michael was landlord to the Galway constabulary, a pillar of conservative, respectable Ireland. His son, witness to Sinn Féin arson and a possible murder, always described himself as 'an extreme Conservative with strong imperialistic ideas'. Later, Joyce claimed a heroic role for himself during the Irish War of Independence, even though he was only 14: 'I served with the irregular forces of the crown in an intelligence capacity, against the Irish guerrillas.'[3] It was an unlikely tale. Many years later, in Berlin in 1940, Joyce rationalised Ireland's troubles through the lens of international conspiracy:

> If one sixth of the money invested and lost outside the empire
> … had been given to Ireland, there might have continued that
> cooperation between her and England which provided British
> history with Burke, Goldsmith, Wellington, Boyle, Roberts,
> French, Beatty and Carson … International finance wound its
> coils through the heart of England, and its venom was carried

throughout the bloodstream to the whole colonial and imperial system.[4]

Unable to get into Oxford or Cambridge, Joyce enrolled at
Battersea Polytechnic, where he became so proficient at boxing,
fencing, riding and swimming that a fellow fascist (Norman
Baillie-Stewart) described him as a 'thug of the first order'. With
his physique formed on the lines of Bulldog Drummond, from
one of 'Sapper's' popular novels,[5] Joyce finally developed his
mind at evening classes at Birkbeck College, where he obtained
a degree in English literature. He might have wondered how he
could combine physical prowess with a love of poetry when,
aged 17, he joined British fascisti to 'protect' the ultra-Tory
candidate for Lambeth, Jack Lazarus, at the hustings in Lambeth
Baths. Attacked by what he maintained was 'a Jewish communist', Joyce had his face badly slashed with a cut-throat razor;
the scar, from ear to mouth on his right side, was a continual
reminder of 'defeat' and humiliation. Lazarus, humiliated too,
came last in the election. Joyce was now at war with 'the Jewish
organisers of the extreme left'.

After attempts to pursue a master's degree (the work somehow 'stolen' by a Jewish scholar) and then a career in the Civil
Service or Foreign Office, Joyce succeeded in something: marrying Hazel Barr on 30 April 1927 (she left him in 1935). At the
same time, he left the British fascisti and joined the Conservative
Party, but left two years later when he encountered Oswald
Mosley at a rally in Brighton in 1934. Joyce was finally matched
to his destiny. Mosley, Joyce enthused, was 'the greatest
Englishman I have ever known'. Mosley's defection from the
Labour Party had led to his creation of the New Party and then
the BUF, which he launched on 1 October 1932. Joyce became
the BUF's West London Area Administrator on a paid salary and
then, in 1934, Director of Propaganda. In order to accompany
Mosley on a diplomatic visit to Hitler, Joyce needed a British
passport, which he applied for on 4 July 1933, an ironic date

for an American citizen to claim another country's citizenship. Later, this would prove damning evidence at his trial. Joyce did not get to see Hitler on that occasion (and Mosley not until 1935) but he had already donned the black shirt of Italian fascism and declared 'war' on the Jews in January 1934.

Unlike Mosley, Joyce was far less interested in economic reconstruction through protectionism for the British Empire than he was in a racial new order, pan-European and transcending economic issues, where the cult of Aryanism led by Germany would lead to a crusade against Soviet-Jewish Bolshevism. Joyce's visionary utopia could be reached only by men of iron will, prepared to wade through blood. At the Olympia rally held on 7 June 1934, communist and Jewish counter-demonstrations outside the hall were accompanied by brawling inside it, where black-shirted guards appeared on newsreels merely as dressed-up yobs. The BUF threw out the infiltrators at a cost, for Lord Rothermere of the *Daily Mail*, their most influential backer, withdrew his support. Jews were behind it all, Joyce explained, and Rothermere had been 'blackmailed' by the 'Oriental confectioner' Sir Isidore Salmon,[6] who threatened to stop advertising in Rothermere's papers. At the Albert Hall on 28 October, Mosley also declared war on the Jews and made Joyce his deputy; on 9 October, Mosley and Joyce found themselves street-fighting in Worthing, Sussex. They were both hauled before the magistrates for affray, but acquitted. Joyce would soon be an out-and-out Hitlerite.

When challenged, Joyce made it clear that Hitler alone would save the 'British' race. In after-dinner speeches, he could become 'luminous with hate' in a way suggestive to his listeners of the advocates of the worst excesses of the French Revolution:

> Thin, pale, intense, he had not been speaking many minutes before we were electrified by this man.... Never before, in any country, had I met a personality so terrifying in its dynamic force, so vituperative, so vitriolic. The words poured from

him in a corrosive spate. He ridiculed our political system, he scarified our leading politicians, seizing upon their vulnerable points with a destructive analysis that left them bereft of merit or morality. We listened in a kind of frozen hypnotism to this cold, stabbing voice. There was the gleam of a Marat in his eyes.[7]

Special Branch reported on 15 September that Joyce

called together the principal party speakers and delivered to them what amounted to a tirade against Jews and the attitude taken up by the government on anti-Semitism... . He exhorted them not to retreat in the face of police persecution and declared that, if necessary, all fascist speakers should be prepared to face imprisonment rather than comply with the dictum of the authorities that they were not to attack Jewry. Large scale arrests would, in his opinion, inevitably tend to intensify antagonism towards Jews.[8]

The victory against the Jewish conspiracy would, in effect, be the victory of the Anglo-Saxon race. The Battle of Cable Street, fought on 4 October 1936, was to be mythologised by anti-fascists as a victory from which fascism could not recover and, although violent clashes continued, Mosley's support began to fall off as violence increased. The Public Order Act stripped Mosley of his uniform. Ironically it also gave him back a measure of civilian respectability during his final pre-war 'peace' campaign.

In 1935 Joyce, estranged from his wife, met Margaret White, a secretary and part-time organiser for the BUF in Manchester. Her new boyfriend was both a part-time lecturer and tutor and a BUF organiser and speaker, often out at evening meetings or on street-corner harangues. The couple joined John MacNab, another BUF organiser, and the three moved into a flat in Kensington, where Joyce and MacNab set up as private tutors and Joyce produced his political testament, *Twilight over England*. As the 1930s progressed, however, and war looked imminent, Joyce and his new wife and friend would travel to Germany, Joyce with another falsely obtained British passport.

On 24 August 1938 Joyce went to the Passport Office and applied for a one-year renewal, declaring himself to be a British citizen. Already under the watchful gaze of the police and aware that, under the Emergency Powers Act then being passed by parliament, he might be arrested and interned, he left for Berlin, where he was assured of a welcome by Goebbels. On 27 August the Joyces arrived at Friedrichstrasse station, having left from Victoria, where the W.H. Smith newspaper kiosk had copies of *Vogue* for sale, advocating holidays in 'Germany – the land of Hospitality'. They settled down in Charlottenburg. Joyce eventually made contact with the Ministry of Propaganda and on 18 September 1939 he became a radio announcer for the English section of Rundfuhk. His companions were Norman Baillie-Stewart, a former-British traitor who had already spent time in prison for selling British secrets, and an oddball, Margaret Bottomley, founder of the Imperial Fascist League. Baillie-Stewart was the first to be called 'Lord Haw-Haw' for his broadcasts to Britain, but Joyce soon took the title, while his wife (a less frequent broadcaster) became 'Lady Haw-Haw', so-called because of the Joyces' rather 'plummy' accents.

Joyce was therefore one of a dozen or so oddly assorted Britons used by the Germans for propaganda or recruitment. None was distinguished and some were decidedly peculiar. One such was John Amery, the son of the eminent intellectual and Conservative politician Leo Amery, himself a lifelong friend of Churchill. John Amery, however, was a well-educated criminal drifter who specialised in fraud, married a prostitute (and others bigamously), and was entirely amoral and quite possibly a paranoid schizophrenic, carrying a gun everywhere he went and insisting on the constant companionship of his teddy bear (a trait suggestive of Sebastian in Evelyn Waugh's *Brideshead*

Revisited, 1945). Amery's bizarre behaviour led to a spell of gun-running and finally to his being washed up in Vichy France. He applauded Hitler's 'crusade' against Stalin. 'It was my considered opinion', he stated on 22 June 1944, 'that Europe was in the greatest peril of a communist invasion, that this invasion would sweep the whole continent and that nothing could stop it, unless the different countries of Europe pushed though a social revolution which would spike the guns of the communists in their world-wide revolutionary activities. It was also [my] view that the Jewish race was ... working hand in glove with Moscow.'[9] Recruited to fascism by the ex-communist, now fascist, Jacques Doriot, Amery offered his services to Germany, left Vichy and began that hopeless attempt to raise a fighting force to spearhead British fascism called the British Legion. Even worse than the useless recruitment figures was Amery's Achilles heel – his grandmother was 'Jewish' (she converted to Protestantism).

Joyce reminisced too about his own attachment to fascism:

When I joined the first fascist movement in Britain on December 6, 1923, I saw that night in Battersea[10] the mob violence, the broken heads and the broken bodies, the typical evidence of the disruption which communism can bring into a nation, and while I heard the dismal wail of 'The Red Flag' intoned by the sub-men out for blood, I thought of Mussolini and of what he had been able to do for Italy. I was not pro-Italian, I was merely pro-human. There were many millions of people throughout the world at about that time who had the same thoughts, and when I look back on these twenty years I can only say that Mussolini has, in that period, become one of the greatest figures in history.[11]

In his last broadcast to Britain on 30 April 1945, Joyce's slurred and exhausted voice sounds much older than the 39-year-old who is speaking. Interrupted by long pauses, the shifting of seat and papers and in a tone of voice that suggested drinking, Joyce rehearsed his creed. Germany was not imperialist but made modest demands, met unreasonably by the Allies. Germans wanted only to 'live their own simple lives' and were innocent victims of aggression. In a peculiarly ironic pastiche of Churchill's own oratorical style, Joyce addressed 'my English listeners' and reiterated the threat of 'Bolshevik attack' against which the 'German legions' were essential allies of the British. Predicting a 'greater world war to come against the menace from the east', Joyce went on to conclude that 'the people of Britain deserve what they get in the future' if they fail to mobilise to save the Third Reich. Should no such undertaking occur, then Joyce accepted that 'The whole of my work has been in vain'. With the conclusion '*Heil Hitler* and farewell', Joyce signed off and vanished.[12]

Almost a month later, while on the run with his wife and holding a false passport under the name of Wilhelm Hansen, a teacher, Joyce bumped into two British officers. Overfatigued, overwrought and perhaps desperate to be recognised and acknowledged, Joyce dropped the German and French with which he began his conversation and reverted to English. Suspicious now, the officers arrested him and found yet another passport, bearing the name William Joyce. Joyce was sent to military hospital and thence home to Bow Street magistrates' court, Brixton prison, Wormwood Scrubs (where prisoners threatened to lynch him) and finally to Wandsworth. Safely behind bars, he was charged with treason under the Act of 1351: helping the king's enemies abroad and 'traitorously contriving and intending to aid and assist the said enemies ... falsely becoming a neutralised German citizen, [and] broadcasting treasonable material'.

Yet Joyce was an American by birth and an American, despite his wishes, by citizenship. For what did he have to answer to a British court? Craving the authenticity of Anglo-Irish origins and determined to be an Englishman, Joyce had no desire to refuse the court and plead as an American. Meanwhile, the court, itself perplexed by its own legalistic dilemma, looked to precedent, finding it in seventeenth- and eighteenth-century law and finally in its own pronouncements: 'If an alien, a subject of a foreign prince in amity with the king, live here, and enjoy the benefit of the king's protection, and commit a treason, he shall be judged and executed, as a traitor, for he owes a local allegiance.'[13]

As Joyce contemplated his fate on the plane returning to England, he was approached by one of his guards, who wanted an autograph from the celebrity prisoner. Joyce, in pensive but oddly elated mood, wrote, 'We are about to pass over the white chalk cliffs England's bulwark. It is a sacred moment in my life – and I can only say whatever my fate may be – God bless Old England.' American, German, loyal Irish Catholic he may be. He was also a twice-born Englishman. Joyce had travelled abroad on a British passport and was thus guilty – an inauthentic man who found authenticity in a false passport.

The journalist Rebecca West attended the trial on 17 September 1945 at the Central Criminal Court, Court No. 1. Like so many others, she had only heard Joyce on the radio as 'Lord Haw-Haw'. Now here he stood, 'a tiny little creature [at least, this was West's perception] … ugly with small dark-blue eyes which were hard and shiny… . His body looked flimsy yet coarse… . A deep scar running across his right cheek … gave a mincing immobility to his mouth, which was extremely small. His smile was pinched and governessy.'[14] With his bad clothes, odd formality and strange genuflection on the judge's entry and departure, Joyce appeared absurd, diminished, a petit-bourgeois snob, clothed in an aura of vulgarity of taste and fashion. Only the voice suggested another class and another physical stature, behind which a more civilised persona could perform in the invisibility of radio. Sentenced to death, Joyce made no statements from the dock, no last testament for posterity, beyond the note he had penned in the German hospital in June 1945 defending his belief that Britain and Germany were natural allies against the tide of Sovietism. He awaited his plea for clemency, first to the Court of Appeal, then to the Lords, found he had been refused and went to his hanging on 3 January 1946 at Wandsworth prison. Outside, a small group of loyal British Nazis gathered to record the moment. John Amery had already gone to oblivion in December 1945.

Rebecca West was quite clear that Joyce was a revolutionary. He had applied himself to the Nazi revolution just as surely as Saint-Just had to the French. Both knew that their revolution had to be born in blood in order to justify the new world from which the people would find the order and discipline that would set them free, but only under the martial law of a transcendent ideology. Like Saint-Just, Joyce was an ideologue and, like the Frenchman, he courted the disaster he argued to prevent.

Both were nihilists to whom the cause was greater than any society that might come to embody it and both were therefore, in West's words, 'metaphysical' murderers for whom governance was of little real interest in the face of the power of the will. Above all, such revolutionaries exalted the triumph of will-power over its material and over the constitutional pragmatism of a new world as it might be lived. The essence of such revolutionary fervour is the mystique of endless struggle: permanent revolution, permanent motion. Both played with the possibility of their own extinction, triumphant at last as dead martyrs: 'Therefore he must have known delight as the German planes went out to destroy England: and anguish too. For though the revolutionary's love of death finds joy in what he does, his love of life knows it to be criminal. That is why he contrives that the drama of the revolution shall develop so that in the end he shall pay for his crime with his life. The scaffolds of Paris took, in the end, all those that set them up.'[15] The bombs fell indiscriminately, annihilating Michael Joyce's home, leaving father and mother temporary exiles alongside their wayward son.

What might Joyce have done if he had returned to Britain in the wake of Operation Sea Lion and the destruction of the Royal Air Force? He might very well have come as Minister for

Information under Mosley, if Mosley had seen the practicality of making a deal with Hitler to preserve the Empire. The British might have trusted him, having heard him broadcast, his voice both reassuring and authoritative. More to the point, Joyce probably could not have coexisted alongside Mosley, who was a rival, and one or other would perhaps have had to yield. To the Germans, Mosley was the better bet, Joyce too extreme and unstable. Yet Mosley might be soft on Jews and communists, Joyce never: a Reich's protector for the British Isles? It seems likely that Mosley, with his nose pressed so long on the window of Number 10, might have capitulated and left Joyce to act out the final solution in the cities, towns and hamlets of Britain, even as they reinstated Edward VIII as puppet monarch of a self-contained empire whose flag was the Union Jack surmounted by a swastika, the party supreme under the BUF lightning flash of a copycat British SS. Because he loved England, he would purge and purify it, remove the betrayers, aliens and *Untermenschen*. Above all, Joyce was an internationalist who tied the fate of the United Kingdom in with the 'European Union' forged under Germany and poised to finish things with the Soviet Union.

Mosley's corporate British Empire, with its autarkic self-sufficiency, would have had no place for its Jewish citizens. As late as his peace rally at Earl's Court during July 1939, Mosley continued to blame Jewish interests for the world situation. The hall, filled with 30,000 adherents, was attended by numerous old 'patriotic' anti-Semites, including Admiral Sir Barry Donville, who recalled, 'We had lovely seats... . The hall was laid out à la Nuremberg... . Masses of the press all giving fascist salute... . O.M. spoke ... perfectly splendid.'[16] Another listener, Francis Yeats-Brown, recalled that Mosley '[was] as good as Goebbels'. All fascist groups and many of their more lukewarm sympathisers blamed Jewish interests alone for the war. Hitler was simply defending German interests, said Mosley: 'It was a Jews' war [...] that we should be asked to fight. Hitler had sworn to destroy the world's No. 1 enemy. He was succeeding beyond measure. The

Jews and their rotten masonic institutions were disappearing under the crusader's hammer blows – and we should be asked to stop them. It was unthinkable.'[17] The growth of upper-middle-class and aristocratic anti-Semitism immediately before and during the early months of the war coincided with the populist appeal of Mosley's BUF and the violently anti-Semitic agitation of Arnold Leese and others in the Nordic League or on its periphery. If this had halted the drift to war on a 'peace' platform that brought Mosley to power, then life would have been intolerable for Jewish Britons.

It is quite likely that Mosley would have had to purge the likes of Joyce if he had decided to pursue a policy of 'soft' anti-Semitism:

> Politics apart, Mosley and Joyce had little enough in common, nor did they greatly like one another personally. Mosley was capable of being urbane, relaxed, and downright frivolous. Women found him charming and attractive, though not in the most conventional way... . Mosley also lived in a private world where there was leisure and a sense of fun. Joyce was rarely anything but intense, impatient, sardonic. He inhabited a narrow world of self-dedication, as surely as the Jesuits who had taught him. In his presence, fun shrivelled and died. Mosley in his autobiography made only one reference to Joyce ... as one who was 'intensely vain'.[18]

Mosley could, however, have tolerated a 'revolutionary' wing of the party dedicated to finishing the Jewish problem on German lines.

Such a crisis would have excluded the possibility of merely enforcing emigration to a 'Zionist' state, as most pre-war anti-Semites were also ardent Arabists. The pressure from people such as Leese and Joyce, and the clear views they held about a possible final solution, might have opened the way to extermination camps in the United Kingdom. Britain's crusade against

Bolshevism as an ally of Germany would have silenced American opposition, which could have been ignored by a self-sufficient empire with London or York as its capital.

The registration of Jewish businesses and their enforced sale to 'real' Englishmen would certainly have followed. Mass Jewish emigration would have been a problem, but some thousands of Jews might have been able to leave (minus their cash, perhaps) to the United States. Leading left-wing opponents and Jewish or liberal voices would be silenced, locked up or liquidated – the latter a real probability for the executive of the CPGB or Jewish anti-fascist organisers. The extremes of the fascist right would certainly have pressurised Mosley towards a German model.

Such thoughts are not simply fantasy, as the Germans did control part of the United Kingdom – the Channel Islands, which had been invaded between 30 June and 1 July 1940 after the evacuation of 30,000 islanders. On 27 September the Germans enforced their anti-Semitic legislation and required all *suspected* Jews to register with the British authorities, represented by the Bailiff on Jersey. Those Jews who remained in Jersey (most had left) were elderly and frightened but still had to go through lengthy registration proceedings with Clifford Orange, the Chief Aliens Officer, who went to great lengths to record family histories in order to find 'tainted' blood. In October all Jews or people with Jewish grandparents had to register. Some hid, others prevaricated, some answered as best they could. Orange dutifully sent the list to the Bailiff, Alexander Coutanche, who followed the German requirement of marking Jewish businesses with 'JU' or 'Jewish Undertaking'. The Bailiff, eager to do his duty, simply asked the Germans the methods by which he might achieve his task; the German commander helped with details.[19] Coutanche and Orange had had an honourable war.

William Joyce also had a good war, which had led by actual and symbolic stages to that martyrdom of the 'last fascist fighting on the barricades'. In January 1947 his friend MacNab remembered to put an 'in memoriam' notice in the *Daily*

Telegraph. Finally, on 18 August 1976, Joyce's body was taken from its grave at Wandsworth Prison and reinterred in the New Cemetery, Bohermore, County Galway in Ireland by his daughter, Heather, who, in a spirit of reconciliation, attempted to atone for her father's anti-Semitism by attending synagogue and sending her own daughter to live on a kibbutz. Meanwhile, Joyce was interred in Ireland as a *victim* of English injustice! Margaret Joyce was not prosecuted, despite also broadcasting from Germany. She died in London in 1972, an unrepentant Nazi and, as a true British citizen, the actual traitor in the family, aware no doubt, that her husband's last actions had included scratching a swastika on his cell wall.

The heady period of acute street warfare between 1934 and 1936 and in 1937, in which the European ideological struggle found its uniquely British character, led neither to widespread insurrection nor even to loss of life (which is not to diminish injury or arrest). Writing of the fight with fascism and of 'Mosley and his pimpled followers', George Orwell offered his own reflection on the political climate and the nature of the British people (the poorest of whom he had visited at the behest of left-wing publisher Victor Gollancz). Hitler, Orwell feared, might just be winning the war of ideas, his appeal more visceral than the 'scientific' (that is, sterile) arguments of left-wing intellectuals who wittered on about 'historic necessity'. In 'times … growing harsher', he thought, 'we could do with a little less talk about "capitalist" and "proletariat" and a little more about the robbers and the robbed'.[20]

Despite 'the howl of glee', as Orwell put it, from the Church of England, the Catholic establishment and the leading right-wing writers of his day (Ezra Pound, Wyndham Lewis, T.S. Eliot), as Franco began his conquest of Spain, there might still be time to create 'Justice and liberty!' It would only be necessary to get rid of 'Marxists chewing polysyllables, escaped Quakers, birth-control fanatics and Labour Party backstairs-crawlers': 'Socialism,' Orwell opined, 'at least [in Britain], does not smell any longer of revolution and the overthrow of tyrants; it smells of crankish, machine-worship and the stupid cult of Russia.' In the absence of a reaching-out to the people, 'fascism may win'. Orwell's appeal to the sense and good nature of the people was also a vision of a community that had 'neither turned revolutionary nor lost their self-respect': 'Of course the post-war development of cheap luxuries has been a very fortunate thing for our rulers. It is quite likely that fish and chips, art-silk stockings, tinned salmon, cut-price chocolate, the movies, the radio, strong tea and the football pools have between them averted revolution.'[21]

It was true, then, that the 'boss' class still remained, but a restored 'moral economy' might also just be possible in a world of full employment in which 'futile massacres and a regime of savage repression' might be avoided and where working-class home life fell into 'a sane and comely shape', a sentiment there-after continuously derided by left-wing intellectuals for whom happiness and contentment were easily ignored in the quest for the 'dictatorship of the proletariat'. It was a sentiment that would have sounded as absurd to Palme Dutt, dictating from Paris the current Communist Party line as directed by Moscow, as it would have been to Joyce, reading the 'news' from Berlin.

Chapter Eighteen

Resist English Rule

Scotland had largely forgotten its radical tradition after the revolution of 1820. There was little taste for either independence or a republic. Things settled down and other issues, such as temperance, occupied radical minds. For the most part, the working-class vote had gone to the Liberals and politics concentrated on issues far smaller, but more pressing, than independence. Nevertheless, in 1871 Arthur Ponsonby produced a pamphlet attacking Victoria's spending. Called 'What Does She Do With It?', it stirred enough interest for Charles Dilworth to set up a republican club in Edinburgh during July. This had been preceded by a Dundee Republican Club, which soon had 150 members. Criticised as being a hotbed of 'aesthetic communism', the movement showed not everybody in Scotland approved of Her Majesty's new love for the country. Issues of Gaelic identity (the Gaelic Society of Inverness was founded in 1871) were coming to the fore. Alongside this was a distaste for British imperial policy, with people like John Murdoch directly linking Scottish interests with those of Afghanistan: 'Our sympathies are with you,' he

said. 'We claim the same patriotism [and] lament ... the inglorious mission of our noble Scottish Highland regiments – to
make war on the noble Highlanders of Afghanistan.'[1] Later,
indeed, there was much agitation on behalf of the Boers as
a 'free community composed of Christian whites'. The earlier disaster surrounding the death of Charles George Gordon
at Khartoum elicited the anti-English, anti-Westminster
comment that 'cockneydom and the nation are once more
at variance'.

With Scotland's large Irish population, it was no wonder
that Michael Davitt was heard with enthusiasm when he came
to preach the nationalisation of land on behalf of the Irish
Land League in 1879, and it was Davitt who made the link
explicit between national issues and class concerns.[2] This came
to a head in the so-called Crofters' War on Skye, in which a
mob of women agitating over tenantry questions had seen off
a force of magistrates and police at the 'Battle of the Braes'.
Some time later, a party of marines and a gunboat had arrived
in Stornoway to put down another crofting rebellion. The
Scottish Land Restoration League was founded on the lines of
the Irish movement. A Crofters' Party emerged in 1885 and,
although its successes were minimal, it did highlight the plight
of Highlanders, enough to get legislation passed in June 1886
(Crofters' Holdings Act). It was, however, socialism that gained
ground in these years, especially among the highly industrial
workers of Glasgow.

Since 1880, socialism had been discussed as a new 'religion'
and Christianity was often equated with it. Yet, as early as
1881, a group of 'social democrats' at a meeting in Hamilton,
and possibly influenced by Engels, had called for a Scottish
Labour Party. Nevertheless, it was not until William Morris and
his Socialist League called for 'complete revolutionary socialism' that things grew, the first conference of Scottish socialist
societies meeting in December 1888 in an attempt to unite the
Social Democratic Federation, the Land and Labour League and

various other Christian socialist groups. When Morris first lectured in Glasgow in 1884, one of those present recalled that the audience contained:

> a few veteran Owenites who had not lost the faith and hopes of their younger days. Those aged radicals, who were in the most instances freethinkers, listened enrapt to the unfolding afresh of the ideas of the communist commonwealth, and were ... eager to communicate their joy in beholding once more in the sunset of their years the glory of the vision which had filled their eyes in the morning glow on the hilltops long ago.[3]

This strange mix of participants had not yet become a movement; instead, it took on the mantle of martyrdom. One delegate recalled, 'Socialists were undoubtedly cranks; they were in a similar category to the strange beings who tore their beards and confessed their sins in public at religious meetings. I became aware of the curious glances of my old companions as they saw me busy selling pamphlets or taking collections at meetings. Plainly they thought my madness had grown upon me... . But with others, I glowed with righteousness in the face of ostracism... . We conceived we were the stuff of martyrs.'[4] Socialism, however, grew and with it a sense of injustice. Needless to say, most Scots were still wedded to the liberalism of the previous forty years, with a belief in free trade, fairness and the 'rights of small nations', as well as a sense of the 'people' and hatred of all hereditary honours, especially represented by the House of Lords. It would take some time to forge this common-sense set of beliefs, which were undermined by the class war which broke out between 1917 and 1919. Meanwhile, there was the slow realisation that working men (there was no common cause with women) should stand up for themselves. As the Revd C.C. MacDonald bluntly pointed out, 'You must represent yourselves!' For many years, therefore, the Scottish

Labour Party (SLP) worked with the Liberal Party, but there was already pressure for a Scottish Independent Party on the lines of the Irish National Party of Parnell. The SLP were less inclined to discuss home rule than unemployment and housing, but in January 1900 they met in the Free Gardeners' Hall in Edinburgh to work 'for direct independent working-class representation in the House of Commons'. On the whole, it was business as usual.

Things changed most rapidly and (for the Establishment) most alarmingly amid the skilled workers of the Clyde, in a situation that came to a head during the First World War. The militancy centred around the Clyde Workers' Council (CWC) and included Arthur McManus and Willie Gallacher, among others, who, we have seen, would later become prominent as founders of the CPGB. Few of these militant leaders called for revolution and they fought primarily for workers' rights alone. Nevertheless, so dangerous was the situation during 1918 and 1919 that the Government had to act with supreme caution, just in case a revolutionary faction arose and formed a soviet (workers' council) on Russian lines. William Bolitho, in his book *The Outlook* (1924), actually coined the phrase 'Red Clyde' to describe the situation: 'No state, however geographically remote, however seemingly secure in possession of an unshakeable constitutional system, can any longer be certain of immunity from violent, bloody change in its body politic.'

It was clear that the Government thought itself on the brink of catastrophe, with continuous strikes, the threat of a general stoppage and soldier mutinies, not to mention the Russian Revolution of 1917. Government was in a continuous state of agitation. Bonar Law, deputy prime minister, reported to the Cabinet on 10 January 1919 that:

> a certain section of the workers (whose names and activities are well known to Scotland Yard and the Home Office) are

only too ready and eager to fan and ferment a passing grievance to inveigle the solders into an alliance with themselves,
on the lines of the soviet committees. The ultimate end of
this manoeuvre would be revolution and a soviet form of
government... . The dangers consequent upon even the
slightest success of such a scheme must be patent to anyone
who has studied the course of events in Russia. The spread
of this spirit is alarming, and evidence can be obtained of a
determined effort to emulate the Russian Bolshevik movement in this country.[5]

On 16 January, Winston Churchill believed that the army was
'liquifying fast' and Sir Henry Wilson, the Chief of the General
Staff (who was finally killed by the IRA), believed that 'we
are sitting on top of a mine'. Basil Thomson, head of Special
Branch, was required every two weeks to produce his 'report on
revolutionary organisations in the United Kingdom and Morale
Abroad'. The reports made gloomy reading. In 1917 even the
police went on strike, defeating the Government and leading
Lloyd George to say that 'the country was nearer Bolshevism
that day [of the strike] than at any other time since'. Half the
men were out in Liverpool and, after much rioting, a battleship and two destroyers were sent up the Mersey. George V
believed that there was a general 'Bolshevist rising'. Churchill,
on 5 February 1919, felt that the 'Bolshevist movement' was
gaining strength in Glasgow and London, and saw Bolshevism
just below the surface of union unrest. Thomson was even more
clear, although he thought the danger had passed: 'During the
first three months of 1919 unrest touched its high watermark. I
do not think that at any other time in history since the Bristol
Riots we have been so near revolution.'[6] It was in Scotland that
this revolution looked like occurring. On 7 February 1919 the
Government put back in place its system of spies, stood down
after the war's end, and in April it established a Directorate of
Intelligence, with Thomson as its head. During September,

General Haig had called a high-level meeting to ensure that plans were complete for martial law and counter-revolutionary struggle. Yet there was no organised party of revolution on the Clyde or elsewhere, and no soviets formed, nor did any revolutionary leaders arise. As Gallacher remembered in 1936, 'For those of us who were leading the strike, we were strike leaders, nothing more: we had forgotten we were revolutionary leaders of the working class.... We were carrying on a strike when we ought to have been making a revolution.'[7]

There was, perhaps, one revolutionary leader in Glasgow whose name is forever linked with 'Red Clydeside'. Even though John Maclean was too much of a maverick to be directly involved with many of the strikes, it was nevertheless he whom Lenin chose as 'Bolshevik Consul for Scotland'.

Maclean was born in Pollokshaws, a small industrial town outside Glasgow, on 24 August 1879, the sixth child of Daniel and Anne Maclean, both of whom were from the Highlands and who regaled their son with stories of the Clearances. Daniel died of silicosis when John was 8, and therefore his mother brought the children up, sending him to the Free Church Training School to get a certificate for teaching. Ambitious, but also by now an atheist, John left religious teaching. However, he did go to Glasgow University to get further qualifications, which he later put to use with his evening classes in Marxism, a doctrine he had come to embrace after his loss of faith in religion. In this, he was one of the first British socialists to work with Marxism, as opposed to a mixture of Christianity and cooperative work that substituted itself for the real thing among many who considered themselves socialists.

In 1903 he formed a Glasgow press committee, which put out leaflets and press releases on social issues and by 1908 was holding nightly classes in Marxist doctrine, with open-air meetings held as far apart as Lerwick, Aberdeen and Hawick. Maclean also met Jim Larkin, then conducting the Belfast Transport Workers' strike, and took in a Russian émigré called Peter Petroff, a lifelong friend and also a communist. Between 1910 and 1913, a series of strikes began to give Glasgow the reputation as a militant centre and Maclean worked as far as possible to foment dissent, especially among the miners, who went on strike during 1912. It was at this time that shop stewards like Gallacher came to Maclean's evening classes, and although Maclean was not directly involved with the CWC, he was arrested under the Defence of the Realm Act in 1915 as a seditious agitator and spent time in jail. It was at this time that he was finally dismissed as a teacher by the Govan School Board, the last regular work he had. Meanwhile, a rent strike broke out, and Maclean, now free, spoke at a vast rally. The cause was won, but Maclean went back to jail for not paying his rent.

By 1916, students at Maclean's evening classes had grown to sufficient numbers for him to form the Labour College Committee, teaching aspects of economics, labour law and history. Nevertheless, the government was watching his activities and he was again arrested on 6 February, alongside Gallacher and others. Petroff had also been put behind bars. Maclean's trial began on 11 April 1916 and he was sentenced to three years' penal servitude – in Scottish jails a virtual death sentence, and Maclean's health declined. Meanwhile, the February Russian Revolution had occurred and Maclean was elected to the Executive of the British Socialist Party (BSP), now finally fully Marxist. On May Day 1917, thousands demonstrated on behalf of the Russians and to have Maclean released. On his early release, he was elected to the All Russian Congress of Soviets and appointed Bolshevik Consul for Scotland, a bizarre title and one that just got him more notice from the authorities.

This notice led to his arrest again in April 1918 when he returned from a talking tour of Durham. He was accused of sedition, specifically by saying that the workers should follow the Russian example and strike for revolution. Again, the sentence was harsh: five years in Peterhead jail. He immediately went on a hunger strike and this may have helped his early release, which occurred on 3 December 1918. His return to Glasgow was triumphant. People lined the streets and his carriage was pulled by his followers, a traditional mark of respect for radicals, Maclean himself waving a red flag all the while. He returned to revolutionary work during the period that Lloyd George and Thomson both thought that Britain was on the brink of a Bolshevik takeover.

Nevertheless, Maclean's fortunes now began to decline and his hard-line, vituperative attitude made him enemies. In 1920 he was forced out of the BSP for his views and formed a small cell of dedicated Marxists who were financed through the sales of his paper and various leaflets, of which 'All Hail the Scottish Communist Republic' was the most famous. Now more than ever, Maclean felt that the Scots, of all the industrial workers of Britain, were ready to rise for communism. He travelled to the Highlands and islands and attended the Highland Land League Conference, where he detected a communistic attitude among the workers. Yet his instinctive trust of Highlanders did not extend to the newly formed CPGB, whose doctrines and members he shunned for their lack of purity. The issue was moot anyway, as Maclean was again arrested, and not released until 25 October 1922. This time, on his release, there were no crowds and no triumph. Maclean was penniless, broken in health and isolated. His revolutionary cell had joined the CPGB while he was in prison and, although he stood for parliament, it was Gallacher (now estranged) who finally got in. Finally, in his latter years Maclean founded the Scottish Workers' Republican Party, with which he contested Glasgow, Gorbals, aided by Sylvia Pankhurst. He lost and, with failing health, finally succumbed to pneumonia in 1923.

Maclean's health declined every time he was in jail. Lloyd George's Cabinet actually discussed his case, because of Lenin's rather odd acknowledgement of Maclean's position as Scotland's leading Marxist. It was decided to release him early on the second occasion of his incarceration because it was believed that he was 'more or less a lunatic'. Maclean certainly believed that his prison food was drugged and he protested after his first spell in prison, so that when he was imprisoned again, he insisted on food being brought in. Yet he refused even this, and was therefore force-fed. By now, he seemed to have sunk into paranoia, especially with regard to Gallacher, who had been to Moscow and whom Maclean thought the misguided 'gramophone of Lenin'. Others, such as Tom Bell, recalled during electioneering that 'persecution obsessions and questions irrelevant to the election made up the subject matter of his speeches. The wild enthusiasm with which he was received at each of his meetings evaporated in the murmurs of sympathetic concern, many people leaving the meetings while he was speaking, obviously disturbed by the state of their friend and comrade's mind.'[8] Thomson in his fortnightly reports assured the Cabinet that Maclean's mental health was such that it would no longer create a threat. Maclean, perhaps rightly, believed that he was the subject of a police plot, his meetings were often broken up by police in plain clothes.

Maclean was one of Britain's few professional revolutionaries. A dedicated and doctrinaire Marxist, he earned his living by collections after meetings and the sale of pamphlets and his paper, *Vanguard*. He was one of the first to see the international dimensions of Scottish independence and the position of the worker in capitalism as a global whole. He made common cause with the Russians, whom he saw as making that successful revolution needed in Scotland, and with Sinn Féiners, who, although not communist, were fighting imperialism and the British capitalist system. He saw that at the 1907 Labour Party Conference, 'a sort of socialist revolution was carried' and that a 'workers' party [was] necessary', but only on communist lines. By 1919, he was calling for a revolution in Britain and already expected the next war, this time American capital versus British imperialism.

Indeed the idea was not wholly fanciful, as, during the 1920s, the United States developed the 'Joint Army and Navy Basic War Plan – Red', which proposed an invasion of Canada and a war with Britain. Only by 'bolshevising the world tomorrow' could such a catastrophe be averted. Yet it was not until 1920 that Maclean openly declared that 'Scotland should strike out for national independence', such independence being a blend of 'old' communism taken from the Highlands and new communism taken from Marxist-Leninist practice. The message was uncompromisingly revolutionary and, in the end, entirely in keeping with his belief that in Glasgow there were all the ingredients of the revolution: 'We on the Clyde have a mighty mission to fulfil. We can make Glasgow a Petrograd, and revolutionary storm-centre second to none. A Scottish break-away at this juncture would bring the empire crashing to the ground and free the waiting workers of the world.'[9]

Although Maclean was among the most extreme and prominent of Home Rulers, there were others. There was Ruairidh Erskine, the Earl of Mar, who early on rejected his title and, in 1892 became the vice-president of the Scottish Home Rule Association and later advocated a Pan-Celtic Association, a 'drawing together of the Gaels of Scotland and Ireland'. In 1911 he formed the Comunn nan Albanach, or the Scottish National League (SNL). There was also Seamus Mac Garaidh (James Car MacDonald Hay), who was born in Arbroath in 1885. He joined the SNL and founded a branch in his home town, refusing to sing the national anthem, because of its rarely sung fourth verse with its anti-Scottish sentiments. Nevertheless, he fought in the First World War (despite getting regular parcels of pro-Sinn Féin journals) and left convinced of Ireland's right to independence. Labelled an extremist, he was finally forced to dream of Scotland in exile from his new home in San Francisco, where he founded a Gaelic class and encouraged the arts and crafts of Scotland, always flying the Scottish saltire and refusing to display the

Union flag. This also made him a focus for pan-Celtic and Irish republican groups until his death on 9 January 1966.

Others helped revive Scottish culture, such as Hugh MacDiarmid (Christopher Murray Grieve) and Wendy Wood, who worked with young people and started Scottish Watch, a rival organisation to the Scouts. She was also involved with Scottish dancing, went to jail twice for minor political offences and was implicated alongside Ian Hamilton for the theft from Westminster Abbey of the Stone of Scone (Stone of Destiny). Meanwhile, in June 1935 a small book appeared called *The Scottish Book of Law and Folklore*, an attempt to redress the balance in the school curriculum in which Scottish mythology had been excluded in favour of English mythology. This work was produced by Ronald MacDonald Douglas, a man whose lifelong efforts on behalf of Scottish culture went hand in hand with armed rebellion.

During the 1930s, Douglas had conceived the idea of an armed insurrection with the help of men who had fought in Ireland's civil war. A number of Scots had either fought in 1916 (like Amhlaidh MacAindreas) or been killed in the Irish civil war (like Ian McKenzie Kennedy) and Scots willingness to align themselves with their Irish cousins still ran high. Along with MacAindreas, Douglas went looking for arms and, in Geneva, he found them. Unfortunately, he also found MI6, who immediately arrested him (and, he claimed, also tortured him) and returned him to Scotland. There he was apparently offered a deal by the Lord Advocate, that permanent exile in the Irish Free State might be better than being hanged for treason. He did not return until 1967, when he edited the magazine *Catalyst* and joined the 1320 Club (named after the Declaration of Arbroath, in which the Scots declared their independence). Although he died in 1984, Douglas never revealed where he kept his cache of weapons, despite the rise of a more violent republican movement, claiming it was unfair for an old man to send young men to their deaths.

The revival of Scottish hopes in the late 1960s grew from the murky world of Scottish frustration among disaffected groups and the presence, early on, of agents provocateurs. The re-emergence of the IRA during the period helped create an imitative atmosphere and a sense of possibility. The situation began in 1968, when the Scottish National Party (SNP) took the largest share of the vote in municipal elections and a sense of a Scottish independent future emerged. A minority of the 1320 Club decided to go one step further and found the Army of the Provisional Government (APG), with Major Frederick Boothby as its head. Boothby, a strange character, may have been a Government agent.[10] 'Tartan terrorism' was born when 'the sudden upsurge in SNP support was paralleled by the rise of the "peace" movement, whose main vehicle was the Campaign for Nuclear Disarmament. CND was highly popular in Scotland where there were close links with the SNP and considerable overlapping of membership. The SNP declared at its June 1968 Conference that an independent Scotland could not remain a member of NATO "in its present form", and would demand the removal of all foreign military bases from Scotland.'[11]

To counter the threat of activists sabotaging installations, there were army manoeuvres in 1975, 1977 and 1978, when the SAS and Commandos played war games outside Edinburgh Airport. Indeed, the threat to NATO installations in Scotland had been recognised in the early 1950s, and at the height of trouble during the 1980s there was regular phone-tapping of potential troublemakers.

The 1320 Club had plans for a 'provisional government' on the lines of the IRA. There was to be a cabinet and full hierarchy, as well as an armed forces committee whose job it was to create an army. This farcical organisation was to be divided into a Highland brigade, a Lowland brigade, an armoured formation and a parachute battalion, as well as a full headquarters staff. The whole pipedream had only a handful of activists, few of whom even had a weapon. Once the plans for the APG were in place, its organisers broke away from the 1320 Club to pursue their war.

These began with bank robberies. John Gillian, a photographer, John Stewart, a bank clerk, and William Murray, a quality surveyor, formed one of the APG's cells or 'schiltroms' (named after the medieval military formations of pikemen) who were willing to rob for independence. Their plans were big, as they wished to take their small army and capture Fort William, Ullapool or Oban in a symbolic occupation that would be defeated by the British government, so outraging the Scots that they would rise and throw out the English. Proclamations of the Provisional Government would be read as soon as the towns were seized and a general rising precipitated. Boothby was to be defence minister in the scheme. Watched by the police, on April Fools Day 1971 the three were captured in a hotel after carrying out several bank raids.

Matt Lygate, a tailor's cutter and a committed Marxist whose grandparents were Irish, was also a dedicated republican who first engaged in communist propaganda while living in New Zealand. Having returned to Scotland, Lygate joined the Committee to Defeat Revisionism for Communist Unity (a far-left organisation critical of the CPGB) who relaunched Maclean's old paper, *Vanguard*. The group intended to establish a 'revolutionary elite', joining Maclean's ideas to those of Maoism and the struggle in Ireland; they formed the John Maclean Society in 1968. The Workers' Party of Scotland (WPS) expanded and eventually went in for its own bank robberies, striking on 7 May, 21 October, 19 November and 17 December 1971; on the last occasion a bank employee was wounded by a shotgun. Six months later, they too were in the dock (March 1972) betrayed by a colleague. Lygate was quite open about keeping guns and engaging in guerrilla tactics. In the end, he dismissed his defence and made an impassioned speech from the dock, which Lord Dunpark was unable to silence. He listened impassively as Lygate finished on a threat: 'I would like to say that in the future a day will come when the roles of this court will be reversed, when the workers will sit on the bench and those people who have judged me now will be judged themselves.'[12] Dunpark replied insouciantly, 'I don't look forward to those days with any longing I must say.' The judge then handed down sentences that ranged from twenty-four years to twenty-six years, Lygate receiving twenty-four years. As he left the dock, Lygate shouted, 'Long live the workers of Scotland.' His trial caused a sensation, being seen as a patently unfair case of class discrimination, and campaigning got him released after thirteen years; he was a 'wee political man' in Lenin cap and jeans.[13]

In 1974 Idi Amin, the President of Uganda, declared himself in favour of an independent Scotland and pledged himself to the Provisional Government. This odd state of affairs followed the emergence of William Anderson, a one-time army sergeant who was living in Aberdeen and who deeply disapproved of the English use of Scottish oil. Soon he had a group around him, discussing the possibility of bombing English towns on the lines of the Provisional IRA. Anderson had hidden 109 sticks of dynamite and fifty detonators. He wanted to join the APG, but was already involved with a more dangerous person, a Special Branch agent called Colin Boyd. A meeting of the Scottish Republican Club in Aberdeen helped the campaign along and recruited more people. Eventually, alongside William Bell, a fanatical Anglophobe, Anderson staged a publicity stunt with journalists to announce 'Tartan Terrorism' by the Tartan Army and Scottish Liberation Army. A wholly fictitious secret set of organisations was announced, and Amin, rather bizarrely, rallied to the cause on Uganda radio. More bank raids followed, but Boyd had shopped the lot and most were rounded up in 1975. Anderson got ten years, and even Boothby went to jail for a few months.

The shadowy force known as the Tartan Army emerged during 1972 (and may have been a complete fiction, a creation

of Special Branch, or a number of actual illicit organisations).
Its activities did not come to an end until 31 May 1976, when
fourteen people were tried. Detonators and dynamite were
burgled and William Wallace's two-handed sword was stolen
from its museum. Edward Heath's government had promised a
Scottish Assembly. It was not forthcoming and Wendy Wood,
the Leader of the Scottish Patriots, had gone on hunger strike
as a protest. She was by this time an elderly woman and her
strike was backed by bombs at Dounreay Nuclear Reactor, ICI
(explosives) and British Petroleum's Grangemouth refinery. A
decision by the Government to create a green paper on devolution stopped the hunger strike and the bombs. Although the
Tartan Army consisted of less than fifty members, it began a
violent bombing campaign almost immediately afterwards, and
certainly sufficient to bring large numbers of police into the
case. The police break came with the arrest of David Sharkey
in 1973 for the stabbing of a seaman at a party. When he was
questioned, it became clear that he was deeply involved with
the Tartan Army. Arrests did not follow until 1976. One of
the men was Donald Currie, a maintenance engineer from
Clackmannanshire, who also added to Sharkey's tale of tartan
terror. In the end, the case collapsed with all the accused walking free, as the idea of a single organisation called the Tartan
Army seemed more and more to be the fevered brainchild of
Currie himself.

Despite the efforts of Special Branch and MI5, bombings
of pipelines, offices and pylons continued, often the work
of teenage activists, as with the campaign of 1974 to 1975.
Much of the activity centred on Glasgow, where memories of
Maclean and the CWC had recently been revived. Moreover,
there was a large population whose origins were Irish, and
sympathetic organisations linked to Sinn Féin had existed for
years. The Scottish Workers' Republican Party (SWRP) was
originally formed by Maclean, but re-formed as a Trotskyist
organisation in 1973 and immediately split when the Scottish

Citizens' Army of the Republic (SCAR) was created as a cell to kidnap politicians. Scottish Republican Clubs remained underground because of political surveillance and because their worlds often overlapped with organised crime, as they did in Ireland. Again, robbery was the method of 'expropriation' and again the perpetrators were hunted down and put on trial. In June 1976 the Stanley Green trial opened in Glasgow, with Green, a typewriter-maker, accused alongside others of robbing a sub-post office. The usual prison sentences followed. Finally, the loose alliance of left-wing republican movements coalesced as the Scottish Republican Socialist Party (SRSP), but, with most of the leaders in jail, things looked as though they might quieten down.

Yet things were not to be quiet. A bomb factory exploded during 1980, suggesting that activities had reopened. This time the main culprit was Peter Wardlaw. He had created the Socialist Republican League (SRL) and, coincidentally, their campaign began after the British government failed to act on the 'yes' vote for devolution. Wardlaw was a 'professional revolutionary', according to the police when he was arrested. A deserter from the British army who would not serve in Northern Ireland, Wardlaw planned his campaign with care and precision and he and other members of the republican movement were in regular contact with Irish and Welsh independence fighters. Their first bank raid on 24 October 1979 did not go well and they escaped with only £978; their plans to blow up the temporary Scottish Assembly building (the Royal High School on Calton Hill) also failed. Another raid, this time on a post office van, netted £100,000 and Wardlaw had his money for his army. The next raid was intended to target Explosives and Chemical Products Limited, in order to gain dynamite and prove to the Provisional IRA that the Army of the Scottish People meant business. This success decided the little army to try to blow up the Scottish Assembly building again on the anniversary of the Battle of Bannockburn. It was this bomb that exploded in the terrorists' flat and led to their arrest. It was all over for the Army of the Scottish People.

In spring 1983 another declaration of war was delivered to *Firinn Albannach*, the official magazine of Sìol Nan Gaidheal. This was from an organisation called Arm Nan Gaidheal, or the Army of the Gaels, which was dedicated to a Highland style of independence and which carried out actions between November 1982 and March 1983 against the 'colonial lackeys' of the English. This group had masonic connections to the Grand Priory in Scotland and the Order of the Templars (reformed in Scotland in 1972). It was Jacobite and monarchical in orientation and championed Prince Michael's return to the Scottish throne. On public displays, their members wore full Highland dress, including the *sgian dhubh* and claymore, despite their being illegal in public places. Their drum corps was dressed in black military uniform with a Nazi-style symbol and '*Saorsa*' (freedom) on their banner. Disrupting SNP meetings with Nazi songs, they vied for attention with the 1320 Club, which, under MacDonald Douglas, was now calling for civil disobedience with the aim of 'complete independence'. The first bomb was planted at the Assembly Rooms in Edinburgh and further bombs followed, but all to no avail because of the actions of a police spy, and Scottish right-wing romanticism came to a halt.

Yet another organisation took its chances when the Scottish National Liberation Army (SNLA) tried to blow up Margaret Thatcher as she came to speak at the Scottish Conservative conference in Perth. The device, a 6lb bomb, radio-controlled, would have killed many inside, including the Prime Minister. A message relayed to the BBC by a contact stated that 'it would have been a turning point in British politics. While the first public reaction would have been shock and revulsion, the assassination would have awakened the political conscience of Scotland in the long term. The rest of the world including England would have alienated Scotland and the Scots. We would then be forced to fend for ourselves in a political sense and it would be then that the people would turn to a socialist republic.'[14] It would finally be the Provisional IRA, however, that would have the dubious privilege of blowing up Mrs Thatcher and her Cabinet as they stayed in Brighton for their party conference in 1984.[15]

Chapter Nineteen

War in the Valleys

Since the 1830s, Wales had remained dormant as a centre for revolutionaries. However, Methodism, temperance and socialism did create the background for the appearance of the Labour Party. Nevertheless, with the coming of the Celtic Revival, independence was again debated. During his tour of the British Isles on behalf of Irish land reform, Michael Davitt spoke at a meeting on Welsh independence. He was thanked by a Welsh lawyer, David Lloyd George. That same year, Thomas Ellis won a 'Welsh Nationalist' seat and joined the Welsh Independent Movement, Cymru Fydd. He was joined on 10 April 1890 by Lloyd George, now MP for Caernarfon, who spoke on Welsh independence on 13 June 1890: 'The current of the time is sweeping to nationalism. Wales, in throwing in her lot with Ireland in the self-government struggle, has struck a blow not only for the national rights of another Celtic country, but also for her own.'[1] Lloyd George went on to form 'Young Wales', but the victory of the Liberal Party in 1906 and Lloyd George's acceptance of a Cabinet post killed the 'dream of an independent party for Wales' and, from then on, especially in his treatment of the Irish, Lloyd George proved himself an enemy of Celticism and was regarded as a traitor to his Welsh roots.

Meanwhile, the Labour Party, aware of the value of Home Rule as a way of cadging votes, declared in 1918 its belief in 'self-government', but in their terms of office during 1923 to 1934 and 1929 to 1931 did nothing to further the cause. The result of this frustrating betrayal was the founding of Byddin Ymreolwyr Cymru (Home Rule Army of Wales) in 1924 and then, a year later, the creation of Plaid Cymru, created from self-government groups and dedicated to '[releasing] Wales from the grip of the English'. Nowadays it stands for the promotion of the 'constitutional advancement of Wales' with a view to obtaining 'full national status' in the European Union, but their first aim was to restore the Welsh language. 'We can aim at nothing less than to do away with the English language in Wales.' So wrote John Saunders Lewis, Plaid Cymru's founder. Yet words seemed to achieve nothing; fire was needed.

In 1936 the Air Ministry had established a Royal Air Force bombing school at Penrhos on the Llyn peninsula, right in the centre of a Welsh-speaking area, an action that was seen as an English provocation. Welsh nationalists were incensed. 'It is a plain historical fact that ... Llyn has been Welsh of the Welsh, and that so long as Llyn remained un-Anglicised, Welsh life and culture was secure.... For Wales, the preservation of the Llyn Peninsula from this Anglicisation is a matter of life and death.'[2] Protests followed but to no avail. The bombing range committee had already rejected a number of English sites, including the Wash and Holy Island. Then there was an arson attack on the Pen-y-Berth farmhouse on the aerodrome. On 8 September, Lewis, a lecturer at University College, Swansea, the Revd Lewis Valentine and D.J. Williams, a teacher of English literature, reported to Pwllheli police station and handed themselves in for the arson attack.

At the trial under English law at Caernarfon, the jury failed to agree a verdict, and so the three accused were hauled off to the

Old Bailey so that their version of 'militant pacifism' should go
neither unexplained nor unpunished. Finally found guilty by an
English jury, they were each sentenced to nine months; it was
the first time since 1839 that Welshmen had resorted to violence
in defence of their homeland. It would not be the last. Lewis's
speech from the dock of Caernarfon on 13 October 1936 was
the first great independence speech in Wales since the fifteenth
century. In it, he firmly blamed the English for the actions of
the Welsh, 'yet we hold the conviction that our action was in
no wise criminal, and that it was an act forced upon us, that it
was done in obedience to conscience and to the moral law, and
that the responsibility for any loss due to our act is the responsibility of the English government'.[3] At the centre of all this
was the survival of the Welsh language: 'Welsh literature', said
Lewis, 'is one of the great literatures of Europe... . And it is
a living, growing literature, and draws its sustenance from a
living language and a traditional social life. It was my sense of
the inestimable value of this tremendous heirloom ... that first
led me ... to the establishment of the Welsh National Party.'[4]
Lewis also reiterated that independence must come through
peaceful means: 'I have repeatedly and publicly declared that the
Welsh Nation must gain its political freedom without resort to
violence or physical force.' Yet there remained a threat, which
carried with it a memory of the Irish troubles: 'Had we wished
to follow the methods of violence ... nothing could have been
easier for us than to ask some of the generous and spirited young
men of the Welsh National Party to set fire to the aerodrome and
get away undiscovered. It would be the beginning of methods of
sabotage and guerrilla turmoil.'[5]

   Lewis himself, with his receding hairline, long face and
beaky nose, was born in Cheshire, England, in 1893, but
brought up among the Welsh community there. It seems it was
his experience of fighting in the First World War alongside
Irishmen whose loyalties were split that convinced him of the
significance of Welsh independence. Twice nominated for the

Nobel Prize, a fierce advocate of the Welsh language (the Welsh Language Society, Cymdeithas yr Iaith Gymraeg, was founded after his radio lecture in 1962[6]) and a moving force behind S4C (the Welsh-language television channel), he was also posthumously influential on the Welsh Language Act of 1993. He finally converted to Catholicism, the ancient religion of Wales, and died in 1985.

Despite Plaid Cymru's stand for independence, some felt it was too 'cultural' in its interests and pushed for a more overtly political stand. At the annual conference in September 1949, fifty members walked out. Thus the Welsh Republican Movement started, with its paper *Y Gweriniaethywr*, which ran between 1950 and 1957 under the editorship of Hari Web and Cliff Bere. This was followed by another paper, *The Welsh Republican*, also edited by Bere. He was born of Welsh parents but brought up in Burnley, Lancashire. He studied at University College, Swansea, but this was interrupted by the Second World War and service in North Africa. Afterwards, he worked for a time in the National Museum of Wales but became radicalised and thereafter fought for Welsh independence, despite a brief period in jail following the burning of a Union Jack. Bere went on to produce a manifesto for the Welsh Republican Movement in 1950.

The document argued for a free, independent Wales, a republic of the 'common people' where 'the king of England [then George VI] … shall have no jurisdiction … or dominion'. Welsh would be restored as the first language and 'cooperatives' would be the means of production. In order to 'take its place and play its part in the international community of nations' and 'live in close cooperation with the other Celtic peoples', it would be necessary to declare Wales a 'sovereign democratic republic'. It was a powerful piece of rhetoric but it rallied few to the cause and Bere returned chastened to Plaid Cymru. Ironically, he was arrested again during the arson campaign of 1980 and died aged 82 in Glamorgan on 16 September 1997.

In 1952 it was decided that a bombing campaign would be initiated to disrupt water supplies from Wales to the Midlands of
England. The Welsh Republican Movement decided to blow up
the pipeline from the new Claerwen reservoir to Birmingham.
Although this was not finally undertaken, on 19 October 1954
there was an attempted bombing on the Fron Aqueduct, also
taking water to England. Then in 1957, despite angry and prolonged protests, Liverpool City Council came up with a plan to
flood the Tryweryn valley to create yet another 'English' reservoir. It was bitterly opposed but went through parliament on
31 July 1957. Together, Owain Williams and Emyr Jones, one
a former British Columbian logger turned café owner, and
the other a poet-student, decided to dynamite the reservoir. It
was the first action of Mudiad Amddiffyn Cymru (MAC), the
Movement for the Defence of Wales. The whole affair was a
farce and both men were arrested and imprisoned. Another
small bomb blew up a power cable, and that seemed to be that.

That was, until the Lord Mayor of Liverpool, with crass
indifference, came to Tryweryn to open the reservoir. Here he
was met by a large, angry crowd and men in a green uniform
sporting an eagle flag – the Free Wales Army (FWA), founded
by Julian Cayo Evans, a horse breeder from Lampeter. On the
fiftieth anniversary of the 1916 Rising in Dublin, the FWA even
marched with its colours flying and in uniform alongside IRA
men. The apparent closeness to the IRA was a constant worry
to the police and Special Branch. There were also links with the
Scottish Liberation Army. Much of the activity of the FWA
centred around the formation of the theoretical 'international
Celtic guard', which remained a powerful concept. Yet the
FWA's activities had practical results, for, at their first meeting
with representatives of the IRA and independence fighters from
Scotland, it was decided to begin a campaign of expropriation
and gun theft.

The Free Wales Army and MAC regularly went on manoeuvres in the hills with their limited arsenal and Nazi-style

uniforms. Indeed, they resembled an uneasy mix of the IRA and British National Front, but were, for all their noise, too small, too weak and too well known to the police to be much trouble. Further bombings, of Inland Revenue offices and pipelines, continued. Meanwhile, Plaid Cymru had expelled the flag-waving, uniformed nationalists from its ranks. From now on, MAC and the FWA would represent the armies of Welsh independence and Welsh resistance. MAC and the FWA continued an occasional war of attrition with the British until July 1969, when they prepared for a showdown. On 1 July, Charles would be made Prince of Wales at a ceremony at Caernarfon Castle.

The FWA and MAC trained together, but planned operations separately. The FWA (and Patriotic Front, made up of English-speaking Welshmen) came up with a plan to invade the town and hold it by force until overwhelmed. It would be a 'blood sacrifice' for Wales in the same vein as that of 1916 in Dublin – futile in itself, but possibly the catalyst to bigger events. It would certainly focus the world's attention on Wales. The FWA was reasonably well organised but it was scattered and had few weapons or decent transport, its 'columns' no more than three or four men. Nevertheless, plans were laid of a spectacular order. Keith Griffiths wrote to Evans, 'The plans are fixed for Caernarfon, we rise! ... we march and take Caernarfon at all costs. Arm ourselves with shot guns, guns, bows, slings, pikes, weapons of all sorts ... we fight our way into the town!'[7] Evans fantasised that 'specially trained and equipped volunteers of 'Cilmeriad' squads will be active throughout the battle. These squads will be responsible for special services and lead the attack on the castle and other key positions in the town held by the enemy [that is, the English]; and also the task of assassinating the Pretender [Charles] if necessary and other key people on the black list.'[8] If all else failed (so the fantasy went), '[Evans was] calling in the IRA'. Unfortunately, the IRA were not about to ride over the horizon and save the day. Infiltrated by spies and

Special Branch, the desperate but comic-opera insurrection was trapped by a series of major arrests. All the leaders were rounded up, their trial coming to court in May and their sentencing to occur on the very day of the Investiture. Evans received fifteen months, Keith Griffiths nine, and so on through the other eight defendants who had been due to lead the uprising. The FWA and Patriotic Front were finished for good.

The commander of MAC, until then unknown to the authorities, had the perfect cover – he was serving as a member of Her Majesty's armed forces. John Jenkins was a sergeant in the Army Dental Corps and later the non-commissioned officer in charge of a Territorial Army drum band whose travels around the country proved perfect cover for MAC reconnoitring. More importantly, Jenkins was one of a handful of professional, dedicated revolutionaries, with a theoretical as well as a practical sense of what needed to be done. He had been brought up by English-speaking parents in Merthyr Tydfil and did not hear Welsh spoken until he left school. Somewhere, his Welshness took hold:

> There was no logical reason that could be accounted for environmentally why I should turn out the way I did… . As I grew older my feelings of Welshness grew stronger… . I am not even Welsh speaking.[9]

Even though a member of the army, Jenkins had an inherent dislike of violence, but he also had a patriotic fervour for an independent Wales:

> I took up arms because … I felt instinctively that the Welsh national identity, our sacred soul … was in the last stages of survival. The military, political and economic wars have long been lost in Wales and the final cultural annihilation [had] … gathered momentum… . The strategy was military, to achieve a short term mental attitude leading to a long term

political settlement. The fight was not to win a military victory, but to create a state of mind.

So, on Investiture Day, MAC's plan was to cause as much mayhem as possible, but without assassinating Charles, which, they believed, quite rightly, would have caused a massively unfavourable reaction in Wales that might have killed the independence movement.[10] Meanwhile, on 30 June 1969, the day before the investiture, the first bomb went off in a post box in Caernarfon. Then two members of MAC, Alwyn Jones and George Taylor, laid a bomb in an alley between government offices.[11] Misconnecting the bombs' wires, the two men were blown apart – MAC's first casualties and the first deaths in the whole campaign since the 1950s.

As part of 'Operation Cricket', thousands of police, soldiers and Special Branch were in the town, two Royal Navy minesweepers swept the Menai Straits and a large boom was laid across Caernarfon harbour. Frogmen and patrol boats also guarded the Royal Yacht. It did not prevent another bomb going off just as the twenty-one gun salute occurred. Twenty-two detonations were counted by onlookers but edited out of television's footage. Other bombs either failed to detonate or went off mysteriously, as when a soldier was killed when his truck blew up for no apparent reason. The police realised they had a second threat to deal with. Clues were scarce but they had interviewed Jenkins before and knew one of his associates, Frederick Alders. In September 1969 they interviewed Jenkins again but found nothing. However, ever persistent, they raided the two men's homes on 2 November, only now to find several sticks of dynamite. Alders, newly married, turned Queen's evidence; Jenkins was sentenced to ten years on 20 April 1970 (and released in 1976). The war was over but the struggle continued.

Indeed, with Plaid Cymru's disappointing showing in the election of 1970, things seemed to have quietened down, but in 1979 an arson campaign began against English holiday homes.

Meanwhile, another bombing campaign had been organised by the Workers' Army of the Welsh Republic, whose acronym 'WAWR' also meant 'Dawn'. Yet another group had left bombs during 1981. This group, called Meibion Glyndw^r (Sons of Glendower), also bombed the Welsh Office in Cardiff. Yet again the police and Special Branch had to go into action, and eight suspects were arrested. One, Dafydd Ladd, was given nine years for possession of explosives; he had been helped by Jenkins, who again went to prison, for two years.

Republican views were not confined to Ireland, Scotland and Wales, but included the wider Celtic community: Cornwall and the Isle of Man also have long associations with republican nationalism. In Cornwall this was first associated with Tyr ha Tavas (Land and Language). In the 1930s Henry Jenner founded the original organisation, which became Mebyon Kernow in 1949. Agitation followed, especially around the use of the Cornish language and the Cornish flag. In 1966 the 'party' (more properly a pressure group) erected a statue to An Gof, a Cornish rebel who had finally been defeated by the English at the Battle of Deptford Bridge in 1497. In 1967 Mebyon Kernow won its first-ever seat on Cornwall County Council, after running a campaign against 'foreigners' moving into the area. Yet it was not until November 1981 that the Perranporth Policy Conference finally came down firmly on a republican message, but a call for the socialist 'Cornish people's eventual ownership of the creation and distribution of wealth' was defeated three to one. Nevertheless, this anti-monarchical stand was 'put on hold' in November 1982, which left the supporters of 'radical autonomism' frustrated.

Two years earlier, a rather more eccentric independence movement had arisen. This group also acknowledged An Gof and exploded a crude bomb in St Austell courthouse on Sunday 7 December 1980. Nevertheless, the shadowy An Gof continued with threats, bombing a hairdresser's in mistake for a building society in January 1981, and making accusations against Mebyon

Kernow members and 'Trotskyists'. Bomb scares emptied a local Tesco supermarket and Woolworths, but left the police no wiser as to the organisation or its personnel. Instead, they concentrated on finding one man – the lone bomber of An Gof. The *Western Morning News* reported that he was thought to be 'About 40 years old, approximately 5ft 8in to 5ft 9in, of slim build, but possibly with a paunch, black or dark coloured hair, probably straight and swept back (it may have been greased), clean shaven with no noticeable sideboards, wearing a black or dark coloured three-quarter-length coat, and dark coloured trousers.'[12]

A suspect having been arrested and then released, all went quiet. An Gof resurfaced in the attempted bombing of Beacon Hill village hall and the arson attack on the Zodiac bingo hall in Redruth, finally putting out threats against Tesco in 1987. Attacks on the Cornish beaches to discourage tourists failed to materialise. It was all very fishy. Who were An Gof? One author has suggested that the organisation was 'the creation of a police "dirty tricks squad" … with the aim of discrediting the Cornish movement. Hoax letter-bombs to government offices in Plymouth and Exeter, and press releases threatening tourists, were guaranteed to cause widespread "horror" coverage in the media which would be made to reflect on both Mebyon Kernow and the Cornish National Party.'[13] After these minor incidents, An Gof was heard of no more. Cornwall remains an English county (not a country) and plans for devolved representation have come to nothing.

The Isle of Man (or Mann), however, enjoys a different status. Despite its small size, Man has spawned a number of independence movements. Man is the only semi-independent Celtic 'country' to survive in the British Isles and has its own government, called the 'Tynwald' (the House of Keys is the lower house), which is considered the oldest in the world. Nevertheless, its position is anomalous because, 'the Isle of Mann is not part of the United Kingdom' but that 'the power of the imperial parliament (Westminster) to legislate for the Isle of

Mann is supreme'.[14] The Celtic League had this story about this anomaly during 1973:

> Mann has a greater degree of devolved government, than any system so far proposed for Scotland and Wales. In all aspects of Manks [*sic*] life except Defence, International Relations and the Customs Union (the so called Common Purse) – the Manks people legislate for themselves. This legislation however, has to have the assent of the Lord of Mann (Elizabeth II, of England). This royal assent effectively castrates [the] democratic government of the nation… . Mann therefore has devolved government… . Its citizens are not regarded as being citizens of the U.K… . The devolution granted to Mann, should technically be capable of extension if the Manks people wish to [have] 'sovereign independence'. However, on more than one occasion, U.K. members of constitutional enquiries, have inferred, that this would be unacceptable.[15]

The two issues that exercised Man's independence movements were the obliteration of the Manx language and the welcoming of wealthy 'come-overs' from mainland England, which pushed house prices up during the 1970s and 1980s. It was against this background of frustration that Man's various republican groups were formed. The first of these was Mec Vannin (Sons of Mann), who wavered between acting as a political lobby group and a fully fledged political party. Nevertheless, they stood for republican independence. In 1974 they issued a statement saying that they stood for the 'rights of self government', and in 1984 they made this unequivocal statement of intent in their newsletter: 'The aim of Mec Vannin is to achieve national independence for Mann as a Democratic Republic. To achieve that aim, the existing system of undemocratic "outside" rule must be abolished and replaced with a system based upon the sovereignty of the Manx nation.'[16]

Mec Vannin participated in the parliamentary process and fielded candidates for the House of Keys during the 1970s, polling nearly 15 per cent of the votes in the various constituencies in which they stood. Yet electioneering and protesting against corrupt practices hardly ingratiated them with more hardline republicans. A new revolutionary group therefore appeared in 1973, called Fo Halloo (Underground). Standing for a tough approach to the issue of independence, the 'party' was also socialist in orientation. Their manifesto read:

> In order for Mannin to survive as an independent nation we must rethink our whole industrial and agricultural policy. Although, as nationalists have pointed out for years, independence does not mean isolation, it does mean we must produce the things we need to live on in our own country.... We therefore recommend that the following steps be implemented.... The removal of all crown representatives and agents from the legislature.... Encouragement to be given to the fostering of our native language & culture ... [and] the establishment of a closer economic and cultural bond between ourselves and the other Celtic nations.[17]

The group's main target was also the 'come-overs', new residents pushing up land and property prices and turning the island into a tax haven. Daubing of homes of come-overs soon began with the Marchioness of Queensbury's modest bungalow, targeted on 11 March 1973. Mild destruction continued across the island, with 1,200 hay bales being slashed open on 2 August 1973. It did not amount to much and certainly looked more like a prank than anything serious. Nevertheless, on 6 July 1973 they also struck at the opening ceremony for the Tynwald, setting fire to a large cross and later a tree. The actions in themselves were virtually harmless, but caused anxiety among residents, and a 'stop and search' policy by the police. Eventually the campaign turned to arson, for which three men, Christopher Sheard, Philip Gawne and Gregory Joughin, were finally brought to trial. The Celtic League recorded the arrests in language that the early republicans would have recognised: 'The Speaker of the House of Keys, personally took action which ended with the fining of three young men for the trivial technical offence of putting up posters which did not bear the printer's name... . These three were probably the first Manxmen to be prosecuted for a patriotic act since the nineteenth century.'[18]

Fo Halloo gave birth to Irree Magh (Passion to the Fore), who produced at least one pamphlet urging the Manx people to 'unite [in] open rebellion' and to look to other Celtic countries to defeat the 'iniquitous imperialistic policy' of the English: 'The day will soon come when the Manx nation will be established in it's [sic] own right and the confiscated assets of the immigrants will be used for the Manx people. When the time comes a department of repatriation will have to be established.'[19]

Last but not least came Poblaght Soshiallagh Vannin (Manx Republican Socialist Party), dedicated to full independence from 'United Kingdom Imperialism'. The PSV produced its own charter, in which it declared, 'We are resolved to assert Mann's independence as a sovereign nation... . To establish a new society in Mann based on ... socialist doctrine. To achieve our aims we are committed to the overthrow and abolition of the existing capitalist political and social regime, with its classes and class antagonisms.'[20]

The concentration and intensification of revolutionary activity from the 1960s to the late 1970s meant that Scottish and Welsh independence groups had meetings with, and were supplied by, the IRA. Although the Scots always remained cash-poor and the Welsh were dedicated to actions that did not threaten life, nevertheless, any alliance of Celtic groups would certainly have destabilised the United Kingdom. The forces of law and order, especially MI5 and Special Branch, had to develop ways and means to combat growing disorder in at least five areas of the United Kingdom.

In the end, the combined forces of the British state have faced and broken each effort at independence and even the IRA have now officially decommissioned. Yet the often aggressive tactics could not efface the memory of sacrifice among the Celtic people, or a feeling that a great wrong had been done and that an identity needed to be preserved. The Scots gained their parliament and the Welsh their assembly in 1997, but Cornwall and Man have still had to wait, while Ireland remains divided. In England, despite the upsurge of left-wing revolutionary groups in the 1970s and 1980s, the forces of republicanism are as isolated and small as ever, their sacrifices largely forgotten, their promise still to be fulfilled.

Notes

PREFACE

1. These are Edward Vallance, *A Radical History of Britain*, and David Horspool, *The English Rebel*.
2. The Assembly and Executive were finally established in 1999 and the IRA decommissioned in 2005.

INTRODUCTION

1. Christopher Brooke, *The Saxon and Norman Kings* (London: Fontana, 1986), p. 31.
2. *Ibid.*, p. p. 32.
3. *Ibid.*, p. 37.
4. *Ibid.*, p. 37–8.
5. Patrick Wormald, *The Making of English Law: King Alfred to the Twelfth Century, Volume 1 Legislation and Its Limits* (Oxford: Blackwell, 1999), p. 448.
6. *Ibid.*, p. 448.
7. Jeremy Paxman, *The English* (London: Penguin, 1999), p. 94.
8. Darren Baker, *Simon de Montfort and the Rise of the English Nation* (Stroud: Amberley, 2018), p. 232; see also Sophie Therese Ambler, *The Song of Simon de Montfort* (London: Picador, 2019).

9. *Ibid.*, p. 232.

10. Chris Skidmore, *Bosworth: The Birth of the Tudors* (London: Phoenix, 2014), p. 13.

11. G.R. Elton, *The Parliament of England 1559–1581* (Cambridge: Cambridge University Press, 1986), p. 341.

12. *Ibid.*, p. 341.

13. *Ibid.*, p. 19.

14. *Ibid.*, p. 321.

15. Algernon Sidney, *Discourses Concerning Government*, ed. Thomas G. West (Indianapolis: Liberty Fund, 1990), p. xxix.

16. *Ibid.*, p. xxxi.

17. *Ibid.*

18. *Ibid.*, p. xvi.

19. M.C. Jacob, *The Newtonians and the English Revolution 1689–1720* (Hassocks: Harvester, 1976), p. 82.

20. *Ibid.*, p. 85.

21. *Ibid.*, p. 87.

22. H.J. Hanham, *The Nineteenth Century Constitution: Documents and Commentary* (Cambridge: Cambridge University Press, 1969), p. 5.

23. *Ibid.*, p. 30.

24. *Ibid.*

25. *Ibid.*, p. 31.

26. *Ibid.*, p. 13.

27. *Ibid.*, pp. 39–40. See also Walter Bagehot, *The English Constitution* (London: Chapman Hall, 1867), p. 103.

28. Richard J. Aldrich and Rory Cormac, *Spying and the Crown* (London: Atlantic Books, 2021), p. 609.

29. Anne Twomey, 'From Bagehot to Brexit: "The Monarchs Rights to be Consulted, to Encourage and to Warn"' in *The Round Table*, 107:4 (2018), pp. 417–28. 'I suspect it really is Bagehot. I've not been able to find the point earlier than him (though I have not dug very, very deeply) and don't think it could in any event be much earlier. It must date from the time of the establishment of the convention that the monarch should act on the advice of her ministers. The relevant bit of Blackstone, a century before Bagehot, is very different in its assumptions' (David Ibettson, Regius Professor of Civil Law (Cambridge), in correspondence with the author).

30. Hanham, p. 36.

31. *Ibid.*, pp. 37–8.

32. Clive Bloom, *Victoria's Madmen: Revolution and Alienation* (London: Macmillan Palgrave, 2013), p. 249.

33. *Ibid.*, p. 250.

34. Hanham, p. 47.

35. Frank Hardie, *The Political Influence of the British Monarchy 1868–1952* (New York: Harper and Row, 1970), p. 77.

36. *Ibid.*, p. 87.

37. *Ibid.*, p. 144.

38. Aldrich, p. 397.

39. *Ibid.*, p. 614.

40. *Financial Times* magazine, 13 November 2021.

41. 'Crown Estate', Wikipedia (accessed 3 September 2022).

42. *The Mail Online* (accessed 3 September 2021).

43. *Ibid.*

44. Russell Brand, *Revolution* (London: Century, 2014), p. 118.

45. See respectively, Gerald Gould, *The Coming Revolution in Great Britain* (London: W. Collins Sons & Co., 1920) and Tariq Ali, *The Coming British Revolution* (London: Jonathan Cape, 1972).

46. www.marxist.com (accessed 3 September 2022).

47. Stratford Caldedott, 'Prince Charles: Imaginative Conservative' (accessed 12 September 2022). Despite Charles's ground-breaking interests, the family are haunted by the accusations of racism, from the Duchess of Sussex and people like Ngozi Fulani. Nevertheless, the attacks are *ad homina* and do not touch the Crown as an institution, despite spurious attempts to link its history to slavery by historians such as David Olusoga.

48. This section reproduced by kind permission of the *Times Higher Education Supplement*. See appendix 2 in Clive Bloom, *Riot City: Protest and Rebellion in the Capital* (London: Palgrave, 2012) for a full breakdown of British republican flags.

49. Charles Dilke quoted in Christopher Rumsey, *The Rise And Fall of British Republican Clubs 1871–1874* (Oswestry: Quinta Press, 2000).

50. *Ibid.*, p. 21.

51. *Ibid.*, p. 3.

52. Murray Armstrong, *The Fight for Scottish Democracy: Rebellion and Reform in 1820* (London: Pluto Press, 2020), p. 7; see also Peter Berresford Ellis and Seuma Mac A'Ghobhainn, *The Scottish Insurrection of 1820* (Edinburgh: John Donald Publishers, 1970).

53. A selection of relevant books on Scottish independence: Angus Calder, *Revolving Culture: Notes from the Scottish Republic* (London, New York:

I.B. Tauris Publishers, 1994); Gavin McCrone, *Scottish Independence: Weighing Up the Economics* (Edinburgh: Birlinn Ltd, 2013); James Foley and Pete Ramand, *Yes: The Radical Case for Scottish Independence* (London: Pluto Press, 2014); John Curtice, David McCrone, Nicola McEwen, Michael Marsh and Rachel Ormston, *Revolution or Evolution? The 2007 Scottish Elections* (Edinburgh: Edinburgh University Press, 2009). For Wales see Kenneth O. Morgan, *Revolution to Devolution: Reflections on Welsh Democracy* (Cardiff: University of Wales Press, 2014).

CHAPTER ONE

1. Michael Joseph Rahilly was born in 1875, became a member of Sinn Fein and the Gaelic League and a founder of the Irish Volunteers. He was killed leading a charge along Moore Street on 28 April 1916. The name 'The' is an honorary clan title.

2. Tim Pat Coogan, *1916: The Easter Rising* (London: Phoenix, 2005), p. 131.

3. This was a Trotskyist cadre within the Labour Party working on the one hand to use parliamentary process for the overthrow of capitalism, while on the other giving support for the nationalist armed struggle of the IRA in Northern Ireland. Militant Tendency was, to all intents and purposes, a revolutionary party joined parasitically with, and often working secretly within, a democratic one.

4. These men were privately sponsored bodies of amateur cavalry paid partly through landowners and through aristocratic patronage. The extraordinary need for regular army volunteers during the French Revolution and Napoleonic Wars meant that a home army of 'territorials' was needed. During 1795, these amateur cavalry put down their first riot near Leicester jail. By 1801, there were 20,000 such volunteers, as well as a militia of 'home guardsmen' used to defend fortresses. Alongside both were volunteer loyal associations of tradesmen and shopkeepers. Even more cavalry were raised through the Provincial Cavalry Act of 1794 and were intended to bolster the yeomanry. Armed with a light cavalry sabre and carbine, the yeomanry were a supplementary force used to support the regular army at home, and therefore first on the scene when a riot was being put down.

5. J. Bowyer Bell, *The Dynamics of the Armed Struggle* (London: Frank Cass, 1998), p. 11.

6. Edward Hyams, *Terrorists and Terrorism* (London: J.M. Dent and Sons, 1975), p. 9.

7. The Elizabethan secret service was expressly created to defeat the internal threat of a Catholic resurgence. The hatred of Catholics lasted long after the end of Elizabeth's reign and has revived intermittently up until the present day. After the rise of the Jacobites, people such as Henry Fielding were quite open in their hatred of 'Popery': 'When Popery without a mask stalks publicly abroad, and Jesuits preach their Doctrines in print, with the same confidence as when the last Popish prince was seated on the throne, it becomes high time for every man, who wishes well to his country, to offer some antidote to the intended poison' ('A Proper Answer to a Late Scurrilous Libel' (London: M Cooper, 1747), p. 1). This hatred has continued to the present day, where in the Orange lodges of Northern Ireland they still (half-humorously) drink to the destruction of 'papists' and 'Jacobites'.

8. E.P. Thompson, *The Making of the English Working Class* (New York: Vintage, 1966), p. 25.

9. *Ibid.*, p. 189.

10. *Ibid.*, p. 25.

11. *Ibid.*

12. The Society was variously known as the Club Breton, the Société des Amis de la Constitution and the Amis de la Liberté et de l'Egalité. They met throughout the French Revolution and by July 1790 had over a thousand members. It was the most extreme of the revolutionary clubs and was an instrument of government, with 5,000 to 8,000 affiliated clubs throughout France at the time of the Terror. Its name became a byword for any violent radical, but especially for republicans. In England, the word 'Jacobin' was usually used as a term of abuse similar to 'bolshie' in the twentieth.

13. Karl Marx and Friedrich Engels, *Manifesto of the Communist Party*, in Marx and Engels, *Selected Works in One Volume* (London: Lawrence and Wishart [1888] 1970), p. 63.

CHAPTER TWO

1. Sir Henry Halford, *Essays and Orations* (London: John Murray, 1831), p. 201.

2. *Ibid.*, p. 202.

3. *Ibid.*, p. 203.

4. Thurloe's activities on behalf of Cromwell were also useful to Charles II on his return, as were those of the Revd John Wallace, a Cambridge mathematician who worked on the decryption of Charles I's despatches but was nevertheless re-employed as a code-breaker and as a royal chaplain after the Restoration. Thurloe was also in charge of the vital Offices of Post for Letters (Foreign and Ireland), where Isaac Dorislaus worked on ciphers. Thurloe's 'allowance for intelligence' dwindled during the latter half of the seventeenth century, even as the post of Principal Secretary rose in significance. In 1711, an Act was passed to permit interception and opening of letters, the department being so secret that it became known to parliament only in 1742, when it had both a budget and a staff of five.

5. James Holstun, 'Ehud's Dagger: Patronage, Tyrannicide and Killing No Murder', in *Cultural Critique* (Oxford; Oxford University Press), no. 22 (Fall 1992), p. 116.

6. The most popular book of the period, however, was *Eikon Basilike* by John Gauden, which was an amalgam of the last writings of Charles I and Gauden's own imaginative thoughts. Despite the attempts of the Republic to suppress the work, it ran to forty English editions and was translated into many foreign languages.

7. Anon, *An Exact and Most Impartial Accompt of the Indictment, Arraignment, Trial, and Judgment etc of Twenty Nine Regicides the Murtherers of His Late Sacred Majesty etc.* (London: R. Scot et al., 1679), pp. 3–4.

8. *Ibid.*, p. 13.

9. Gerrard Winstanley, 'The True Levellers Standard Advanced', in *The Law of Freedom and Other Writings* (Harmondsworth: Penguin, 1973), p. 78.

10. John Sainsbury, *Disaffected Patriots* (Gloucester: Alan Sutton, 1987), p. 6.

11. *Ibid.*, p. 61.

12. *Ibid.*, p. 85.

13. Burke was one of the two sitting members of parliament for Bristol. He was for the most part an absentee from the city that had voted for him and got involved in its affairs only reluctantly.

14. Sainsbury, *Disaffected Patriots*, p. 48.

15. Letter to William Smith, Esq., 'In Ireland, on Catholic Emancipation', 29 January 1795, in *Edmund Burke: Selected Prose*, ed. Sir Philip Magnus (London: Falcon Press, 1948).

Chapter Three

1. Anon. (possibly Isaiah Thomas), *Narrative of the Excursions and Ravages of the King's Troops under the Command of General Gage* (Philadelphia, 1775), p. 2.

2. Christopher Duffy, *The Military Experience in the Age of Reason* (London: Routledge & Kegan Paul, 1987), p. 209.

3. *Ibid.*, p. 208. Farmer soldiers might cry murder, but for all its momentary terror the war in America was a small affair compared to the numbers involved in later European battles of the French Revolutionary and Napoleonic wars, and American casualties, while proportionally high, were usually numerically negligible. At Yorktown in 1781 an American army of 17,233 men lost 271 killed or wounded while the British lost 596 out of a force of 8,225. Such losses represent only twice the death toll of all the civilian combatants of the Gordon Riots.

4. John Sainsbury, *London Supporters of Revolutionary America 1769–1782* (Gloucester: Alan Sutton, 1987), p. 90.

5. Michael Walzer, *Regicide and Revolution* (Cambridge: Cambridge University Press, 1974), p. 122. See this edition also for this and other references to the trial of Louis XVI.

6. *Ibid.*, p. 128.

7. *Ibid.*, p. 131.

8. Samuel Bamford, *Passages in the Life of a Radical* (Oxford: Oxford University Press, [1842] 1967), p. 26.

9. Edward Pearce, *Reform!* (London: Pimlico, 2004), p. 218.

10. *Ibid.*, p. 259.

11. *Ibid.*, p. 292.

12. *Ibid.*, p. 266.

13. H.T. Dickinson (ed.), *The Political Writings of Thomas Spence* (Newcastle upon Tyne: Avero, 1984), p. 19.

Chapter Four

1. Much of the French Revolution was plotted at Le Procope, in the rue de l'Ancienne Comédie. In the alley behind, Marat had his printing press and the first guillotine was built. Marat's own home, where he was murdered by Charlotte Corday, was at 30 rue des Cordeliers. His bath was preserved at the Grévin waxworks. The Cordeliers Club remains preserved in the University of Paris, Faculty of Medicine, while the

Jacobin Club has long vanished, but was originally in the chapel at the place du Marché Saint-Honoré. Robespierre lived just down the road at an apartment on the rue Saint-Honoré. The guillotine itself was set up on the place de la Révolution, while those awaiting execution, including Brissot, Saint-Just, the Girondins, Robespierre and Marie Antoinette, were housed at the ancient prison of the Conciergerie, part of the palais de la Cité. 'La Marseillaise' was composed in a single night by Claude Joseph Rouget de Lisle while he was stationed in Strasbourg in 1792. The Convention accepted it as the national anthem on 14 July 1795 but, ironically, it was banned by Napoleon and not officially reinstated until 1879.

2. Thomas Paine, *The Age of Reason*, Part II (New York: Prometheus Press, 1984), p. 73. Paine died on 8 June 1809, having been invited to America to take up residence by Thomas Jefferson. He died abandoned and largely forgotten by the American nation he had helped to found.

3. Ordnance of 1649.

4. Derek Jarrett, *The Begetters of Revolution* (Harlow: Longman, 1973), p. 92.

5. Robert Harvey, *Liberators* (London: John Murray, 2000), p. 34.

6. *Ibid.*, p. 47.

7. Like Brissot, Marat also believed in the equality of the Negro – the rights of man were universal. French San Domingo (now Haiti) was a slave-owning society. It was also the gold mine of the West Indies. When Brissot's Girondins came to power, San Domingo declared for the Republic and, after some vacillation, slavery was abolished. Jamaica, 50 miles away by sea, was alerted and Pitt was persuaded that an invasion would restore slavery and capture the wealthiest island in the world for the British Empire. The excuse came with the declaration of war by France on Britain. An expedition was sent out and, by 1794, seemed to be fulfilling its mission. However, fever and military defeats slowly wore it down, until the biggest army Britain had ever mobilised sank without trace trying to defeat republicans and freedom. Of 100,000 troops, 50,000 died and most of the rest were incapacitated. Britain had fatally weakened its war with the Revolution by squandering men and munitions to fight a 'war for security', as Pitt put it. This was, perhaps, a rather disingenuous excuse for an invasion that had proved fruitless, except, of course, to keep Jamaica a slave-owning island and prevent the Haitian revolution from spreading.

8. Louis Gottschalk, *Jean Paul Marat* (Chicago: University of Chicago Press, 1967), p. 16.

9. *Ibid.*, p. 23.

10. *Ibid.*, p. 105.

11. *Ibid.*, p. 131.

12. *Ibid.*

13. Ray Watkinson, 'Thomas Bewick, 1753–1828', in Lionel M. Munby (ed.), *The Luddites and Other Essays* (London: Michael Katanka Books, 1971), pp. 11–33, at pp. 28–9.

CHAPTER FIVE

1. Despite the apparent improvement of the law in cases of treason, things remained entirely unremedied when judges went on circuit. Fifty years later on 18 January 1840 during the trial of Samuel Horberry at the Town Hall in Sheffield there were six magistrates available as well as Colonel Marten commanding the First Royal Dragoons, Lieutenant Nichol commanding the local militia as well as several officers of cavalry. Total magistrates and others therefore numbered between eight and fifteen. There was also a Mr Palfreyman and Mr Thomas Rodgers prosecuting. The indictment was 'high treason' but 'none of the prisoners had any professional assistance' (*Leeds Intelligencer*, 18 January 1840).

2. John Hawkes, quoted in John H. Langbein, *The Origins of the Adversarial Criminal Trial* (Oxford: Oxford University Press, 2003), p. 84.

3. Stella Tillyard, *Citizen Lord* (London:Chatto and Windus, 1997), p. 81.

4. For this, and the information on Edward Fitzgerald, see *ibid.*, p. 298.

CHAPTER SIX

1. Australia was a dumping ground for the potentially disaffected until October 1867, when sixty-three Fenians arrived in Western Australia on board the *Hougoumont*. Meanwhile, apart from the Scottish 'martyrs' Maurice Magarot, Thomas Muir, Thomas Parker, William Skirving and Joseph Gerrald, transported in 1794, there were also transportees of the Nore and Spithead mutinies. The Irish who formed the backbone of the Castle Hill rebellion were brought in eight ships between 1797 and 1802, with more rebels arriving in the *Polla* (1803) and the *Tellichery* (1806). In all, 1,025 political prisoners of the Irish revolts of 1798 and 1803 have been identified. Two ships at least, the *Eleanor* and the *Eliza*, transported Luddites. During 1820 the Scottish rebels joined the Irish, as did twelve Yorkshire rebels who arrived between 1820 and 1822. The Tolpuddle Martyrs followed in 1834, in addition to the Swing Rioters, 475 of whom were transported from rural areas of England. Following the Newport rising, sixty Chartists

were transported to Van Diemen's Land (Tasmania), as were the Canadian convicts who arrived on HMS *Buffalo*. Of these, eighty-two were actually American, fifty-eight French, and only five were English.

2. Leonard Guttridge, *Mutiny* (New York: Berkeley, 1992), p. 49.

3. *Ibid.*, p. 58; information regarding Richard Parker comes from contemporary pamphlets and the court records.

4. R.W. Postgate, *Revolution from 1789 to 1906* (New York: Harpertorch Books, 1962), pp. 104–5.

5. *Ibid.*, pp. 73–4.

6. *Ibid.*, p. 73.

7. Anon., *Memoir of Richard Parker, the Mutineer etc., and Trial by Court Martial* (London: George Cawthorn, 1797), p. 4.

8. Anon., *The Trial of Richard Parker* (London: JS, 1797(?)), p. 28.

9. The Netherlands was a republic and hence the red flag flown at the mastheads of their fleet in the Texel may have been mistaken for a republican standard.

10. John Foster, *Class Struggle and the Industrial Revolution* (London: Methuen, 1974), p. 35.

CHAPTER SEVEN

1. Strictly speaking, the agitation for reform was begun by the Revd Christopher Wyvill and his Association Movement.

2. R. Hemmings, *Liberty or Death* (London: Lawrence & Wishart, 2000), p. 13.

3. Gwyn A. Williams, *Artisans and Sans-Culottes* (London: Edward Arnold, 1968), p. 13.

4. Norman Hampson, *The Terror in the French Revolution* (London: Historical Association, 1981), p. 25.

5. There is still uncertainty about the exact number of executions. See Graeme Fife, *The Terror* (London: Portrait, 2004), p. 415.

6. Williams, *Artisans and Sans-Culottes*, p. 13.

7. *Ibid.*, p. 9.

8. William Godwin, *Caleb Williams* (Oxford: Oxford University Press, [1794] 1982), p. 202.

9. David Williams, *John Frost: A Study in Chartism* (New York: Augustus M. Kelley, 1969), p. 9.

10. Lord North to the Country Gentleman, 18 April 1785, in A. Aspinall (ed.), *English Historical Documents 1783–1832*, vol. 10 (London: Eyre and Spottiswood, 1959), p. 306.

11. Ray Hemmings, *Liberty or Death* (London: Lawrence and Wishart, 2000), p. 68.

12. John Ehrman, *The Younger Pitt* (London: Constable, 1983), p. 230.

13. Lord North to the Country Gentleman, in *Aspinal* (ed.), *English Historical Documents*, vol. 10, p. 313.

14. *Ibid*.

15. R. J. White, *Waterloo to Peterloo* (New York: Russell and Russell, 1957), p. 3.

16. *Ibid*.

17. Scotland lost her ancient independence amid rioting and unrest on 1 May 1707, when the Act of Union was ratified. Scotland's own parliament met for the last time on 25 March and the first British parliament met on 23 October.

18. Hemmings, *Liberty or Death*, p. 82.

19. Penelope J. Corfield and Chris Evans (eds), *Youth and Revolution in the 1790s* (Stroud: Alan Sutton, 1996), p. 53.

20. *Ibid*.

21. Roger Scruton, *England: An Elegy* (London: Pimlico, 2001), p. 12.

Chapter Eight

1. John Wardroper, *Kings, Lords and Wicked Libellers* (London: John Murray, 1973), p. 2.

2. *Ibid*., p. 3.

3. The identity of Junius is still a matter of debate, Sir Philip Francis being one of the candidates.

4. Articles of Act of Union.

5. *Ibid*.

6. Wardroper, *Kings, Lords and Wicked Libellers*, p. 177.

7. A. Aspinall and E. Anthony Smith (eds), *English Historical Documents 1783–1832*, vol. 11 (London: Eyre & Spottiswoode, 1959), p. 317.

8. *Ibid*., p. 318.

9. *Ibid*., p. 319.

10. Also rounded up as a dangerous subversive was James Parkinson, the English physician and palaeontologist who went on to discover 'Parkinson's disease'.

11. Aspinall (ed.), *English Historical Documents 1783–1832*, vol. 10, p. 319.

12. *Ibid*., p. 320.

13. Mike Jay, *The Air Loom Gang* (London; Bantam, 2003), p. 273.

14. Mike Gay, *The Unfortunate Colonel Despard* (London: Bantam Books, 2004), p. 310.

15. Lord Sidmouth, Henry Addington was born on 13 May 1757 and was prime minister from 17 March 1801 to 10 May 1804. It was Sidmouth who introduced the Gagging Acts and suspended habeas corpus, and it was Sidmouth (after Castlereagh) who was also finally responsible for the passing of the Six Acts and for overseeing the events following the Cato Street conspiracy. Unlike Castlereagh, his unpopularity did not deny him a long life and he died in 1844, aged 87.

16. Aspinall (ed.), *English Historical Documents 1783–1832*, vol. 10, p. 95.

17. *Ibid.*, p. 334.

18. Wardroper, *Kings, Lords and Wicked Libellers*, p. 210.

CHAPTER NINE

1. R.A. Leeson, *Travelling Brothers* (London: Granada, 1979) p. 90.

2. *Ibid.*, p. 88.

3. *Ibid.*, p. 140.

4. John Foster, *Class Struggle and the Industrial Revolution* (London: Methuen, 1979), p. 39.

5. *Ibid.*

6. *Ibid.*, p. 50.

7. *Ibid.*, p. 47.

8. *Ibid.*, p. 40.

9. During the first decade of Chartism, which led to the rising in Newport, the Government had deployed as many as 30,000 soldiers on internal garrison duties just to watch the population. Sometimes, however, military intervention at political or union rallies was reduced to farce. At Rochdale the soldiers attempted to stop a meeting during a very wet and dreary day, the rain running into the musket barrels shouldered by the troops, allowing one droll woollen-weaver to remark that the 'poor redcoat' might 'squirt us … but could not shoot us'.

10. Mollie Gillen, *Assassination of the Prime Minister* (London: Sidgwick & Jackson, 1972), pp. 35–6.

11. *Ibid.*, p. 36.

12. Eventually, Lord Cochrane took the petition, but it was on the day that the Prince Regent was attacked in his carriage and the whole reform movement fell under suspicion.

13. David Johnson, *Revolution: The Case of Arthur Thistlewood* (London: Compton Russell, 1974), p. 5.

14. Masonism had been 'revived' in Scotland in the sixteenth century. By the early nineteenth century, the influence of Masonic symbolism and the importance of secrecy were widely copied and were endemic to the working class and its various clandestine activities, including the union movement. What Masonic lodges were to the middle class, unions were to the working class.

15. It was always the Government's position that Oliver never fomented anything that would not have happened anyway. Lord Liverpool called him simply 'the informer'. Perhaps Oliver was both detective and spy in an age that could not separate the two.

16 A. Aspinall (ed.), *English Historical Documents 1783–1832*, vol. 10 (London: Eyre & Spottiswoode, 1959), p. 319.

17. The Brandreth name, however, did not die out. In 1992 his descendant Gyles Brandreth became Conservative MP for Chester.

18. It was ironic that the guillotine began its life as the 'Halifax gibbet' in Yorkshire in 1286 (continuing there until 1650), and was subsequently adopted as a Scottish means of execution between 1556 and 1710 in Edinburgh. It was finally used by the British military authorities in Germany after the Second World War (1945/6) when *Werwolf* insurgents were guillotined on old Nazi stock. On 10 September 1977 the French used the guillotine for the last time, on the murderer Hamida Djandoubi.

Chapter Ten

1. Nothing now remains of St Peter's Fields in Manchester, the site of Peterloo, except a faded blue plaque recording the visit of Henry Hunt, his audience of '60,000' and the attack of the yeomanry. By the mid-1840s, the area was being rapidly built over with warehouses and civic buildings, such as a theatre and corn exchange. Later on, an LNER goods yard and depot came to dominate the area and dwarf the Georgian houses and business premises in Castlefield and Deansgate. By the 1970s, the area was derelict and it was rehabilitated only in the 1990s.

2. Samuel Bamford, *Passages in the Life of a Radical* (Oxford: Oxford University Press, 1984), pp. 19–20.

3. *Ibid.*, p. 21.

4. *Ibid.*, p. 26.

5. George Edwards was a sculptor who made models of heads and plaster casts and had at one time been secretary of the Spencean Society. He

certainly made a bust of the head of Paine for the republican Richard Carlile, but was considered a man of such violent temper that he was nicknamed 'blood and thunder' and by degrees his business suffered. He worked from a shop in Windsor, where he appears to have made contact with the Government, probably because of financial worries. Nevertheless, when Thistlewood met him he was certainly dressed in the height of fashion. After the conspirators were caught, Edwards escaped to Guernsey, thereafter apparently getting a job at Somerset House. Many years later, he possibly reappears as Thomas Haydon Green, involved in the murder of his landlord and his own suicide. Interestingly, by this time his name and the name of the cow keeper had become conflated and it is no longer possible to work out who actually committed the crime. See T.H.R. Cashmore, 'The Mystery of Thomas Haydon Green, The Whitton Murder and the Cato Street Conspiracy' (Twickenham Local History Society, Paper No. 23), February 1972.

6. David Johnson, *Regency Revolutionary* (London: Compton Russell, 1974), p. 89.
7. Bamford, *Passages in the Life of a Radical*, p. 63.
8. *Ibid.*, p. 63.
9. *Ibid.*, p. 68.
10. *Ibid.*, p. 16.
11. Tim Hilton, 'Preface', in *ibid.*, p. 5.
12. Robert Owen, Manifesto (1840), in Robert Owen, *A New View of Society and Other Writings*, ed. Gregory Claeys (Harmondsworth: Penguin, 1991), p. 358.

Chapter Eleven

1. Such was the interest in the country in reform that even places such as Sutton Scotney, a small hamlet 7 miles from Winchester, found time for its parishioners to sign a petition in September 1830, which was then taken on foot by one of the inhabitants all the way to Brighton to be presented to King William IV.
2. Barry Reay, 'The Last Rising of the Agricultural Labourers', *History Workshop*, no. 26 (Autumn 1988), p. 86.
3. 'Wise men', 'diviners', 'cunning folk', 'charmers' and the like were endemic to the nineteenth century, which obstinately refused to give up its low magic despite modernity's inroads. Such wisdom was handed down and lasted into the twentieth century. More significantly it was

centred not in remote rural areas but in the heart of London. See Ronald Hutton, *The Triumph of the Moon* (Oxford: Oxford University Press, 1999), pp. 87–109.

4. Things faired differently in Scotland. The Chartist agitation in Scotland dates from 10 April 1838 with a meeting in Glasgow. In June 1838, radicals, including republicans John Taylor and Thomas Gillespie, gathered again in Glasgow to 'show contempt' for the coronation preparations of Queen Victoria. Nevertheless, such apparent violent attitudes were never in the Scottish Chartist agenda, the movement soon becoming middle class and Christian in its orientation and reformist in its outlook. Even the revolutions in Europe during 1848 failed to stir action, despite John Grant's calling for 'every man [to] arm himself'.

5. Frost was finally captured and tried. It is a measure of the change in the times that he was not sentenced to be hanged and beheaded, but instead to transportation for life. While in Australia, he was employed as a clerk and schoolmaster but, on being pardoned in 1854, he went to the United States. Finally granted an unconditional pardon, he returned to Newport but he alienated people with his aggressive stance. He therefore moved to Bristol and died there on 28 July 1877 at the age of 93.

Chapter Twelve

1. William Blackstone (1723–80) wrote *Commentaries on the Laws of England*.
2. *The Operative*, 16 December 1838.
3. Max Morris (ed.), *From Cobbett to the Chartists* (London: Lawrence & Wishart, 1951), p. 144.
4. Because of the importance of freehold and land ownership to voting rights, O'Connor's scheme was not the only one. There was also James Taylor's Freehold Land Movement in Birmingham, started in 1847. By 1850 there were fifty such societies.
5. Donald Read, *Cobden and Bright* (London: Edward Arnold, 1967), pp. 36–7.
6. This was known as the 'Battle of the Forth'.
7. The phrase refers to the action of the Highland Brigade at the Battle of the Alma commanded by Campbell. The phrase 'thin red line' was first used by W.H. Russell in 1877.
8. *Leeds Intelligencer*, 18 January 1840, p. 8.

9. It was a time of momentous events. Alongside reporting the 'downright infatuation' of the Chartists at Sheffield, the *Leeds Mercury* of 25 January 1840 also carried news of Canadian Union, an anti-Corn Law banquet at Manchester and the beginning of the penny post. There was even a report on a Mr Magnus Klein, 'whose resemblance to Napoleon is so remarkable'.

10. *Leeds Mercury*, 18 January 1840.

11. The activities of the early units of yeomanry and militia came too often near to licensed thuggery. Nevertheless, such associations did survive into respectability, with 'amateur' soldiers learning their new trade in the village drill halls and shooting ranges that grew up during the Crimean War. The yeomanry went on to fight in the Boer War and the First World War. The regular army, when garrisoned at home, was always the prime agent of order during periods of riot or insurrection.

12. F.B. Smith, *Radical Artisan* (Manchester: Manchester University Press, 1973), p. 94.

13. *Ibid.*, p. 156.

Chapter Thirteen

1. Quoted in Asa Briggs, *Victorian Cities* (Harmondsworth: Penguin, 1982), p. 90.

2. Ruth and Edmund Frow, *Karl Marx in Manchester* (Manchester: Manchester Free Press, 1985), p. 26.

3. Edmund and Ruth Frow, *Frederick Engels in Manchester* (Manchester: Manchester Free Press, 1995), pp. 4–5.

4. By May 1864 Wolff was suffering from the serious hallucinations and amnesia that would kill him.

5. Ruth and Edmund Frow, *Karl Marx in Manchester* (Manchester: Working Class Movement Library, 1985), p. 47.

6. Friedrich Engels, *The Condition of the Working Class in England* (Harmondsworth: Penguin, [1845]1987), p. 27.

7. *Ibid.*, p. 72.

8. In April 1848 the Chartist Convention moved to London, where it convened at the Literary Institute, Fitzroy Square. The number of delegates was forty-nine, 'in order to escape the penalties of the Convention Act'. The leading lights were Ernest Jones and the son of St Kitts slaves, William Cuffay. The meeting was intended to prepare the charter, which would be ratified by a monster meeting on Kennington Common,

494 *A History of Britain's Fight For A Republic*

whence it would be taken to the House of Commons. The speeches became more inflammatory and were reported daily by *The Times*. The third and last charter failed after the meeting at Kennington Common. Cuffay and others became even more militant and organised for an armed insurrection in London planned for 16–18 June 1848, but the Chartist Executive worked against the London Committee and the whole thing was riddled with police spies such as Thomas Reading, the Irish correspondent for the *Northern Star*. Arrests were made, including Jones. Another plot was immediately hatched by Chartist renegades and Irish republicans, but it was again foiled when the conspirators met in the Orange Tree public house on 16 August and all the leaders were arrested. A gathering in anticipation of the rising was also dispersed at Seven Dials. Cuffay, although only recently appointed as secretary of the 'ulterior committee' and therefore not central to the plot, became the patsy for the enterprise, and after weapons were found in pubs and church yards, he was sentenced with others to transportation to Australia. He is best known for his courtroom defence, which he gave after a prejudiced trial, but he was nevertheless sentenced to transportation.

9. The so-called Plug Riots, named because boiler plugs were removed, was a continuation of the idea of a general strike. We still retain the phrase 'pulling the plug' from these disturbances.

10. Peter Washington, *Madame Blavatsky's Baboon* (London: Secker & Warburg, 1993), p. 11.

11. Briggs, *Victorian Cities*, p. 194.

12. Hamish McPherson, *To Stand Truly by Each Other* (International Socialist Organisation, 2004).

13. The flag itself was sewn by Anastasia Withers and Anne Duke.

14. Raffaello Carboni, *The Eureka Stockade* (Melbourne: Melbourne University Press, 2005), p. 71.

15. *Neue Oder Zeitung*.

Chapter Fourteen

1. Stanley H. Palmer, *Police and Protest in England and Ireland 1780–1850* (Cambridge: Cambridge University Press, 1988), p. 435.

2. *Ibid*., pp. 437–8.

3. *Ibid*., p. 438.

4. *Ibid*., p. 484.

5. *Ibid.*

6. *Ibid.*, p. 252.

7. The tricolour to be found in St Aidan's Cathedral in Enniscorthy is claimed to have been carried by the 1798 insurgents at Wexford on 9 May. This is not likely. The style of the flag and its manner of manufacture suggest the date of 7 March 1848, the second time the flag was carried. It therefore may be the oldest Irish flag in existence.

8. The Fenian movement was already full of British spies. One was Thomas Miller Beach (originally from Colchester), who went under the name Henri Le Caron, having spent some time in France. Le Caron was employed by the British to spy on the New York network, from where he warned the Canadians that they would be invaded. Indeed he got very close to O'Neill. Although his warning was ignored, he continued his activities, rising high in the Fenian movement. Once the Fenian cause started to decline, he moved to Ireland, where he was part of the attempt to discredit Charles Stewart Parnell. The attempt, which included a forged letter, broke Parnell and ended his career. Afterwards, however, Le Caron was dropped, and he died in 1894.

9. Peter F. Stevens, *The Voyage of the Catalpa* (New York: Carroll & Graf, 2002), p. 33.

10. Peter Berresford Ellis, *The Celtic Revolution* (Ceredigion: Y Lolfa Cyf, 1985), p. 141.

11. Cleveland Moffatt, 'The Overthrow of the Molly Maguires', *McClure's Magazine* (1894), p. 95.

12. Allan Pinkerton was born in Glasgow and emigrated to the United States in 1842. He died in 1884.

13. Christy Campbell, *Fenian Fire* (London: Harper Collins, 2002), p. 93.

CHAPTER FIFTEEN

1. Christy Campbell, *Fenian Fire* (London: Harper Collins, 2002), p. 7.

2. Peter F. Stevens, *The Voyage of the Catalpa* (New York: Carroll & Graf, 2002), p. 338.

3. Only later did the Electric Boat Company exploit Holland's invention, selling it to both the US Navy and the Royal Navy. Forty days after Holland died in 1914, three British cruisers were sunk by the U-boat *U-9*.

4. The original target was to be the outgoing Secretary, who was to be murdered on a station platform, but he had caught an earlier train.

5. The murders sparked a parliamentary crisis. The morning of the incident, Parnell was at Portland prison, welcoming Davitt, and knew nothing of the affair until later, when he realised that all his party had worked for might vanish in light of the outrage. The debate over a new Coercion Bill was held directly after Cavendish's funeral. The events also exposed Parnell's secret deal to support the Liberals.

6. The image of the terrorist as essentially an Irishman with a bomb remained enshrined in legislation right up to the late twentieth century. In 1989, for instance, the Prevention of Terrorism (Temporary Provisions) Act strengthened the police powers that had existed since 1978 in order to 'prevent the establishment of new explosive factories, magazines and stores in Northern Ireland'. In 1996 a further Additional Powers Act strengthened 'powers of search in connection with acts of terrorism', as well as establishing rules for police cordons and restrictions of vehicle movement, while in 1998 the Criminal Justice (Terrorism and Conspiracy) Act made 'provision about procedure and forfeiture concerning proscribed organisations, and about conspiring to commit offences outside the United Kingdom'. The Terrorism Act 2000 continued to widen and also define police powers, especially in Northern Ireland. The Act defined the meaning of the term 'terrorism' where the use or threat of action was intended 'to influence the government' or 'intimidate the public' in order to promote a 'political, religious or ideological cause', in which there might be 'serious violence against the person', 'damage to property', the endangerment of 'a person's life, other than that of the person committing the act' or where there existed a 'serious risk to the health or safety of the public' or where there was an attempt to 'disrupt an electrical system' (that is, a communication or supply network). Uniforms were again banned in Northern Ireland, as they had been in 1937 in the rest of the United Kingdom after the rise of Oswald Mosley's black-shirted British Union of Fascists. A terrorist was, of course, defined as anyone engaged in the listed activities, all of which looked towards the conflict in Ireland, the catalogue of proscribed organisations, both Catholic and Protestant, being entirely Irish.

7. Christopher Andrew, *Secret Service* (London: Sceptre, 1992), p. 35.

8. Bribery was also of major significance with the creation of a Secret Service fund in the 1660s. This, in turn, was backed by private funds out of the pockets of spymasters, some of whom (like the Elizabethan

Francis Walsingham) went bankrupt in the process. Robert Walpole spent much of the fund on political advancement, while both Lord Bute and Pitt the Younger used the money for bribery abroad. The parcels of money handed over were known as the 'cavalry of St George', because of the stamped impression on the gold sovereigns. Yet the money spent by William Wickham, Britain's envoy to Switzerland, in trying to counter the French Revolution all went to waste. Burke's promotion of the Economic Reform Bill was intended to curb political bribery and promote good order in the payment of spying. It became law in 1782, creating an annual budget and also bringing into being the Home, Foreign and Colonial Offices. The original budget of £25,000 rose, however, to over £172,000 as the threat from Napoleon increased. Once peace was re-established, the Secret Service fund rapidly declined and was well below the 1782 figure as late as the Boer War, not rising significantly even during the Fenian bombing campaign of 1883 to 1885, the Government complacent in its belief that intelligence work was 'dirty work' only done by foreign governments. The French *cabinet noir* interrupted British diplomatic post (as did the Russians) and even read Gladstone's correspondence when he was prime minister holidaying in Cannes.

9. David Vincent, *The Culture of Secrecy* (Oxford: Oxford University Press, 1998), p. 5.

10. *Ibid.*, p. 44.

11. The recourse by secret groups of artisans or labourers to anonymous letter-writing, which often contained exhortations to followers or threats to employers, was punishable by death until 1823 and transportation thereafter. The practice of writing threatening letters fell into abeyance after the 1830s.

12. Vincent, *The Culture of Secrecy*, p. 57.

13. The modern Special Branch specialises, among other things, in gathering and collating information regarding extremist political or terrorist activity, providing armed protection for ministers of state, policing the ports in order to detect foreign terrorists, watching for Irish terrorist groups or espionage from foreign infiltrators, looking for weapons of mass destruction and keeping public order.

14. Tony Gray, *The Orange Order* (London: Bodley Head, 1972), p. 160.

15. *Ibid.*, pp. 167–8.

16. He, too, was executed on 12 May 1916.

17. Interestingly, the war that finally achieved 'dominion' status for Southern Ireland never carried an explicit demand for a republic nor for the abolition of the monarchy on Irish soil. This came much later and almost by accident as a *de facto* result of partition.

CHAPTER SIXTEEN

1. Hermia Oliver, *The International Anarchist Movement in Late Victorian London* (London: Croom Helm, 1983), p. 76.
2. Krupskaya's reminiscences of London are taken from Tish Collins, 69th Marx Memorial Lecture; 'Lenin, Iskra and Clerkenwell', n.d., n.p.
3. *Ibid*.
4. Bernard Porter, *The Origins of the Vigilant State* (London: Weidenfeld and Nicolson, 1987), p. 112.
5. Michael Collins, *The Likes of Us* (London: Granta, 2004), p. 83.
6. Kell's equivalent in foreign intelligence (eventually MI6) was Captain (later Sir) Mansfield George Smith-Cumming. A naval officer with a knowledge of French, photography and electricity, he was brought out of semi-retirement to head the new branch. A car accident that killed his son also left him with an artificial leg. With his penchant for green ink (still used by his equivalent today), he remained head of the service until 1923.
7. Sheila Rowbotham, *Friends of Alice Wheeldon* (London: Pluto Press, 1986), p. 76.
8. *Ibid*., p. 8.
9. *Ibid*., p. 56.
10. Harry Pollitt, *Serving my Time* (London: Lawrence & Wishart, 1940), p. 167.
11. *Ibid*.
12. Francis Beckett, *Enemy Within* (London: John Murray, 1995), p. 113.
13. Fear of revolution was confirmed when the soldiers mutinied at Etaples base during 1917. The grievances were numerous but for the most part not seditious. Offences ranged from drunkenness to threatening a superior officer, but army intelligence was determined to find more. Red flags were discovered but could have come from a nearby train signal hut. Nevertheless, it was considered that the soldiers were 'very republican'. James Cullen, a private in the Argyll and Sutherland Highlanders, claimed that he was one of the soldiers who formed a communist cell to create a general mutiny, but there is little direct evidence.

Notwithstanding any evidence, General Haig believed that the army had been infiltrated by Bolshevism and was determined to stamp it out, the scapegoat being Corporal Robert Jesse Short, who was shot.

Yet it was between November 1918 and June 1919, coinciding with the worst of the Glasgow industrial unrest, that the most mutinies occurred. Of the hundred or so recorded, the majority were about the speed of demobilisation. Some of the disturbances happened at Kinmel Camp, between Bodelwyddan village and Abergele in Wales, where Canadian and British troops were stationed. Among the troops were men of Russian extraction, and Regimental Sergeant Major Lawrence Wilson, giving evidence at the inquiry, stated that 'some of the mob were led by men carrying red flags and had the general appearance of a bunch of anarchists'. Furthermore, a Major Langford also recalled that 'an officer reported to me that he had seen a union jack pulled down ... a red flag put up in its place, and this pulled down again and two American flags hoisted by two Frenchmen, one of whom shouted *"Vive la République"*.' Both of these incidents were finally played down, partly because the evidence was circumstantial and partly because, in the atmosphere of the time, mention of Bolshevism among the troops would be unnecessarily alarmist.

14. Pollitt, *Serving my Time*, pp. 212–13.
15. *For Soviet Britain* (London: Communist Action Group, n.d.), p. ii.
16. *Ibid.*, p. 4.
17. Andrew Thorpe, 'The Communist International and the British Communist Party', in Tim Rees and Andrew Thorpe (eds), *International Communism and the Communist International 1919–1943* (Manchester: Manchester University Press, 1988), pp. 67–87, at pp. 67–8.
18. Here he predicted the far future rather than the immediate situation, dominated as it was to be by the tactics of blitzkrieg.
19. George Orwell, *The Road to Wigan Pier* (London: Gollancz, 1937).

CHAPTER SEVENTEEN

1. Board of Deputies of British Jews: HO45-25383.
2. The term was used by right-wing opponents of Mosley who thought his policies favoured Jewish interests.
3. Francis Selwyn, *Hitler's Englishman* (London: Routledge & Kegan Paul, 1987), p. 18.

4. *Ibid.*

5. 'Sapper' was the pen name of Herman Cyril McNeile, who wrote popular patriotic conspiracy books around his hero, Bulldog Drummond.

6. Owner of J. Lyons & Co., the catering company.

7. Selwyn, *Hitler's Englishman*, p. 61.

8. *Ibid.*, p. 63.

9. Adrian Weale, *Patriot Traitors* (London: Viking, 2001), p. 137.

10. He may have been thinking about the fight to defend Lazarus at Lambeth Baths.

11. J.A. Cole, *Lord Haw-Haw* (London: Faber & Faber, 1987), p. 210.

12. Imperial War Museum: Archive 5224/1.

13. Rebecca West, *The Meaning of Treason* (London: MacMillan, 1949), p. 25.

14. *Ibid.*

15. *Ibid.*, p. 127.

16. Richard Griffiths, *Patriotism Perverted* (London: Constable, 1998), p. 68.

17. *Ibid.*, p. 133.

18. Selwyn, *Hitler's Englishman*, p. 37.

19. On 11 December 1940 all Jewish property was to be 'Aryanised' and the Bailiff again complied. Finally under virtual house arrest, Jews had their property forcibly sold and were put under curfew. Some on Guernsey were sent off to die at Auschwitz during 1942. In everything, the Bailiff and his officers acted with scrupulous, bureaucratic correctness and total inhuman indifference; it mattered little if some Jews were left on the islands (though harassed) or deported to concentration or death camps. At the end of their tether and awaiting deportation in 1943, some of the few remaining Jews (all old) died of heart attacks brought on by fear, or committed suicide. Some few lived through the occupation and survived the terror. When the war ended, Alexander Coutanche, as a good government administrator, helped Jewish evacuees to pursue their claims.

20. Orwell, *The Road to Wigan Pier*, p. 211.

21. *Ibid.*, p. 83.

Chapter Eighteen

1. W. Hamish Fraser, *Scottish Popular Politics* (Edinburgh: Polygon, 2000), p. 95. After the Second Afghan War of 1879, the new emir, Yakub Khan,

actually clothed his Household Guard in a form of kilt in honour of the Scots troops deployed during the campaign.

2. So popular was Davitt that when they opened the Parkhead Ground of Celtic Football Club in 1892, it was he who planted a symbolic turf of shamrock (later stolen). There was every reason for Davitt's popularity, for, during 1847–8, over 33,000 Irish travelled to Glasgow and in 1871 even Liverpool was overtaken by Greenock and Dumbarton in numbers of immigrants, many from Ulster. By 1881, the census gave 5.8 per cent of the Scottish population as being of Irish origin.

3. Fraser, *Scottish Popular Politics*, p. 120.

4. *Ibid.*, p. 122.

5. Chanie Rosenberg, *Britain on the Brink of Revolution* (London: Bookmarks, 1987), p. 16.

6. *Ibid.*, p. 42.

7. *Ibid.*, p. 37.

8. Iain McLean, *The Legend of Red Clydeside* (Edinburgh: John Donald Publishers, 1999), p. 147.

9. John Mclean, 'The Irish Tragedy: Up Scottish Revolutionists', *Vanguard* (November 1922).

10. Boothby was a major in the army and the son of a soldier, and to all accounts was a perfectly well-bred Englishman. Nevertheless, having fought in the war and gained experience of guerrilla warfare, he settled down in Dorset, protected by Dobermanns and living in a wooden hut decorated with skulls! Here, he founded a folklore society, apparently a cover for a witches' coven. He next surfaced in Scotland, reinvented as an ardent nationalist and activist for the SNP. His broadsheet, *Sgian Dhubh*, advocated terrorist methods for Scotland's independence, calling for an armed revolution. Boothby was a member of the 1320 Club, which also advocated a 'Provisional Government' headed by a Scottish cabinet and council of the realm. This would take full responsibility for administering Scotland in the 'interregnum'. This dictatorial directorate was to be filled with hand-picked men and women of 'vision, courage, ability and determination', who were 'prepared if necessary to spend the next ten years in jail'. In April 1972 Douglas named Boothby as an agent provocateur, and in January 1973 Boothby was threatened with assassination and fled to England, cutting his ties with the 1320 Club and the APG.

11. Andrew Murray Scott and Iain Macleay, *Britain's Secret War* (Edinburgh: Mainstream Publishing, 1990), p. 17.

12. *Ibid.*, p. 45.

13. *Ibid.*

14. *Ibid.*, p. 144.

15. The bomb exploded at the Grand Hotel at 2.54 a.m. on 12 October. It killed five and injured at least thirty.

Chapter Nineteen

1. Peter Berresford Ellis, *The Celtic Revolution* (Ceredigion: Y Lolfa Cyf, 1993), p. 83.

2. Saunders Lewis, 'Why we Burnt the Bombing School', in Reginald Reynolds (ed.), *British Pamphleteers*, vol. 2 (London: Allan Wingate, 1951), pp. 289–300, at p. 291.

3. *Ibid.*, p. 289.

4. *Ibid.*

5. *Ibid.*, p. 290.

6. The talk was called 'The Fate of the Welsh Language' and was broadcast on 13 February 1962.

7. Roy Clews, *To Dream of Freedom* (Ceredigion: Y Lolfa Cyf, 1980), p. 225.

8. *Ibid.*

9. *Ibid.*, p. 119.

10. A bombing campaign told the police that, although the FWA were out of action, another force was active. Actually there were two forces, as a lone bomber, more violent than MAC, was also on the loose during 1969. When caught, he turned out to be Robert Trigg, a Sheffield student from Cardiff. He was sentenced to five years.

11. George Taylor and Alwyn Jones (neither of whom spoke Welsh) were known as the 'Abergele martyrs'.

12. *Western Morning News*, 133, vol. 47, p. 70.

13. Berresford Ellis, *The Celtic Revolution*, p. 40.

14. *Ibid.*, p. 149.

15. *Celtic and Republican Nations Magazine*, vols 1–2 (Summer 1973), p. 9.

16. Manx Museum archive, L6/MNP.

17. Manx Museum archive, MS09618

18. *Celtic and Republican Nations Magazine*, vols. 1–2, p. 9.

19. Manx Museum archive, MS09618

20. Manx Museum archive, L3/POB.

Index

You may also enjoy …

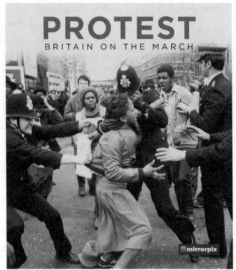

978 0 7509 9072 1

'Never doubt that a small group of thoughtful, committed citizens can change the world. Indeed, it is the only thing that ever has.' – Margaret Mead

Britain was built on protest. From Magna Carta to the suffragettes, the Peasants' Revolt to the Iraq War; British people have never been afraid to take to the street. *Protest: Britain on the March* takes a look at the lengths to which ordinary people will go to make their voices heard, all through the lens of Mirrorpix's incredible photo archive.

The History Press

The destination for history
www.thehistorypress.co.uk